· 2022 ·

# 何梁何利奖

HLHL PRIZE

何梁何利基金评选委员会 编

THE SELECTION BOARD OF HO LEUNG HO LEE FOUNDATION

中国科学技术出版社
· 北 京 ·

图书在版编目（CIP）数据

2022何梁何利奖 / 何梁何利基金评选委员会编. --
北京：中国科学技术出版社，2025.2. -- ISBN 978-7
-5236-0858-6

Ⅰ. K826.1

中国国家版本馆CIP数据核字第20249PE510号

| 责任编辑 | 韩　颖 |
| --- | --- |
| 责任校对 | 吕传新 |
| 责任印制 | 徐　飞 |

| 出　　版 | 中国科学技术出版社 |
| --- | --- |
| 发　　行 | 中国科学技术出版社有限公司 |
| 地　　址 | 北京市海淀区中关村南大街16号 |
| 邮　　编 | 100081 |
| 发行电话 | 010-62173865 |
| 传　　真 | 010-62173081 |
| 网　　址 | http://www.cspbooks.com.cn |

| 开　　本 | 787mm×1092mm　1/16 |
| --- | --- |
| 字　　数 | 447千字 |
| 印　　张 | 19 |
| 插　　页 | 4 |
| 印　　数 | 1—3000册 |
| 版　　次 | 2025年2月第1版 |
| 印　　次 | 2025年2月第1次印刷 |
| 印　　刷 | 北京荣泰印刷有限公司 |
| 书　　号 | ISBN 978-7-5236-0858-6 / K·408 |
| 定　　价 | 80.00元 |

（凡购买本社图书，如有缺页、倒页、脱页者，本社销售中心负责调换）

# 编辑委员会

顾　　问：朱丽兰　钟登华　霍泰辉
主　　编：段瑞春
编　　委：（按姓氏笔画排序）
　　　　　马永生　王小凡　杨纲凯　吴伟仁
　　　　　张立同　张恭庆　陈佳洱　郝吉明
　　　　　赵宇亮　钱绍钧　倪　军　桑国卫
　　　　　曹雪涛　程　序　曾庆存　蒲慕明
执行编辑：李存军　任晓明

## EDITORIAL BOARD

Advisers:　Zhu Lilan　Zhong Denghua　Huo Taihui
Chief Editor:　Duan Ruichun
Board Directors:　Ma Yongsheng　Wang Xiaofan　Kenneth Young
　　　　　　　　Wu Weiren　Zhang Litong　Zhang Gongqing
　　　　　　　　Chen Jiaer　Hao Jiming　Zhao Yuliang
　　　　　　　　Qian Shaojun　Ni Jun　Sang Guowei
　　　　　　　　Cao Xuetao　Cheng Xu　Zeng Qingcun
　　　　　　　　Pu Muming
Executive Editor:　Li Cunjun　Ren Xiaoming

## 内 容 提 要

本书是何梁何利基金出版物——《何梁何利奖》的第二十九集。书中简要介绍了2022年度何梁何利基金56位获奖人的生平经历和主要科技成就。为了便于海内外人士了解本奖背景，书中同时收入了反映何梁何利基金及其科技奖励情况的资料，作为附录刊出。

This is the twenty-nine collection of the publications of Ho Leung Ho Lee Foundation—*Ho Leung Ho Lee Prize*. In this book, the biographical notes on the 56 awardees of the year 2022 and their main scientific and technological achievements are accounted briefly. This collection includes appendices concerning Ho Leung Ho Lee Foundation and its scientific and technological award in order to help the readers both in China and abroad to understand the background of this prize.

2023年2月17日，何梁何利基金2021和2022年度颁奖大会（第二十八届、第二十九届）在北京钓鱼台国宾馆举行。国务院副总理刘鹤出席大会并讲话。

On February 17, 2023, the 2021 (28th) and 2022 (29th) Award Ceremony of HLHL Foundation is held at Diaoyutai State Guesthouse in Beijing. Liu He, the Vice Premier of the State Council, attends and delivers a speech.

国家领导人、各界嘉宾与何梁何利基金2021年度、2022年度获奖人合影。

The state leaders and the honored guests have a group photo taken with the winners of 2021 HLHL Prize and 2022 HLHL Prize.

何梁何利基金信托委员会主席、评选委员会主任朱丽兰在何梁何利基金 2021 和 2022 年度颁奖大会上作评选委员会工作报告。

Zhu Lilan, Chairwoman of the Board of Trustees and Director of the Selection Board of HLHL Foundation, delivers a report on the work of the Selection Board at the 2021 and 2022 Award Ceremony of HLHL Foundation.

何梁何利基金（北京）代表处首席代表、何梁何利基金评选委员会秘书长段瑞春主持大会。

Duan Ruichun, the chief representative of the Beijing Representative Office of the Ho Leung Ho Lee Foundation (Hong Kong), and the Secretary-General of the Selection Board of HLHL Foundation, presides over the 2021 and 2022 Award Ceremony of HLHL Foundation.

国务院副总理刘鹤为何梁何利基金 2022 年度科学与技术成就奖获奖科学家林鸣颁奖。

Liu He, the Vice Premier of the State Council, presents prize to Lin Ming, the winner of 2022 HLHL Prize for Scientific and Technology Achievements.

国务院副总理刘鹤与何梁何利基金科学与技术成就奖获奖科学家胡思得（2021年度）、林鸣（2022年度）合影。

Liu He, the Vice Premier of the State Council, has a photo taken with Hu Side and Lin Ming, the winners of 2021 HLHL Prize and 2022 HLHL Prize for Scientific and Technology Achievements.

何梁何利基金 2022 年度科学与技术成就奖获得者林鸣院士在颁奖大会上发言。

Lin Ming, the winner of 2022 HLHL Prize for Scientific and Technology Achievements and academician of the Chinese Academy of Engineering, delivers a speech at the 2021 and 2022 Award Ceremony of HLHL Foundation.

何梁何利基金捐款人代表梁祥彪先生在 2021 和 2022 年度颁奖大会上视频致辞。

Mr. Leung Cheung Biu, representative of donors of the HLHL Foundation, delivers a video speech to the 2021 and 2022 Award Ceremony of HLHL Foundation.

国家领导人、各界嘉宾为何梁何利基金 2021 和 2022 年度获奖人颁奖并合影。
The state leaders and the honored guests present prizes to and have a group photo taken with the winners of 2021 HLHL Prize and 2022 HLHL Prize.

国家领导人、各界嘉宾为何梁何利基金 2021 和 2022 年度获奖人颁奖并合影。
The state leaders and the honored guests present prizes to and have a group photo taken with the winners of 2021 HLHL Prize and 2022 HLHL Prize.

国家领导人、各界嘉宾为何梁何利基金 2021 和 2022 年度获奖人颁奖并合影。
The state leaders and the honored guests present prizes to and have a group photo taken with the winners of 2021 HLHL Prize and 2022 HLHL Prize.

国家领导人、各界嘉宾为何梁何利基金 2021 和 2022 年度获奖人颁奖并合影。
The state leaders and the honored guests present prizes to and have a group photo taken with the winners of 2021 HLHL Prize and 2022 HLHL Prize.

国家领导人、各界嘉宾为何梁何利基金 2021 和 2022 年度获奖人颁奖并合影。
The state leaders and the honored guests present prizes to and have a group photo taken with the winners of 2021 HLHL Prize and 2022 HLHL Prize.

国家领导人、各界嘉宾为何梁何利基金 2021 和 2022 年度获奖人颁奖并合影。
The state leaders and the honored guests present prizes to and have a group photo taken with the winners of 2021 HLHL Prize and 2022 HLHL Prize.

何梁何利基金 2021 和 2022 年度颁奖大会会场。
The meeting hall of the 2021 and 2022 Award Ceremony of HLHL Foundation.

何梁何利基金 2021 和 2022 年度颁奖大会会场。
The meeting hall of the 2021 and 2022 Award Ceremony of HLHL Foundation.

# 在何梁何利基金 2021 和 2022 年度颁奖大会上的讲话

刘 鹤

（2023 年 2 月 17 日）

尊敬的吉炳轩副委员长，

尊敬的万钢副主席，

尊敬的朱丽兰主席，

尊敬的胡思得院士、林鸣院士，

尊敬的何梁何利基金赞助人、代表、各位科学家，

各位嘉宾，女士们、先生们：

大家上午好！

经过党中央批准，我很荣幸出席这次对国家意义重大的颁奖大会。这充分体现了以习近平同志为核心的党中央，对这个奖项、对科技创新伟大事业和对科学家创新精神的高度重视。在此，我代表国务院向所有获奖的科学家表示热烈的祝贺，对这个奖项的所有的支持者表示衷心的感谢。刚才，我也听了胡思得院士、林鸣院士发表的讲演，我很受感动和教育。下面借这个机会，我也谈几点想法和大家分享。

第一点，我们要高度重视科技创新对国家高质量发展的引领作用。中共二十大对科技创新做了全面的战略部署，把科技创新作为国家的核心发展战略。第一次把科技、教育、人才放在一起，提出非常明确的要求。我们一定要深入领会、认真学习，坚定不移地贯彻落实。特别要看到当今世界科技进步速度全面加快，人工智能、生命科学等领域已经出现颠覆性的巨大变化。中国经济发展需要有

强有力的科技支撑。在这样关键的历史始点上，我们由衷希望中国的科学家、科技人员发挥重要的历史支撑作用。

第二点，我们要提倡科学精神。最近几年，我非常荣幸联系中国的科技工作，接触了很多在这个领域作出重要成就的人，包括获得何梁何利基金奖项的人才。我发现成功的人士有几个特点：一是具有强烈的使命意识和责任感。刚才两位老师发言，大家都可以听到这一点，他们对国家负责、对人民负责、对全人类的命运负责。正是这种责任感，使他们获得了巨大的研究动力。二是有着十分执着的意志力。在自己的领域顽强地拼搏，不达到目的绝不罢休。有时可能是好奇心驱动，有时是荣誉感驱动，但最终是一定要成功，绝不放弃。三是有十分严谨的工作作风，实事求是，遵循规律，脚踏实地，发扬民主。同时，我发现这些成功人士还有一个重要的特点，就是都有较强的人文精神。人文精神和科学精神相互促进，推动事业的发展。

第三点，我呼吁科技领域的干部要进一步发挥好作用，科学技术对中国十分重要，在这个领域工作的干部们，我认为有几点至关重要。一是要坚持党的领导，充分发挥制度优势，有强烈的国家意识，在引导战略方向、创造有利于科学发展的环境上发挥更大的作用。二是要敬畏科学规律，努力补充自己的知识结构。尊重科学家和各类人才，要和业内人士建立真正的共同语言。三是要树立强烈的公仆意识，真正当好后勤部长。

最后，我再次向获奖的科学家表示热烈的祝贺，再次感谢何梁何利基金一直以来对我国科研事业的大力支持。让我们更加紧密地团结在以习近平同志为核心的党中央周围，为祖国、为人民、为全人类的科学事业作出更多更大的贡献。

谢谢大家！

# Address at the 2021 and 2022 Award Ceremony of Ho Leung Ho Lee Foundation

Liu He, Vice Premier of the State Council

(February 17, 2023)

Dear Mr. Ji Bingxuan, Vice Chairman of the Standing Committee of the National People's Congress,

Dear Mr. Wan Gang, Vice Chairman of the Chinese People's Political Consultative Conference,

Dear Ms. Zhu Lilan, Chairperson of the Trust Board of HLHL Foundation,

Dear Academician Hu Side and Lin Ming,

Dear donors and representatives of HLHL Foundation,

Dear scientists, guests, ladies and gentlemen:

Good morning, everybody!

I feel honored to attend the prize-awarding ceremony that is of important significance for the country with the approval of the Party Central Committee. The approval fully reflects that the Party Central Committee with comrade Xi Jinping at its core attaches high importance to the prizes of the HLHL Foundation, the great undertaking of scientific and technological innovation and the enterprising spirit of scientists. Here I would like to extend my warm congratulations to all prize-winning scientists on behalf of the State Council, and express my heartfelt thanks to all those supporting the prizes of the HLHL foundation. Just now, I was deeply moved and inspired by the speeches made by academician Hu Side and academician Lin Ming. I will avail myself of this opportunity to share with you some of my views.

First, we should accord high importance to the guiding role of scientific and technological innovation in the high-quality national development. The 20th National Congress of the CPC maps out a comprehensive strategic plan on scientific and technological innovation, and puts scientific and technological innovation the core strategy of national development. For the first time in history, it puts together science and technology, education and talents when mentioning them, and puts forward specific demands on them. We should have a keen understanding of the significance of these demands, and meet them through earnest study and firm implementation. What is particularly worthy of our attention is that global scientific and technological progress is gaining speed in an all-round way, and that there have appeared subversive and drastic changes in the fields of human intelligence and bioscience. China's economic development calls for powerful support from science and technology. We sincerely hope that, at this critical historical juncture, scientists as well as other science and technology workers in China can play an important, historic and supportive role.

Next, we should advocate a scientific mindset. In recent years, while getting involved in the work related to China's science and technology, I am honored to get to know many people who have made important achievements, including winners of the prizes granted by the HLHL Foundation. I discover that successful people share the following characteristics. First, they boast a strong sense of mission and responsibility. We can learn from the speeches made by two prizewinners that they are aware of the responsibilities they take for the State, the people and even the fate of the whole humanity. It is such a sense of responsibility that greatly motivates them to do research. Second, they demonstrate sheer willpower. They make tremendous efforts in their own fields of research, and they would never give up until they achieve their goals. Driven by curiosity or a sense of reputation, they will never lose heart in the pursuit of their goals until they finally attain them. Third, they do research with a rigorous style of work, seek truth from facts, follow the laws of things, adopt a down-to-earth approach and promote democracy. As I see, another characteristic shared by these successful people is that they have a strong spirit of humanism. The spirit of humanism and the spirit of science mutually promote each other and advance the research career development of scientists.

Third, I appeal to officials in the field of science and technology to bring their roles into better play. Science and technology are vital importance to China. I believe it is critically important for them to do a good job in the following aspects. First, they should adhere to the leadership of the Party, fully bring into play the institutional advantages, and foster a stronger sense of national identity. They should play a greater role in guiding the strategic orientation and creating an environment favorable for the scientific development. Second, they should hold the law of science in reverence, and equip themselves with new knowledge to improve their knowledge structure. They should respect scientists and various kinds of talents, and establish a common language with the people in science and technology circle. Third, they should foster a stronger sense of service to the people, and do a real good job in providing rear services.

Finally, let me extend my warm congratulations again to prize-winning scientists. Let me express my thanks again to the HLHL Foundation for its energetic support to China's scientific research. Let us rally even more closely around the Central Committee of the Communist Party of China with comrade Xi Jinping at its core to make still more and greater contributions to the scientific development of our motherland, our people and the whole humanity.

Thank you.

# 序

踏入 2023 年，新冠疫情威胁终于过去，社会运作及市民生活也渐回正轨。回顾疫情于 2019 年暴发，迅即蔓延至全球，除导致大量染疫者死亡，对环球经济更造成史无前例的冲击。然而，何梁何利基金凭借多年来建立的稳固基础，在信托委员会朱丽兰主席、孙煜副主席、钟登华委员、霍泰辉教授和施颖茵委员的带领，以及评选委员会和投资委员会同人的努力协调，并在基金顾问的指导下，基金的活动虽然亦受到疫情影响，但各项工作基本上都能够如常进行，各捐款人深表欣慰。

即使受到疫情影响，2022 年评选委员会收到有效提名数目突破 1000 人，达到 1073 名，是基金成立以来首次，除了反映我国科技进步和科研人才辈出这个可喜现象之外，也证明了何梁何利基金越来越受到社会各界的支持和认同。

在过去数年疫情期间，全球经济和投资环境都面对极大挑战。现时疫情虽然过去，但经济复苏仍是差强人意，加上地缘政治局势持续紧张、国际贸易矛盾和经济制裁、美国通胀及息率上升等因素，都继续为环球金融市场带来波动，经济前景仍不明朗。

然而基金自成立以来，在历任投资委员会成员的努力下，财务状况一直维持稳健，为基金的长远有效运作打造了良好条件。至今，基金共奖励了 1526 位中国杰出科学工作者，授出奖金超过港币 3.2 亿元，各捐款人对投资委员会及有关工作人员的贡献非常感谢。

今年 3 月初，国家主席习近平在第十四届全国人大会议中强调："要坚持'四个面向'，加快实施创新驱动发展战略，推动产学研深度合作，着力强化重大科技创新平台建设，支持顶尖科学家领衔进行原创性、引领性科技攻关，努力突破关键核心技术难题，在重点领域、关键环节实现自主可控。"

2021 年，国家制定"十四五规划纲要"，为中国未来五年（2021—2025 年）指明了前进方向和蓝图，将"坚持创新、加快建设科技强国"作为重点之一。当中提出的"3+4"区域创新布局，即建设 3 个国际科技创新中心（北京、上海、大湾区），以及 4 个综合性国家科学中心（北京怀柔、上海张江、安徽合肥、大湾区），同时将大湾区建设成为具有国际竞争力的科技成果转化基地。

香港是大湾区中心城市之一，何梁何利基金作为在香港成立的民间奖励基金，同人会继续在尊重知识、尊重人才、尊重创新的基础上，发挥弘扬科学精神和奖励科技人才的宗旨，配合国家以创新驱动发展战略，为建设中国成为世界科技强国的目标尽一份力。

**何梁何利基金捐款人**

何善衡慈善基金会有限公司　　梁銶琚慈善基金会有限公司
何添基金有限公司　　　　　　伟伦基金有限公司

2023 年 6 月于香港

# Preface

With the threat of the COVID-19 pandemic finally beginning to subside in 2023, the normal activities of everyday life have been getting back on track.

When the pandemic erupted in 2019, its rapid spread around the world led to a significant loss of life and had an unprecedented impact on the global economy. Amid these tremendous challenges, the Ho Leung Ho Lee Foundation benefitted from its well-established operational structure; the expert leadership of the Trustee Committee Chairman Zhu Lilan, Vice Chairman Sun Yu, and Members Zhong Denghua, Professor Fok Tai Fai, and Diana Cesar; the concerted efforts of the Selection Committee and Investment Committee, and the guidance of the Advisors. These combined strengths enabled the Foundation to proceed largely as usual with its important work. The Donors wish to express their deep gratitude to everyone involved in facilitating the Foundation's successful operation under such difficult circumstances.

Indeed, the Donors are delighted to note that the number of valid nominations received in 2022 surpassed 1000 to reach a new high of 1073 individuals. Not only does this reflect the upward trend in technological advancements and the continued emergence of talented researchers in our country, it also demonstrates the growing support and recognition the Ho Leung Ho Lee Foundation is receiving from various sectors of society.

Over the past few years, the pandemic has created formidable challenges for the global economy and the investment environment. Although the pandemic has subsided, the economy is still in the early stages of recovery. Moreover, factors such as tense geopolitical situations, international trade conflicts, economic sanctions, and rising inflation and interest rates in the United States continue to create volatility in global financial markets, which is further contributing to the uncertain economic outlook.

Nevertheless, thanks to the efforts of past and present members of the Investment Committee, the Ho Leung Ho Lee Foundation's financial situation remains robust. This will continue to facilitate the Foundation's effective long-term operation. To date, the Foundation has awarded honours to 1526 outstanding Chinese scientists, granting total prize money of over HKD 320 million. The Donors are immensely grateful to the Investment Committee and related staff for their dedication.

During the 14th National People's Congress in early March this year, President Xi Jinping emphasized that "we must adhere to the 'four aspects'; accelerate the implementation of the innovation-driven development strategy; promote deep collaboration between industry, academia and research; strengthen the construction of major scientific and technological innovation platforms; support top scientists in leading original and pioneering scientific and technological breakthroughs; strive to overcome key and core technological challenges; and achieve self-reliance and controllability in key areas and critical sectors."

The National 14th Five-Year Plan formulated in 2021 set the direction and blueprint for China's next five years (2021—2025), with "insisting on innovation and accelerating the construction of a technology powerhouse" as one of the key focuses. It proposed a "3+4" regional innovation structure, consisting of building three international science and technology innovation centres (in Beijing, Shanghai, and the Greater Bay Area) and four comprehensive national science centres (Huairou, Beijing; Zhangjiang, Shanghai; Hefei, Anhui; and the Greater Bay Area). Additionally, the plan aims to transform the Greater Bay Area into an internationally competitive hub for the conversion of scientific and technological achievements.

Hong Kong is one of the core cities in the Greater Bay Area. As a private award foundation established in Hong Kong, the Ho Leung Ho Lee Foundation will continue to uphold the principles of respecting knowledge, talent, and innovation. We are committed to promoting the spirit of science and rewarding scientific talents. In alignment with the country's strategy of innovation-driven development, we will contribute our efforts towards the goal of building China into a world-leading science and technology powerhouse.

**Donors of Ho Leung Ho Lee Foundation**

S. H. Ho Foundation Limited    Leung Kau Kui Foundation Limited
Ho Tim Foundation Limited    Wei Lun Foundation Limited

June 2023, Hong Kong

# 何梁何利基金评选委员会
# 2021和2022年度工作报告

信托委员会主席、评选委员会主任　朱丽兰

（2023年2月17日）

尊敬的刘鹤副总理，

尊敬的吉炳轩副委员长，

尊敬的万钢副主席，

同志们，朋友们：

春回大地，万物复苏。在全面贯彻落实党的二十大精神的开局之年，我们相聚北京钓鱼台国宾馆，隆重举行何梁何利基金2021和2022年度颁奖大会，向112位优秀科技工作者授予何梁何利基金科学技术奖励的崇高荣誉。这是我国科技界、教育界和社会各界的一大盛事。

国务院副总理刘鹤同志，全国人大常委会副委员长吉炳轩同志，全国政协副主席万钢同志，科技部党组书记、部长王志刚同志以及各部门领导亲临大会指导，给予我们莫大鼓舞。在此，我谨代表何梁何利基金，对党和国家领导同志的亲切关怀和悉心指导表示衷心感谢，对科技界、教育界和社会各界嘉宾和代表光临本次盛典表示热烈欢迎。

下面，我代表何梁何利基金做工作报告。

## 一、关于2021和2022年度基金信托委员会的有关决定

何梁何利基金适用中国香港法律。信托委员会为基金决策机构，投资委员会为基金资本运营机构，评选委员会为基金评审执行

机构。依据《信托契约》，一年一度的信托委员会全体会议听取、审核投资委员会、评选委员会工作报告，就基金发展的重要事项作出决定。

过去两年，由于疫情影响，2021和2022年度信托委员会全体会议均在香港和北京两地通过视频方式举行。

在2021年度信托委员会会议上，基金捐款人代表梁祥彪先生致辞，热情赞扬在信托委员会、评选委员会、投资委员会同人的共同努力下，各项工作稳步开展，取得良好业绩。基金捐款人向各位评委、各位志愿者表示衷心感谢。

在2022年度信托委员会会议上，梁祥彪先生致辞强调，2022年是香港特别行政区成立25周年。香港将更好地融入国家发展大局，共享民族复兴伟大荣光。何梁何利基金将会继续发挥自身优势，鼓励更多青年科技人才研发高新科技，推动我国科技的自立自强和创新发展。

香港捐款人代表的讲话鼓舞人心、催人奋进，得到与会同人一致赞同。

两年的信托委员会全体会议均在和谐、务实的气氛中，审议通过了相应的决定。

（一）审议并接受基金投资委员会工作报告

近年来，世界经济形势复杂，投资环境持续波动，金融市场起伏动荡。基金资本运营面临较大挑战。投资委员会把握变局，沉着应对，科学审慎管理，使得基金财务状况总体稳定向好。其中，截至2021年3月底，基金市值从上年7.42亿港元上升到7.66亿港元。截至2021年12月底和2022年3月底的基金市值始终维持在7亿至7.2亿港元的合理区间。与创立之初总值3.9亿港元相比，基金始终保持着较高增值。

考虑到未来经济形势尚存诸多变数，信托委员会会议决定：2021年度和2022年度基金的奖金总额，均按过去五年（即2016年至2020年）的平均数确定为1200万港元。这笔资金来之不易。在此，我们要感谢投资委员会面对复杂经济环境付出的艰苦努力。

## （二）审议并通过基金评选委员会工作报告

以习近平同志为核心的党中央始终把科技创新摆在国家发展核心地位。我国科技战线为实现科技自立自强、建设现代化科技强国只争朝夕、砥砺前行，科技创新发展进入跃升期。杰出人才脱颖而出，创新成果日新月异，何梁何利基金提名人数也逐年增多。2021年共收到提名推荐书1017份，有效被提名人976人。2022年共收到提名推荐书1120份，有效被提名人达到1073人，首次突破千人。获奖入选比率高达20:1，竞争十分激烈。

评选委员会全体委员和专业评委遵循《何梁何利基金评选章程》，把贯彻"公平、公正、公开"的评选方针作为基金的铁律，作为科技大奖的立业之本、权威之根、公信力之源，严格履行评审程序，优中选优，保障评选结果经得起历史考验。

适应形势发展，基金管理工作加快数字化、网络化建设，由优秀志愿者开发完成的"评选委员会科技奖网络管理系统"经公安部第三研究所信息安全高等级测评通过，于2021年专业评审会试用成功，自2022年起正式投入使用，从而使评选工作克服疫情影响，通过线下、线上相结合的方式顺利完成。

## （三）审议并通过何梁何利基金其他决定

一是毕马威会计师事务所自2006年至2021年义务承担何梁何利基金审计工作。现因运营成本原因，提出将于2021年年底终止该项业务。信托委员会感谢毕马威会计师事务所多年志愿担任基金审计师，对基金财务管理贡献良多，理解并接受其终止上述业务。

著名国际会计审计机构——罗兵咸永道会计师事务所赞赏何梁何利基金的崇高事业，同意自2022年会计年度起担任基金审计师，豁免收取所有服务费用。信托委员会对此表示衷心感谢，决定从2022年度起聘任罗兵咸永道会计师事务所义务担任本基金审计师。

二是基金信托委员会委员、评选委员会副主任沈祖尧教授因离开香港中文大学赴新加坡任职，提请辞去基金职务。信托委员会感谢沈祖尧教授多年为基金服务，贡献良多，理解并接受其辞呈。决定聘任香港中文大学原副校长、著名医学家霍泰辉教授担任信托委员会委员、评选委员会副主任。

三是评选委员会委员朱道本教授因个人身体原因，提请辞去基金职务。基金理解和接受其辞呈，决定聘任中国科学院纳米技术中心主任赵宇亮教授为评选委员会委员。

## 二、关于 2021 和 2022 年度获奖科学家的介绍

2021 和 2022 年，评选委员会在严格遵守北京市疫情防控规定的前提下，抓住"窗口期"，组织完成了初评和终评工作，各评选产生"科学与技术成就奖" 1 名、"科学与技术进步奖" 33 名、"科学与技术创新奖" 22 名，获奖人数两年合计 112 名。

（一）关于科学与技术成就奖

"科学与技术成就奖"是何梁何利基金的最高奖项，是每年评选工作的重中之重。由评选委员会委员提名，评选委员会成立预审小组进行考察、听证，形成预审报告提请评选委员会全体会议审议。

2021 年度何梁何利基金"科学与技术成就奖"得主落户中国工程物理研究院。他是我国著名核物理学家、中国工程院院士。他 1958 年于复旦大学物理系毕业，分配到二机部第九研究所，加入核科学研究和工程设计战线。20 世纪 60 年代，在国外数据严格保密、国内缺少实验条件的困难情况下，他担任课题组组长，参与第一颗原子弹的研制，成功解码复杂技术参数，架起从方案到产品的桥梁；他历任主任设计师、副院长、院长，攻克多项关键技术难题，带领团队无私拼搏、志在必得，铸就了多项科技辉煌，用较少的研究经费、较少的实验次数实现国家战略科技力量大幅提升。他作为著名核军控学者，在国际舞台上宣传中国核不扩散和核安全的政策主张，推动中外核军控领域合作研究，为维护国家安全和世界和平作出了宝贵贡献。

2022 年度何梁何利基金"科学与技术成就奖"得主为中国交通建设集团首席科学家、中国工程院院士。他 40 年如一日，在桥隧工程一线从事国家重大桥梁工程建设，参建润扬长江大桥、南京长江三桥、港珠澳大桥等重大工程，创造多项中国桥梁建设纪录。港

珠澳大桥采用桥、岛、隧组合设计方案，被誉为"新世界七大奇迹"。他领衔担任该项目的岛隧工程总设计师，带领团队守正创新、开拓进取，攻克了外海岛隧工程多项世界级难题，创造了跨海沉管安装、深插大直径钢圆筒快速筑岛等多项先进技术，形成了具有自主知识产权的跨海沉管隧道建造技术体系，主持建成了我国首条、世界最长的跨海公路沉管隧道，为我国公路沉管隧道达到国际领先水平作出了重要贡献。

（二）关于科学与技术进步奖和科学与技术创新奖

2021年和2022年"科学与技术进步奖"和"科学与技术创新奖"的110位获奖科学家，是在新时代面向科技前沿、面向经济主战场、面向国家重大需求、面向人民生命健康，在向科学技术深度和广度进军的赛道上脱颖而出的科技人员的杰出代表。人人都有一张值得骄傲的成绩单。

归纳起来，有以下亮点和特点：一是在基础研究、应用基础研究领域崭露头角，实现多项从"0到1"的原始创新、从"1到多"的应用研究成果，可喜可贺；二是打破封锁、突破瓶颈，实现技术链产业链营销链全程畅通、亮点频闪，为经济发展提供支撑和保障；三是以企业为主体、市场为导向，产学研深度融合再上台阶，赋能新兴产业发展和加速传统产业改造升级；四是区域创新催生边远、贫困和少数民族地区特色科技发展，赋能经济转型升级，推进乡村振兴战略跃升；五是医学药学、生命科学领域协同创新硕果累累，人民至上、生命至上，为人民生命健康带来福音；六是面向国家重大需求，打赢多项关键技术攻坚战，抢占科技制高点，为实现高科技自立自强迈出坚实步伐；七是获奖人员结构基本合理，获奖者年龄最大85岁、最小37岁，平均57岁，中青年科技工作者成为获奖人主体；八是自主知识产权出现质的跃升，高水平科学论文、高质量发明专利、PCT国际专利的比重有所增加；九是经过初步评估，获奖人的主要科技成果均居于国际先进行列，越来越多地从跟跑、并跑进入领跑方阵。

让我们为获奖科学家的杰出成绩表示衷心祝贺。

## 三、结语

不忘初心，方得始终。何梁何利基金创立至今，已经走过了29载春秋。1997年香港回归之年，时任中共中央政治局常委的朱镕基同志专程赴香港出席在恒生银行举行的何梁何利基金第四届颁奖大会，他挥毫为捐款人何善衡、梁銶琚、何添、利国伟先生题词："何梁何利基金奖励祖国科技人才，高谊可风，功在当代，泽被永远。"我想，这是对何梁何利基金崇高宗旨的精辟概括和深刻诠释。

令人遗憾的是，当年四位基金创立者都已在九旬高龄驾鹤仙逝。我们深深地怀念他们。而今，四位捐款人的后辈秉承先辈的志向，爱国、爱港、爱科学、爱人才，协力推进何梁何利基金承前启后、继往开来、行稳致远。在此，我向新一代捐款人代表致以崇高的敬意。

路虽远，行则将至；事虽难，做则必成。伟大时代需要伟大精神，伟大精神需要榜样引领。习近平总书记曾经指出，"用好科研人员，既要用事业激发其创新勇气和毅力，也要重视必要的物质激励"。我国科技界、教育界和社会各界人士唯有踔厉奋发、笃行不怠，持续推进科技奖励事业健康发展，方能不负历史、不负时代、不负人民。

各位领导、各位嘉宾，中华人民共和国宪法庄严宣布"国家发展自然科学和社会科学事业，普及科学和技术知识，奖励科学研究成果和技术发明创造"。奖励杰出科技人才是国家和全社会的神圣使命，是一项功在当代、泽被永远的崇高事业。让我们以习近平新时代中国特色社会主义思想为指导，努力把何梁何利基金科学与技术奖办成国际一流科技大奖，加快科技自立自强步伐，为建设富强民主文明和谐美丽的社会主义现代化国家、以中国式现代化实现中华民族的伟大复兴而努力奋斗！

谢谢大家！

# 2021 and 2022 Work Report of the Selection Board of Ho Leung Ho Lee Foundation

Zhu Lilan, Chairperson of the Trust Board and Director of the Selection Board

(February 17, 2023)

Dear Mr. Liu He, Vice Premier of the State Council,

Dear Mr. Ji Bingxuan, Vice Chairman of the Standing Committee of the National People's Congress,

Dear Mr. Wan Gang, Vice Chairman of the Chinese People's Political Consultative Conference,

Comrades and friends:

Spring returns to the earth and everything comes back to life. We are in the first year of fully implementing the guiding principles laid down at the 20th National Congress of the Communist Party of China. Today we hold the prize awarding ceremony of the HLHL Foundation for the years of 2021 and 2022 at the Diaoyutai State Guesthouse in Beijing, when we will award the prestigious scientific and technological prizes of the HLHL Foundation to 112 excellent scientists. This is a grand event for people from the science and technology circle, education circle and all other walks of life.

Mr. Liu He, vice premier of the State Council, Mr. Ji Bingxuan, vice chairman of the Standing Committee of the National People's Congress, Mr. Wan Gang, vice chairman of the Chinese People's Political Consultative Conference, Mr. Wang Zhigang, secretary of the Leading Party Members' Group of the Ministry of Science and Technology and Minister of Science and Technology, and leaders of many other departments come to this meeting to give their guidance. Their arrival brings great joy and encouragement to us. On behalf of all my colleagues at the HLHL Foundation, I would express my heartfelt thanks to the leaders of the CPC and the State for their care and guidance, and extend my warmest welcome to the distinguished guests from the education circle, science and technology circle and all other walks of life for their presence at this ceremony.

Next, I will deliver the work report on behalf of the HLHL Foundation.

## I. Decisions of the Trust Board of HLHL Foundation in 2021 and 2022

The laws of Hong Kong, China apply to the HLHL Foundation. Under the HLHL Foundation, the Trust Board is the decision-making organization, the Investment Board is the capital operating organization, and the Selection Board is the evaluation-making organization. In accordance with the Trust Deed, the plenary session of the Trust Board is held annually to hear and deliberate the work reports of the Investment Board and the Selection Board, and to make decisions on important matters concerning the development of the HLHL Foundation.

Affected by the COVID-19 epidemic, the plenary sessions of the Trust Board for the years of 2021 and 2022 were held in Hong Kong and Beijing respectively in the form of online conferencing.

In his speech delivered at the plenary session of the Trust Board in 2021, Mr. Leung Cheung Biu, representative of the donors of the HLHL Foundation, sang high praise of the colleagues in the Trust Board, the Selection Board and the Investment Board who, through their joint efforts, contributed to the steady progress and sound performance of the HLHL Foundation. The representatives of the donors expressed their heartfelt thanks to all judges and volunteers.

In his speech delivered at the plenary session of the Trust Board in 2022, Mr. Leung Cheung Biu stressed that the year of 2022 marked the 25th anniversary of the founding of the Hong Kong Special Administrative Region (HKSAR). Hong Kong would be better integrated into the development of the country, and share the glory of national rejuvenation. The HLHL Foundation will continue to bring into play its advantages to encourage still more young science and technology talents to engage in the research into high and new technologies and promote the self-reliance and self-improvement and the innovative development of science and technology in China.

The speeches made by the representative of donors from Hong Kong were encouraging and inspiring, and won the unanimous agreement of all colleagues present at the meeting.

The plenary sessions of the Trust Board over the past two years deliberated and approved corresponding decisions in a harmonious and down-to-earth atmosphere.

i. Deliberated and approved the work reports made by the Investment Board

The capital operation of the HLHL Foundation has met severe challenges as a result of the complicated international economic situation, continued fluctuation of investment environment and volatile financial market. The Investment Board handled the situation by calmly responding to changes and exercising scientific and prudent management. Thanks to these efforts, the overall financial situation of the HLHL Foundation remains steady and improving. By the end of March 2021, the market value of the HLHL Foundation went up from 742 million HK dollars in 2020 to 766 million HK dollars. It was kept within an appropriate range from 700 million HK dollars to 720 million HK dollars up to the end of December 2021 and the end of March 2022. Compared with the initial market value which stood at 390 million HK dollars when the HLHL Foundation was established, the market value today has seen considerable increases over the years.

Considering the uncertainties in the future economic situation, the Trust Board decided that the total amount of prizes in 2021 and 2022 remained 12 million HK dollars respectively, which was the average number of the total amounts allocated to each of the five years from 2016 to 2020. It is hard to obtain such a sum of money. Here we would express our thanks to the Investment Board for its hard work to deal with the complicated economic situation.

ii. Deliberated and approved the work reports made by the Selection Board

The Central Committee of the Communist Party of China with comrade Xi Jinping at its core always puts scientific and technological innovation at the core of national development. China's science and technology workers forge ahead without delay to achieve self-reliance and self-improvement in science and technology and build China into a modernized country with developed science and technology. China has entered a period of leapfrog development in innovative science and technology when excellent talents come to the fore and innovative achievements are scored every day. The numbers of nominees for the prizes of the HLHL Foundation also increase with each passing year. In 2021, a total of 1017 letters of recommendations were received, with 976 effective nominees recommended. In 2022, a total of 1120 letters of recommendation were received, with 1073 effective nominees recommended. It was the first time that the effective nominees exceeded 1000. As the ratio between nominees and prize winners reached as high as 20 : 1, the competition among nominees became fierce.

In compliance with the Selection Regulation, all members of the Selection Board and professional judges regard the adherence to the principles of justice, fairness and openness as the fundamental rules to follow in selecting prize winners. In their eyes, these principles are the basis of establishing the prizes, the root of authority of the prizes, and the origin of the credibility of the prizes. They strictly follow the procedures of evaluation, and, upholding the principle of "selecting the top from among the excellent candidates", they see to it that the selection results would withstand the test of history.

In response to the development of situation, the HLHL Foundation moved faster to adopt the digitalized and network-based approach in exercising management. Developed by excellent volunteers, the Network Management System of the Selection Board on Scientific and Technological Prizes (the management system) passed the high-degree information security test and evaluation conducted by the Third Research Institute of the Ministry of Public Security. Following its successful trial use at a professional evaluation meeting held in 2021, the management system was put into formal use from 2022. Thanks to the use of such a system, the selection of prize winners could overcome the difficulties caused by the COVID-19 epidemic, and was smoothly completed both online and offline.

iii. Deliberated and approved other decisions made by the HLHL Foundation

First, having served as the auditor of the HLHL Foundation on a voluntary basis from 2006 to 2021, KPMG LLP proposed that it would stop to serve as the auditor at the end of 2021 out of the consideration for operating costs. The Trust Board expressed thanks to KPMG LLP for its many years of voluntary auditing of the HLHL Foundation and its huge contributions to the financial management of the HLHL Foundation, and it understood and accepted the termination of the above auditing business on the part of KPMG LLP.

A world well-known accounting and auditing company, PricewaterhouseCoopers (PwC) thinks highly of the lofty mission undertaken by the HLHL Foundation, and agreed to serve as the auditor of the HLHL Foundation from the accounting year of 2022. It would also exempt the HLHL Foundation from paying all service fees. The Trust Board expressed heartfelt thanks to PwC, and decided to engage PwC as the auditor of the HLHL Foundation from 2022.

Second, professor Joseph J.Y. Sung, member of the Trust Board and deputy director of the Selection Board tendered his resignation from the HLHL Foundation since he would leave the Chinese University of Hong Kong for assuming a post in Singapore. The Trust Board expressed thanks to him for his many years of service for and substantial contributions to the HLHL Foundation, and understood and accepted his resignation. The Trust Board decided to engage professor Tai-fai Fok, former Pro-Vice-Chancellor of the Chinese University of Hong Kong and an eminent expert in medicine to serve as a member of the Trust Board and deputy director of the Selection Board.

Third, professor Zhu Daoben, a member of the Selection Board, tendered his resignation from the HLHL Foundation because of his physical health. The HLHL Foundation understood and accepted his resignation, and decided to engage professor Zhao Yuliang, director-general of the National Center for Nanoscience and Technology under the Chinese Academy of Sciences, to serve as a member of the Selection Board.

**II. About the Prize-winning Scientists in 2021 and 2022**

In each of 2021 and 2022, under the precondition of strictly observing the rules of Beijing Municipality on COVID-19 epidemic prevention and control, the Selection Board lost no time in organizing the preliminary and final evaluation, whereby it selected one winner of the Prize for Scientific and Technological Achievements, 33 winners of the Prize for Scientific and Technological Progress and 22 winners of the Prize for Scientific and Technological Innovation. The prizewinners of these two years totaled 112. Below is an introduction to these prizewinners.

i. About the Prize for Scientific and Technological Achievements

As the Prize for Scientific and Technological Achievements is the highest prize granted by the HLHL Foundation, selecting its winner is the most important task of selection each year. The Selection Board nominates candidates, and forms a pre-examination team to investigate and hear the pre-examination results. It then forms the pre-examination report and submits it to the plenary session of the Selection Board for deliberation.

The winner of the Prize for Scientific and Technological Achievements in 2021 came from China Academy of Engineering Physics, who is a renowned nuclear physicist and an academician of the Chinese Academy of Engineering. After graduating from Fudan University in 1958, he was assigned to work in the Ninth Institute of the Second Ministry of Machine Industry, where he engaged in the research of nuclear science and engineering design. In the 1960s, the countries other than China strictly kept in confidential the data related to atomic bombs from China while the conditions for doing experiments with atomic bombs were not available in China. Despite these difficulties, he participated in developing the first atomic bomb in China as the leader of a research group. He successfully decoded complicated technical specifications, and turned product solutions into real products. In those days when he was the chief designer, vice president and president of the China Academy of Engineering Physics, he addressed many difficulties in developing key technologies. In the spirit of selfless struggle and with a determination to win, he and the research teams under his leadership made several brilliant achievements. With less research expenditures and experiments, they managed to improve considerably the national strength in strategic science and technology. As an eminent scholar in nuclear arms control, he introduces China's policies and position on nuclear non-proliferation and nuclear security, and promotes the collaborative research between China and other countries on nuclear arms control. All his efforts make valuable contributions to safeguarding national security and world peace.

The winner of the Prize for Scientific and Technological Achievements in 2022 was the chief scientist of China Communications Construction Company Limited and an academician of the Chinese Academy of Engineering. Over the past 40 years, he engaged in the construction of many major bridge and tunnel engineering projects in China, for instance, the Runyang Yangtze River Bridge, the 3rd Nanjing Yangtze River

Bridge and Hong Kong–Zhuhai–Macao Bridge. These projects break many records in China's bridge construction. Combining the scheme of bridge, island and tunnel, the design solution of Hong Kong–Zhuhai–Macao Bridge is reputed as one of the "seven wonders of the modern world." While serving as the chief designer of the island and tunnel construction of Hong Kong–Zhuhai–Macao Bridge, he and the team under his leadership resolved many world-class difficulties in constructing offshore island and tunnel projects in a spirit of breaking new ground while upholding fundamental principles and blazing trails. The creation of many advanced technologies such as cross-sea immersed tunnel completes tube installation and deep submerging of large-diameter steel cylinders for fast island building forms a technical system of constructing cross-sea immersed tube tunnel, which boasts independent intellectual property rights. He presided over the construction of China's first and world's longest cross-sea immersed tunnel for road traffic, making important contributions to elevating China to the rank of world's leading powers of building immersed tunnel for road traffic.

ii. About the Prize for Scientific and Technological Progress and the Prize for Scientific and Technological Innovation

In 2021 and 2022, 110 scientists were presented with the Prize for Scientific and Technological Progress or the Prize for Scientific and Technological Innovation. They were selected from among the scientists who target global scientific and technological frontiers, serve the economy, meet major national needs, and strive to improve people's lives and health in the new era. They came to the fore on the racetrack of exploring science and technology at deeper levels and on wider scale. Each prizewinner has proud achievements to his or her credit.

In summary, the highlights and characteristics of these prizewinners and their achievements are as follows.

First, they come into prominence in the fields of basic research and basic applied research. They made a number of original innovative achievements that did not exist before or applied research results that can be used under diverse conditions and circumstances. Both prizewinners and their achievements deserve to be congratulated.

Second, the achievements of prizewinners break blockades and bottlenecks, with highlights scattered at every stage of the chains of technology, industrial chains and marketing chains, supporting and ensuring technical development.

Third, in the efforts to make achievements, the principal position of enterprises is reinforced, the market orientation is emphasized, and in-depth integration between enterprises, universities and research institutes is further promoted. All these efforts enable the development of emerging industries and accelerate the transformation and upgrading of traditional industries.

Fourth, regional innovation facilitates the development of technologies with distinctive characteristics in outlying, impoverished places and places inhabited by people of ethnic minorities, enables economic transformation and upgrading, and drives the implementation of rural rejuvenation strategy to a new level.

Fifth, fruitful achievements through collaborative innovation have been registered in the fields of medicine, pharmacy and bioscience. Acting on the belief that the people come first, and life matters most, the prizewinners bring good news on improving people's lives and health with their achievements.

Sixth, to meet major national needs, the prizewinners crack many difficulties in creating key technologies and gain an edge in developing leading technologies, making solid steps in achieving self-reliance and self-improvement in high technologies.

Seventh, the age structure of prizewinners remains reasonable. The oldest prizewinner is 85 years old, the youngest one is 37 years old, and the average age of prizewinners is 57 years. The middle-aged and young scientists constitute the majority of prizewinners.

Eighth, remarkable qualitative improvements are recorded in terms of independent intellectual property rights. High-level science papers, high-quality inventions and patents, and PCT international patents occupy a larger proportion of the prize-winning achievements than before.

Ninth, preliminary evaluation shows that the major scientific achievements made by prizewinners have entered the advanced ranks in the world. Initially running after international competitors and then running side by side with them, more and more prizewinners have become frontrunners in the competition for making scientific and technological achievements.

Let us congratulate prize-winning scientists on their outstanding achievements.

## III. Concluding Remarks

Never forget why you started, and you can accomplish your mission. Twenty-nine years have passed since the establishment of the HLHL Foundation. In 1997 when China resumed its sovereignty over Hong Kong, comrade Zhu Rongji, then a member of the Standing Committee of the Political Bureau of the Central Committee of the CPC, paid a special visit to Hang Seng Bank in Hong Kong to attend the fourth prize-awarding ceremony of the HLHL Foundation. For the four donors of HLHL Foundation—Mr. Ho Sin-Hang, Mr. Leung Kau-kui, Mr. Ho Tim and Mr. Lee Quo-Wei, Zhu Rongji wrote the following words with a writing brush, "That the HLHL Foundation rewards scientific and technological talents of China is a highly noble deed. It will benefit not only this generation, but many more to come." In my eyes, these words give a pithy summary and profound interpretation of the lofty purpose of the HLHL Foundation.

It is a pity that the four founders of the HLHL Foundation passed away in their nineties. We cherish the lasting memory of them. Today, cherishing the ambition of their predecessors and the love for the motherland, Hong Kong, science and talents, the descendants of the founders work together to carry forward the cause pioneered by their fathers for promoting the sound and steady development of the HLHL Foundation. Here I will pay high tribute to the new-generation representatives of donors.

Long as the journey is, we will reach our destination if we stay the course; difficult as the task is, we will get the job done if we keep working at it. Great era calls for great spirit, and great cause needs models to lead. President Xi Jinping pointed out that "To make good use of scientific research personnel, we should place importance on giving them necessary material incentives in addition to inspiring them to make innovations courageously and persistently with the opportunities in their career." Only through vigorous and determined endeavor, can the people from the education circle, science and technology circle and all other walks of life continue to promote the healthy development of rewarding the scientific and technological achievements, fulfill their responsibility toward history, prove worthy of their times and live up to people's expectations.

Leaders and distinguished guests, the Constitution of the People's Republic of

China solemnly proclaims that "The state shall develop the natural and social sciences, disseminate scientific and technological knowledge, and commend and award research achievements and technological discoveries and inventions." Rewarding outstanding scientific and technological talents is a sacred mission of the State and the society at large, and it is also a lofty undertaking that will benefit not only this generation, but many more to come. Let's work hard to build the scientific and technological prizes of the HLHL Foundation into internationally first-class prizes under the guidance of the Xi Jinping Thought on Socialism with Chinese Characteristics for a New Era, move faster to achieve self-reliance and self-improvement in science and technology, and work still harder to build China into a great modern socialist country that is prosperous, strong, democratic, culturally advanced, harmonious, and beautiful, and promote national rejuvenation through a Chinese path to modernization.

Thank you!

# 目 录

在何梁何利基金2021和2022年度颁奖大会上的讲话 …… 刘　鹤

序 ……………………………………………… 何梁何利基金捐款人

何梁何利基金评选委员会2021和2022年度工作报告 …… 朱丽兰

**何梁何利基金科学与技术成就奖获得者传略**
  林　鸣 ……………………………………………………（3）

**何梁何利基金科学与技术进步奖获得者传略**
  数　学　力　学　奖　获　得　者　周　刚 ………………（11）
  物　理　学　奖　获　得　者　封东来 ……………………（14）
  物　理　学　奖　获　得　者　赵红卫 ……………………（17）
  化　学　奖　获　得　者　涂永强 …………………………（20）
  地　球　科　学　奖　获　得　者　侯增谦 ………………（23）
  古生物学、考古学奖获得者　沈树忠 ……………………（26）
  生　命　科　学　奖　获　得　者　刘志杰 ………………（29）
  生　命　科　学　奖　获　得　者　宋保亮 ………………（32）
  农　学　奖　获　得　者　陈绍江 …………………………（35）
  农　学　奖　获　得　者　罗利军 …………………………（38）
  农　学　奖　获　得　者　张佳宝 …………………………（41）
  医　学　药　学　奖　获　得　者　刘德培 ………………（44）
  医　学　药　学　奖　获　得　者　马　骏 ………………（47）
  医　学　药　学　奖　获　得　者　史伟云 ………………（51）
  医　学　药　学　奖　获　得　者　王拥军 ………………（54）
  医　学　药　学　奖　获　得　者　郑晓瑛 ………………（57）

机械电力技术奖获得者　苑伟政……………………（60）
机械电力技术奖获得者　张旭辉……………………（63）
电子信息技术奖获得者　高　文……………………（66）
电子信息技术奖获得者　王振常……………………（69）
电子信息技术奖获得者　谢胜利……………………（72）
电子信息技术奖获得者　郑庆华……………………（76）
电子信息技术奖获得者　张荣桥……………………（79）
交通运输技术奖获得者　冯江华……………………（82）
冶金材料技术奖获得者　曲选辉……………………（85）
冶金材料技术奖获得者　张福成……………………（88）
化学工程技术奖获得者　袁晴棠……………………（91）
资源能源技术奖获得者　郭彤楼……………………（94）
生态环保技术奖获得者　徐祖信……………………（97）
工程建设技术奖获得者　龚晓南……………………（100）
工程建设技术奖获得者　谭永华……………………（103）
工程建设技术奖获得者　吴宏伟……………………（106）
工程建设技术奖获得者　张锦岚……………………（109）

## 何梁何利基金科学与技术创新奖获得者传略

青年创新奖获得者　戴　庆……………………（115）
青年创新奖获得者　冯　雪……………………（118）
青年创新奖获得者　刘建锋……………………（121）
青年创新奖获得者　林学春……………………（124）
青年创新奖获得者　彭　艳……………………（127）
青年创新奖获得者　杨元合……………………（131）
青年创新奖获得者　詹祥江……………………（133）
区域创新奖获得者　方创琳……………………（137）
区域创新奖获得者　李　星……………………（140）
区域创新奖获得者　欧　珠……………………（143）
区域创新奖获得者　赵永祥……………………（146）

产业创新奖获得者 丁建宁 …………………………（149）
产业创新奖获得者 董书宁 …………………………（152）
产业创新奖获得者 蒋官澄 …………………………（155）
产业创新奖获得者 骆建军 …………………………（158）
产业创新奖获得者 廉玉波 …………………………（161）
产业创新奖获得者 石　碧 …………………………（164）
产业创新奖获得者 王爱杰 …………………………（167）
产业创新奖获得者 王　军 …………………………（170）
产业创新奖获得者 王如竹 …………………………（173）
产业创新奖获得者 徐文伟 …………………………（177）
产业创新奖获得者 徐　佐 …………………………（180）

## 附　录

何梁何利基金评选章程 ………………………………（185）
关于何梁何利基金获奖科学家异议处理若干规定 ……（195）
关于何梁何利基金评选工作若干问题的说明 …………（200）
关于何梁何利基金（香港）北京代表处公告 …………（219）
何梁何利基金捐款人简历 ………………………………（221）
　何善衡 ……………………………………………（221）
　梁銶琚 ……………………………………………（221）
　何　添 ……………………………………………（223）
　利国伟 ……………………………………………（223）
何梁何利基金信托人简历 ………………………………（230）
　朱丽兰 ……………………………………………（230）
　孙　煜 ……………………………………………（231）
　钟登华 ……………………………………………（231）
　郑慧敏 ……………………………………………（232）
　霍泰辉 ……………………………………………（233）
何梁何利基金评选委员会成员简历 ……………………（239）

# CONTENTS

Address at the 2021 and 2022 Award Ceremony of Ho Leung Ho Lee Foundation
................................................................................ Liu He

Preface ........................................ Donors of Ho Leung Ho Lee Foundation

2021 and 2022 Work Report of the Selection Board of Ho Leung Ho Lee Foundation
................................................................................ Zhu Lilan

## PROFILES OF THE AWARDEES OF PRIZE FOR SCIENTIFIC AND TECHNOLOGICAL ACHIEVEMENTS OF HO LEUNG HO LEE FOUNDATION

Profile of Lin Ming ................................................................ ( 6 )

## PROFILES OF THE AWARDEES OF PRIZE FOR SCIENTIFIC AND TECHNOLOGICAL PROGRESS OF HO LEUNG HO LEE FOUNDATION

Awardee of Mathematics and Mechanics Prize, Zhou Gang ................ ( 12 )

Awardee of Physics Prize, Feng Donglai ................................... ( 16 )

Awardee of Physics Prize, Zhao Hongwei ................................. ( 19 )

Awardee of Chemistry Prize, Tu Yongqiang ................................ ( 22 )

Awardee of Earth Sciences Prize, Hou Zengqian .......................... ( 24 )

Awardee of Paleontology and Archaeology Prize, Shen Shuzhong ........ ( 27 )

Awardee of Life Sciences Prize, Liu Zhijie ................................ ( 31 )

Awardee of Life Sciences Prize, Song Baoliang ........................... ( 34 )

Awardee of Agronomy Prize, Chen Shaojiang .............................. ( 36 )

Awardee of Agronomy Prize, Luo Lijun .................................... ( 39 )

Awardee of Agronomy Prize, Zhang Jiabao ................................ ( 43 )

Awardee of Medical Sciences and Materia Medica Prize, Liu Depei ...... ( 45 )

Awardee of Medical Sciences and Materia Medica Prize, Ma Jun ........ ( 49 )

Awardee of Medical Sciences and Materia Medica Prize, Shi Weiyun ……… ( 53 )
Awardee of Medical Sciences and Materia Medica Prize, Wang Yongjun …… ( 56 )
Awardee of Medical Sciences and Materia Medica Prize, Zheng Xiaoying … ( 59 )
Awardee of Machinery and Electric Technology Prize, Yuan Weizheng …… ( 62 )
Awardee of Machinery and Electric Technology Prize, Zhang Xuhui ……… ( 64 )
Awardee of Electronics and Information Technology Prize, Gao Wen ……… ( 67 )
Awardee of Electronics and Information Technology Prize,
  Wang Zhenchang ……………………………………………………… ( 71 )
Awardee of Electronics and Information Technology Prize, Xie Shengli …… ( 73 )
Awardee of Electronics and Information Technology Prize,
  Zheng Qinghua ……………………………………………………… ( 77 )
Awardee of Electronics and Information Technology Prize,
  Zhang Rongqiao ……………………………………………………… ( 81 )
Awardee of Communication and Transportation Technology Prize,
  Feng Jianghua ……………………………………………………… ( 84 )
Awardee of Metallurgy and Materials Technology Prize, Qu Xuanhui ……… ( 87 )
Awardee of Metallurgy and Materials Technology Prize, Zhang Fucheng …… ( 90 )
Awardee of Chemical Engineering Technology Prize, Yuan Qingtang ……… ( 92 )
Awardee of Resources and Energies Technology Prize, Guo Tonglou ……… ( 96 )
Awardee of Ecology and Environmental Protection Technology Prize,
  Xu Zuxin ……………………………………………………………… ( 99 )
Awardee of Engineering and Construction Technology Prize,
  Gong Xiaonan ……………………………………………………… ( 102 )
Awardee of Engineering and Construction Technology Prize,
  Tan Yonghua ……………………………………………………… ( 105 )
Awardee of Engineering and Construction Technology Prize,
  Ng Wang Wai ……………………………………………………… ( 107 )
Awardee of Engineering and Construction Technology Prize,
  Zhang Jinlan ……………………………………………………… ( 110 )

PROFILES OF THE AWARDEES OF PRIZE FOR SCIENTIFIC AND
TECHNOLOGICAL INNOVATION OF HO LEUNG HO LEE FOUNDATION

 Awardee of Youth Innovation Prize, Dai Qing ································ ( 116 )
 Awardee of Youth Innovation Prize, Feng Xue ································ ( 120 )
 Awardee of Youth Innovation Prize, Liu Jianfeng ···························· ( 122 )
 Awardee of Youth Innovation Prize, Lin Xuechun ··························· ( 125 )
 Awardee of Youth Innovation Prize, Peng Yan ································ ( 128 )
 Awardee of Youth Innovation Prize, Yang Yuanhe ··························· ( 132 )
 Awardee of Youth Innovation Prize, Zhan Xiangjiang ······················· ( 134 )
 Awardee of Region Innovation Prize, Fang Chuanglin ······················· ( 138 )
 Awardee of Region Innovation Prize, Li Xing ································ ( 141 )
 Awardee of Region Innovation Prize, Ngodrup ······························· ( 144 )
 Awardee of Region Innovation Prize, Zhao Yongxiang ······················ ( 147 )
 Awardee of Industrial Innovation Prize, Ding Jianning ······················ ( 150 )
 Awardee of Industrial Innovation Prize, Dong Shuning ····················· ( 154 )
 Awardee of Industrial Innovation Prize, Jiang Guancheng ·················· ( 156 )
 Awardee of Industrial Innovation Prize, Luo Jianjun ························ ( 159 )
 Awardee of Industrial Innovation Prize, Lian Yubo ························· ( 163 )
 Awardee of Industrial Innovation Prize, Shi Bi ······························· ( 166 )
 Awardee of Industrial Innovation Prize, Wang Aijie ························ ( 169 )
 Awardee of Industrial Innovation Prize, Wang Jun ·························· ( 171 )
 Awardee of Industrial Innovation Prize, Wang Ruzhu ······················ ( 174 )
 Awardee of Industrial Innovation Prize, Xu Wenwei ······················· ( 179 )
 Awardee of Industrial Innovation Prize, Xu Zuo ···························· ( 182 )

APPENDICES
 REGULATIONS OF HO LEUNG HO LEE FOUNDATION ON THE EVALUATION
  AND EXAMINATION OF ITS PRIZES AND AWARDS ················ ( 189 )
 REGULATIONS ON HANDLING THE COMPLAINT LODGED AGAINST
  THE PRIZE-WINNER WITH HO LEUNG HO LEE FOUNDATION ···· ( 197 )

EXPLANATIONS ON SEVERAL ISSUES ON THE SELECTION WORK OF
   HO LEUNG HO LEE FOUNDATION ················ ( 207 )
PUBLIC ANNOUNCEMENT OF THE BEIJING REPRESENTATIVE
   OFFICE OF THE HO LEUNG HO LEE FOUNDATION (HONG KONG)
   ················································································ ( 220 )
BRIEF INTRODUCTION TO THE DONORS TO HO LEUNG HO LEE
   FOUNDATION ······························································ ( 225 )
   Brief Biography of Dr. S. H. Ho ······································ ( 225 )
   Brief Biography of Dr. Leung Kau-Kui ······························ ( 225 )
   Brief Biography of Dr. Ho Tim ········································ ( 227 )
   Brief Biography of Dr. Lee Quo-Wei ································· ( 228 )
BRIEF INTRODUCTION TO THE TRUSTEES OF HO LEUNG HO LEE
   FOUNDATION ······························································ ( 234 )
   Brief Biography of Professor Zhu Lilan ······························ ( 234 )
   Brief Biography of Mr. Sun Yu ········································ ( 235 )
   Brief Biography of Mr. Zhong Denghua ······························ ( 236 )
   Brief Biography of Ms Louisa Cheang ······························· ( 236 )
   Brief Biography of Mr. Fok Tai-Fai ·································· ( 237 )
BRIEF INTRODUCTION TO THE MEMBERS OF THE SELECTION BOARD OF
   HO LEUNG HO LEE FOUNDATION ································· ( 253 )

# 何梁何利基金科学与技术成就奖获得者传略

PROFILES OF THE AWARDEES OF PRIZE FOR
SCIENTIFIC AND TECHNOLOGICAL ACHIEVEMENTS OF
HO LEUNG HO LEE FOUNDATION

# 林　鸣

　　林鸣，1957年10月出生于江苏省扬州市。1981年毕业于南京航务工程专科学校（现已并入东南大学）港口水工建筑专业。1981—2003年就职于交通部第二航务工程局，先后参与建设了武汉三桥、润扬大桥等多座大型桥梁工程，担任技术员、项目经理、副局长等；2003—2005年任南京三桥建设指挥部副指挥长、总工程师；2005年任中国交通建设股份有限公司总工程师，历时12年主持建成港珠澳大桥岛隧工程。2021年当选中国工程院院士。现任中交集团首席科学家、上海交通大学讲席教授、东南大学博士生导师。

林鸣是桥隧及海工工程技术创新与工程管理的优秀带头人，长期坚持在一线从事国家重大桥梁工程建设，坚持自主创新，不断创造中国桥梁建设纪录。他参建的润扬长江大桥、南京长江三桥、港珠澳大桥等工程都是我国重大工程的典范，引领着当时我国工程建设的技术与管理。他在岛隧技术自主创新上取得重大突破，主持建成了我国首条、世界最长的跨海公路沉管隧道，为我国公路沉管隧道赶超国际领先作出了重大贡献。

## 一、主持攻克多座国家重点公路桥梁工程关键难题

2000年前后，林鸣在当时具有代表性的武汉三桥、润扬大桥、南京三桥等国家重点工程中主持攻克多项关键技术，提出"动态联盟"工程项目管理方法。

武汉三桥主跨618m，时为我国最大跨径斜拉桥。面对90年代大跨径桥梁建设能力与经验不足的情况，林鸣主持研发空间索定位挂设关键技术，创新采用平台法深水基础取代惯用的双壁钢围堰，为我国大跨径斜拉桥建造技术创造了重要经验。润扬大桥主跨1490m，时为我国最大跨径悬索桥。林鸣提出北锚碇嵌硬岩地连墙止水围护结构方案，主持创新千吨钢套箱工厂制造、整体安装及高塔液压爬模技术，解决了大桥重大关键技术难题。南京三桥主跨648m，为我国首座钢塔斜拉桥。林鸣组织研发钢塔制振、大节段吊装、线型控制等关键技术，填补了我国大跨径桥梁钢塔技术空白。相关成果获国家科技进步奖二等奖2项。

在桥梁管理方面，林鸣结合大型复杂工程建设实践，提出"动态联盟"工程项目管理方法，主持创新公路行业深基坑工程信息化施工成套技术，14个月建成润扬大桥"神州第一锚"；整合优质资源实现精细管理，提前22个月建成南京三桥，直接经济效益5.47亿元。

## 二、主持研发港珠澳大桥岛隧工程关键技术，形成具有自主知识产权的跨海岛隧建造技术体系

作为中交集团总工程师，林鸣从2005年开始组织港珠澳大桥前期工作研究和筹备工作。为了不影响香港机场通航及珠江口出海航道的远期发展，港珠澳大桥主通航孔采用了6.7km沉管隧道方案。港珠澳大桥沉管隧道是世界最长的公路沉管隧道，也是世界唯一的深埋沉管隧道和我国第一条跨海沉管隧道，与世界已有的沉管隧道相比有四方面的突出难点：①沉管隧道单节重量80000t，超过以往沉管的1倍；②工程海域每年遭遇多次台风，灾害性风险极大；③建设条件特别复杂，表现在珠江洪汛导致复杂的海流及海水温盐变化、地质情况复杂多变、回淤影响严重；④珠江口是中华白海豚核心保护区，而且跨香港水域，环保极具挑战。

世界沉管隧道历史近200年，当时只有美国、荷兰、日本具备建造能力。在港珠澳大桥之前，世界最长的公路沉管隧道——韩国釜山沉管长3.4km，是由荷兰、日本、韩国合作建设的。国内沉管隧道发展历史还不到20年，建成的沉管隧道总长不到4km，平均

长度 370m，平均工期 6.4 年。港珠澳沉管隧道长 6.7km、单段重 80000t、工期 7 年，港珠澳大桥不仅是我国第一次建设跨海沉管隧道，而且是建世界规模最大、最复杂的沉管隧道，为确保工程顺利建成，国家决定采用设计施工总承包模式。林鸣作为前期策划人和央企的技术负责人，担负起了工程建设重任，带领团队自主研发跨海岛隧建造技术体系，攻克了深埋沉管、超厚软土沉降控制、海上快速筑岛等世界性工程技术难题。作为岛隧工程项目总经理、总工程师，林鸣主持完成了一系列关键技术创新，创建"模式、技术、方法"深度融合的工程管理体系，为港珠澳大桥建设作出了重要贡献。

1. 主持发明"半刚性"沉管新结构

沉管隧道一般埋深 1～2m，港珠澳沉管隧道最大埋深 22m，基础荷载增加 3～5 倍，传统柔性与刚性沉管结构均不适用。为此，林鸣提出"半刚性"沉管构想及利用预应力改善沉管接头抗力和变形能力总体方案，主持接头传力机理试验研究，确定合理预应力度、接头摩擦系数等重要参数，研发沉管结构部分无粘结纵向预应力和剪力键超限保护"记忆支座"等关键技术，解决了沉管深埋难题。相关成果获授权发明专利 6 项、省部级科技特等奖 1 项。

2. 主持研发"复合地基+组合基床"隧道基础新技术

港珠澳沉管隧道水下基础长约 6km，软土地基最厚 40m，沉降风险极大。林鸣创新"复合地基+组合基床"隧道基础结构，主持试验研究揭示了超固结地基条件下沉管隧道基础"瞬时沉降"规律，研发基础抛石夯实、基床面清淤等系统，形成了深水基础精细化施工成套技术。相关成果获授权发明专利 7 项、省部级科技特等奖 1 项。

3. 主持研发跨海沉管隧道建造技术

跨海沉管隧道建造技术是港珠澳大桥"卡脖子"技术。他发明单测量塔管尾绝对定位关键方法，主持试验揭示先铺法沉管轴线运动规律及控制机理，创新免精调无潜水作业对接沉管安装技术，实现了跨海沉管安装核心技术突破。主持发明整体式主动止水最终接头新结构，创造一天完成对接（传统止水板法半年以上）、贯通精度 2.6mm 的工程纪录，实现了沉管隧道合龙技术的重大突破。相关成果获授权发明专利 15 项、国家级工法 1 项、省部级科技特等奖 2 项。

4. 主持创新深插大直径钢圆筒快速筑岛技术

人工岛建设同时受台风等极端天气、白海豚保护、通航安全和工期等条件限制。林鸣首创深插大直径钢圆筒快速筑岛兼作围护结构同步形成海中大型深基坑的技术；主持攻克结构体系和设计方法，研发八锤联动振沉、数字化定位纠偏快速筑岛工法体系。相关成果获授权发明专利 3 项、省部级科技特等奖 1 项。

港珠澳大桥被英国卫报评为"新世界七大奇迹"，岛隧工程在 2018 年一举获得了英国土木工程师协会 NCE、美国承包商协会 ENR、国际隧协 ITA 三项年度工程大奖。

林鸣个人获授权发明专利 67 项（国外 9 项），中国优秀专利奖 2 项；国家科技进步奖二等奖 2 项，省部级科技进步奖特等奖 5 项、一等奖 11 项；获第四届中国质量奖（个人奖）、全国企业管理现代化创新成果一等奖（主创人）。

# Profile of Lin Ming

Lin Ming was born in Yangzhou City of Jiangsu Province in October 1957. In 1981, he graduated from Nanjing Aviation Engineering College ( now merged into Southeast University ), majoring in port hydraulic architecture. From 1981 to 2003, he worked in the Second Harbor Engineering Bureau of the Ministry of Transportations, and successively participated in the construction of many large-scale bridge projects such as Wuhan Three Bridges and Runyang Bridge, serving as technician, project manager and deputy director. From 2003 to 2005, he served as the deputy commander and chief engineer of Nanjing Three Bridges Construction Headquarters. In 2005, he served as the chief engineer of China Communications Construction Co., Ltd., and presided over the construction of the Hong Kong-Zhuhai-Macao Bridge Island Tunnel Project for 12 years. In 2021, he was elected as an academician of the Chinese Academy of Engineering. He is currently the chief scientist of CCCC, a chair professor of Shanghai Jiao Tong University, and a doctoral supervisor of Southeast University.

Lin Ming is an excellent leader in bridge-tunnel and offshore engineering technology innovation and project management, and has long been engaged in the construction of major national bridge projects in the front line, adhered to independent innovation, and constantly created a record of bridge construction in China. The projects he participated in the construction of Runyang Yangtze River Bridge, Nanjing Yangtze River Three Bridge, Hong Kong-Zhuhai-Macao Bridge and other projects are all models of major projects in China, leading the technology and management of China's engineering construction at that time. He has made a major breakthrough in the independent innovation of island tunnel technology, presided over the construction of China's first and the world's longest cross-sea highway immersed tunnel, and made significant contributions to China's highway immersed tunnel catching up with the international leading level.

**1. Presided over overcoming key problems in a number of national key highway and bridge projects**

Around 2000, Lin Ming presided over a number of key technologies in the representative national key projects such as Wuhan the Third Bridge, Runyang Bridge, and Nanjing the Third Bridges, and proposed the "Dynamic Alliance" project management method.

## 2. Preside over the research and development of the key technologies of the Hong Kong-Zhuhai-Macao Bridge Island Tunnel Project, and form a cross-sea island tunnel construction technology system with independent intellectual property rights

As the general manager and chief engineer of the island tunnel project, Lin Ming personally presided over the completion of a series of key technological innovations, created an engineering management system that deeply integrates "mode, technology and method", and made important contributions to building the Hong Kong–Zhuhai–Macao Bridge.

Lin Ming has personally obtained 67 authorized invention patents (9 abroad), and 2 China Excellent Patent Awards; 2 second prizes of National Science and Technology Progress Award, 5 special prizes of provincial and ministerial science and technology progress awards, and 11 first prizes; Won the 4th China Quality Award (Individual Award), the first prize of National Enterprise Management Modernization Innovation Achievement (main creator). Lin Ming has a firm political stance, loves the Party and the country, has a decent study style, good conduct, strives for technical excellence, is willing to dedicate himself to work, builds bridges and educates people, and has cultivated a number of backbone national major project construction for the industry, and has been awarded the national model worker and the national outstanding Communist Party member.

# 何梁何利基金科学与技术进步奖获得者传略

PROFILES OF THE AWARDEES OF PRIZE FOR SCIENTIFIC AND TECHNOLOGICAL PROGRESS OF HO LEUNG HO LEE FOUNDATION

# 数学力学奖获得者

# 周　　刚

周刚，1964年6月出生于陕西省西安市。北京理工大学毕业。1986—1999年在中国人民解放军原89801部队（1998年10月改为63672部队）工作，历任研究实习员、研究室副主任，副研究员。1999—2014年在中国人民解放军63672部队，历任研究室主任、副总工程师、副所长、所长，研究员。2014年至今在中国人民解放军63650部队工作，任总工程师、研究员。2021年当选中国工程院院士。

周刚是核科学技术与工程专业、核材料与核燃料学科、爆炸力学方向的知名专家，63650部队总工程师、军委装备发展部与军委科技委四个技术专家组成员。他围绕国家安全重大需求，主持相关科研试验攻关并取得突出成绩。35年来，获国家科技进步奖二等奖3项、军队科技进步奖一等奖2项和二等奖5项；获授权国家发明专利11件。

### 一、成功研制系列爆炸密封装备并在重大国家科研试验中应用

分别主持和参与研制成功强约束条件下系列爆炸密封重大装备，攻克封闭冲击、破片与气体产物关键技术难题，为开展重大国家实验、形成新的国家研究能力提供了基础和前提，彻底改变了动态实验方式。

### 二、建立了国家唯一特种材料动能装备试验场技术系统

主持国家唯一大型特种材料动能装备试验场技术系统设计和建设，攻克系列关键技术，为我国新型特种材料动能装备体系建立、威力提升提供前提与验证条件，为试验场建立奠定技术基础。初步建成试验场试验、测试与装备性能评价鉴定技术系统，已分别成功开展两型特材动能装备的科研与鉴定试验。

三、研制多型先进高效动能装备，其中两型列装部队

主持研制成功并列装两型装备。正在主持研制四型先进高效动能装备，探索了基于未来作战平台的动能装备，作为项目负责人，主持了两项重大（点）项目的研究。

# Awardee of Mathematics and Mechanics Prize, Zhou Gang

Zhou Gang was born in Xi'an City of Shaanxi Province in June 1964. He graduated from Beijing Institute of Technology. From 1986 to 1999, he worked in the former 89801 Unit (renamed 63672 Unit in October 1998) of the People's Liberation Army of China, serving successively as a research intern, deputy director of the research office, and associate research fellow. From 1999 to 2014, he successively held the posts of director of the research office, deputy chief engineer, deputy director of the institute, director of the institute, and research fellow in the 63672 Unit of the People's Liberation Army of China. Since 2014, he has been working in the 63650 Unit of the People's Liberation Army of China, serving as chief engineer and research fellow. In 2021, he was elected as an academician of the Chinese Academy of Engineering.

Zhou Gang is a well-known expert in the field of nuclear science, technology and engineering, nuclear materials and nuclear fuels, and mechanics of explosion. He is currently chief engineer of the 63650 Unit, and a member of four technical expert groups of the Equipment Development Department and the Science and Technology Commission under the Military Commission. He has led relevant scientific research experiments and achieved outstanding results around major national security needs. Over the past 35 years, Zhou has won three National Science and Technology Progress Awards (second class), two Military Science and Technology Progress Awards (first class), and five Military Science and Technology Progress Awards (second class); and has been granted with 11 national invention patents.

**I. He successfully developed a series of explosion sealing equipment and applied them in major national scientific research experiments**

He led and participated in the successful development of a series of major equipment for explosion sealing under strong constraint conditions, and overcame key technical difficulties in confined shock, fragments, and gaseous products, providing a foundation and prerequisite for conducting major national experiments and the formation of new national research capabilities, and completely changing the method of dynamic experiment.

## II. He established the only technology system in China for testing ground of special material-kinetic energy equipment

He led the design and construction of the only technology system in China for large-scale testing ground of special material-kinetic energy equipment, and overcame a series of key technical difficulties, providing a prerequisite and verification condition for the establishment and power enhancement of China's new special material-kinetic energy equipment systems, and laying a technical foundation for the establishment of such testing grounds. The technical systems for experiments and tests at testing grounds and the evaluation and appraisal of equipment performance have been initially established, and scientific research and appraisal tests for two types of special material-kinetic energy equipment have been successfully carried out.

## III. He developed several types of advanced and efficient kinetic energy equipment, two of which are now used in troops

He successfully led the development of two types of equipment which are now used in troops. He is currently leading the development of four types of advanced and efficient kinetic energy equipment, and exploring kinetic energy equipment based on future combat platforms. As a project leader, he also led the research on two major (key) projects.

# 物理学奖获得者

# 封 东 来

封东来，1972年10月出生于江苏省盐城市。于1994、1996年先后获中国科学技术大学近代物理系学士和硕士学位，2001年获得美国斯坦福大学物理系博士学位。先后在加拿大不列颠哥伦比亚大学物理和天文系、复旦大学物理系、中国科学技术大学从事科研和教学。现任中国科学技术大学国家同步辐射实验室主任、核科学技术学院执行院长、合肥微尺度物质科学国家研究中心教授。中国科学院院士、美国物理学会会士。

封东来长期从事凝聚态体系微观机理的实验研究，发展了电子结构测量技术，在揭示关联材料的实验图像和观测材料新奇性质等方面取得了系列原创成果。

## 一、实验探索高温超导机理

1. 系统揭示两大类铁基超导的电子结构，阐明了复杂表象背后统一的实验图像，为建立当前铁基超导理论提供了系统的实验依据

铁基超导发现之初，曾被认为是与铜氧化物高温超导迥异的新一类高温超导。随着研究深入，发现铁基超导具有多样的电子结构、能隙分布、母体相和相图，而能否建立统一的物理图像是高温超导领域的核心问题。封东来和合作者发现铁硒类超导 $K_xFe_{2-y}Se_2$ 仅具有电子型费米面，超导能隙无节点，这一发现无法被早期铁基超导主流的弱耦合理论解释；发现含节点铁砷类超导的能隙分布与无节点铁砷类超导的能隙对称性一致；发现 $K_xFe_{2-y}Se_2$ 超导的母体是莫特绝缘体，且铁砷类超导的自旋密度波母体来自局域磁性，并揭示了多样的铁基超导相图演化形式是基于电子关联演化的实质。这些工作阐明了铁基超导多个复杂表象下统一的物理图像，否定了弱耦合理论，表明铁基和铜基两类高温超导机理的本质是一致的，均可用局域强耦合图像描述，推动了高温超导统一机理的探索。

2. 在铜氧化物高温超导中发现铜氧层间耦合和电子态相干分量的演化规律，为理论模型的建立提供了关键事实

铜氧化物中的铜氧层间耦合是诺贝尔奖得主菲利普·安德森等提出的一类高温超导理论的基础，但长期未被实验观测到。封东来等首次证实了层间耦合的存在，发现铜氧化物超导单电子激发谱中的相干分量的演化规律符合基于莫特绝缘体的超导理论，被列为高温超导领域重要实验结果之一。

### 二、发现电声子耦合与电子关联协同增强超导机制

电声子耦合和电子关联分别是常规超导理论和非常规超导理论的核心，但对于两者能否协同作用、产生更高温的超导一直没有定论。封东来等在两类重要超导体系中发现了电声子耦合与电子关联协同作用产生并增强超导的两种机制，拓展了现有超导物理图像，为设计和寻找更高温的超导提供了新思路。

1. 揭示界面电声子耦合和短程电子关联协同增强高温超导的机制

生长于钛酸锶衬底上的单层铁硒具有界面超导和铁基超导中最大的超导能隙。封东来等实现铁硒/氧化物界面的生长、调控与原位测量，得到其电子结构及超导配对信息，说明了磁性不是导致界面超导配对增强的主要因素；通过同位素效应，确定了界面电声子的耦合，并证明其与电子关联协同提高了超导能隙。通过构筑铁硒/铁酸镧异质结，获得80K的该类超导能隙闭合温度纪录。

2. 证明电子长程关联可增强铋氧化物超导中的电声子耦合，解释了其高超导温度

铋氧化物超导体最早发现于1976年，1988年人们在$Ba_{1-x}K_xBiO_3$中发现了32K的超导转变温度（在氧化物超导体中仅次于铜氧化物）。有计算表明：电声子耦合很弱，远不足以解释这么高的超导转变温度，其机理一直存疑。封东来等解决了立方体系电子结构测量难题，首次获得了$Ba_{1-x}K_xBiO_3$的能带与能隙结构，证实了电子长程关联大大增强了电声子耦合的理论预言，从而证明其超导电性仍然来自电声子耦合机制。

### 三、实验研究凝聚态体系拓扑特性

封东来等在探索新型拓扑材料方面取得了系列成果。发现了（Li，Fe）OHFeSe是目前最高超导转变温度的拓扑超导体的证据，在其磁通涡旋中观察到马约拉纳零能模，首次测得该马约拉纳零能模的量子化电导；揭示了重费米子体系电子结构的近藤效应，给出$SmB_6$作为首个拓扑近藤绝缘体的直接实验证据；率先给出NbP为外尔半金属的证据。

封东来在《科学》和《自然》（4篇）及其子刊（20篇）、《现代物理评论》（1篇）、《物理评论快报》（32篇）和《物理评论X》（8篇）等刊物共发表论文180余篇，相关成果曾获国家自然科学奖二等奖、联合国教科文组织侯赛因青年科学家奖、海外华人物理学会亚洲成就奖、亚太物理学会联盟杨振宁奖、中国物理学会叶企孙奖、上海市青年科技杰出贡献奖和上海市自然科学奖一等奖等奖项。

# Awardee of Physics Prize, Feng Donglai

Feng Donglai was born in Yancheng City of Jiangsu Province in October 1972. He has received his BS and MS degrees in Physics from the University of Science and Technology of China (USTC) in 1994 and 1996 respectively, and PhD degree in physics from Stanford University in 2001. He is currently the director of the National Synchrotron Radiation Laboratory, executive dean of the School of Nuclear Science and Technology, and Yan-Jici Chair professor of the School of Physics at USTC. In 2021, he was elected as an academician of the Chinese Academy of Sciences.

Feng Donglai has been long engaged in experimental research on the microscopic mechanism of condensed matter system. He developed electronic structure measurement techniques, and made a series of original achievements in revealing experimental pictures and novel properties of various quantum materials. His work helped to shape the understanding of iron-based superconductors and provided a systematic experimental basis for establishing the current theory of iron-based superconductivity. He revealed cooperative mechanisms of electron phonon coupling and electron correlation for enhancing superconductivity in FeSe/oxide interfacial superconductors and bismuthates. His work also deepened the understanding of charge density wave, heavy fermion system and Mott phase transition. Moreover, he has found the experimental evidence for the Majorana zero mode in novel topological superconductors, topological Kondo insulators, and Weyl semi-metals.

Feng Donglai has published more than 180 papers. He has been awarded the second prize of the National Natural Science Award, the Javed Husain Prize for Young Scientist of UNESCO, Asian Achievement Award of the Overseas Chinese Physics Association, Ye Qisun Award of Chinese Physical Society, and the first prize of Shanghai Municipal Natural Science Award etc.

# 物理学奖获得者

# 赵红卫

赵红卫，1966年1月出生于甘肃省宁县。1984年毕业于成都科技大学（现四川大学）应用物理系，1995年在俄罗斯杜布纳核联合研究所获科学技术博士学位，1996年在中国科学院近代物理研究所获理学博士学位。1991年至今在中国科学院近代物理研究所工作。2003年3月至今任中国科学院近代物理研究所副所长。兰州大学、中国科学院大学、中国科技大学兼职教授。2019年当选中国科学院院士。

赵红卫主要从事离子加速器物理相关领域的研究工作，在高电荷态离子源、质子超导直线加速器和重离子回旋加速器等方面作出了系统的、具有原创性和重要国际影响的工作。曾获国家科技进步奖二等奖2项、中国科学院科技进步奖一等奖1项、甘肃省科技进步奖特等奖1项、甘肃省科技进步奖一等奖3项以及国际离子源领域最高奖Brightness Award等学术奖励。

## 一、强流高电荷态重离子束产生

自20世纪90年代末，赵红卫先后主持研制成功水冷常温线圈磁体、全永磁磁体、蒸发冷却线圈磁体和全铌钛超导磁体的系列高电荷态ECR（电子回旋共振）离子源。其领导的团队在国际上首次提出了一种把三个螺线管置于六极磁体内部的ECR等离子体超导磁约束新结构和高磁镜比"最小B"磁场新构形以及微波耦合加热等离子体新模式。这些创新有效地提高了ECR等离子体密度、电子能量和离子约束时间，产生了持续稳定的高密度高电荷态ECR等离子体，解决了等离子体约束和电子碰撞电离产生强流高电荷态离子束的关键问题。主持研制成功世界上性能最好的基于NbTi超导磁体的高电荷态ECR离子源（SECRAL和SECRAL II），产生了从氧到铀元素绝大部分高电荷态重离子束流强度的世界纪录，如 $^{16}O^{6+}$ 6.7 emA，$^{40}Ar^{18+}$ 15 eμA，$^{129}Xe^{30+}$ 365 eμA，$^{209}Bi^{31+}$ 680 eμA，$^{238}U^{33+}$ 450 eμA，$^{238}U^{35+}$ 315 eμA 等。2007—2018年，SECRAL超导离子源已为兰州重离子加速器累计提供各种高电荷态重离子束流超过 35000 小时，SECRAL Ⅱ 截至目前已供束约 17000 小时，并创造了为加速器单次不间断连续供束超过 1000 小时的世界纪录。10 多年里，赵红卫领导的团队把极重离子束流强度提高了约两个量级，一直处于强流高电荷态离子束产生国际领先水平。近期提出并正在研制世界首台 45GHz Nb3Sn 高场新结构超导磁体的高电荷态 ECR 离子源，已取得突破性进展，引领国际 ECR 离子源领域从第三代向第四代发展。

20 多年来，赵红卫领导的团队为国内外实验室研制了 10 多台高电荷态 ECR 离子源，这些离子源全部投入兰州重离子加速器 HIRFL 或国内外其他离子束装置上稳定运行供束。研制的高电荷态离子源为 HIRFL 提供了 $Ca^{11+}$、$Kr^{26+}$、$Xe^{32+}$、$Sn^{26+}$、$Bi^{31+}$、$U^{32+}$ 等高流强高电荷态重离子束，使 HIRFL 实现了从碳到铀全离子加速，并显著提高了加速器束流强度，使兰州重离子冷却储存环能够在世界上首次对 30 多个短寿命核素质量进行高精度测量，解决了一些核天体物理学重要科学问题；提供的各种高流强重离子束为我国在世界上首次合成 30 多种新核素等成果的取得创造了必要条件。

### 二、强流质子超导直线加速器

作为项目负责人，领导团队设计并建成世界首台 17—25 MeV 连续波强流质子超导直线加速器。提出了极低束流损失和极低纵向发射度的超导直线加速器动力学设计方法，研制出高性能极低 β 半波长超导腔，实现了 4K 低温下的微弱束损和束流轨道在线监测技术以及高功率连续束秒量级自动加载与故障快速恢复技术，突破了低能量段强流高功率连续波质子束极低损失传输、加速和长时间稳定运行的难题。研制成功国际上束流强度和束流功率最高的连续波质子超导直线加速器，首次实现束流强度 10mA 连续波质子束 174kW 稳定运行，在 126kW 束流功率下连续运行 108 小时，验证了全超导直线加速器稳定加速 10mA 连续波质子束的可行性，为加速器驱动的先进核裂变能、高通量中子源、稀有同位素制备等重大核技术应用奠定了基础。

### 三、紧凑型重离子回旋加速器

作为项目负责人，主持研制成功用于重离子束治癌的高性价比紧凑型回旋加速器注入器，把碳离子 $^{12}C^{5+}$ 加速到能量 6.5 MeV/A，引出碳离子束流强度 10—15 eμA。该回旋加速器的特点和创新之处在于采用全永磁高电荷态离子源轴向注入、加速器结构紧凑、无任何垫补线圈。以该回旋加速器为注入器的重离子治疗装置规避了国外专利的限制，为我国首台具有完全自主知识产权的重离子治癌专用装置的成功研发发挥了关键作用。该重离子治癌专用装置已在医院稳定运行两年多，临床治疗肿瘤患者 600 多例。配有该回旋加速器的重离子治癌专用装置已在国内推广建设 7 台。

# Awardee of Physics Prize, Zhao Hongwei

Zhao Hongwei was born in Ning County of Gansu Province in January 1966. He received his Doctor's degree in Science and Technology from Joint Institute of Nuclear Research, Russia in 1995, and received another Doctor's degree in Physics from Institute of Modern Physics (IMP), Chinese Academy of Sciences (CAS) in 1996. He has conducted research work at IMP since 1991, an outstanding senior physicist. He has been a Deputy-Director of IMP since March 2003. He was entitled an academician of CAS in 2019. He has been engaged in ion accelerator physics and related research work. He has made original and internationally significant achievements in the research fields of highly-charged ion source, superconducting proton linac and heavy ion cyclotron accelerators.

Zhao Hongwei has accomplished and led successfully design, construction and development of highly-charged ECR ion sources based on water-cooling normal-conducting magnet, all permanent magnet, evaporation-cooling magnet and NbTi superconducting magnet. He and his team have conceived, developed and demonstrated an innovative NbTi superconducting magnet structure for highly-charged ECR plasma confinement by moving the sextupole magnet outside the three solenoids. On basis of the innovation, he and his team have designed and built two highly-charged ECR ion sources based on the NbTi superconducting magnet (SECRAL and SECRAL II). SECRAL and SECRAL II have demonstrated the world best performance at the world leading levels of highly-charged ECR ion source by producing many of highly-charged heavy-ion record beam intensities from oxygen to uranium elements and long-term operation to the accelerator facility. More recently, he and his team are building a world first 4th generation highly-charged ECR ion source based on $Nb_3Sn$ high field superconducting magnet and 45 GHz high power microwave, leading a transition from the 3rd generation to the 4th generation for the world ECR ion source community.

As a project leader, He has led a team to accomplish design, construction and demonstration of a world first 17-25 MeV continuous-wave (CW) high-intensity proton superconducting linac accelerator. The team has proposed and demonstrated a new beam-dynamics design with extremely low beam loss and low longitudinal emittance. CW 10 mA proton beam stable acceleration at energy 17.4 MeV has been demonstrated, and 126 kW CW proton beam at energy 17.2 MeV has been run continuously for 108 hours with availability 93%. All of these are the world first demonstrations at the world leading levels of CW proton superconducting linac accelerator. He has led a team to accomplish design, construction and demonstration of a compact high-intensity heavy-ion cyclotron injector dedicated to a synchrotron medical accelerator for tumor treatment. The cyclotron with $^{12}C^{5+}$ energy 6.5 MeV/A and extracted beam intensity 10-15 eμA has been put into long-term routine operation for the China first carbon ion therapy facility by which more than 600 patients were treated.

# 化学奖获得者

# 涂永强

涂永强，1958年10月出生于贵州省遵义市。1982年毕业于兰州大学化学系有机化学专业，1989年在兰州大学获得博士学位；1993—1995年在澳大利亚昆士兰大学作博士后研究，主要从事天然产物的分离、结构和生物活性研究。1995年回国后在兰州大学任教授，独立开展有机合成研究；2005年受聘教育部"长江学者特聘教授"；1996—1998年任兰州大学化学系副主任，2001—2010年任功能有机分子化学国家重点实验室主任，2018—2022年任上海交通大学化学化工学院院长。2009年当选中国科学院院士。2012—2018年任英国皇家化学会杂志 Chem. Commun. 副主编。2015—2020年任教育部科技委化学化工学部副主任。现任中国化学会常务理事，中国化学会会士，英国皇家化学会会士。

涂永强长期致力于有机合成领域研究，取得了具有重要影响的研究成果，主要包括碳–碳键重排反应及其合成应用研究，新型手性催化剂和金属有机催化剂的设计、制备和反应性质研究，药物和生物活性天然产物的高效合成策略研究。曾获中国化学会青年化学奖、合成化学奖和手性化学奖，香港求是基金会杰出青年学者奖，以及3次省部级科技奖一等奖。2012年被授予"全国优秀科技工作者"称号。2016年获国家自然科学奖二等奖。

## 一、发展新型碳–碳重排反应

如何通过碳–碳键迁移或重排，一步构建较为复杂的结构单元，是有机合成研究追求的目标之一。涂永强瞄准了一个沉睡上百年的频哪醇重排反应，首次设计了还原、氧化、亲电、亲核等多类反应与之串接，系统发展了近30种新型、高选择性的反应和方法。由此创建了一系列高效构建"多立体中心、多官能团结构单元"的新策略，并首次实现了这类重排反应的催化不对称模式。同时，还实现了抗癌药物紫杉醇和三尖杉碱、止咳中药百部碱、治疗老年痴呆病药物加兰他敏等30多种药物、生物活性天然产物及关键中间体的合成。

自 20 世纪 90 年代，涂永强团队不断把这一反应研究推向新的制高点，成为这一领域的领跑者。部分工作被英国皇家化学会评为 20 个最具代表性合成策略。目前，越来越多的国内外学者正在跟进这一反应研究，并设计了许多高效的天然产物分子合成策略，必将为有机合成和药物化学的研究产生更大影响。

在创新有机化学反应方面，自 2018 年，涂永强设计开发更具挑战的有机合成反应——构建多环多中心的"环化/扩环"反应。这个反应的原理是基于交叉学科中物质的"团簇与扩散，或压缩与膨胀"原理，一步转化即可构建较为复杂的多环多中心的结构单元。实现这一转化过程面临极大的挑战性，因为过渡态中相邻季碳中心空间位阻极大、能垒高，使得反应难以进行。最终，借助小环的扩环动力，并通过基团的电负性调节和共轭效应驱动，实现了预期转化。他还对反应规律和普适性进行研究，已成功用于罗汉松油的四环二萜快捷合成。这一反应已成为有机合成的高效、普适性的构环新方法。

### 二、发展新型催化剂，开辟手性药物合成策略

自 2012 年，涂永强设计和发展了一类具有我国自主知识产权的新型氮-杂螺环手性催化剂。其优点是结构刚柔并济、分子量小，即可用作有机催化，又可为配体形成金属配合物实现金属催化。目前已衍生出 100 多个催化剂物种，用于 20 多个重要有机反应中，并实现了吗啡、可待因等 10 多个镇痛药物或中间体的高效不对称合成。通过进一步优化、拓展，有望成为国内外最优势的催化剂之一。

### 三、发展新型金属有机催化剂，探索有机合成新反应

许多高附加值的化工原料或药物中间体，例如制备尼龙-66 的己内酰胺等，可以利用金属有机配合物催化，从炼油、炼焦炭或来自天然气中的小分子转化合成。这对减少温室气体、缓解全球变暖问题也具有重要价值。实现这些转化的关键是发展性能优越的金属有机催化剂，把惰性的碳-氢键活化、断裂，使之形成各种有价值的化工原料。

针对这一科学问题，涂永强设计制备了一类结构独特的螺环稠合的六元环氮杂卡宾（SNHC）配体，其亲电性较强，可以通过氧化还原制成许多高价的金属配合物；有的配合物初步表现出独特的化学性质，如催化较为惰性的碳-氢键、活化乙炔选择性制备氯乙烯等。

### 四、发挥有机合成优势，助力新药研发

涂永强与中国医学科学院药物研究所合作承担了科技部十三五"重大新药创制"专项"天然产物来源创新药物新品种研发及其关键创新技术体系"的第 5 课题，建立了一系列构建天然产物骨架的新技术，完成了 39 个活性天然产物高效和多样性的全合成，为新药研发提供了物质基础和科技支撑。相关工作发表高水平研究论文近 100 篇，发明 10 多项专利，新获得临床批件 1 项，为我国的新药创制和药物合成新工艺开发作出了突出贡献。

# Awardee of Chemistry Prize, Tu Yongqiang

Tu Yongqiang was born in Zunyi City of Guizhou Province in October 1958. He now works for Lanzhou University and Shanghai Jiao Tong University. He graduated from Lanzhou University in 1982, and then obtained his M.S. and Ph.D. at LU in 1985 and 1989. He undertook the postdoctoral research in chemo-ecology at the University of Queensland, Australia, working with Prof. William Kitching (1993—1995). During 2004—2005, he worked as an academic visiting professor at Bielefeld University, Germany. He obtained a full professor position and began his independent research since 1995 at Department of Chemistry of Lanzhou University. Then he served as the vice-Dean of this department (1996—1998) and the Director of State Key Laboratory of Applied Organic Chemistry (2001—2010) at Lanzhou University. In 2009. He was elected as an academician member of Chinese Academy of Sciences. During 2012—2018, he served as an Associate Editor for *Chem. Commun.* Since 2014, he joined part-time in Shanghai Jiao Tong University, and then served as the Dean of the School of Chemistry and Chemical Engineering (2018—2022). Currently, he is a fellow of Chinese Chemical Society and the Royal Society of Chemistry.

**About Organic Synthesis**: Prof. Tu began his research on synthetic organic chemistry since his graduate study of Master degree in 1982. During his 40 years' research career, he has mainly conducted three research topics: ① structure and biological activity of natural products isolated from plants and insects (1982—1998); ② C-C bond rearrangement-based synthetic methodology and total synthesis of organic bioactive natural and pharmaceutical molecules (1993—present); ③ design and development of new chiral organic and organometallic catalysts, their catalytic effective asymmetric or C-C bond formation reactions as well as the synthetic applications (2012—present). In particular, Prof. Tu favorites the exploration of new catalysts, new organic reaction, synthetic methodology and total synthesis of complex and bioactive organic molecules as well as pharmaceutical molecules. He has completed a series of projects around these fields.

# 地球科学奖获得者

# 侯 增 谦

侯增谦，1961年6月出生于河北省藁城市。1988年毕业于中国地质大学获理学博士学位，之后进入中国地质科学院矿床地质研究所工作；1993—1994年赴日本地质调查所从事博士后研究，同时担任客座研究员。1998—2000年担任中国地质科学院研究员、院长助理；2000—2005年任中国地质科学院矿产资源所副所长（主持工作）；2005—2018年任中国地质科学院地质研究所所长；2018年2月任第八届国家自然科学基金委员会副主任。先后担任西澳大学、南京大学、中国地质大学（北京）兼职教授，国际应用矿床地质学会区域副主席，国际地学计划中国委员会主任等。荣获国家科技进步奖特等奖1项、国家科技进步奖一等奖1项、国家自然科学奖二等奖1项，以及李四光地质科学奖和国际经济地质学会区域副主席讲席奖等。中国科学院院士，国际经济地质学会会士，发展中国家科学院院士。

侯增谦长期从事碰撞带成矿规律及成矿理论研究，在大陆成矿理论、矿床成矿模型和勘查评价方法等方面作出了一系列开创性研究工作。

**一、系统揭示青藏高原大陆碰撞成矿机制，发展了大陆碰撞成矿理论**

"大陆碰撞能否成大矿"一直是国际矿床界关注的重大理论问题。国际主流观点认为碰撞难以形成大矿，国内学者则对碰撞如何成大矿颇有争议。针对这一科学问题，侯增谦带领团队以全球最典型的大陆碰撞带——青藏高原为突破口，取得以下重大进展：①通过系统精细测年和地质证据标定，查明众多大型-超大型矿床形成于65Ma之后，用事实证明大陆碰撞可以形成大矿；②基于碰撞过程与成矿耦合的系统研究，揭示印-亚大陆碰撞经历主碰撞大陆俯冲、晚碰撞构造转换和后碰撞地壳伸展三段式过程，分别对应发育铅锌锡、金铜铅锌和铜钼锑等成矿作用，证明不同碰撞阶段造就不同的成矿系统，并揭示碰撞成矿系统形成的深部驱动机制；③通过 Hf 同位素填图和岩石圈三维架构重建，发现冈底斯斑岩铜矿带下存在新生地壳，提出大陆碰撞引发不同时代地壳的活化与再造，从根本上控制着成矿金属来源、主要矿床类型和空间分布规律。在此基础上，提出青藏高原"大陆碰撞成矿论"，回答了大陆碰撞如何成大矿的理论问题，为青藏高原实现重大找矿突破提供了重要理论指导。

### 二、建立碰撞型斑岩铜矿成矿理论，推动了冈底斯带找铜重大突破

斑岩铜矿是全球最重要的矿床类型。经典理论强调斑岩铜矿产于岩浆弧环境，其形成与大洋俯冲有关。侯增谦与团队通过西藏、三江、伊朗等地斑岩铜矿的典型解剖和对比研究，发现大陆碰撞造山带是产出斑岩铜矿的另一重要新环境，证实铜成矿作用贯穿于大陆碰撞的全过程；发现含矿斑岩起源于早期弧岩浆底侵而成的镁铁质新生下地壳，成矿主要组分 $Cu$、$S$ 和 $H_2O$ 分别来自新生下地壳硫化物重熔和角闪石分解等。据此建立碰撞型斑岩铜矿成矿理论，阐明了碰撞成铜新机制，2019 年获国家自然科学奖二等奖。

侯增谦率先撰文系统论证了冈底斯带具有巨大的成矿潜力，引起国家相关部门的高度重视。中国地调局以此为主要理论依据，部署实施了大规模矿产勘查；西藏地勘局据此调整战略方向，将勘查重点转向斑岩铜矿。随着理论深化，侯增谦又带领团队建立勘查模型和评价方法，为冈底斯带大型－超大型铜矿的重大突破提供有力支撑。

### 三、建立逆冲褶皱系铅锌成矿新模型和找矿新方法，指导找矿获突破

"密西西比河谷型"铅锌矿是全球最重要的后生层控矿床，经典理论认为其发育于前陆盆地环境，重力驱动成矿流体长距离迁移，张性断层控制矿床就位。侯增谦及其团队通过研究三江地区并对比伊朗超大型铅锌矿，发现其产于逆冲褶皱系而非前陆盆地，挤压应力驱动地壳流体侧向运移并沿途萃取成矿金属，应力松弛导致含矿地壳流体与原位还原流体混合并诱发硫化物淀积，碰撞相关构造（如盐穹构造）控制矿床矿体就位。据此建立了逆冲褶皱系铅锌成矿新模型。

基于上述成矿模型和区域调查成果，侯增谦于 2008 年撰文率先提出青藏高原东北缘发育一条上千千米的巨型铅锌矿化带，指明了找矿突破方向。针对青海多才玛找矿困局，带领团队开展矿区构造－岩相填图和物探测量，提出"逆冲推覆构造控矿＋音频大地电磁测深定位"找矿方法和具体钻探建议，指导发现了厚大富矿体，控制铅锌资源量达 620 万吨，一跃成为超大型矿床，2016 年获部级科技成果一等奖。

# Awardee of Earth Sciences Prize, Hou Zengqian

Hou Zengqian was born in Gaocheng City of Hebei Province in June 1961. He obtained his doctorate degree in 1988 from China University of Geosciences, Beijing (CUGB), and then worked as research fellow in Institute of Mineral Resources, Chinese Academy of Geological Sciences (CAGS). During period of 1993—1994, Zengqian worked in Geological Survey of Japan as post-doc research fellow. In 2000, he was appointed as deputy director of Institute of Mineral Resources, CAGS, and got promotion in 2005 to be director of Institute of Geology, CAGS in. He quit the position of director until 2018, and was then appointed as deputy director of the National Natural Science Foundation of China. Zengqian was guest professor at University of West Australia and regional vice president of SGA (Society for Geology Applied to Mineral Deposits), and is currently guest professor at Nanjing University and China University of Geosciences Beijing (CUGB) of China, and director of China National Committee for IGCP. He is the winner of the SEG Regional Vice President Lecturer (2014), Grand and First Prize of National Science and Technology Progress Award, and Second Prize of National Natural Science Award of China. He is academician of Chinese Academy of Sciences (CAS) and The Third World Academy of Sciences (TWAS).

Zengqian's research interests mainly focus on metallogenesis of the Tethyan belt. He made a series of pioneering research work in the aspects of metallogenesis of continental collision, ore deposit model, and mineral exploration, which is briefly summarized as follows.

He conducted systematic precise dating on main ore deposits in the Qinghai-Tibet Plateau, and confirmed that most giant to large deposits formed after 65 Ma and in continental collisional setting. Then he systematically revealed mineralization mechanism of these deposits, and finally proposed metallogenesis theory of continental collision, which answers well the questions on how continental collision can produce large ore deposit.

He found the continental collision orogenic belt is another important new environment for producing porphyry copper deposit through comparative study of porphyry copper deposits worldwide, and then established the theory to interpret the generation of porphyry copper systems in collisional orogens, promoting the breakthrough of copper exploration in southern Tibet.

Based on systematical study of the Pb-Zn deposits in the Sanjing belt and comparison with some giant deposits in Iran, he found that these Mississippi Valley-type deposits in Tethyan belt were produced in fold-thrust systems rather than foreland basins. Then he proposed a new genetic model for Mississippi Valley-type Pb-Zn deposits in thrust-fold systems and established a new method for their prospecting. His work guided the discovery of the giant Duocaima deposit (6.2 Mt Pb+Zn).

# 古生物学、考古学奖获得者

# 沈 树 忠

沈树忠，1961年10月出生于浙江省湖州市。1989年获中国矿业大学地质系理学博士学位。1996—2000年分别在日本和澳大利亚从事博士后研究。2000年年底进入南京地质古生物研究所工作。2006—2015年任现代古生物学和地层学国家重点实验室主任，2012—2020年任国际地层委员会二叠纪地层分会主席，2020年至今任国际地层委员会副主席。现任南京大学地球科学与工程学院教授、安邦书院院长，生物演化与环境科教融合中心主任。2015年当选中国科学院院士。

沈树忠从事地层古生物研究，在二叠纪地层学、二叠纪末生物大灭绝与环境变化、腕足动物和牙形类古生物学等方面取得了系统性和创新性成果。曾获国家自然科学奖二等奖和省部级科技进步奖一等奖各1项、李四光地质科学奖、尹赞勋地层古生物学奖等荣誉。由于在二叠纪地层学方面作出的贡献，于2019年被国际地层委员会授予个人杰出成就奖，这是迄今首位亚洲科学家获此殊荣。

一、系统古生物和地层学研究

深入研究十多个国家的腕足类和牙形类动物群，描述了一批具有重要演化意义的腕足类和牙形类化石新类群，包括220余属430余种，建立一个新亚科和18个新属，在《中国腕足动物化石属志》中完成了石炭纪和二叠纪261个属的重新描述和厘定工作。带领团队建立石炭纪至三叠纪的全球腕足动物数据库，并进行系统的定量学分析，建立了全球生物古地理和多样性演变模式，恢复全球各主要块体的古地理位置，揭示当时海洋底栖生态系统演变过程，提出了前乐平世生物灭绝事件与当时全球大海退造成的大规模栖息地减少相关等新认识。

沈树忠多次深入西藏喜马拉雅地区开展广泛的野外地质调查，采集了大量化石和岩石样品，建立了以藏南为代表的冈瓦纳北缘二叠纪–三叠纪之交连续的生物地层、化学地层和岩石地层序列，研究结果改变了藏南地区缺失中、上二叠统沉积的传统认识，并通过比较藏南喜马拉雅地区与雅鲁藏布江缝合带的动物群特征，提出雅鲁藏布江缝合带外来体和拉萨地块二叠纪地层及动物群与冈瓦纳大陆北缘有本质区别，中、新特提斯洋在瓜达鲁普世（中二叠世）业已形成等观点，对理解特提斯洋中各块体的古地理演化具有重要意义。

对华南二叠纪地层及生物群开展广泛研究，是二叠系乐平统和长兴阶底界两枚"金钉子"的野外工作组织者和主要完成人之一。担任国际二叠纪地层分会主席和国际地层委员会副主席期间，组织和领导国际工作组完成了乌拉尔统（下二叠统）的萨克马尔阶，瓜达鲁普统（中二叠统）的鲁德阶、沃德阶、开匹顿阶以及乐平统（上二叠统）底界的"金钉子"定义或再研究工作。

**二、生物大灭绝、生物多样性变化与环境背景研究**

2.52 亿年前的二叠纪末发生了地质历史时期最大的一次生物灭绝事件。沈树忠带领团队深入研究华南、西藏等地海相、海陆过渡相和陆相二叠系–三叠系剖面，建立高精度综合年代地层框架，运用大数据及最新的多样性定量统计和多种古环境指标分析，论证了二叠纪末海陆生物大灭绝的同时性和瞬时性，指出特提斯洋中酸性岩浆弧火山喷发和西伯利亚火山喷发造成大规模岩浆活动和地表环境巨变，在极短的时间内引发全球海、陆生态系统同时崩溃，导致生物大灭绝。成果入选 2012 年度"中国科学十大进展"，相关内容被编入美国大学的古生物学和生物学教材。2020 年通过利用大数据平台、开发人工智能新算法、进行高性能计算等，构建了古生代 3 亿多年的高分辨率生物多样性演变曲线，其分辨率比以往同类研究提高了 400 多倍，成果入选 2020 年度"中国科学十大进展"。

沈树忠带领研究团队广泛开展生物与环境协同演化研究，在南京大学成立生物演化与环境研究中心，该中心形成了以古生物与地层学研究为基础，古环境与古气候、古生物大数据和地球系统模型等多方向交叉融合发展的生物演化与环境科研团队，跻身国际相关研究方向第一梯队，建设完成了与国际一流同步的古生物大数据超算平台和金属同位素地球化学实验室，在相关学科发展和人才培养方面发挥了重要作用。

# Awardee of Paleontology and Archaeology Prize, Shen Shuzhong

Shen Shuzhong was born in Huzhou City of Zhejiang Province in October 1961. He graduated from China University of Mining and Technology and got his Ph.D. in 1989 and later did his postdoctoral research in Japan and Australia between the years of 1996 and 2000. He worked as a research professor at the Nanjing Institute of Geology and Palaeontology From 2000. Prof. Shen was elected as an Academician by the CAS in 2015 based on his significant research achievements on stratigraphy and palaeontology, and he furthered his career in 2019 by joining Nanjing University where he currently serves as the dean of Anbang College and the director of the Centre for Research and Education on Biological Evolution and Environment.

Prof. Shen's is mainly engaged in paleontology and stratigraphy with his primary research program over the last three decades centered around the Permian stratigraphy, the end-Permian mass extinction and environmental changes, and the systematic paleontology of brachiopods and conodonts.

Prof. Shen's contribution to Stratigraphy goes above and beyond the two GSSPs established in China. In particular, his passion in serving and leading the Permian global research community is most notably marked by him serving the Subcommission on Permian Stratigraphy first as its Chair between 2012-2020 and then the Vice-chair of International Commission on Stratigraphy from 2020 with the result that the timescale from Lopingian to the Permian-Triassic boundary has become one of the best-refined examples in the Phanerozoic. Under Prof. Shen's determined leadership and guidance, four other Permian stage-level GSSPs have been refined and established with formal publications for two of these.

Prof. Shen has studied the brachiopod and conodont faunas with important evolutionary implications from more than ten different countries including more than 220 genera and 430 species, of which one new family and 18 new genera were established. More recently, working with international peers, Prof. Shen has been leading an research group to provide a new and more finely resolved age model for the end-Permian and end-Guadalupian mass extinctions, which in turn has allowed exploration of the links between global environmental perturbation, carbon cycle disruption, mass extinction, and recovery at millennial timescales.

Prof. Shen's research team established a large palaeontological database for the Phanerozoic, which so far represents the most complete and precise records of marine fossils of China. Based on the database and high-resolution biostratigraphic framework, Prof. Shen, together with their big data team constructed a biodiversity curve with an unprecedented resolution to ~20,000 years through high performance computing technology and artificial intelligence algorithm in 2020. The two papers published in Science in 2011 and 2020 were voted as the top 10 most important progresses in Science respectively in 2012 and 2020 in China. The above contributions represent science of highest international caliber and will no doubt leave a lasting impact, for his findings Prof. Shen was awarded of the International Commission on Stratigraphy (ICS) Medal in 2019, the only Asian scholar to receive this honor so far.

# 生命科学奖获得者

# 刘志杰

刘志杰，1962年10月出生于天津市。1995年毕业于中国科学院生物物理研究所获生物物理学博士学位。1995年在美国匹兹堡大学进行博士后研究，同年转入美国佐治亚大学继续博士后研究，之后继续担任助理研究员、副研究员直至2006年。2006—2013年在中国科学院生物物理研究所工作。2013年5月至今任上海科技大学iHuman研究所执行所长，2020年12月至今任上海科技大学大道书院院长。兼职南开大学教授，中国生物物理学会副理事长，中国晶体学会常务理事，亚洲晶体学会理事，国际生物大分子结晶组织理事。2021年当选国际欧亚科学院院士。

刘志杰长期聚焦人体细胞信号转导的分子机制研究，在天然免疫信号转导及G蛋白偶联受体（GPCR）和新药研发领域取得了国际公认的系统性研究成果，是我国蛋白质科学领域的领军人才之一。曾获得上海市科学技术奖自然科学奖一等奖（2020年）、上海市先进工作者（2020年）、上海市科技精英提名奖（2017年）、上海领军人才（2019年）、药明康德生命化学研究奖学者奖（2013年）等。

## 一、人源大麻素受体的系统研究

CB1和CB2是人体内源性大麻素系统的重要成员，CB1是中枢神经系统中分布最广的GPCR，是治疗多种精神类和情绪类疾病以及疼痛、炎症、药物滥用、多发性硬化症等的重要靶点；CB2主要存在于免疫系统中并负责免疫系统调控，是治疗免疫调节类疾病、炎性神经痛、神经性炎症和神经退行性疾病等的治疗靶点。刘志杰团队率先解析了CB1与拮抗剂的三维精细结构，揭示其相互作用方式和复杂的配体结合口袋。该成果入选2017年 *Cell* 的十篇最佳论文，也是当年中国科学家唯一入选的论文，同时获评当年上海市十大科技事件。随后解析了CB1分别与两种新型激动剂复合物的三维精细结构，首次提出 CB1 的激活依赖"双耦合开关"。在此基础上，对两个受体 CB1 和 CB2 在不同配体调控下的结构与功能进行了更加深入的系统研究，解析了它们与拮抗剂、激动剂及下游 G 蛋白复合物的高分辨率结构，揭示了两种大麻素受体与配体相互作用机制以及与下游信号转导分子 G 蛋白接头方式的异同。该研究成果不但提升了我国在 GPCR 领域的研究水平，也直接促进了我国在 GPCR 领域的新药研发能力。

## 二、苦味受体的结构基础研究

苦味受体 TAS2R46 在口腔、呼吸道、肠道、脑和心脏等组织有显著表达，被认为是哮喘的潜在药物靶点。刘志杰和华甜团队在国际上首次解析了苦味受体 TAS2R46 与激动剂士的宁的三维结构，为探索苦味受体的结构和作用机制开创了新途径，填补了 T 类 GPCR 结构的空白。

## 三、糖尿病重要靶点胰高血糖素样肽 –1 受体的结构与功能研究

胰高血糖素样肽 –1 受体（GLP-1R）是维持人体血糖平衡的重要调节蛋白。刘志杰与合作团队巧妙设计并获得了小分子别构抑制剂与 GLP-1R 复合物的晶体结构。该成果揭示了 GLP-1R 的别构调节机理，为小分子别构调节口服药物研发奠定了重要基础。

## 四、肥胖、精神类疾病密切相关靶点五羟色胺的多重药理学研究

刘志杰团队以与肥胖、精神类疾病密切相关的血清素受体五羟色胺 5-HT2C 为靶点，解析了其与激动剂和拮抗剂复合物的晶体结构，揭示两种药物分子分别获得多重药理学和高选择性的结构基础，为设计具有多重药理学特性药物打下了坚实基础。

## 五、解析"趋化因子受体复合物"三维结构，助力抗癌药物研发

趋化因子受体介导细胞迁移，与炎症和癌症的发生发展密切相关。趋化因子白介素 8（IL-8）作用于 G 蛋白偶联受体 CXCR2，趋化中性粒细胞以及 T、B 等淋巴细胞的游走、脱颗粒等一系列生物学效应，在炎症、细胞发育和肿瘤细胞的趋化等方面发挥重要作用。刘志杰团队利用冷冻电镜技术，首次成功解析了 CXCR2 与两种形式的内源型配体 IL-8 及下游 Gi 复合物的三维结构，从原子水平揭示了内源趋化因子 IL-8 独特的浅口袋耦合模式和对受体的激活机制，为癌症治疗提供了新的理论依据。

## 六、天然免疫信号识别与转导机制

刘志杰团队在国际上率先解析并发表干扰素刺激因子 STING 及其与 c-di-GMP 二元复合物的晶体结构。该结构显示 STING CTD 具有独特的三维架构，阐明了其形成功能性二聚体的分子机制，纠正了人们对其二级结构的错误预测。该工作有助于深入了解 STING 在天然免疫信号通路中的核心作用，为揭示宿主细胞感知病原菌入侵的分子机制提供了

直接的结构生物学证据，同时也为设计新的环鸟苷二磷酸类似物疫苗佐剂或免疫治疗药物奠定了基础。该成果引起国内外同行广泛关注，被中国科学院《科学发展报告》收录为当年"中国科学家具有影响力的部分工作"，被《中国科学院重大成果年报（2012）》收录，入选《中国科学院国际科技合作年度述评》2012年度报告的《国际科技合作重要进展》。

# Awardee of Life Sciences Prize, Liu Zhijie

Liu Zhijie was born in Tianjin, China in October of 1962. He obtained PhD in Biophysics at the Institute of Biophysics, CAS in 1995. He started his research career as Postdoctoral Fellow at University of Pittsburgh, Postdoctoral Fellow, Research Assistant Scientist, Research Associate Scientist at University of Georgia. Liu returned back to China in 2006 and worked at the Institute of Biophysics of CAS, as a research professor of the "Hundred Talents Program" until 2013. Liu joined ShanghaiTech University in 2013 and is working as the Executive Director of iHuman Institute and the Dean of Dadao College. Liu is also serving many organizations, including Adjunct Professor of Nankai University, Vice President of the Chinese Society of Biophysics, Council member of the Chinese Crystallography Society, Asian Crystallographic Association, International Organization for Biological Crystallization (IOBCr). In 2021, he was elected as an Academician of the International Eurasian Academy of Sciences.

Liu Zhijie has focused his research on structure and function of human cell signaling and development of new methods and new technologies in structural biology. He is one of the leaders in the field of protein science in China and has made numerous internationally recognized scientific achievements.

Liu Zhijie has won many awards, such as the Special Allowance of the State Council, the 1st Prize of Natural Science Award of Shanghai Science & Technology Award, Shanghai Science & Technology Elite Nomination Award, Shanghai Leading Talent, and the Scholar Award of WuXi AppTec Life Chemistry Research Award.

# 生命科学奖获得者

# 宋保亮

宋保亮，1975年1月出生于河南省林州市。1997年毕业于南京大学生物科学与技术系获理学学士学位。2002年毕业于中国科学院上海生命科学研究院生物化学与细胞生物学研究所获理学博士学位。2002—2005年在美国得克萨斯大学西南医学中心从事博士后科研工作。2005年回国加入中国科学院上海生命科学研究院生物化学与细胞生物学研究所，任研究组长、研究员。2014年3月加入武汉大学至今，任生命科学学院院长；2021年当选中国科学院院士；2022年担任武汉大学副校长、泰康医学院（基础医学院）院长、泰康生命医学中心主任。兼任中国细胞生物学会副理事长、国家自然科学基金委员会"糖脂代谢的时空网络调控"重大研究计划专家组组长。

宋保亮长期从事胆固醇代谢和代谢性疾病研究，取得了一系列重要原创发现，其研究成果推动了胆固醇代谢领域的发展，为降脂药物研发提供了新的思路和理论基础，为我国脂代谢研究作出了重要贡献。

## 一、小肠胆固醇吸收调控

宋保亮鉴定出小肠胆固醇吸收途径中的一系列重要蛋白，证明胆固醇由小肠细胞主动运输并阐明详细机制；从新疆哈萨克低血脂家系中发现了新的胆固醇吸收基因LIMA1，揭示其变异造成NPC1L1转运异常，最终导致胆固醇吸收减少与血脂降低；证明临床药物依折麦布通过阻断NPC1L1内吞而降低胆固醇吸收；揭示胆固醇和脂肪酸增强胆固醇酯合成酶的稳定性，促进脂质吸收。其有关LIMA1的研究工作入选2018年"国内十大医学研究"及"中国心血管领域十大影响力事件"。

## 二、胆固醇合成调控

宋保亮阐明了胆固醇合成限速酶HMGCR泛素化修饰与降解的核心机制；鉴定出羊

毛甾醇为内源调控信号，纠正了长期认为胆固醇是调控分子的错误概念；揭示胆固醇合成两个负反馈调控通路——HMGCR 降解和 SREBP 剪切——的交互调控。发现 USP20 是饥饿—进食转化中调控胆固醇合成的关键蛋白，能响应进食后升高的葡萄糖和胰岛素，通过稳定 HMGCR 上调胆固醇合成；提出并证明靶向负反馈调控通路的降脂新策略，并获得活性小分子白桦酯醇。其有关 USP20 的研究工作被评为"2020 年中国生命科学十大进展"。白桦酯醇已被广泛接收并成为降脂新药研发热点，并作为降脂活性分子被 Merck 等公司广为销售。

### 三、胆固醇运输调控

宋保亮发现了细胞内胆固醇运输的新途径与方式，即胆固醇通过溶酶体—过氧化物酶体—内质网形成的膜接触运输至内质网并转化成胆固醇酯；阐明胞内脂质运输的调控机制；揭示胆固醇运输异常是"过氧化物酶体紊乱疾病"的病因之一；提出膜性细胞器过氧化物酶体可作为胆固醇转运体的新概念，开拓胆固醇运输研究的新领域；发现调控低密度脂蛋白受体蛋白稳定性的新因子 PK，证明抑制其表达是降脂和抗栓的新策略。其有关膜接触的研究工作被评为"2015 年中国生命科学领域十大进展"。

### 四、胆固醇外排调控

由于胆固醇的环戊烷多氢菲结构，人体细胞很难高效降解胆固醇分子，如能将胆固醇外排出人体将是理想的降脂策略。宋保亮揭示抑制糖蛋白受体 ASGR1 可以促使胆固醇外排而降低血脂和肝脂；发展 ASGR1 的中和抗体，该中和抗体可以有效促使胆固醇外排，并与他汀及依折麦布有良好的协同降脂效果。基于该工作，ASGR1 已成为各制药公司的热点靶标。

### 五、新胆固醇修饰蛋白

宋保亮利用自主研发的胆固醇探针，发现了新型胆固醇共价修饰蛋白 SMO，颠覆了二十多年来 Hedgehog 被认为唯一被胆固醇共价修饰的错误观念；揭示 SMO 胆固醇修饰的全新生化反应机制，并鉴定出关键胆固醇结合和修饰位点。这些结果不仅揭示了胆固醇可作为共价配体调控信号转导和胚胎发育，而且开拓了蛋白质胆固醇修饰研究新方向。

宋保亮曾荣获国家杰出青年科学基金（2009 年）、陈嘉庚青年科学奖（2012 年）、中国青年科技奖（2013 年）、谈家桢生命科学创新奖（2014 年）、首届全国创新争先奖（2017 年）、药明康德生命化学研究奖杰出成就奖（2018 年）等奖项和荣誉。

# Awardee of Life Sciences Prize, Song Baoliang

Song Baoliang was born in Linzhou City of Henan Province in January 1975, Academician of Chinese Academy of Sciences. Prof. Song received his B.S. degree from Nanjing University in 1997, and Ph.D. degree from Chinese Academy of Sciences in 2002. He did his postdoctoral training in the Brown-Goldstein lab at UT Southwestern Medical Center from 2002 to 2005. He then joined in the Shanghai Institutes for Biological Sciences at Chinese Academy of Sciences as a Principle Investigator. In 2014, he moved to Wuhan University and has been the Dean of College of Life Sciences since then. He is the Vice President of Wuhan University, the Dean of Taikang Medical School, and the Director of Taikang Center for Life and Medical Sciences.

Prof. Song focuses on cholesterol metabolism and the associated diseases. He had published about 100 scientific papers, including those in *Nature*, *Science*, and *Cell*. His work has been included in several classic textbooks such as *Lehninger Principles of Biochemistry*, *Molecular Cell Biology* and *Williams Textbook of Endocrinology*. These pioneer studies have significant impacts on the cholesterol field and shed new light on cholesterol-lowering drug development.

On intestinal cholesterol absorption, Song illustrates the molecular pathway of NPC1L1-mediated cholesterol endocytosis, and identifies *LIMA1* as a new regulation of intestinal cholesterol absorption through regulating NPC1L1 transport back to the cell surface. On cholesterol biosynthesis regulation, Song delineates the mechanism of sterol-induced degradation of HMGCR, a rate-limiting enzyme in cholesterol biosynthesis. He identifies the ubiquitin ligases and cofactors as well as the endogenous regulator of HMGCR degradation. He also finds that USP20 is the key protein controlling cholesterol biosynthesis in the starvation-feeding transition state. On intracellular cholesterol transport, Song finds that cholesterol is transported through lysosome-peroxisome membrane-endoplasmic reticulum membrane contacts. He shows that lysosomal cholesterol accumulation can be a major contributing factor to peroxisomal diseases. On cholesterol efflux, Song recently finds a pathway to promote cholesterol excretion through inhibiting ASGR1. On cholesterol modification, Song identifies SMO as a new protein subjected to cholesterol modification, and demonstrates that SMO cholesterylation is a $Ca^{2+}$-boosted autoreaction.

Prof. Song has won many influential prizes including China National Funds for Distinguished Young Scientists(2009), and Arthur Kornberg Memorial Award(2013).

# 农学奖获得者

# 陈 绍 江

陈绍江，1963年11月出生于河南省永城市。1995年获东北农业大学农学博士学位。1995—1997年在中国农业大学进行博士后研究，并于1998年留校任教。1999—2000年赴国际遗传工程中心进行访学研究。2003年被聘为中国农业大学教授，曾主持"十一五""十二五"国家"863"计划和"十三五"重点研发计划等，任重点研发计划项目首席科学家、国家玉米产业技术体系岗位科学家、国家玉米改良中心副主任。曾获教育部技术发明奖一等奖1项，国家技术发明奖二等奖2项，国家科技进步奖二等奖1项等奖项，并入选农业部首批科研杰出人才。

陈绍江长期从事作物遗传育种研究与教学工作，在作物育种前沿核心技术方面创建了系统的玉米单倍体快速育种技术体系并实现规模化应用，为推进种业关键技术的自主创新及转型升级作出了突出贡献。

**一、研发玉米单倍体快速育种技术体系，实现整体性创新，开启育种新速度**

作为杂种优势利用的基本形式，杂交品种选育是玉米育种的核心内容，而选育杂交种的基础是自交系的培育。传统选育方法已延续超过百年，一般需要连续自交8代以上才能获得高度纯合的自交系，而单倍体技术则可以在两个世代实现纯合，显著加快育种进程，促进亲本纯系创制和育种模式的变革。

陈绍江带领团队瞄准这一重要方向，经过20多年攻关，发明了诱导系高效分子选育方法并选育了系列单倍体高频诱导系，使诱导效率大幅提高；在国际上首创以籽粒高油分标记与核磁共振相结合的单倍体自动化鉴别技术，准确率达90%以上；建成的单倍体芽苗加倍法、幼胚组培高效加倍及一步成系技术，实现了育种技术上的整体性创新和纯系高通量创制。该技术可实现育种基础材料的快速成系，被誉为作物育种领域的"高铁"技术。

## 二、克隆单倍体诱导关键基因，解析基础性原理，催生技术新跨度

历经十多年持续攻关，成功克隆两个玉米母本单倍体诱导关键基因 *ZmPLA1* 和 *ZmDMP*，阐明了单倍体高频诱导的遗传基础，占领关键技术制高点；由此进一步突破诱导基因利用的物种界限，使该技术体系拓展至小麦、番茄、油菜、水稻和烟草等作物，为创建跨作物通用型快速育种技术体系开辟了新路径，呈现出更为广阔的应用前景。

## 三、推动单倍体技术工程化应用，促进育种系统重塑，形成发展新力度

为进一步提升我国种业研发人员的理论和技术，陈绍江于2008年创办竞雄玉米育种学校，至今已经连续举办14期，累计培训玉米遗传育种技术骨干1200余人次。此外，陈绍江在国际上出版了首部单倍体育种技术专著，该书已成为我国作物育种从业人员必备的技术手册，大大促进了单倍体育种技术在全国主要企事业育种单位的普及和应用，显著增强了选择的时效性和准确性。

为便于企事业单位规模化应用单倍体育种技术，陈绍江提出工程化新思路，在三亚建立了全国首个自助共享式单倍体育种技术工程化应用和示范平台，有效促进了单倍体育种技术的规模化应用，形成了科技成果应用和科企合作新模式，为工程化高通量的育种流程重塑提供了新动能。目前，单倍体育种技术已作为关键育种技术，有力促进了现代玉米育种的转型与升级，被评为近十年农业科技领域的标志性成果。据不完全统计，应用该技术育成的新品种数量已超过200个，这些品种的种植范围覆盖了黄淮海、东北、华北、西北等玉米主产区，为农民增产增收和保障粮食安全作出了贡献。

# Awardee of Agronomy Prize, Chen Shaojiang

Chen Shaojiang was born in Yongcheng City of Henan Province in November 1963. He got his Ph.D. degree in agronomy from Northeast Agricultural University in 1995. He worked as a postdoctoral researcher at China Agricultural University from 1995 to 1997, and he was a visiting scholar at ICGEB from 1999 to 2000. He has been a professor at China Agricultural University since 2003 and was a chief scientist from 11th to 13th Five-Year National Key R&D Programs, deputy director of the National Maize Improvement Center of China, and scientist of China Agricultural Research System (CARS). He received the first prize of technical invention from the Ministry of Education, two second prizes of the National Technology Invention Award, one second prize of the State Scientific and Technological Progress Award respectively. He was selected as one of the first batches of outstanding talents in scientific research from the Ministry of Agriculture.

Prof. Chen was engaged in crop genetics and breeding for a long time and made a great contribution to maize doubled haploid (DH) breeding technology.

## 1. The establishment of DH breeding technology significantly speeds up the breeding cycle

Prof. Chen developed a series of high-efficiency haploid inducer lines, invented a novel haploid seed sorting system by determining the kernel oil content and developed a NMR-based sorting equipment that allowed for the automatic, high-throughput and accurate selection of haploid kernels. To improve the chromosome doubling rate, he developed efficient chromosome doubling protocols with efficiency 5-10 times higher than that of spontaneous ways. With these breakthroughs, DH technology was widely applied in both breeding companies and institutes. This technique was also known as "high-speed rail technology" in crop breeding.

## 2. The discovery of the key haploid induction genes expands the DH technology to work beyond maize

Prof. Chen leads his team successfully cloned two crucial genes, *ZmPLA1* and *ZmDMP*, that control haploid induction in maize. These works deciphered the mystery of haploid induction in maize that lasted for several decades, and marked another new milestone in DH technology. More importantly, the discovery of the genes led to the finding of orthologues, which have been proved with similar function in haploid induction in different crop species. Using gene editing, the induction gene-based haploid induction system was established in wheat, tomato, rapeseed, rice, etc. This work contributed to a wide range of international influences and will open up a new space for DH technology.

## 3. Renewed the traditional breeding system by promoting the new technology application at a large scale

Prof. Chen was engaged in educating and training of breeders. Since 2008, he has started and held 14 sessions of the Jingxiong Breeding School. More than 1200 breeders from different institutions and companies were trained. He also published 2 editions of monographs about the DH breeding of maize. The books had become an important reference book for every corn breeder. To facilitate the large-scale application of haploid breeding technology in enterprises and institutions, Prof. Chen established the first self-service and shared engineering DH line production laboratory for the winter nursery in Sanya, which promoted haploid breeding technology application effectively.

Up to now, more than 200 new DH hybrids covering the main planting regions have been released, which brings significant increase in both yield and income for farmers directly, as well as strengthened the food supply and security at the national level.

# 农学奖获得者

# 罗利军

罗利军，1961年7月出生于湖北省崇阳县。1978年考入华中农业大学，先后获农学学士、硕士和博士学位。1986—2000年在中国水稻研究所从事稻种资源的收集保存、研究评价与创新利用，先后被聘为助理研究员、副研究员和研究员。其间，先后在国际水稻研究所、美国得州农工大学以访问学者身份进行合作研究。1998年被聘为华中农业大学博士生导师。2001年带领团队到上海市农业科学院筹建上海农业种质库。2002年上海市农业生物基因中心成立后，任中心主任、首席科学家。

罗利军长期从事农业基因资源的保护创新与评价利用研究，建立了国际一流的种质资源保护与利用体系，解决了水稻高产优质与节水抗旱难以兼顾的技术难题，取得了节水抗旱稻从0到1的重大原创性科技成果。

## 一、遗传资源的保护创新与研究利用

罗利军于1986年起开始水稻种质资源研究，至2020年，带领团队共收集、整理、保存各类水稻遗传资源20余万份，使我国稻种资源保存量增加130%。建立了具有自主知识产权的基于库位管理、数据管理和用户管理的"一库三系统"种质资源保护与利用体系，实现了种质资源从收集鉴定、种子处理、入库贮存、监测到分发利用的安全高效管理，实现了种质资源的全社会共享，解决了我国水稻育种和基础研究中遗传资源缺乏的重大问题。主编出版《稻种资源学》，是第一部系统地对稻种资源研究进行高度概括和探索的著作，被认为是稻种资源研究的里程碑。

## 二、节水抗旱稻的基础理论研究

罗利军团队制定了《节水抗旱稻术语》行业标准，提出了旱稻早于水稻分化、在旱稻向水稻的演变过程中抗旱性丢失的新观点，揭示出抗旱性分化是水陆稻遗传分化的主要因子，阐明了抗旱性与产量之间的 tradeoff 及其遗传基础；建立了基于大田的抗旱性精准鉴定设施、方法与评价标准，制定了《节水抗旱稻抗旱性鉴定技术规范》行业标准，鉴定和定位一批重要的抗旱 QTLs，克隆 *OsRINFzif1*、*OsAHL1*、*OsGRAS23*、*OsSNB* 等重要抗旱基因，揭示了水稻抗旱性的多组学特征。

### 三、节水抗旱稻的育种与应用研究

罗利军团队首次提出了发展节水抗旱稻的理念与策略，发明了在目标环境中实行"双向选择"以整合耐旱性、避旱性、水分利用效率和产量、米质、抗病性状的育种新技术。育成首个旱稻不育系沪旱 1A 等 18 个不育系并实现三系配套；育成沪优 2 号等 31 个节水抗旱稻，普遍表现高产稳产、节水抗旱特性，其中旱优 73 是目前我国单个杂交水稻年推广面积最大的品种之一。阐明了节水抗旱稻肥水高效利用的遗传与生理基础，针对水田、旱地和山坡地研制了"旱直播旱管"栽培技术，实现了在水田不需要移栽和淹水种植，可节水 50%、减少碳排放 90% 以上。节水抗旱稻可在旱地、山坡地种植，产量米质与一般水稻相近，拓展了水稻的种植区域，取得显著的社会、经济与生态效益，并在亚非多国示范推广，产生了积极的国际影响。

# Awardee of Agronomy Prize, Luo Lijun

Luo Lijun was born in Chongyang County of Hubei Province in July 1961. He was admitted to Huazhong Agricultural University in 1978 and received his bachelor's degree, master's degree and PhD in agronomy successively. From 1986 to 2000, he was engaged in rice germplasm resources conservation in China Rice Research Institute and employed as an assistant researcher, associate researcher and researchersuccessively. During this period, he successively conducted cooperative research in the International Rice Research Institute and Texas A & M University as a visiting scholar. In 2001, he led his team to Shanghai Academy of Agricultural Sciences to set up the "Shanghai Agricultural Germplasm Bank". After the establishment of Shanghai Agricultural Biological Gene Center in 2002, he became the director and chief scientist of the center.

Luo Lijun has been engaged in the protection, innovation, evaluation and utilization of agricultural genetic resources for a long time. He has established a world-class germplasm resources protection and utilization system, solved the technical problems of combining high yield and good quality with water saving and drought resistance, and made the original scientific and technological achievements in water-saving and drought-resistant rice.

### 1. The germplasm resources conservation and utilization

Luo Lijun led the team to collect and preserve more than 200000 copies of various rice genetic resources, increasing the amount of rice germplasm resources preserved in China by 130%. He established an "one storage and three systems" germplasm resources protection and utilization system and realized the safe and efficient management of germplasm resources from collection and identification, seed processing, storage, monitoring to distribution and utilization.It promotes the sharing of germplasm resources among the whole society, and solves the major problem of the lack of genetic resources in rice breeding and basic research in China. As an chief editor, he published a book *Rice Germplasm Resources*, which was the first work to systematically and highly summarize and explore the research of rice germplasm resources, was considered as a milestone in this area.

## 2. The Theory Research of Water-saving and Drought-resistant Rice（WDR）

Luo's team formulated the industry standard of *Terminology of Water Saving and Drought-resistant Rice*, and put forward the new view that upland rice has differentiated before paddy rice and the drought resistance ability was lost in the evolution.They revealed that drought resistance differentiation is the major factor in the genetic differentiation of upland rice and lowland rice, elucidating the trade-off and its genetic basis between drought resistance and yield. They set up a accurate identification facilities, methods and evaluation criteria for drought resistance based on the field. They also formulated the industry standard of *Technical Specification for the Identification of Drought Resistance in WDR*, identified a number of important drought-resistant QTLs and cloned many important drought resistance genes such as *OsRINFzif1*, *OsAHL1*, *OsGRAS23*, and *OsSNB*, and revealed the multi-omics characteristics of rice drought resistance.

## 3. The Breeding and Application of WDR

Luo's team put forward the concept and strategy of developing WDR and invented a new breeding technology to implement "two-way selection" in the target environment to integrate drought tolerance, drought avoidance, water use efficiency, yield, rice quality and disease resistance traits. They bred 18 CMS sterile line including the first upland CMS sterile lines Huhan 1A and 31 WDR varieties, such as Huyou 2 and Hanyou73, generally showing the characteristics of high and stable yield, water saving and drought resistance. They also clarified the genetic and physiological basis of the efficient utilization of fertilizer and water of WDR, and developed the cultivation technology of "dry directly seedling with aerobic management" for paddy fields, dry land and hillside land, which can save water by 50% and reduce carbon emission by 90%. The WDR can be planted in dry land and hillside land, and the yield of WDR is similar to that of lowland rice, which expands the planting area of rice and achieves remarkable social, economic and ecological benefits. It has also been demonstrated and promoted in many countries in Asia and Africa, exerting a positive international influence.

# 农学奖获得者

# 张 佳 宝

张佳宝，1957年9月出生于江苏省高邮市。1982年在南京农业大学土壤农业化学系本科毕业，1985年在中国科学院南京土壤研究所获理学硕士学位，1990年在国际水稻研究所/菲律宾大学获土壤学博士学位。1990年至今，在中国科学院南京土壤研究所工作，历任副研究员、研究员。1994—1995年在美国加州大学河滨分校高访一年，1997—2005年每年在墨尔本大学或德国海德堡大学或日本九州大学开展2～3个月合作研究。先后担任封丘国家试验站站长、土壤养分管理国家工程实验室主任、中国科学院大学南京学院资环与地科学院院长/教授、浙江大学求是讲座教授。国家"973"项目首席科学家，第三次全国土壤普查专家指导组长，国家重点研发专项"黑土地保护与利用科技创新"专家组长，第14届中国土壤学会理事长，第22届国际土壤学联合会土壤工程与技术委员会主席，第23届国际土壤学联合会副主席等。中国土壤学会会士，中国工程院院士。

张佳宝长期从事土壤物质循环规律、土壤信息快速获取、土壤改良及地力提升方面的研究。针对我国中低产田土壤障碍多、地力水平低两大难题进行突破，创建土壤障碍分类消减、内稳性地力提升、富养-激发式和相似增效型快速培肥地力、易涝渍农田水土联治等理论与技术体系，研发土壤参数探测技术与设备，牵头建立我国农田站联网观测研究平台和土壤养分管理国家工程实验室，形成新一代土壤改良保育的理论基础-核心技术-支撑设备-研发平台体系。研究成果获国家科技进步奖二等奖3项、国家科技进步奖一等奖1项。

**一、创建土壤障碍因子分类消减理论与技术，推进我国改土向精准对症跨越**

消减土壤障碍因子是我国中低产田治理面临的第一大难题。张佳宝通过系统研究障碍因子发生规律发现，众多障碍因子可分为立地条件衍生、土壤属性原生、管理不当次生三类，衍生障碍如旱涝渍、冷冻、水土流失等主要由水土迁移和能量转换产生；属性和次生障碍都是由障碍原物质和障碍发生过程叠加而成，如土壤酸化由酸质子和制酸过程耦合而来。提出以调控水、热、光、势/动能过程为核心消减土壤衍生性障碍，以改性障碍原物质和阻控障碍发生过程为双靶点消减土壤属性障碍的新理论，创建土壤旱涝渍、冷冻、水土流失等衍生性障碍工程化消减共性技术和土壤属性障碍双靶点消减技术，化解土壤改良技术繁杂缺共性抓手问题，推进全国改土向精准对症跨越。

**二、创建增碳沃土培肥耕地地力理论与技术，支撑国家耕地质量提升行动**

中低产田普遍地力水平低，培肥地力成为中低产田治理的第二大难题。张佳宝通过逆向研究地力衰减规律和长期试验发现，地力具有内稳性，内稳性地力提升的核心是增加土壤有机质，即增碳沃土。其中，充分有机碳源供应是一个必要条件，土壤微生物群落结构沃土化和土壤团聚化是两个关键协同推进过程。依据上述理论，研发系列激发剂，创建富养型－激发式秸秆还田快速培肥地力技术和富养型－激发式秸秆错位轮还全耕层培肥技术，成为行业主推技术；同时提出"相似增效理论"，模拟自然生态系统创建增碳沃土技术模式，以相似土壤有机质组分的天然腐殖质材料工程化快速构建优质耕作层。

**三、创建沿淮易涝渍农田水土联治理论与技术，保障沿淮地区粮食生产能力**

淮河两岸农田长期遭受涝渍困扰，研究发现南北过渡带强降雨、大面积低洼地和黏闭砂姜黑土耦合导致经常快速涝渍。张佳宝提出针对传统除涝排水量算法因土壤空间变异而失真的问题，建立了土壤水力参数转换平台，以流域土壤数据转换出土壤水力参数分布图；创新层状土入渗算法，解决了大面积层状潮土入渗计算问题；建立栅格化产流－运动波汇流耦合模型，精确预测除涝排水量，设计出快速排水系统。同时，揭示砂姜黑土涝渍源于高含量膨胀黏粒遇水产生大量纳米孔隙黏闭渍水；发现粉煤灰等刚性颗粒材料能降低膨胀，秸秆、生物炭等柔性材料能降低水化力、增强键合力，并在此基础上创建刚－柔耦合改土增渗技术模式。应用以上水土联治理论与技术，改变了沿淮农田长期易涝渍的局面。

**四、创新土壤参数探测关键技术与设备，牵头建立我国农田试验站联网观测研究平台和土壤养分管理国家工程实验室**

聚焦传感器、激光、雷达高技术，持续开展土壤探测研究，已有多种型号产品投放市场应用，其中新型土壤传感器和多通道雷达探测技术具有国际领先水平。创建多通道雷达探测土壤模式以及土壤参数反演算法，实现高精度二维、三维探测多个土壤参数，成为国际领先技术。作为中国生态系统研究网络科学委员会副主任，牵头建设和运行农田站分网，成为国际上第一个统一规范的农田站网络，并最先组织规范联网观测—研究—示范，解决国家关注的重大问题。前瞻性自主设计和建设土壤养分管理国家工程实验室，成为首批服务于农业的国家工程实验室。

# Awardee of Agronomy Prize, Zhang Jiabao

  Zhang Jiabao was born in Gaoyou City of Jiangsu Province in September 1957. He received a bachelor's degree from the Department of Soil Agricultural Chemistry of Nanjing Agricultural University in 1982, a master of science degree from the Institute of Soil Science, Chinese Academy of Sciences in 1985, and a doctor's degree in soil science from the International Rice Research Institute/University of the Philippines in 1990. He works as an associate professor and professor in the Institute of Soil Science, Chinese Academy of Sciences since 1990. He visited the University of California, Riverside in the United States for one year from 1994 to 1995. From 1997 to 2005, he conducted two to three months of collaborative research annually at the University of Melbourne in Australia, the University of Heidelberg in Germany, or the Kyushu University in Japan. He has successively served as the station chairman of the Fengqiu National Experimental Station, the director of the National Engineering Laboratory of Soil Nutrient Management, the dean/professor of the Nanjing College of Resources Environment and Earth Sciences, University of Chinese Academy of Sciences, and the Qiushi Chair Professor of Zhejiang University; the Chief Scientist of the National 973 Project, the expert leader of the third National Soil Survey, and the expert leader of the National Key Research and Development Project "Scientific and Technological Innovation of Black Land Protection and Utilization"; the president of the 14th Soil Science Society of China, the chairman of Soil Engineering and Technology Committee of the 22nd International Union of Soil Science, the vice President of the 23rd International Union of Soil Science, the fellow of Soil Science Society of China and the academician of Chinese Academy of Engineering.

  Zhang Jiabao focuses on the research fields including soil material and energy cycle laws, rapid access of soil information, soil improvement and soil fertility enhancement. Aiming at the two major problems of multiple soil obstacles and low fertility level in low and medium yield fields, he created a series of theories and technologies such as classified reduction of soil obstacles, improvement of inherent soil productivity, rapid soil fertility improvement based on copiotrophic-activated straw returning and "similarly increasing efficiency", and water-soil joint treatment along the waterlogging prone farmland, and developed technologies and equipment for soil parameter detection. In addition, he leads the establishment of the National Observation and Research Network for China's Farmland Experimental Stations and the National Engineering Laboratory for Soil Nutrients Management, forming the new system of foundation theories related to soil improvement and conservation, core technology, support equipment and research and development platform. Due to the important contribution, he has won the Second Prize of National Science and Technology Progress Award three times, the First Prize of National Science and Technology Progress Award one time.

# 医学药学奖获得者

# 刘德培

刘德培，1950年5月出生于安徽省阜南县。1981年获湖南医科大学（现中南大学湘雅医学院）生物化学专业硕士学位。1986年获中国协和医科大学生物化学与分子生物学专业博士学位。1987—1990年在美国加州大学旧金山分校做博士后研究工作。1992年12月至今任中国医学科学院基础医学研究所生物化学与分子生物学专业教授、研究员、博士生导师。1996年当选中国工程院医药卫生学部院士，2000年当选中国工程院工程管理学部院士。2008年当选美国医学科学院与第三世界科学院院士，2016年当选国际医学科学院组织共同主席，2019年连任。现任医学分子生物学国家重点实验室主任。

刘德培主要从事心血管疾病发病机制、基因表达调控和基因治疗研究。先后承担国家自然科学基金委重大、重点项目和国家"863"重点项目等，1993年被评为"全国首届中青年医学科技之星"；1994年被评为国家级有突出贡献的中青年专家，获国家教委跨世纪优秀人才基金以及国家自然科学基金委优秀中青年人才基金；1995年获国家自然科学基金委杰出青年科学基金，被评为求是基金会杰出青年学者。

## 一、心血管疾病发病机制研究

心血管疾病是衰老相关疾病，刘德培从能量限制和长寿基因延缓衰老的角度入手，系统研究低等动物长寿基因Sir2在高等动物的同源物–Sirt表观调节因子家族各成员对心血管疾病的影响。

发现Sirt1抑制p66shc的表达，预防高血糖诱导的内皮功能障碍；Sirt1抑制血管损伤后新生内膜形成。内皮功能障碍和新生内膜形成是影响动脉粥样硬化、血管狭窄等的重要血管改变。发现能量限制升高Sirt1的表达，抑制腹主动脉瘤的发生与严重程度；而衰老抑制Sirt1表达，促进腹主动脉瘤的发生。刘德培关于能量限制及表观遗传因子调节动脉粥样硬化、腹主动脉瘤的研究处于国际先进水平。

发现 Sirt2 激活心脏中的 LKB1-AMPK 信号途径以抵抗衰老和血管紧张素 Ⅱ 引起的心肌肥厚，且 Sirt2 对介导二甲双胍的作用不可忽视。发现线粒体 Sirt4 抑制 Sirt3 对 MnSOD 的去乙酰化，降低 MnSOD 抗氧化活性，在病理情况下增加线粒体氧化应激水平、促进心肌肥厚发生，颠覆了以往认为 Sirt 家族成员都是抑制心血管疾病的观点，并为将来设计针对线粒体抗氧化应激类药物提供了新思路。刘德培首次揭示氧化还原信号在一个近日节律周期（24小时）内的变化规律，受 p66shc 影响的氧化应激水平节律性调控 CLOCK 的修饰状态并调节生物节律。刘德培关于代谢、氧化还原稳态调节心肌肥厚、生物节律的研究处于国际领先水平。同时创新性地提出衰老四层理论，阐述衰老的作用机制。

二、基因表达调控与基因治疗研究

刘德培从 20 世纪 90 年代开始，对地中海贫血和珠蛋白基因的表达调控和基因治疗进行了系统深入的研究。在基因表达调控与基因治疗研究中，刘德培发现 β 珠蛋白基因簇红系增强子 HS2 及其关键位点，建立 BAC 介导的 α/β 珠蛋白基因簇转基因动物模型，发现 α- 基因簇活性染色质构象（ACH）中珠蛋白基因与看家基因共用转录工厂，发现 β 基因簇 MAR 间协同染色质高级构象，发现马利兰可显著增强贫血恒河猴与地贫患儿的胎儿型珠蛋白表达，用杂合寡核苷酸实现了 β 基因的定点修复，并提出复制叉渗漏寡核苷酸掺入假说等。在基因表达调控研究中，刘德培获得卫生部科技进步奖一等奖、中华医学科技奖一等奖以及国家自然科学奖四等奖等奖项。

# Awardee of Medical Sciences and Materia Medica Prize, Liu Depei

Liu Depei was born in Funan County of Anhui Province in May 1950. He graduated with a Ph.D. from CAMS & PUMC in 1986, and completed his Postdoctoral Fellowship in molecular biology at University of California, San Francisco (UCSF). Dr. Liu is currently a professor of National Laboratory of Medical Molecular Biology, Institute of Basic Medical Sciences, Chinese Academy of Medical Sciences (CAMS) & Peking Union Medical College (PUMC). He is also serving as a member of Chinese Academy of Engineering (CAE), member of National Academy of Medicine (NAM) of USA, member of Third World Academy of Sciences (TWAS), and Cochair of IAPH (InterAcademy Panel for Health).

Dr. Liu's research expertise is gene regulation, gene therapy and molecular mechanisms of cardiovascular diseases. He discovered the hypersensitive site 2 and the key regulatory sites in beta-globin gene cluster. Dr. Liu found that myleran could increase gene expression of fetal globin in anemic rhesus monkeys and patients. He and his group discovered that thymidine treatment of cells could increase efficiency of oligonucleotide-mediated gene repair and thus raised the hypothesis of "replication fork leakage". His works systematically characterized the higher-order chromatin structure organization and its roles in gene transcriptional regulation, using the alpha-, beta-globin gene clusters and other clustered genes as the models. He and his group found that the actively transcribed genes and multiple hypersensitive sites of alpha-globin gene cluster forms an active chromatin hub (ACH) in erythroid cells and that the alpha-globin ACH co-localizes with transcriptional factory formed by surrounding housekeeping genes.

Cardiovascular diseases are the leading cause of death. He and his group work on the molecular mechanisms of cardiovascular diseases. They found that human paraoxonase gene cluster transgenic overexpression not only represses atherogenesis but also promotes atherosclerotic plaque stability in vivo, thus they summarize that the paraoxonase gene cluster as a target in the treatment of atherosclerosis. They demonstrated for the first time the beneficial effects for histone deacetylase Sirt1 in preventing atherosclerotic diseases and in inhibiting neointima formation, found that Sirt2 acts as a cardioprotective deacetylase in pathological cardiac hypertrophy, and demonstrated that Sirt4 plays crucial roles in mediating AngII-induced cardiac hypertrophy, thus acting as a potential therapeutic target. They found that calorie restriction increases Sirt1 expression and ameliorate abdominal aortic aneurysm while aging decreases Sirt1 expression and accelerates abdominal aortic aneurysm. They also found that oxidative modification of CLOCK is involved in circadian regulation. They published a review about the four layers of aging.

# 医学药学奖获得者

# 马 骏

马骏，1963年8月出生于湖南省株洲市。1990年获中山医科大学（现中山大学）肿瘤学专业硕士学位。2000—2002年于美国得州大学M.D.安德森癌症中心接受博士后训练。2013年至今担任中山大学肿瘤防治中心常务副院长，现为广东省鼻咽癌临床研究中心主任、二级教授/一级主任医师、博士生导师。同时兼任中国临床肿瘤学会鼻咽癌专业委员会首任主委、中国抗癌协会鼻咽癌专业委员会主委、国务院学位委员会特种医学学科评议组召集人、第八届教育部科技委员会生命医学部委员，以及中国-美国临床肿瘤协会鼻咽癌临床诊治指南委员会联合主席、欧洲肿瘤内科学会头颈肿瘤学术委员会委员。

马骏依托中山大学肿瘤防治中心&华南肿瘤学国家重点实验室，围绕中国高发鼻咽癌（占全球47%）临床诊治关键问题，带领团队取得了系列创新性成果，将鼻咽癌生存率由20世纪90年代的60%提高到86%，建立行业内广泛应用的国际标准，实现了我国鼻咽癌诊疗"跟跑"到"领跑"的跨越，惠及全球患者。以第一完成人荣获国家科技进步奖二等奖、中华医学科技进步奖一等奖及教育部高校科技进步奖一等奖各两项，并获全国首届创新争优奖奖状、吴阶平医药创新奖及广东省突出贡献奖等荣誉称号。

**一、提出鼻咽癌临床分期诊断新标准，纠正了30%患者的不合理分期；修正国际标准，指导行业内临床治疗决策**

临床分期是评价肿瘤严重程度、制定治疗方案的重要依据。中国鼻咽癌未分化型肿瘤比例（95%）较欧美高（70%），其特点是增殖快、转移风险高，而现行的国际分期标准对此特点未予以重视，因此不适合中国患者情况。马骏通过死亡风险度的研究，发现调高淋巴结转移的风险级别（咽后、IV/Vb区及>6cm颈部淋巴结）、降低局部侵犯的风险级别（鼻腔和口咽），能够纠正30%患者的不合理分期，避免了治疗不足或过度治疗。上述5项修订已证明同样适用于西方患者，因此被国际通用的分期标准采纳（同期仅做9

项修订）。

马骏进一步把临床分期深入分子层面。组织多中心队列研究证实 miRNA 及其调控靶点 mRNA 可作为转移预警分子标签，从而将转移预测准确性由 61% 提高到 80%。

**二、创立晚期鼻咽癌化疗联合放疗增效新方案，改善患者预后**

1. 研制放疗前使用"吉西他滨＋顺铂"的高效低毒新方案，患者 3 年生存率提高 8.8%、严重毒副反应发生率低于 5%

超过 70% 的鼻咽癌患者就诊时已是中晚期，转移率高，需要联合全身化疗，但"何时启动化疗"一直是焦点问题。1998 年国际通用的美国指南推荐"放疗后大剂量化疗"，但马骏观察到该方案毒性大、患者难以完成，并通过多中心、前瞻性临床试验发现该方案并不能提高疗效。研究成果发表次年（2013 年）被美国指南采用，改变了国际上沿用了 15 年的"放疗后化疗"这一教科书式方案。

针对何时启动化疗，马骏提出应将化疗提至放疗前进行。"放疗前化疗"的有效性通过另一项前瞻性、多中心临床试验得到了证实。美国指南再次采纳其研究成果，"放疗前化疗"成为首选的化疗时机。

上述"放疗前化疗"方案同时使用多西他赛＋顺铂＋氟尿嘧啶，虽效果好，但毒性大、难以在基层推广。为此，马骏提出了"吉西他滨＋顺铂"新方案，临床试验证实该方案不仅能够将患者生存率提高 8%，且严重毒副作用低于 5%。研究成果被美国指南第三次采纳，"吉西他滨＋顺铂"成为首选化疗方案。

2. 提出放疗后"卡培他滨"低剂量、长期、口服的维持治疗新模式，患者 3 年生存率提高 9%

患者接受上述治疗后，仍有 20% 的患者出现远处转移，原因是潜伏的全身微小转移灶。对此，马骏创新提出采用放疗后"卡培他滨"低剂量、长期、口服维持治疗模式或可进一步提高疗效。团队通过一项 406 例的多中心、前瞻性临床试验，证实了该方案不仅可将高危人群 3 年生存率提高 9%，且使用方便、价格便宜，依从性高达 74%，易于向基层推广。研究成果第四次被美国 NCCN 指南采纳。

基于学术影响，马骏牵头制定了国内首部《中国临床肿瘤学会鼻咽癌诊疗指南》，作为主席制定了《中国－美国临床肿瘤学会鼻咽癌临床诊治国际指南》，这也是医学领域内首个由中国学者牵头、联合美国学术组织合作制定的国际循证指南，为国际鼻咽癌诊疗提供了"中国智慧"。

**三、打造低风险患者"缩小颈部照射范围"及"化疗豁免"减毒新策略，提高患者生活质量**

1. 首创可量化、导航式、个体化颈部放疗新技术，降低后遗症发生率

鼻咽癌的主要治疗方法是放疗。对于颈部放疗，以往国内外教科书推荐，无论患者

颈部淋巴结是否转移，均采用全颈照射，而甲状腺、颌下腺受到照射后会带来口干、吞咽困难、甲状腺功能减退、颈部纤维化等后遗症。

针对该问题，马骏通过磁共振图像数据挖掘技术，首次阐明了鼻咽癌颈部淋巴结"由上颈向下颈部转移，跳跃性少"的规律，首创了"缩小颈部照射范围"的放疗新技术：①对有淋巴结转移但小于2cm者，可豁免颌下区照射；②对无淋巴结转移者，可进一步豁免下颈部（含甲状腺）照射。该技术在不增加颈部复发的同时，将甲状腺功能减退发生率由39%降低到30%，口干、吞咽困难等严重放疗后遗症发生率降低15%左右。研究结果被国际临床决策支持系统UpToDate采纳。

2. 创立低危鼻咽癌综合治疗"减毒"新策略，避免过度化疗

既往所有中晚期患者均推荐在放疗期间联合同期化疗。由于精准放疗技术的发展，鼻咽癌生存率已明显提高，低危患者通过额外化疗得到的生存获益明显减少，反而增加了骨髓抑制、口腔黏膜炎、体重减轻等急性反应以及肾功能不全和听力下降等晚期毒性，并加重经济负担。

针对这个问题，马骏通过一项多中心、随机对照临床试验证实部分低危中晚期患者可以豁免化疗，将在不改变疗效的同时有效提高其生活质量。研究成果再次被UpToDate临床决策系统采纳。

# Awardee of Medical Sciences and Materia Medica Prize, Ma Jun

Ma Jun was born in Zhuzhou City of Hunan Province in August 1963. He received his master's degree (Oncology) at Sun Yat-sen University of Medical Sciences in 1990, then he continued his postdoctoral training at M.D. Anderson Cancer Center, Houston, TX from 2000 to 2002. From 2013 to present, he works as the executive deputy president of the Sun Yat-sen University Cancer Center, doctoral supervisor, the level-II professor/level-I chief physician and director of the Nasopharyngeal Cancer Clinical Research Center of Guangdong Province, the chairman of the first Committee of the Nasopharyngeal Carcinoma of the Chinese Society of Clinical Oncology (CSCO), the chairman of the Committee of the Nasopharyngeal Carcinoma of Chinese Anti-Cancer Association (CACA), the convener of the Review Committee of Special Medical Disciplines of the Academic Degrees Committee of China State Council, the member of the Life Medicine Department of the 8th Science and Technology Commission of the Ministry of Education, the co-chairman of the Guidelines Committee for Clinical Management of Nasopharyngeal Carcinoma of the China-American Society of Clinical Oncology (CSCO-ASCO), and the member of the Head and neck cancer Sub-Committee of the European Society for Medical Oncology (ESMO). He was awarded second prize of National Science and Technology Progress Award, National Office for Science and Technology Awards (2009, 2015), first prize of Chinese Medical Science & Technology Award

(2015, 2007), first prize of National Higher Education Science & Technology Progress Award (2021, 2015), certificate of National Innovation & Competition Awards (2017), Wu Jieping Medical Innovation Award (2020) and Guangdong Province Outstanding Contribution Award (2019).

Based on the Sun Yat-sen University Cancer Center and the State Key Laboratory of Oncology in South China, Ma Jun and his team focuses on a cancer called nasopharyngeal carcinoma, which is a unique head and neck cancer with extremely high incidence rate in south China. Ma Jun made a series of innovative achievements on this disease and successfully improved the patient 5-year survival from 60% (1990) to 80% (2020). He established the standard treatment of nasopharyngeal carcinoma, which is now widely adopted as the international standards. These original innovations make China become the leading edge of the clinical diagnosis and treatment of nasopharyngeal carcinoma worldwide.

# 医学药学奖获得者

# 史伟云

史伟云，1959年4月出生于安徽省黟县。2005年获青岛大学医学博士学位。1992—1995年在安徽皖南医学院附属医院工作；1996—2002年在青岛眼科医院工作，先后任科主任、副院长；2001—2016年任山东省眼科研究所副所长；2006年至今任山东省眼科医院院长；2016年至今任山东省眼科研究所所长、省部共建国家重点实验室培育基地主任。现任中华医学会眼科学分会常务委员和角膜病学组组长、亚洲角膜病学会理事、中国民族卫生协会眼学科分会主任委员、中国医师协会眼科学分会角膜病委员会主任委员等。组建我国首个国际角膜移植培训中心、眼科博物馆和眼库联盟。2022年入选俄罗斯自然科学院外籍院士。

史伟云专注眼科角膜盲防治相关临床和基础研究40年，在创新角膜病诊疗技术和解决角膜供体匮乏方面作出系列开创性贡献。荣获国家科技进步奖二等奖2项、山东省科学技术最高奖、山东省科技进步奖一等奖等10余项奖项。

## 一、研发系列角膜修复材料，解决供体匮乏难题

我国现有角膜盲患者400多万人，95%可通过角膜移植复明。但由于供体严重匮乏，年均复明患者仅1万例，角膜供体是限制我国角膜盲复明的瓶颈难题。

1. 研发新型生物角膜产品

针对动物角膜临床应用存在的异种排斥、不透明和术后视力差三项难题，历经15年研发，提出胶体渗透压平衡的新理论，发明脱细胞保护液，创新脉冲高静压和飞秒激光精确切削关键技术，获得符合临床要求的新型生物角膜产品。目前已在全国100多家医院应用，使6000余名患者复明，临床效果达到人供体角膜水平，极大缓解了我国角膜供体匮乏局面。

2. 研发我国首个人工角膜产品

终末期角膜盲在我国被认为是绝症。史伟云团队经过10年研发，攻克人工角膜材料合成、镜柱光学偏心等8项关键技术，成功研发首个符合国人眼解剖结构的领扣型人工角膜产品。获4项国家发明专利和Ⅲ类植入医疗器械注册证，填补了国内空白，临床效果明显优于国际同类产品，并建立了我国人工角膜的制造标准和临床应用规范。

3. 研发新型生物羊膜产品

发明新鲜羊膜长效保存液，解决了羊膜活性成分长期保存难的问题，获Ⅲ类植入医疗器械注册证，产品已在全国近百家医院应用，治愈患者10000余例，效果明显优于干燥保存产品。首次成功研发生物结膜产品，解决严重结膜缺损无修复材料的临床难题，已进入临床多中心阶段。

4. 创建角膜原位捐献模式

受传统观念束缚，我国难以实行国际眼库摘除眼球捐献角膜的标准流程。针对原位捐献污染率高和活性保存难的问题，发明角膜保存液，创建了"只取角膜，维持遗容"的角膜原位捐献新模式，并在全国眼库推广，使角膜年捐献量从200枚增加到5000多枚。

## 二、创新系列角膜移植手术，形成规范化诊疗体系

角膜移植是眼科最具代表性的精细复杂手术。针对传统手术并发症多、复明率低的难题，史伟云先后创新28项手术，牵头制定专家共识16项，形成适合我国的角膜病诊治规范体系。

1. 系列圆锥角膜治疗新手术

针对经典角膜移植需多次手术的问题，开创深板层角膜移植联合逐渐加压缝合技术，解决术后视力差的难题；首创热成形联合深板层角膜移植，改写了急性圆锥角膜必须行穿透角膜移植的常规；应用飞秒激光板层角膜移植治疗圆锥角膜，快速恢复最佳视力。系列创新手术在全国推广应用，实现1次手术可终生复明。

2. 边缘和基质角膜疾病新手术

首次应用OCT指导手术，提出角膜供受体精确匹配的个体化角膜移植原则，开创精确修复的角膜移植手术先河，使1枚角膜供体治疗3～5名患者，节省供体，降低治疗费用，减少并发症，达到精确解剖复位和快速恢复视力的治疗目的。发明的"环形角膜移植术"被英国皇家外科医学院院士命名推广。

3. 真菌性角膜炎发病机制与临床应用

提出并证明"不同真菌菌丝在角膜内存在不同生长方式"的创新理论，打破传统板层角膜移植不能治疗真菌性角膜炎的手术禁区，术后长期成功率显著提升；系统研究真菌性角膜炎术后复发特点并提出防治策略，治愈率大幅提高。相关成果被国际经典教科书 *Cornea* 多次引用，并写入美国感染病学会指南。

4. 建立国内常见致盲性角膜病的影像学标准

针对感染性角膜炎早期误诊率高的难题，率先建立活体共焦显微镜诊断的影像学标准，制定指导临床用药原则和判断治疗转归的整体方案，显著提高阳性诊断率、缩短诊断时间，在100多家医院推广应用。发现春季角结膜炎复发的关键机制，建立共焦显微镜指导用药规范，使复发率明显下降。

5. 发明眼内植入缓释免疫抑制剂

针对高危角膜移植免疫排斥率高的临床难题，首次发现并证明"眼内房水通路"是角膜移植免疫排斥的新途径。进一步发明系列眼内植入免疫抑制缓释剂，其中环孢素缓释片获国家药物临床试验批件，临床应用显著优于现有产品。

# Awardee of Medical Sciences and Materia Medica Prize, Shi Weiyun

Shi Weiyun was born in Yixian County of Anhui Province in April 1959. Before he gained his doctorate from Qingdao University in 2005, he worked at the Affiliated Hospital of Southern Anhui Medical College from 1992 to 1995 and at the Qingdao Eye Hospital, successively serving as department head and vice president of the hospital, from 1996 to 2002. Prof. Shi served as deputy director of Shandong Eye Institute from 2001 to 2016 and began to concurrently serve as president of Shandong Eye Hospital from 2006. Since 2016, he has been the director of Shandong Eye Institute and the director of the State Key Laboratory Cultivation Base, Shandong Provincial Key Laboratory of Ophthalmology. Currently, Prof. Shi is the standing committee member of Chinese Ophthalmological Society, president of Chinese Cornea Society, board member of Asian Cornea Society, chairman of the Ophthalmology Branch of Chinese National Health Association, and chairman of the Cornea Group of Ophthalmology Branch of Chinese Medical Doctor Association. He is the founder of China's first international corneal transplantation training center and ophthalmology museum, as well as the National Eye Bank Alliance. Prof. Shi has won 2 Second Prizes of National Science and Technology Progress as first and second investigators, respectively, Top Science and Technology Award of Shandong Province, and First Prizes of Shandong Science and Technology Progress over more than 10 of these prizes. He was elected as foreign academician of Russian Academy of Natural Sciences in 2022.

Prof. Shi has been engaged in the clinical and basic research related to the prevention and treatment of corneal blindness for four decades, making pioneering contributions to both the improvement in the diagnosis and treatment of corneal disease and the alleviation of human donor corneal shortage. He innovative series of corneal repair materials with solution of donor corneal shortage, and has developed and modified 28 surgical procedures and led the formulation of 16 expert consensuses. A standard system of diagnosis and treatment of corneal disease suitable for China has been established.

# 医学药学奖获得者

# 王 拥 军

王拥军，1962年9月出生于河北省邯郸市。1989年获首都医科大学神经病学硕士学位。1989—1999年在首都医科大学宣武医院工作，历任神经内科医师、主治医师、副主任医师、实验室副主任等职务。1999年赴美国阿肯色医科大学访问学习。2000年任首都医科大学附属北京天坛医院神经内科主任，并先后担任北京天坛医院院长助理、副院长和院长，主任医师、教授和博士研究生导师。同时兼任国家神经系统疾病医疗质量控制中心主任、国家神经系统疾病临床医学研究中心副主任、中华医学会神经病学分会主任委员和中国卒中学会执行副会长等。2020年始任中国医学科学院学部委员。他是科技部"十二五"脑血管病、"十三五"重大慢病和"十四五"常见多发病战略规划专家组组长，是国家"重大新药创制"科技重大专项和科技创新2030"脑科学与类脑研究"重大项目总体专家组成员。曾获国家科技进步奖二等奖2项和省部级一等奖3项，同时获得首批全国创新争先奖章、吴阶平医药创新奖、第十三届谈家桢生命科学临床医学奖和2022年度世界卒中组织主席奖。

王拥军长期致力于脑血管病的临床诊疗和科学研究，在联合抗血小板治疗、基于药物基因组学的精准医疗和推动指南向临床转化等领域取得了一系列原创性学术成果。

**一、创立缺血性脑血管病短程双通道双效应联合治疗方案，改写了多国指南和临床实践**

高复发是缺血性脑血管病防治的世界难题，但各国指南推荐的阿司匹林单一抗血小板治疗效果有限，而叠加其他药物的联合抗血小板治疗的临床研究均因无效或增加严重出血风险而失败，因此联合治疗曾被国际指南禁用于缺血性脑血管病。王拥军发现vWF凝血因子及hsCRP等炎性标志物是影响发病和复发的重要因素，并结合临床和研究数据再分析，提出了阿司匹林叠加氯吡格雷的短程双通道双效应联合治疗方案（即CHANCE

方案）。经 5170 例受试者的临床试验证实，该方案可使缺血性脑血管病患者复发风险相对下降 32% 且不增加出血风险，解决了缺血性脑血管病抗血小板联合用药的临床难题，以最高级别推荐改写了我国和美、加等多国脑血管病临床指南。该方案被写入美国执业医师考试教材和经典专著，并入选 NEJM "2013 年度国际医学领域重大进展"和 Lancet Neurology "脑血管病治疗领域年度新进展"。欧洲药品管理局将该方案作为核心依据拓展了氯吡格雷主适应证。研究成果获 2016 年度国家科技进步奖二等奖，及国家药物发明专利 1 项。

## 二、系统研究联合治疗中氯吡格雷疗效的药物基因组学，创立了精准医疗方案

王拥军应用药物基因组学技术对联合治疗药物相关的 9 个基因 28 个位点进行了系统研究，发现 3 个基因的相关位点与 CHANCE 方案疗效显著相关，分别为影响氯吡格雷吸收或代谢的关键基因 *ABCB1*、*CYP2C19* 和 *F2R*。

其中，影响吸收的 *ABCB1* 在基因型为 –154TT 和 3435CC 时，与单用阿司匹林相比，联合治疗可使复发风险相对下降 51%；*CYP2C19* 在基因型为 *1/*1 时，则联合治疗可使复发风险相对下降 49%；*F2R* 在基因型为 AT 或 TT 时，联合治疗同样使复发风险显著下降。他还发现携带 *CYP2C19* 功能缺失等位基因的数量与氯吡格雷疗效呈明显的反向"量效关系"。上述成果被美国食品药品管理局引用，成为其修订氯吡格雷药物说明书的重要支持数据。针对携带 *CYP2C19* 功能缺失等位基因的人群，王拥军提出了"绕行基因"的替格瑞洛替代治疗方案，该方案可显著抑制血小板活性，使抗血小板疗效提升 60%、临床复发率相对降低 23%，研究结果已改写美国 NIH 临床药物基因组学实施联盟国际指南。

## 三、创建推动指南向临床实践转化的新策略，研发了针对新靶点的创新药物

针对部分患者无法从已有治疗手段获益的临床难题，王拥军开展了 31 个省份的流行病学调查和医疗质量研究，发现指南推荐的溶栓和抗凝等治疗手段临床执行率低，找到了指南向临床实践转化不畅的症结，创建了基于整合临床路径、持续质量改进和大数据监测与反馈的推动转化的"金桥"策略，该策略可使缺血性脑血管病复发等血管事件相对下降 28%。"金桥"策略核心内容被作为最高级别推荐写入《中国脑血管病临床管理指南》。相关成果获 2020 年度国家科技进步奖二等奖。

针对经规范治疗后仍有残余复发的问题，他用时 10 余年建立了超过 6 万人的国家脑血管病队列，发现与国际普遍认为的"颅外动脉狭窄"是脑血管病主要病因不同，中国人脑血管病的最主要致病基础是"颅内动脉狭窄"，这也是残余复发的重要原因；进一步发现 PDE3A 基因位点等靶点与残余复发相关，研发了新型 PDE3A 抑制剂并实现产业转化。

# Awardee of Medical Sciences and Materia Medica Prize, Wang Yongjun

Wang Yongjun was born in Handan City of Hebei Province in September 1962. He received his Master Degree of Neurology from the Capital Medical University (CMU) in 1989 and was trained as a neurologist in Xuanwu Hospital, CMU for a decade. During 1999 to 2000, he had his oversea training for Medical Sciences at University of Arkansas in the United States and was hired as an administrative director of the Department of Neurology in Beijing Tiantan Hospital, CMU in 2000. He is now the President of Beijing Tiantan Hospital, the chief scientist of the Neurology Center, the director of the National Center for Healthcare Quality Management in Neurological Diseases and the deputy director of the National Clinical Research Center for Neurological Diseases in Beijing Tiantan Hospital. He is also the executive vice president of the Chinese Stroke Association. As a team leader of strategic planning in the Ministry of Science and Technology, he guided the drafts of Cerebrovascular diseases in the 12th Five-Year Plan, the Key chronic diseases in the 13th Five-Year Plan and the Common diseases in the 14th Five-Year Plan. He has been a member of the Faculty of the Chinese Academy of Medical Sciences since 2020 and has been recognized the "President Award" of World Stroke Organization in October 2022.

Professor Wang has dedicated most of his time in clinical research of cerebrovascular disease for 40 years as a neurologist and a scientist and has made a series of original academic achievements in the fields of dual-antiplatelet therapy, precision medicine based on pharmacogenomics and promoting the translation of guidelines into clinical practice.

# 医学药学奖获得者

# 郑晓瑛

郑晓瑛，女，1956年8月出生于河北省张家口市。1991年获北京大学历史学博士学位。1994—1995年分别在伦敦大学伦敦卫生与热带医学院人口研究中心和哈佛大学公共卫生学院人口与发展研究中心进行合作研究。1995年至今在北京大学人口研究所工作，先后任北京大学人口研究所所长、北京大学APEC健康科学研究院院长。兼任中国残疾人康复协会副理事长、中国老年学与老年医学学会副会长、中华预防医学会残疾预防与控制专委会主任委员、联合国华盛顿小组中国代表。发展中国家科学院院士。

郑晓瑛从事人口健康研究，在人口增龄健康流行病交叉学科的方法和应用等方面取得一系列开创性研究成果。

**一、突破人口健康流行病交叉学科研究中以横截面数据仿真队列重组的难题，完成中国全人口全生命周期残疾谱系，为精准识别和防控残疾风险奠定了我国自主创新的数据平台**

攻克外部信息调整和历史数据缺失"卡点"，利用人口、医学和环境科学交叉学科方法进行仿真队列重组，建立了分层矩阵队列。系统完成中国百年人口残障发生轨迹的复原，以1987年为原点的20年间控制时间效应混杂后的中国人口残障原因、类别、等级和趋势，以及以2006年为原点的65年间基于人口、发展与环境预测模型的中国人口残障趋势预测，解决多次横断面对接形成长时间大跨度队列仿真数据并利用的方法难题。

改良地理空间分异性归因测量方法，利用中华人民共和国成立以来人口、医学、环境等公开数据信息，在国际上完成第一部国家级全人口全生命周期县级小尺度残障归因谱系，是精准防控残疾发生、延缓残疾程度升级和配置医疗卫生资源投入指南的基本依据。

**二、创新"胎龄-增龄-老龄"三龄一体识别致残关键风险的交叉学科系统判定方法，精确定位出生源头在增龄残障累积效应的证据，率先发现中国人叶酸源-运输力间的代谢通路堵点、地理空间归因、人口特征风险点、风险暴露印记年龄以及宏观风险作用于残障表征的因果判定机制，为精准防控累积到老年的残障井喷提供强大科学依据**

首次发现我国北方叶酸干预出生残障效果不佳的机理为叶酸源和运输力代谢链存在通路堵点，即在神经发育缺陷儿母亲的代谢途径中，线粒体呼吸链、神经递质 γ-氨基丁酸和蛋氨酸循环受损；线粒体缺陷与琥珀酸脱氢酶抑制有关；分型发病机制涉及胆碱缺乏，而与叶酸联系微弱，揭示足量补充叶酸但叶酸代谢途径特征性中断并无法被利用于正常甲基化的机理，填补了国际分型神经发育缺陷的碳水化合物、氨基酸、脂类和核酸代谢紊乱模式差异的空白，也是中国贫困地区叶酸通路特定潜在临床标志物的重要依据。

首次完成早期残障空间归因研究，发现胎龄神经发育异常与地质地理自然危险因素之间的关系，明确标识环境痕量元素在生态圈累积后所造成的严重不良健康结局，为医学地理学方法和疾病空间归因技术相结合的创新研究作出贡献。

系统识别中国全人口增龄分期残障的人口特征风险点、风险暴露印记年龄以及宏观风险作用于残障表征的因果判定机制，包括精准发布中国全人口增龄分期残障规模、分类、等级与主要致残原因及相关的年龄和病种特征等。利用建立的中国"事件-残障"自然实验矩阵队列，系统验证了生命早期饥荒、战争、洪水、地震等逆向事件对人口增龄到老年期躯体和精神残障的影响，由此创建了"事件人口学"新的学科方向。根据系统研究成果，提出促进我国全人口全生命周期健康水平的"人口增龄健康组学"理论依据和框架。

**三、创新"三龄一体"多维残疾防控理论和技术体系，推动相关政策制定并领导增龄政策落地工程实施，取得良好社会和经济效益**

主持"0 岁健老"全人口出生缺陷干预工程。最早提出"建立全年龄综合性社会化残障预防机制势在必行"观点及依据，在覆盖 2 亿人口出生发育缺陷高频印记区引入复合营养素干预后，发育残障风险降低 27%；在高发贫困地区防控后发生率降低 68%、疾病负担降低 59%，大人群反复干预实验互印叶酸利用障碍机理，成为全国推广依据。

领导首部国务院《国家残疾预防行动计划》编制技术的研究。作为专家组组长，领导《国家残疾预防行动计划》的编制研究工作，并推动政策条例出台、实施与落地。完成确立 33 个部委、31 个省（自治区、直辖市）253 个生命历程出生、病残、伤害、康复防控技术指标和监评方案。

专业领导和评估全人口全生命周期累积残障风险防控示范工程。作为技术指导组组长，成功建立中国残疾防控的"三龄一体化模式"体系，并被"十三五"国务院残疾预防行动计划全国百县试点应用；建立中国特色的残疾监测体系，完成《中国残疾预防对策研究》和《残疾报告制度研究》，突破"残、老、贫"三维失能导致叠变的识别和预防的技术路径。成果荣获发展中国家科学院科学奖。

# Awardee of Medical Sciences and Materia Medica Prize, Zheng Xiaoying

Zheng Xiaoying, female, was born in Zhangjiakou City of Hebei Province in August 1956. She received her Ph.D. in History from Peking University in 1991. From 1994 to 1995, she conducted collaborative research at the Centre for Population Research, the London School of Hygiene & Tropical Medicine at London University, and the Centre for Population and Development Studies, the School of Public Health at Harvard University, respectively. She has been working at the Institute of Population Research, Peking University since returning to China in 1995. Prof. Zheng has served as the Director of the Institute of Population Research of Peking University and the Dean of PKU-APEC Health Science Academy and other positions. She also serves as the Vice President of the China Association of Rehabilitation of Disabled Persons, the Vice President of the China Association of Gerontology and Geriatrics, the Chairman of the Special Committee on Disability Prevention and Control of the Chinese Preventive Medicine Association, and the Chinese representative of the Washington Group on Disability Statistics of the United Nations. In 2016, she was elected a Fellow of The World Academy of Sciences.

Prof. Zheng has broken through the challenge of reconstructing synthetic simulative cohorts with cross-sectional data in the interdisciplinary research on population health epidemiology and completed a full life-cycle disability spectrum for the whole population in China, laying down China's own innovative data platform for the accurate identification as well as prevention and control of disability risks.

Prof. Zheng has innovated a cross-disciplinary systematic approach to identify the key risks of disability in the "gestational age-aging age-elderly age", pinpointed the evidence of the birth source in the accumulation effect of disability in the accretion age, and she was the first to discover the metabolic pathway "blockage" between folic acid source and transport in Chinese people, the causal mechanism of geospatial attribution, demographic characteristics risks, risk exposure imprinting age, and the causal mechanisms of macroscopic risk effect on disability representation, which provides a strong scientific basis for precise prevention and control of the cumulative disability blowout in old age.

Prof. Zheng has innovatively put forward the multi-dimensional disability prevention and control theory and technical system of the "three-age-stage integrated model", promoted the formulation of relevant policies, and led the implementation of the projects related aging policy, achieving good social and economic benefits.

# 机械电力技术奖获得者

# 苑伟政

苑伟政，1961年出生于天津市。现任西北工业大学空天微纳系统教育部重点实验室主任。兼任军口某领域专家委员会委员、教育部科技委先进制造学部委员、中国机械工程学会常务理事、中国微纳米技术学会常务理事等。

苑伟政是我国微机电系统（MEMS）领域著名专家，长期致力于自主发展MEMS芯片设计与制造技术，在航空航天特种MEMS等方面取得一系列突出成果，获国家技术发明奖二等奖3项、国家教学成果奖一等奖1项；获授权国家技术发明专利86件。研究成果成功用于航空航天等领域3个国家重大专项、16个重点工程。

## 一、提出MEMS"泛结构化"设计模式，研发首套国产专用集成设计工具，设计研制高性能MEMS产品

提出"任意流程、创成式"的"泛结构化"MEMS集成设计模式，解决了微机械结构、芯片制造和驱动检测电路多学科交叉设计难题；发明多端口三维组件系统级建模方法，实现了微结构—静电力—薄膜阻尼等多域耦合仿真分析；建立非线性微结构的数值与解析异构模型，实现了非规则微结构的创成式设计。

主持研发专用集成设计工具MEMS GARDEN，使我国成为继美、法后拥有专用MEMS设计软件的国家，支撑22种复杂MEMS设计。设计工具在航空、航天、兵器等国防单位及高校推广应用，为惯性MEMS等产品开发和优化提供设计和服务支撑。

自主设计静电驱动式微扫描振镜，主要技术指标与美、德等先进产品水平相当，为宽视场、大景深目标的快速三维建模提供了关键核心器件；成功用于某航天单位的激光雷达三维成像系统研制，提升抗诱饵主动识别能力；实现产业化，国内外用户超百家。

提出"基于模态局部化效应的加速度敏感机理"，主持研制国际首款模态局部化微加速度计，分辨力达$640ng/\sqrt{Hz}$，为我国在惯性MEMS新原理方面率先取得突破，相关成

果获 2020 年教育部自然科学奖一等奖。

研究成果"微机电系统的泛结构化设计方法与技术"获 2011 年国家技术发明奖二等奖。

## 二、发明"单掩膜刻蚀与结构选择性释放"等 SOI 基 MEMS 制造方法，制定相应的国家工艺标准，研制航空航天特种 MEMS

发明"单掩膜刻蚀与结构选择性释放"制造方法，运用等离子刻蚀的根侧蚀效应产生纳米"草"表面的疏水特性，解决了微米间隙悬置结构可靠释放的难题，实现了微机械结构无黏附长时稳定运动；突破窄槽刻蚀迟滞效应等约束，实现高深宽比和大异宽比微结构可控刻蚀。

设计建立小批量、多品种制造平台，开发出适合惯性、压力和光学 MEMS 的 3 套制造工艺；牵头制定《基于 SOI 硅片的 MEMS 工艺规范》国家标准，支撑 15 种特种 MEMS 制造，将独特制造技术推广用于多个领域 60 多个单位。

自主研制浮动式微剪应力传感器，具有抗干扰性强、分辨率高的特点，已成功应用并实现某发动机超高温、超高速极端条件下内壁剪应力瞬态测量，为表征燃烧流场的时/频变化特征提供重要实验依据。

定制加工超高过载加速度测量芯片，装备某导弹；定制加工微机械陀螺芯片，装备某型飞机逃逸系统姿态测量装置；定制加工微夹持器芯片，保障某工程关键部件的调节定位。

研究成果"航空航天特种 MEMS 制造技术及其应用"获 2019 年国家技术发明奖二等奖。

## 三、发明聚合物基柔性 MEMS 的"热敏微传感器阵列结构制造"等方法，研制飞行器曲面剪应力感知蒙皮

发明"非平坦表面张紧光刻"等柔性微传感器阵列制造方法，解决了变曲率表面柔性微纳结构精确成形成性等难题，研制出曲面保型剪应力感知蒙皮，为飞行器曲面剪应力分布式测量和边界层状态表征提供了器件保障。研究成果"飞行器流动测控灵巧蒙皮技术"获 2010 年国家技术发明奖二等奖。

主持开发与感知蒙皮配套的流体壁面剪应力测试仪，被中国商飞等 10 余家单位成功用于空气、水及泥沙介质的流动测量，实现了 C919、ARJ21 等民用客机超临界翼型摩阻分布精确测量、边界层分离和转捩判定，支撑减阻增升设计；实飞测定某型飞机短距离、大迎角爬升的分离特征等。研究成果"流体壁面剪应力测试仪及其应用"获 2020 年陕西省技术发明奖一等奖。

发现秦岭高山箭竹叶疏冰特征，发明仿竹叶表面的多层不等高微纳结构及其制造方法，解决了跨尺度多层柔性微纳结构制造难题，研制出疏冰蒙皮，满足了高寒环境安全飞行的急需。

# Awardee of Machinery and Electric Technology Prize, Yuan Weizheng

Yuan Weizheng born in Tianjin City in 1961. He is currently the director of MOE Key Laboratory of Micro and Nano Systems for Aerospace. He is a member of the Expert Committee in an important department, a member of the Department of Advanced Manufacturing of the Science and Technology Commission of the Ministry of Education, an executive director of the Chinese Society of Mechanical Engineering, and an executive director of the Chinese Society of Micro and Nanotechnology.

In the past 30 years, Yuan Weizheng has always focused on the study of MEMS, aimed at the high-end MEMS chip technology urgently needed by the country in order to solve the "neck" problem, and made outstanding achievements in the field of design & manufacturing of MEMS chip for aerospace, flexible MEMS smart skin, ect. He had von National Award for Technological Invention 3 times. His research have been successfully applied in 3 major national projects and 16 key projects in aerospace fields: ① The MEMS pan-structured design method was invented, the first set of MEMS integrated design tools in China was developed, multiple MEMS sensors were designed and used for the inertial measurement in multiple field. ② A new SOI based MEMS manufacturing method was invented, the national standard methods of SOI based MEMS process was established, and industrialization of the micro scanning mirror was realized. ③ Customized MEMS chip has been used in batch for several important projects; A new manufacturing method of flexible MEMS was invented, and the anti/de-icing skin was deployed on an unmanned aerial vehicles; The sensing skin was developed to measure and analyze the friction distribution of C919 aircraft, etc.

# 机械电力技术奖获得者

# 张 旭 辉

张旭辉，1975年2月出生于黑龙江省林口县。1998年从哈尔滨工业大学毕业后，进入航天科技集团一院一部攻读研究生，于2000年和2009年分别获得硕士和博士学位。2008—2012年任CZ-2F载人运载火箭总体主任设计师。2012—2022年先后任航天科技一院研究发展中心主任助理、副主任、党委书记、主任，发展部部长兼党委副书记，航天科技一院副院长。2022年6月任航天科技创新研究院常务副院长，同年11月至今任航天科技创新研究院党委书记。先后担任军委科技委某领域专家委员会副主任、战略支援部队航天系统部太空安全领域专家组专家、国防科工局航天运输专家组组长、中国宇航学会第七届理事。

张旭辉是航天运载器总体技术专家，长期从事航天科研创新与型号研制工作，在空间操控飞行器、智变飞行器、航天系统创新等领域作出了一系列开创性工作。

**一、集成创新，主持空间碎片清除在轨验证**

空间碎片的主动清除，需要解决空间碎片的在轨探测、实时定位、形貌和质量特性测量、引导清除和离轨等一系列难题。张旭辉带领团队在碎片在轨探测方面，针对形貌未知的空间碎片，采用光学探测和引导方案，建立双目相机＋手眼相机复合探测识别方法，解决了空间复杂环境下双目点云匹配三维重建、单目结构光及可见光融合测量难题，实现"看得准"；提出"平台＋机械臂"组合体分时控制策略，有效解决多体特征飞行器动力学耦合效应带来的强干扰问题，实现"控得精"；提出基于智能视觉切换的导引策略与搜索路径方法，解决了多约束下机械臂在线运动规划难题，实现"抓得稳"。在此基础上，开展"遨龙一号"空间碎片主动清除飞行器研制攻关，利用两年零九个月时间完成了从方案设计到飞行演示验证的全流程设计研制攻关工作。2016年6月，"遨龙一号"搭载"长征七号"运载火箭发射入轨并开展在轨试验，对模拟的非合作空间碎片目标进行光学成像和精确的位置探测，并利用所获得的信息引导机械臂在轨采用优化路径对目标进行相关操作，试验取得圆满成功。此次试验是国际首次以非合作物体为目标的空间碎片在轨主动清除演示验证，为我国空间碎片主动清除能力的形成奠定了技术基础，也为空间环境治理作出了重要贡献。

## 二、理技融合，开拓智变飞行器技术领域

智变飞行器是指飞行器的外形和物理属性能够根据飞行任务、飞行速度、飞行环境等智能、适时、自主发生改变，从而以不同的气动布局、结构形式、感知特征适应不同的任务需要。智变飞行器能够突破传统飞行器的性能天花板，实现陆、海、空、天多域融合，是下一代飞行器技术发展的重要发展方向。目前国内智变飞行器技术领域研究工作相对分散，也没有相关型号应用案例。张旭辉带领团队聚焦智变飞行器技术领域，通过变形飞行+人工智能融合创新，研究提出以"变外形、变特征、变功能"为核心的未来智变飞行器新形态。据此梳理形成涵盖变形结构与机构、先进动力灵巧调节、以人工智能决策等为核心的技术体系。作为项目首席科学家，带领团队聚焦高超智变飞行器，提出兼具高超滑行与长时巡弋的飞行器方案，组织开展高马赫数飞行器耐温承载可变形结构、变形飞行自适应控制、多维多层智能决策等关键技术研究攻关并取得突破性进展。

## 三、理论归纳，提出"创新五步法"新范式

针对如何推进航天科技原始创新的时代命题，张旭辉带领团队创造性地提出"创新五步法"，对航天科技创新活动进行解耦和提炼，提出场景构建—短板分析—技术供给—方案拟制—评估验证的"创新五步法"。场景构建是顶层牵引，从需求视角构设创新场景，面向创新对象确定其使命任务和应用场景；短板分析是根本驱动，从矛盾视角聚焦创新对象，深入剖析构设场景下对手的弱点，形成我方创新活动的应对策略，同时分析已有系统尚不具备的能力短板，形成我方创新提升焦点；技术供给是创新关键，从技术视角驱动创新活动，面向需求场景下的短板问题，找出解决问题需要的突破性技术，并给出可能的技术途径；方案拟制是创新主体，从系统视角生成创新方案，面向构设的应用场景，围绕短板分析形成的对策、技术供给形成的途径，给出整体性、系统化解决方案；评估验证是创新回归，从价值视角审视创新结果，基于推演仿真结果分析创新对象的效能，形成对创新活动的评判，指导下一轮创新工作。"创新五步法"是在长期从事创新活动的实践中提炼出的方法论，为推进原始创新提供了新的思维范式。

# Awardee of Machinery and Electric Technology Prize, Zhang Xuhui

Zhang Xuhui was born in Linkou County of Heilongjiang Province in February 1975. After graduating from Harbin Institute of Technology in 1998, he entered China Academy of Launch Vehicle Technology (CALT) to study for a postgraduate degree and got his master's degree in August 2000 and a doctorate in June 2009.

From 2008 to 2012, he served as chief designer of CZ-2F manned launch vehicle. From 2012 to 2018, he served as director assistant, deputy director, party secretary and director of the Research and Development Center of CALT. From 2018 to 2020, he served as minister and deputy secretary of the Party committee of Research and Development Department of CALT. From April 2020 to June 2022, he served as vice president of CALT. Since June 2022, he has served as executive vice president of China Academy of Aerospace Science and Innovation (CAASI). Since November 2022, he has served as secretary of the Party committee of CAASI. He has successively served as deputy director of a certain field expert committee of the Science and Technology Commission of the Central Military Commission, expert of the space security field expert group of the Space Systems Department of the Strategic Support Force, leader of the space transportation expert group of the State Administration of Science. Technology and Industry for National Defense, and the seventh director of the China Aerospace Society. He is also the winner of the first National Defense Outstanding Youth Fund Program.

Zhang Xuhui is the expert of spacecraft's overall technics, who has been engaged in space scientific research innovation and model development for years and has made a series of pioneering research work in the fields of space control vehicle, intelligent morphing spacecraft and space system innovation.

# 电子信息技术奖获得者

# 高　文

高文，1956年3月出生于辽宁省大连市。1991年获日本东京大学电子学博士学位。1991—1996年在哈尔滨工业大学工作，历任计算机系主任、学院副院长、校长助理。1996—2006年先后担任中国科学院计算所所长、中国科学院研究生院常务副院长、中国科技大学副校长等。2006年至今在北京大学工作，先后担任视频编解码技术国家工程实验室主任、视频与视觉技术国家工程研究中心主任、信息学院院长、信息与工程学部主任等。2013—2018年任国家自然科学基金委副主任，2016—2020年任中国计算机学会理事长，2018年至今任鹏城实验室主任。中国工程院院士，国际计算机协会会士、电气与电子工程师协会会士。

高文是多媒体领域著名专家，学术领域涉及计算机网络、图像处理、模式识别、多媒体、虚拟现实、计算机视觉、大规模人工智能系统等。曾主导标准研制及产业应用，牵头制定国际国内标准30余项，其中国家标准12项、行业标准2项、IEEE标准11项、ISO/IEC标准4项、团体标准5项；授权发明国际国内专利286项。为实现我国数字视频产业从跟跑到领跑的历史性跨越、开创我国超高清数字电视行业国际领先发展的新局面作出了重要贡献。

曾获中国计算机学会王选奖、国家技术发明奖一等奖和二等奖各1项、国家科技进步奖二等奖6项、国家自然科学奖二等奖1项等，研究成果两次入选教育部"中国高等学校十大科技进展"。

一、破解行业技术标准难题，创立我国自主视频编码技术和标准体系

高文对数字视频领域的贡献主要在视频编码、视频检索与分析、特征表达与编码等方面。历时二十年，他领导创立了我国自主的视频编解码技术标准体系AVS，推动我国数字视频产业实现了从核心技术空白到国际领先的巨大跨越，使我国成为唯一拥有自主

标准的数字电视强国，成功打破国外标准技术垄断。AVS 系列标准不仅满足了中国国内数字电视产业的需求，还被包括国际电联 ITU IPTV 特别工作组、国际超高清联盟、欧广联 DVB 等国际组织采用。带领团队研制了 AVS 8K 超高清实时编码器和解码芯片，发明了超高清视频多态基元编解码技术体系，突破了传统编码框架要素固化的难题，实现了视频编解码从单一压缩到多层次表达的跨越。其构建的自主可控"技术－标准－芯片－系统"体系，推动了中国首个超高清 4K 频道成功开播，在 2022 冬奥会实现了世界首次奥运会 8K 直播，成果规模化应用于电视台以及高清电视机与机顶盒等核心产品中，实现了超高清数字电视编解码技术世界领先。

## 二、深耕模式识别，创建数字视网膜理论和方法体系

高文对模式识别领域的早期贡献主要在人脸识别和手语识别两个方面。他带领团队提出人脸描述子方法以及大规模开放人脸数据库，获得同行大量引用；设计实现了最大词汇量的中国手语识别与合成系统，在很多电视台获得应用。近年来，为了满足工业视觉智能的需求，高文领导创建了完整的"视频＋特征＋模型"的数字视网膜理论框架、方法体系和计算架构，主持研制全球首款数字视网膜芯片 GV9531，分别在城市管理、安防监控、智慧医疗、智能制造等场景示范应用。借鉴生物视网膜结构与机理，发明了千倍率监控视频编码技术和万倍率视频特征紧凑表达技术，实现了视频编解码从信号压缩到多层次表达的跨越，节省超过 90% 的网络带宽和云计算资源；突破了城市大脑中视觉大数据汇聚分析瓶颈，为安防、城市精细管理、工业互联网等领域开展产业升级和数字经济建设提供关键技术支撑。

## 三、打造国之重器，研发国际领先智能超级计算机"鹏城云脑"

高文作为战略科学家，参与我国新一代人工智能顶层设计和发展规划，主持研制了全球首个人工智能技术国际标准，创建并领导新一代人工智能产业技术创新战略联盟。高文带领团队与华为联合研发的鹏城云脑 II 智能计算机，突破了智能芯片架构、高扩展系统架构、人工智能软件全栈等一系列关键技术难题，实现了人工智能算力突出、能效比高的先进计算系统。鹏城云脑 II 在 IO 性能、AI 性能、图计算性能等方面世界领先。鹏城云脑技术体系支持了智慧城市、智能交通、智慧医疗、智能制造等方面若干大规模人工智能应用系统，形成了具有影响力的应用技术体系，在与学术界合作的同时支撑了我国人工智能产业的快速发展，铸造了人工智能的算力基座国之重器。

# Awardee of Electronics and Information Technology Prize, Gao Wen

Gao Wen was born in Dalian City of Liaoning Province in March 1956. He is the member of

Chinese Academy of Engineering, ACM Fellow and IEEE Fellow. In 1991, he graduated from the University of Tokyo, Japan, with a PhD degree in Electronics Engineering. He worked for the Harbin Institute of Technology as a professor, head of computer science department, and assistant to the university president during 1991 to 1996. He was with Chinese Academy of Sciences (CAS) as professor from 1996 to 2006. During his career at CAS, he served as the managing director of Institute of Computing Technology, the executive vice president of Graduate School of CAS, the vice president of University of Science and Technology of China. He joined with the Peking University as a professor since 2006. He was the founding director of NELVT (National Engineering Lab. on Video Technology) at Peking University, and the Chief Scientist of the National Basic Research Program of China (973 Program) on Video Coding Technology. He was also the President of China Computer Federation from 2016 to 2020. He has been the director of Peng Cheng Laboratory since 2018.

Wen Gao is a well-known expert in the field of multimedia. He has a research career of nearly 40 years in the fields of computer networks, image processing, pattern recognition, multimedia, virtual reality, computer vision, large-scale artificial intelligence systems, etc. He established the Audio Video Coding Standard (AVS) workgroup in China and developed a series of standards invented the Digital Retina computational methodology, chip, and system. He also developed the world-leading intelligent supercomputer in China, named Pengcheng Cloud Brain. He led the industrial application and the formulation of more than 30 domestic and international standards, including 12 national standards, 2 industrial standards, 11 IEEE standards, 4 ISO/IEC standards and 5 group standards. It developed a leading situation of China's ultra-high definition digital TV industry. In 2010, he received the CCF Wang Xuan Award. He was awarded the National Technology Innovation Awards by China State Council twice, a first class award in 2020 and a second class award in 2006. He was also the recipient of the second class National Science and Technology Awards by China State Council for six times. He also won the second prize of the National Natural Science Award. And his research achievements was selected into the "Top Ten Scientific and Technological Progress of Chinese Universities" twice by the Ministry of Education.

# 电子信息技术奖获得者

# 王振常

王振常，1964年9月出生于河北省保定市。2000年获天津医科大学影像医学与核医学专业博士学位。2001—2012年在首都医科大学附属北京同仁医院担任放射科主任、医学影像中心主任；2013年至今在首都医科大学附属北京友谊医院担任副院长、医学影像中心主任；2018年至今任首都医科大学医学影像学系主任。兼任北京航空航天大学、中南大学等教授或博士生导师，中国医学影像技术研究会副会长，中国医师协会第四届放射医师分会会长。作为第一完成人获国家科技进步奖二等奖2项，作为主要完成人获国家科技进步奖二等奖1项；2014年入选北京学者，2015年被授予埃博拉防控全国先进个人，2018年被授予全国优秀科技工作者称号。

王振常是我国听觉和视觉系统影像感知与解析领域的带头人，在人体复杂系统生理病理信息多要素关联诊断体系构建、临床精细影像仪器研制技术及信息获取能力方面取得突破，推动了医学影像学的重构。

**一、建立以多模式多维度协同探测感知为基础的生理病理多要素信息关联诊断体系，实现人体精细结构与隐匿病变识别能力的大幅跃升，为解决搏动性耳鸣、神经眼科疾病等世界性难症的精准探测感知提供了中国方案**

建立多模式多维度协同的生理病理多要素信息关联诊断体系。基于常规毫米级CT/MR仪器，提出生理病理多要素信息与多模式多维度影像信息的关联分析方法，突破多模式探测、多维度解析、多要素关联等关键技术，建立了针对不同器官不同病症的一系列影像信息探测感知方法。通过阐明器官功能链路上相关结构或组织生理病理信息的内在关联关系，揭示其病理发生机制，大幅提升了病变检出及解析效能。由此，形成了多模式多维度协同的生理病理多要素信息关联诊断体系。

针对耳部病症，基于该体系建立听觉传导通路多要素协同探测感知方法。提出双期增强高分辨信息采集技术及骨质血管交互评判方法、四维静脉血流采集技术及压力预测方法、定域曝光式听神经采集参数优化技术、听觉中枢的有向连接非平稳动态贝叶斯分析方法，并构建了基于探测感知信息的搏动性耳鸣多要素关联数值模型。首次发现血管、血流、骨质、中枢多要素耦合致鸣机理，揭示了致鸣诱因，有效解决了听觉传导通路上的微弱信息探知难题，实现"检可显，显可见，见可治"，搏动性耳鸣诱因检出率由44%跃升到94%，引领了该方向国际前沿研究。

针对眼部病症，基于该体系建立视觉传导通路多要素协同探测感知方法。突破了面向不稳定微环境的眼眶容物信息采集、基于水分子布朗运动的白质纤维束示踪成像及定量研判、眼眶内神经分支检测等关键技术，提出了视神经管信息提取、外侧膝状体的精准定位及体积测量、眼运动神经可视化方法，解析了青光眼、外伤后失明等视力障碍诱因及机理，实现了大量"同症异病"的神经眼科病症跨域信息的"可探知、可定位、可解析"。视力下降、复视及外伤后失明的诱因检出率分别达到76%、75%和78%，实现了低漏诊和早发现，大幅降低了失明风险。开拓了基于影像信息的神经眼科学研究新领域。

## 二、创新超分辨力 CT 系统研制思路和方案，主持研制出全球首台专用骨质微结构 CT 仪器，创建听觉传导通路微米级结构探测感知新方法，实现了听觉微小结构与隐匿病变探测感知能力的重要突破

针对骨质微小结构清晰显示及影像解析的需要，提出人体骨质微米级结构信息的宽视与详视相结合 X 射线探测及其影像被扰动的可见光补偿重建技术路线和方法。使用常规 X 射线发生器和大面阵探测器用以实现宽视扫描探知，选择关注靶区；以自研的大功率小焦点 X 射线发生器和高分辨力面阵探测器相组合，实现详视成像；运用可见光立体视觉手段进行精密机电伺服跟踪及时空坐标解算，通过运动数据补偿提高图像清晰度，消除呼吸、心跳等不可控扰动影响，实现了骨质微米级结构的准确定位和精细成像的技术跨越。主持研制出全球首台微米级专用骨质 CT 仪器，实现了影像信息各向同性的采集与重建，体素达 $50\mu m \times 50\mu m \times 50\mu m$。与通用电气、西门子与飞利浦等国际高端仪器相比，空间分辨力提升 6 倍、辐射剂量下降 2/3，一举解决了常规高端仪器的微小结构及隐匿病变"显不出"的国际性难题。

基于自主研制的专用骨质 CT 仪器，建立听觉传导通路微米级结构探测感知新方法，为听觉系统微小结构隐匿病变的探测感知提供了临床"利器"。针对耳部微小结构，开发出光源参数 100 kV/120 mAs、面阵探测器单元尺寸 $0.0748mm \times 0.0748mm$、重建视野达 $65mm \times 65mm$ 的标准化信息采集方案，实现图像优良率达 100%、辐射剂量不高于 0.08 mSv 的微米级结构高清探测。构建标准化空间坐标系，对多种微小结构进行同步精准分割，重合度最高达 83%，形成基于正常解剖模板的病症探测感知的智能判读方法，实现了微小结构隐匿病变的精准定位定量。

在临床实践中首次清晰显示出镫骨底板、前庭导水管内口、耳蜗导水管内口等引起

耳聋、眩晕的重要微小结构，显示率分别为100%、100%、72%；发现了诱发耳鸣、眩晕症状的硬脑膜动静脉瘘、梅尼埃病等常见病症的微弱病理信息，发现了特发性传导聋的新诱因，将耳硬化症检出率由45%提升至100%，实现了微小结构上隐匿病变识别质的跨越，进一步推动了影响人类听觉健康的常见疾病早期精准甄别的跨越式提升。

# Awardee of Electronics and Information Technology Prize, Wang Zhenchang

Wang Zhenchang was born in Baoding City of Hebei Province in September 1964. He graduated from Tianjin Medical University in 2000 with a Doctor degree in Medical Imaging and Nuclear Medicine. From 2001 to 2012, he served as the director of the Department of Radiology and the director of the Medical Imaging Center at Beijing Tongren Hospital, Capital Medical University. Since 2013, he has served as the vice president and director of the Medical Imaging Center at Beijing Friendship Hospital, Capital Medical University. Since 2018, he has been the director of the Department of Medical Imaging at Capital Medical University. He is a guest professor at Beihang University and a doctoral supervisor at Central South University. He is the vice president of the China Medical Imaging Technology Research Association and the president of the fourth radiologist branch of the China Medical Doctor Association.

Zhenchang Wang is a pioneer in the research of medical imaging perception and analysis of auditory and visual systems. He promotes the reformation of medical imaging. He established a physiological and pathological multi-factor information-associated diagnosis system based on multi-mode and multi-dimensional cooperative detection and perception. He also achieved a breakthrough in the recognition of human fine structure and hidden lesions. Additionally, he provided a Chinese solution for the precise detection and perception of pulsatile tinnitus and neuro-ophthalmic diseases.

He conceived the idea and scheme of ultra-high-resolution computed tomography (U-HRCT), presided over the development of the world's first bone micron-scale CT, created a new method for the detection and perception of micro-structures of the auditory pathway, and achieved an important breakthrough in the detection and perception of auditory micro-structures and hidden lesions.

# 电子信息技术奖获得者

# 谢 胜 利

谢胜利，1956年12月出生于湖北省公安县。1981年毕业于湖北荆州师范学院数学系，1995年毕业于华中师范大学数学系获理学硕士学位，1997年毕业于华南理工大学自动化系获工学博士学位。于1992年、1997年先后在武汉大学数学系和中国科学院系统科学研究所做高级访问学者。2011年起任广东省物联网信息技术重点实验室主任，2016年起任教育部物联网智能信息处理与系统集成重点实验室主任，2017年起任国家111学科创新引智基地主任，2019年起任粤港澳离散制造智能化联合实验室主任。先后获得国家自然科学奖二等奖、中国专利银奖、教育部科学技术奖一等奖12项。2019年入选美国电气电子工程师协会会士，2022年当选俄罗斯工程院外籍院士。

谢胜利从事盲信号处理理论与应用研究，在盲信号可分性基本理论和自适应分离方法领域作出了卓越贡献，并由此建立了新的盲检测技术体系且应用于多个工程领域。

## 一、Stone猜想与Xie-定理

Stone猜想是国际上盲信号处理领域中关于"可分性"的基本问题，谢胜利带领团队证明了Stone猜想的不完整性，并发现方差比是一个信号在时域上的本质特征，从数学逻辑上建立了完整的方差比理论，为盲信号处理的可分性理论奠定了坚实基础，该理论被国际同行称为"Xie-定理"，作为盲信号分离的理论基础被应用于不同工程领域。此外，在盲信号处理领域，美国两院院士Sejnowski构造了欠定系统的自然梯度表示，创立了欠定盲分离系统的自适应分离方法。谢胜利带领团队证明了Sejnowski所建立的自然梯度表示的不完备性，首次发现并从数学上严格证明了全新逆矩阵微分公式，给出了欠定盲信号系统的完备自然梯度表示，以此建立了欠定自适应盲信号处理理论体系与方法，突破了统计相关源信号盲分离的瓶颈问题。发现的全新逆矩阵微分公式被经典工具书 *Matrix Cookbook* 收录作为矩阵论基本工具之一。

谢胜利根据建立的盲信号方差比理论及自适应分离方法，发明了单通道多源盲检测、相关源信号盲检测、复杂环境下微弱信号盲检测等系列盲检测关键技术，为盲信号处理的理论应用打下坚实基础。

### 二、单通道多源盲检测技术与北斗卫星信号的快速捕获和高效选星

基于接收的北斗信号多普勒效应和混叠特点，谢胜利带领团队构建时变时延的北斗卫星信号单通道盲分离模型；并根据北斗卫星伪码正交性，提出基于卫星接收信号分区积分的快速盲搜索方法，实现北斗卫星的快速高精度盲捕获。

此外，针对北斗同步"授时难准"问题，提出基于卫星传输链路时延补偿、电路级时延补偿、反馈时延补偿的三重精确同步授时体系架构，发明北斗信号稀疏抗干扰处理方法，提出联合卫星钟差和本地钟漂反馈的数压高精度时延补偿技术，授时精度可达到 6 纳秒；在高精度定位方面，他们发明了融合信号强度和相位模糊度的北斗卫星选星模型，实现在复杂环境下的快速有效选星；提出了基于历元间差分的单频周跳估计方法，实现相位模糊度的可靠固定；发明的基于相位模糊度和伪距的自适应融合定位方法可实现厘米级高精度定位。

### 三、微弱信号盲检测技术与病理特征波提取和心肺音分离

谢胜利带领团队在国际上率先系统开展心电信号盲检测研究和技术攻关，发明了微伏级心电特征波的精确提取技术，突破了微弱心电特征波被掩盖而"测不准"的难题，实现微伏级心电特征波实时高精度提取。

基于盲检测技术和人工智能方法，谢胜利带领团队成功研制了国际首款具有心肺音分离功能的数字智能听诊器，并牵头制定了国家团体标准。产品获得国家医疗器械注册证书和欧盟 CE 认证。

# Awardee of Electronics and Information Technology Prize, Xie Shengli

Xie Shengli was born in Gong'an County of Hubei Province in December 1956. He graduated from the Department of Mathematics of Jingzhou Normal College in Hubei Province in 1981, received the Master of Science degree from the Department of Mathematics of Huazhong Normal University in 1995, and the Ph.D. degree in Engineering from the Department of Automation of South China University of Technology in 1997. He was a senior visiting scholar with the Department of Mathematics of Wuhan University in 1992, and with the Institute of Systems Science, Chinese Academy of Sciences in 1997. He has been the director of the Guangdong Key Laboratory of Internet of Things Information Technology since 2011, the director of the Key Laboratory of

Intelligent Information Processing and System Integration, Ministry of Education of China since 2016, the director of the National 111 Overseas Expertise Introduction Center for Discipline Innovation since 2017, and the director of Guangdong-Hong Kong-Macao Joint Laboratory for Smart Discrete Manufacturing since 2019. He has won the second prize in the National Natural Science Award of China, the China Patent Silver Award, and the first prize in the Science and Technology Award of the Ministry of Education of China twelve times. He has been elected as Fellow of the Institute of Electrical and Electronics Engineers since 2019, and is elected as a Foreign Full Member (Academician) of the Russian Academy of Engineering in 2022.

Professor Shengli Xie is engaged in blind signal processing theory and its application research. He has made outstanding contributions to the fundamental theory of blind signal separability and adaptive separation methods, and thus established a new blind detection technology system that has been applied to many engineering fields.

### 1. Stone conjecture and Xie-theorem

Shengli Xie led his research team in establishing a systematic variance ratio theory, which was called as Xie-theorem, seen as a solid basis of separability of blind source separation and successfully applied to different engineering problems, by pointing out the incompleteness of Stone conjecture, originally finding that the variance ratio is an intrinsic character of signal in the time domain and then mathematically proven a corrected conjecture regarding the separability of blind source separation.

Besides, for the problem of blind source processing, Shengli Xie led his team to point out the incompleteness of such a natural gradient, improved it, and mathematically proved it by finding a new differential formula with respect to an inverse matrix. In this way, Shengli Xie et al established a systematic theoretical architecture and method for underdetermined BSS and broke the bottleneck of BSS of statistically correlated sources. Additionally, such a differential formula for inverse matrix found by Professor Xie's team was verified to be new and collected to *Matrix Cookbook*, a classic toolbox in the field of matrix analysis.

Professor Shengli Xie established blind signal variance ratio theory and self-adaptive separation method, and further invented a series of blind detection key technologies such as single-channel multi-source blind detection, correlated sources signal blind detection, and weak signal blind detection in complex environments. His scientific and technological works have laid a solid foundation for applications of blind signal processing theory.

### 2. Single-channel multi-source blind detection technology and fast acquisition and efficient star selection of Beidou satellite signals

For the problem of slow acquisition speed and low accuracy faced by existing grid search-based satellite acquisition methods arises, Shengli Xie and his team utilized the Dropper effect and aliasing characteristic of receiving satellite signals, and then established a single-channel blind separation model with time-varying and time-delaying for the Beidou satellite signal. According to the orthogonality of the code phase, a fast-blind search method was proposed based on the partition integral of the satellite receiving signal.

In addition, the Beidou PNT system may have a timing accuracy problem. To solve this problem, Shengli Xie and his team proposed a triple precise synchronous timing architecture based on satellite transmission delay compensation, circuit-level delay compensation, and feedback delay compensation. To reduce the impact of interference, a sparsity-based interference-mitigation processing method for Beidou signals was developed. To reduce the influence on accuracy from satellite clock offset and local clock skew, a numerically-controlled oscillator-based (NCO) high-precision delay compensation technology based on satellite clock offset and local clock skew feedback was proposed, in which the timing accuracy can reach 6 nanoseconds. To achieve high-precision positioning, the Beidou satellite selection model was proposed to integrate signal intensity and phase ambiguity, which can realize fast and effective satellite selection in complex environments. Moreover, a single-frequency cycle-slip estimation method based on epoch difference was proposed to achieve reliable fixation of phase ambiguity. Finally, the centimeter-level high-precision positioning can be realized due to the invention of the adaptive fusion positioning method based on phase ambiguity and pseudo-range.

## 3. Weak signal blind detection technology for pathological characteristic wave extraction and separation of heart and lung sounds

Shengli Xie's team invented the precise extraction techniques of microvolt level ECG characteristic wave, which broke through the challenge of extracting weak characteristic waves from mixed non-stationary components and realized the high-precision measurement of ECG characteristic waves at the microvolt level.

Shengli Xie led his team to successfully develop the world's first digital intelligent stethoscope integrated with a function of cardiopulmonary sound separation by leveraging blind detection technology and artificial intelligence methods, and also leads the formulation of national group standards. This product licensed with the Medical Device Registration Certificate of China and the CE certification of the European Union.

# 电子信息技术奖获得者

# 郑庆华

郑庆华，1969年1月出生于浙江省嵊州市。1990年获西安交通大学学士学位，1993年获西安交通大学硕士学位并留校任教，1997年获西安交通大学博士学位，先后担任计算机系主任、校长助理。2002年1—10月在哈佛大学进行博士后研究。2006年起担任智能网络与网络安全教育部重点实验室主任，2014年9月任西安交通大学党委常委、副校长，2021年12月起任西安交通大学常务副校长。国家自然科学基金委信息学部咨询专家委员会、中央网信办内容安全科技专家委员会、教育部科学技术委员会委员，教育部大学计算机教学指导委员会主任。

郑庆华从事知识工程研究，是该领域学术带头人、大数据知识工程新领域的主要开拓者。建立了知识森林原创概念与模型，提出了知识森林构建和推理两大核心方法，形成了大数据知识工程理论与方法原创性成果，并在国家金税工程、国家在线教育实现重大应用。成果获得国家科技进步奖二等奖3次，国家教学成果一等奖、二等奖各1次，以及2019年IEEE智慧世界大会杰出成就奖（华人首次）。

## 一、创建大数据知识工程理论

碎片化是大数据环境下知识分布的共性问题。通过对维基百科等4亿余条碎片知识进行拓扑、时序、语义等量化分析，发现碎片知识具有散、杂、乱的特点，进一步深层挖掘发现散、杂、乱表象下隐含的主题聚集性、局部依赖性、分面同构性三个时空特性，揭示了知识结构的拓扑演化规律，为知识森林构建与推理提供了理论依据。

受到认识论中"既见树木又见森林"的启发，提出"用树叶表示碎片知识、树木表示某个主题知识、森林表示领域知识体系"的原创思路，提出知识森林原创性概念，从理论上回答了"知识森林"是什么，解决了散、杂、乱碎片知识如何表征为层次化、主题化、结构化知识体系的难题。形成了一套以知识森林为核心，包括碎片知识时空规律、表征模型、计算代数三位一体的大数据知识工程理论,得到国际知识工程界的认可。

### 二、实现大数据知识工程核心技术自主创新

发明知识森林构建方法。模拟人类"由易到难"的认知机理,提出基于自步学习的"一致性+互补性"跨模态表示学习算法,解决碎片知识的富语义表征难题;设计标签传播的半监督主题树生成算法,解决了"碎片知识→主题树"装配优化子集选择组合爆炸问题;提出拓扑融合的学习依赖挖掘方法,破解了"主题树→知识森林"构建中稀疏关系挖掘的草堆寻针难题。

研究出"多元融合-递阶推理"两阶段知识森林推理方法,解决了知识森林"如何用"的问题;提出多元融合线索识别算法,解决了深层隐匿线索的识别、表征和对齐等难题;提出生成对抗网络架构可微编程搜索算法,将线索依据时序、依赖、因果等关系递阶推理生成证据链,解决了可解释证据链生成难题。

授权发明专利86项、美国专利2项,形成自主可控的专利群,获中国专利优秀奖。

### 三、实现金税工程、在线教育等领域的重大应用

运用知识森林模型和构建方法,挖掘融合1994年以来数万亿条税收历史大数据,建立了5000万纳税人、270万个偷逃骗税案例、3万部税法的三大税收基础知识库,并在此基础上采用"知识引导+数据驱动"策略,研制出具有偷逃骗税行为识别、证据链生成等功能的国家税收风险管理系统。2016年起在全国部署应用,每年为国家挽回数千亿的巨额税款。

研制出知识森林导学系统,实现基础教育、高等教育和"一带一路"线上培训等重大应用,为缩小教育数字鸿沟、促进教育公平、提升教育质量作出贡献。列举两个案例:一是应用于国家教育资源公共服务云平台,服务全国11000所中小学,为解决老少边穷岛地区优质教育资源短缺作出贡献。新冠疫情期间,服务全国1.2亿师生。二是应用于"一带一路"国际工程科技的在线培训,为113个国家培训4万余工程技术人才,被联合国教科文组织评价为"中国方案"。

# Awardee of Electronics and Information Technology Prize, Zheng Qinghua

Zheng Qinghua was born in Shengzhou City of Zhejiang Province in January 1969. He received the B.S. degree in computer software in 1990, the M.S. degree in computer organization and architecture in 1993, and the Ph.D. degree in system engineering in 1997 from Xi'an Jiaotong University, China. He was a Post-Doctoral Researcher with Harvard University, in 2002. He is currently a professor in School of Computer Science and Technology of Xi'an Jiaotong University. He is serving as the Executive Vice President of Xi'an Jiaotong University, the chairman of the Steering Committee on Computer Instruction of Ministry of Education, and the director of Ministry of Education key lab for Intelligent Networks and Network Security.

Professor Zheng is an academic leader in the field of Knowledge Engineering in China, and has opened up the new field of Knowledge Engineering with Big Data. He establishes the original concept and model of the knowledge forest, which consists of facet trees and learning dependencies. Knowledge forest organizes knowledge fragments in a way that is more consistent with human cognition and learning. In addition, he proposes two core methods of knowledge forest, including knowledge forest construction and reasoning. Knowledge forest theory and methods have achieved major applications in the National Golden Tax Project and National Online Education.

Professor Zheng has won several awards, including three Second Prize of the State Science and Technology Progress Awards, one First Class of the National Teaching Achievement Award, and two Second Class of the National Teaching Achievement Awards.

# 电子信息技术奖获得者

# 张 荣 桥

张荣桥，1966年4月出生于安徽省祁门县。1988年获西安电子科技大学电磁场与微波技术专业学士学位，1991年获电子科技大学电磁场与微波技术专业硕士学位。1991年在航空航天部第五研究院五〇三所工作，历任监测站上行站站长、双星室副主任、科技处副处长、科技处处长、副所长、所长。2004在国防科工委月球探测工程中心工作，历任总工程师、副主任、探月工程副总设计师、深空探测论证工程总设计师、高分辨率对地观测系统重大专项（民用部分）工程总设计师、首次火星探测任务工程总设计师。现任中国行星探测工程总设计师、天问二号任务总设计师、天问四号任务总设计师。

张荣桥长期在一线从事深空探测技术研究，作为我国行星探测工程总设计师，主持完成了我国行星探测工程的规划和实施方案论证，主持完成我国首次火星探测（天问一号）任务的研制和实施，在国际上首次通过一次任务实现火星环绕、着陆、巡视探测，使我国成为世界第二个实现火面巡视的国家，一举跨入国际先进行列。

## 一、任工程总设计师，圆满完成中国首次火星探测任务

1. 创新提出"通过一次任务实现火星环绕、着陆、巡视"的总体技术方案

针对我国火星探测尚属空白、与国外存在较大差距的现实，考虑对航天技术的发展和科学研究的牵引和带动作用，对标国际先进水平，大胆创新提出"通过一次任务实现火星环绕、着陆、巡视"的总体技术方案并组织实施，在国际上首次成功实现，使我国成为世界上第二个在火星开展巡视探测的国家，并跨入行星探测领域世界先进行列。

2. 负责工程顶层设计和关键技术攻关，研究决策系统间重大技术问题

针对火星探测发射每隔26个月仅有一次发射机会及海南夏季台风多发极端天气等情况，为确保可靠发射，主持研究提出固定射向、固定滑行时间的多弹道（42条）奔火发射方案，解决了过去使用的变射向、变滑行时间多弹道方案所导致的飞行诸元临射切

换、测控布船、航落区管控、子级残骸落区安全方面的难题。针对我国首次实施行星发射（双曲线轨道），解决了双曲线轨道关机量畸变的问题，消除了误关风险，提高了关机精度，实现了首次火星探测任务的可靠发射、精准入轨，成功实现我国首次第二宇宙速度火箭发射；火星探测测控通信距离4亿千米，相比我国原有的40万千米测控通信，信号强度衰减了100万倍（60dB），同时最大时延达到23分钟；针对首次火星探测遇到的新难题，提出采用星上高灵敏应答机、地面异地组阵接收、全球VLBI测量、UHF和X双频中继的整体解决方案。组织攻关突破了大动态、超低信噪比、低码速率的信号捕获跟踪与解调和–157dBm灵敏度星载X频段深空应答机等关键技术（美国MAVEN灵敏度–156dBm），实现了4亿千米超远距离微弱信号的接收解调。主持研究突破了天线异地组阵信号合成关键技术，攻克了亚洲最大70m口径全可动天线研制难关，实现4亿千米数传码速率达到2Mbit/s（美国MRO数传码速率为1Mbit/s）。在国际上首次采用UHF/X双频段全自主中继通信技术，解决了火星车数据高速传输难题，器间中继数传能力达到500Mbit/天（美国MRO中继能力为170Mbit/天）；针对火星大气、火星表面等自然环境不确知的世界难题及我国缺少一手先验数据的现实，组织研究提出了采用火箭弹进行降落伞开伞和减速验证、着陆悬停和避障试验方案，解决了火星大气剖面结构和风场模型等环境因素不确定情况下试验验证难的问题，验证了着陆火星这一关键技术方案的正确性和适应性，实现了首次成功在地外行星软着陆和巡视；提出并利用我国首次火星探测任务中太阳–地球–火星夹角小于5°（日凌）的机会，通过深空网35m和66m测控设备开展日凌期间的太阳噪声对天问一号测控通信链路影响的研究，获取了我国自主的一手试验成果，为后续深空探测活动中太阳噪声影响分析提供了更加精确的指导依据。

3. 创新工作理念，统筹技术、质量和进度管理

针对火星探测任务技术新、飞行时间长等特点，提出"只要火箭不点火，设计完善不停止""验收合格不等于可靠，产品交付不等于完事""飞行控制是方案、初样、正样之后的第四个研制阶段"等创新管理理念，实现准时发射、可靠飞行、有效探测。

**二、作为工程论证总设计师，组织完成行星探测重大工程论证立项**

从创新驱动、跨越发展、持续推动的维度，统筹考虑技术跨越、经济承受、工程实现、能力提升，在深入总结探月工程发展经验的基础上，提出行星探测以火星探测为主线，"一步实现绕着巡，两步完成取样回"的跨越发展路线；围绕"打造探测太阳系的工程能力"技术需求和小行星探测"精"、木星系探测"远"的能力需求，提出小行星探测、木星系和行星穿越探测等任务，形成了我国2030年前行星探测发展蓝图。2021年11月，行星探测重大工程通过国家立项批复。

# Awardee of Electronics and Information Technology Prize, Zhang Rongqiao

Zhang Rongqiao was born in Qimen County of Anhui Province in April 1966. In 1988, he graduated from Xidian University's Department of Electromagnetic Field Engineering, majoring in electromagnetic field and microwave technology. After completing a master's degree in the same major from the Institute of Applied Physics of the University of Electronic Science and Technology of China in 1991, he began his career at the 503$^{rd}$ Research Institute of the Fifth Academy of the former Ministry of Aerospace Industry, and successively served as the head of the monitoring station's uplink station, deputy director of the Double Star Mission Office, deputy director and director of the Science and Technology Department, and deputy director and director of the Institute. In 2004, he worked at the Lunar Exploration Center of the former Commission for Science, Technology and Industry for National Defense, and served successively as chief engineer, deputy director, deputy chief designer of the Lunar Exploration Project, chief designer of the Deep Space Exploration Demonstration Project, chief designer of the High-resolution Earth Observation System (civilian use), chief designer of Tianwen-1, China's first Mars mission, as well as Tianwen-2 and Tianwen-4 missions, chief engineer of China's Planetary Exploration Project, and member of the Tenth Standing Committee of China Association for Science and Technology.

Since 2000, Zhang Rongqiao has been engaged in the front-line research of deep space exploration technology. As the chief designer, he presided over the planning and implementation plan demonstration of China's Planetary Exploration Project. Zhang also presided over the development and implementation of China's first Mars exploration (Tianwen-1) mission, the world's first successful endeavor to perform orbiting, landing and roving in a single mission, making China the second country in history to patrol the Martian surface, and scaling new heights in the international arena.

# 交通运输技术奖获得者

# 冯江华

冯江华，1964年11月出生于湖南省隆回县。1989年、2008年分别获得浙江大学硕士学位和中南大学博士学位，毕业后一直在中车株洲电力机车研究所工作，先后任研发中心主任、副总工程师、正高级工程师，下属单位时代电气股份有限公司副总裁、技术总监，以及副总经理、总工程师。他是新型功率半导体器件国家重点实验室主任、科技部"列车网络控制与信息系统创新团队"及"创新人才培养示范基地"负责人。兼任IEEE高速列车和磁浮标委会主席、轨道电气系统特别委员会主席、全国轨道电气标委会副主任委员。

冯江华是轨道交通列车控制与信息技术专家，长期从事应用基础研究、关键技术攻关、产品平台研制，取得系列原创性成果，为我国高速列车核心技术实现从无到有、从追赶到领跑作出突出贡献。

**一、攻克第一代高速列车"中华之星"异步牵引控制关键技术，填补国内空白**

20世纪七八十年代，西方发达国家竞相发展高速列车并形成技术垄断，我国轨道装备技术严重落后。特别是在高速牵引必需的异步交流传动等技术上尚属空白。冯江华从零起步，带领团队攻克了大功率低开关频率直接转矩控制、四象限电能变换控制等关键技术难题，确立了自主异步牵引控制技术模式，填补了国内空白。成果达到国外同期先进水平，产品装备于我国第一代高速列车"中华之星"，并为后来的"和谐号"高速动车组批量应用奠定了坚实基础。

**二、主持研发"复兴号"高速牵引与控制技术，实现世界最高商业运营速度，"复兴号"高速列车迈出从追赶到领跑的关键一步**

冯江华担纲主持研制"复兴号"高速牵引与控制系统关键技术攻关，创建逆变器–

电机 - 齿轮 - 轮轨一体化优化控制技术，攻克高功率密度牵引动力全局高效难题。与国外控制算法对比试验，电机输出功率增加 20% 时，温升反而降低 25K。在同等温升约束下，"复兴号"实现单轴牵引功率 625kW、密度 0.868 kW/kg，优于国外最高指标；创建列车电力变换主动控制技术，攻克列车群 - 电网 - 电源不确定性复杂大系统稳定难题。列车半载以上功率运行时，网侧电流总畸变率≤0.75%、等效干扰电流≤0.77A，优于国外最佳指标（1.16%、1.03）；共网运行列/机车达 50 辆（国外 12 辆）；创建宽带实时控制网络与安全诊断技术，全面升级高速列车安全监测、功能安全与安全诊断能力，监测与诊断信息从 3000 余项跃升到 11000 余项。为我国高速列车从追赶到引领迈出了关键一步。

目前，该项技术已经在"复兴号"系列高速列车上得到批量应用，并推广应用于重载机车、城轨列车等其他领域，产品出口到亚、欧、美、非等 14 个国家和地区，销售收入逾 200 亿元，创造良好的经济效益和社会效益。

**三、主持研究永磁牵引技术，创建新一代高速牵引技术平台，被评选为"2015 年中国十大科技进展新闻"**

永磁传动具有更高的效率优势，成为牵引动力的发展方向，在国际上引发高速列车等装备的新一轮技术竞争。21 世纪初，冯江华在国内最早开展该领域理论研究和关键技术攻关，结合高速度、强电磁环境、分段供电等轨道交通运用要求，攻克了反电势过压限速、磁极信息失真失控、高速动力重构冲击等业界前沿难题。

他发明高速主动弱磁控制技术，突破电机反电势超过最大电压（方波供电）时对速度的限制：电机效率 98%（国外 97%），运用转速范围 0 ~ 5890rpm、弱磁深度 0.71（国外 0~3150、无弱磁）；发明磁极位置（控制基准）多模辨识技术，消除因传感信号 mV 级失真引发的系统失控危害：稳态误差 <0.01rad、动态误差 <0.05rad（国外分别为 0.02rad、0.1rad）；摆脱对位置传感器的依赖，保障复杂电磁环境下系统可靠性；发明列车越行无电区后动力重构技术，保障列车在分段供电条件下高速运行能力：重构时间 <10ms，转矩冲击 <2.8%。

成果已装备 350km/h 和 400km/h（世界最高）永磁高速列车，能耗较异步牵引降低 10% 以上，功率密度提升 20% 以上；应用于地铁列车，能耗较异步牵引降低 35% 以上；推广应用于电动汽车、船舶电驱等领域。

基于上述成果积淀，跨界融合胶轮车辆技术，首创自主导向虚拟轨道列车。发明虚拟轨道精确生成、列车轨迹跟随控制等技术。在没有实体轨道约束下，创造性解决了长编组列车存在的弯道难转、长车扫尾等固有难题。开创城市交通新制式，入选"中国改革开放 40 周年成果展"。

冯江华先后荣获国家科学技术奖 3 项，国际/国家专利金奖 2 项、银奖 1 项，省部级特/一等奖 9 项；授权发明专利 55 件；主持制订国际标准 3 项、国家标准 7 项；个人获全国创新争先奖章、光华工程科技奖、詹天佑大奖、茅以升科学技术奖等荣誉。

# Awardee of Communication and Transportation Technology Prize, Feng Jianghua

Feng Jianghua was born in Longhui County of Hunan Province in November 1964. As an expert in train control and information technology, he has been devoted in applied fundamental research, key technology research, and product platform development for several decades, who has achieved a series of original scientific and technological achievements. He organized the R&D of traction and control system for high-speed train, that built a product platform with proprietary intellectual property rights which supports the Chinese "Fuxing" EMU (Electric Multiple Units) that achieve the world's highest commercial operation speed. The technological results have been widely applied in rail transit, new energy, industrial transmission and etc., which have been exported to 14 countries across Asia, Europe, America, and Africa. He developed the permanent magnet traction technology for high-speed train which has been selected as "The top 10 news stories of scientific and technological progress" by academicians of both the Chinese Academy of Sciences and the Chinese Academy of Engineering in 2015. He invented Autonomous-rail Rapid Transit (ART) which has been selected into the national "Large-scale Exhibition Celebrating the 40th Anniversary of Reform and Opening up". His outstanding contributions make the key technologies of China high-speed train from scratch to commercial application, and from following to leading.

Feng Jianghua has won plenty awards in his career, including 3 National Science and Technology Awards, IEC 1906 Award, 2 International/National Patent Gold and 1 Silver Awards, and 9 provincial/ministerial level special/first prize. Moreover, 55 invention patents were authorized. He is the convener of 3 International Standards and 7 National Standards. He also won numbers of other awards, such as Medal of National Innovation, Guanghua Engineering Technology Award, and etc.

# 冶金材料技术奖获得者

# 曲 选 辉

曲选辉，1960年9月出生于湖南省澧县。1981年、1984年和1992年先后获中南大学学士、硕士和博士学位，后留校任教。1986—1988年在加拿大英属哥伦比亚大学进行访学工作。2001年调入北京科技大学，先后任材料科学与工程学院副院长、院长，新材料技术研究院院长，现任先进粉末冶金材料与技术北京市重点实验室主任。兼任国际科技数据委员会中国全国委员会执行委员会委员，亚洲材料数据委员会主席，国务院学位委员会学科评议组成员，中国新材料产业技术创新战略联盟副理事长，中国材料研究学会常务理事，中国金属学会常务理事兼粉末冶金分会主任委员。

曲选辉主要从事金属材料和粉末冶金专业方向的教学与研究工作，先后主持完成国家自然基金、"973""863"、重点研发计划等国家项目40余项。在粉体材料近终形成形技术、高铁刹车材料、难熔金属和高温合金、特种和新型储能材料等研究方面取得了突出成绩。获授权发明专利200余件；获世界粉末冶金大会中国粉末冶金贡献奖、全国优秀科技工作者、中国青年科技奖等荣誉，以及国家级教学成果一等奖1项、国家技术发明奖二等奖1项、国家科技进步奖二等奖1项、省部级教学和科技成果奖30余项。

## 一、粉末注射成形技术研发与应用

曲选辉是我国最早提出和开展金属粉末注射成形技术研究的学者之一，并为我国粉末注射成形产业的形成和壮大提供了不可或缺的技术和人才支撑。二十多年来，团队建立了粉末注射成形系统理论，发明了多种特种材料的粉末注射成形新工艺。研制的产品成功应用于国家重要型号装备中，解决了多个重点装备研制和发展的瓶颈问题。相关技术通过专利转让，在江苏精研、上海富驰、扬州海昌等20余家企业产业化，产品在华为、联想、小米、苹果、特斯拉、三星等国际知名企业获得应用，其技术水平和生产规模均进入世界前列。"高性能特种粉体材料近终形制造技术及应用"获2019年度国家技术发明奖二等奖。

## 二、高性能粉末冶金摩擦材料研究

曲选辉团队承担了"复兴号"动车组摩擦材料和闸片的攻关工作。在探明高速列车闸片失效机理的基础上，提出了发挥粉末冶金工艺特色、研发新型复合摩擦材料的新思路。突破了多功能多组元粉末冶金复合材料设计、材料高致密化和组织精确调控、产业化关键装备和质量监控等关键科学和技术问题，研发的产品成功用于"复兴号"动车组。高寒闸片用于哈大线动车组，解决了制动盘异常磨耗难题，为实现高寒地区冬季不减速运行提供了安全保障。开发的静音型闸片成功应用于京张高铁"奥运版"智慧动车组，助力北京冬奥会。实现了我国高铁制动材料和技术的完全自主可控。"复兴号"350Km/h级动车组闸片获世界粉末冶金大会杰出创新产品奖。相关技术成果先后获2021年度中国有色金属工业科学技术奖（发明）一等奖和2022年度教育部科技进步奖一等奖。

## 三、耐高温结构材料研究

针对我国高端装备发展的迫切需求，曲选辉团队开展了大尺寸高纯难熔金属制品制备新原理新方法研究。揭示了难熔金属中杂质元素来源、存在形式和走向规律，建立难熔金属高纯化系统技术；创立了难熔金属高致密化、细晶化和组织均匀化的烧结理论与新方法。产品成功应用于大型高纯石英连熔炉、蓝宝石晶体生长炉、热等静压机和高温烧结炉、磁控溅射、MOCVD等高端装备，支撑和引领了我国高端装备和难熔金属产业的发展。该成果获2022年度中国有色金属工业科学技术奖（发明）一等奖。

此外，团队还开展了粉末冶金高温合金杂质来源与演化规律、纯净化原理与新方法等研究，获授权发明专利10余件，为我国粉末冶金高温合金的发展和应用提供了理论和技术支撑。研发的新型钴基高温合金成功应用于某装备中并定型批量生产供货，解决了该重点装备研发和生产的"卡脖子"问题。相关材料配方和制备技术分别获得国防发明专利和国家发明专利，技术成果获得教育部技术发明奖一等奖。

## 四、特种和新型储能材料研究

20世纪90年代中期，曲选辉针对我国重点国防装备国产化的急需，开展了热电池用锂-硼合金阴极材料的研制工作。突破了锂-硼合金粉末合成反应剧烈、组织不均匀等关键科学和技术问题，研制的材料满足了"鱼雷""重弹"等型号装备的需要，从此改变了该材料依赖进口的被动局面。该成果获1999年度中国有色金属工业科学技术奖二等奖。近年来，团队在锂离子、钠离子、钾离子等新型金属离子电池材料方面开展了系列研究工作，提出了通过调控粉体内部结构减少电极材料在充放电过程中的尺寸效应的新思路，取得了很好的效果。获授权发明专利20余项，其中2项专利已转让山西企业，实现了工业化生产。

# Awardee of Metallurgy and Materials Technology Prize, Qu Xuanhui

Qu Xuanhui was born in Lixian County of Hunan Province in September 1960. Qu earned his bachelor, master, and doctor degrees from Central South University in 1981, 1984 and 1992. During that time, he was a visiting scholar at University of British Columbia Canada from 1986 to 1988. Prof. Qu joined University of Science and Technology Beijing in 2001, where he was successively appointed as the Dean of School of Materials Science and Engineering, and the Dean of Institute for Advanced Materials and Technology. Currently, he is the director of Beijing Key Laboratory for Advanced Powder Metallurgy Materials and Technology. He also serves as an executive member of China Branch of the Committee on Data (CODATA) of the International Science Council, the president of Asian Materials Data Committee (AMDC), a member of the Discipline Evaluation Group for the Academic Degrees Committee of the State Council, the deputy president of China Innovation Alliance of New Materials Industry, the executive director of Chinese Materials Research Society, and the executive director of The Chinese Society for Metals and chairman of its Powder Metallurgy Branch.

Over the years, Prof. Qu has focused on teaching and research of metallic materials and powder metallurgy under the support of over 40 funded projects including NSFC, 973, 863, and National Key R&D Program of China, etc. He has acquired outstanding accomplishments in the reform of education and teaching in Materials, powder metallurgy near net shaping technology, brake materials for high-speed train, energy storage materials, and powder superalloys, etc. So far, he authorized over 200 patents and has won numerous awards, including a First Prize of National Teaching Achievements, a Second Prize of State Technological Invention, a Second Prize of State Scientific and Technological Progress, over 30 provincial and ministerial awards, the China Powder Metallurgy Contribution Award of World PM' 2018 the National Outstanding Scientific and Technological Workers, the China Youth Science and Technology Award, etc.

# 冶金材料技术奖获得者

# 张 福 成

张福成，1964年8月出生于吉林省蛟河市。1993年获哈尔滨工业大学金属材料及热处理专业博士学位。1993—2019年在燕山大学工作，先后任材料科学与工程学院讲师、副教授、教授、学校副校长。2003年3—10月、2004年9月—2005年6月在牛津大学进行合作研究。2019年4月起任华北理工大学校长，并兼任燕山大学亚稳材料制备技术与科学国家重点实验室教授。中国金属学会第十一届常务理事，中国金属学会材料科学分会第七、八届副主任委员。

张福成从事钢铁材料及其冶金技术相关领域研究，在先进钢铁基础理论研究和钢铁冶金全流程技术开发等方面作出了一系列开创性工作。承担和完成国家"863"计划和重点项目等科研任务40多项，作为第一完成人获国家技术发明奖二等奖2项、国家科技进步奖二等奖1项及教育部和河北省等省部级科技一等奖4项、十三届光华工程科技奖项。

**一、发明难焊高锰钢辙叉焊接用钢及焊接技术，解决了我国铁路发展中的一项"卡脖子"技术难题，为实现我国高速、重载跨区间无缝线路的技术跨越创造了条件**

发现奥氏体锰钢中合金原子以C–Me形式呈短程有序偏聚，导致焊接热影响区易析出碳化物；硫和磷在晶界处偏聚形成低熔点共晶物，产生焊接液化裂纹，是高锰钢辙叉难焊的主要原因。提出异质难焊材料加过渡连接材料焊接的新思路。

开发高锰钢变质净化技术，提高其可焊性，并制定了焊接高锰钢硫、磷含量控制标准；发明焊接高锰钢辙叉与钢轨用导热率低、相稳定、高温强度高的连接材料，保证焊接辙叉时热输入钢轨少，使钢轨组织和性能焊接前后不变，并焊接顶锻时排除熔合区高锰钢中的有害组织，获得纳米晶凝固组织焊缝，实现辙叉与钢轨高质量焊接。

目前，我国高锰钢辙叉焊接企业均采用该技术成果进行工业化生产，为实现我国铁路跨越式发展作出了重要贡献。

**二、发明铁路辙叉用新型高锰钢冶金全流程技术，制造出洁净、致密、均质、纳米孪晶高锰钢，使辙叉服役稳定、长寿，为我国铁路快速发展提供保障**

发现高锰钢难锻和疲劳破坏的关键控制因素及提高性能的技术路径：①凝固组织粗大和杂质元素偏析导致锻造开裂；②微观铸造缺陷间交互作用加剧疲劳裂纹形成，超高应变速率下位错穿越孪晶后塞积于奥氏体晶界诱导裂纹萌生，降低疲劳性能；③钢中平面位错结构和孪晶吸收位错可有效防止局域应力应变集中，提高疲劳性能；④调控高锰奥氏体钢层错能和晶粒尺寸，可获得强塑性组合达 1.0GPa/109% 或者 1.6GPa/40% 的优异性能。

建立了辙叉用新型高锰钢成分设计准则和冶金全流程技术创新路径，发明多项技术：①高锰钢加重稀土、吹氮精炼和微合金化技术，可净化钢液、细化晶粒、强化晶界，提高其可锻性；②高致密铸造、选择性锻造技术，可消除缩松、气孔缺陷及铸态粗晶组织，提高抗疲劳性；③冲击预硬化技术，可实现钢高密度可动位错和纳米孪晶化，提高耐磨性。制造出新型高质量高锰钢辙叉，解决了传统辙叉寿命短且离散的难题。

成果在铁路辙叉制造企业实现工业化生产，大幅提升了我国高锰钢辙叉制造技术水平，为打造高锰钢辙叉中国品牌作出贡献。

**三、发明系列贝氏体新钢种及其冶金系统技术，解决了贝氏体相变周期长、性能不稳定以及超大尺寸轴承均质化的技术难题，推动了贝氏体钢应用技术的发展**

利用钢铁化学冶金和物理冶金全流程协同创新获得钢均质化短流程技术，解决了超大尺寸轴承钢均质化和淬透性难题。建立了基于异质共格形核缩短贝氏体相变孕育期、调控过冷奥氏体组织和性能实现快速相变的理论和方法。利用铝提高氢扩散能垒，显著降低了贝氏体钢的氢脆敏感性；调控贝氏体钢组织，获得强塑性达 2.4GPa/15% 的优异性能。阐明贝氏体钢性能及其稳定性与过冷和残余奥氏体成分、结构、含量、尺寸、形态及层错能的关系，构建了贝氏体钢获得优异性能的控制策略和方法。基于此，发明了高性能超细贝氏体轴承钢、辙叉钢、耐磨钢等系列新钢种及其冶金系统技术。

发明的三个新钢种及热加工技术已纳入 2 项国家标准、3 项行业标准。成果在多家铁路辙叉、轴承和耐磨钢制造企业工业化应用。生产的超细贝氏钢辙叉寿命稳定达 3.5 亿吨，较传统贝氏体钢辙叉寿命提高 1 倍以上；生产的超细贝氏体钢轴承较传统马氏体钢轴承寿命提高 50% 以上，被中国轴承工业协会称为"第二代贝氏体轴承"；贝氏体耐磨钢板达到国际著名 Hardox600 钢板水平，技术产品占国内港口市场 70% 并批量出口。

# Awardee of Metallurgy and Materials Technology Prize, Zhang Fucheng

Zhang Fucheng was born in Jiaohe City of Jilin Province in August 1964. He received his Ph.D. degree in metal materials and heat treatment from Harbin institute of Technology in 1993. His career began at Yanshan University in 1993 in the area of steel material and the related metallurgical technology, as an teacher until 2019. From March 2003 to October 2003, and from September 2004 to June 2005, he worked at University of Oxford as a senior visiting scholar. From 2006 to 2019, he held the position of vice-president of Yanshan University. And from 2019, he holds the position of president of North China University of Science and Technology, and the professor of State Key Laboratory of Metastable Materials Science and Technology of Yanshan University, at the same time.

Zhang Fucheng focus his research on steel material and the related metallurgical technology, and has carried out a series of pioneering researches in the area of basic theory of advanced steel and whole process of steel metallurgy. He had led or participated more then 40 national research projects, and was awarded three national awards and four provincial awards, including 2 State Technological Invention Awards and 1 State Science and Technology Award from the Chinese government. He also obtained Guanghua Engineering Science and Technology award.

Zhang has developed a novel welding steel and corresponding welding technology for difficult-to-weld high manganese steel frogs, solved a bottleneck problem in the development of China's railway, and created conditions for the technological leapfrogging of high-speed and heavy-haul trans-sectional jointless track in China. This invention was awarded by State Science and Technology Award in 2002, and Technological Invention Award of Ministry of Education in 2008.

Zhang has developed a metallurgical full-flow technology of novel high manganese steel for railway frogs, produced a clean, dense, homogeneous and nano-twinned high manganese steel, achieving a stable and long-life service performance of frogs, and providing a security guarantee for the rapid development of China's railway. This achievement was awarded by State Technological Invention Award in 2020, and Technological Invention Award of Hebei province in 2016.

Zhang has developed a series of novel bainitic steel and metallurgical technologies, working out the problems of long transformation time, unstable performance of conventional bainite steel, and homogeneity difficulty of ultra-large size bearing steel, and promoting the progress of applied technology of bainitic steel. This study was awarded by State Technological Invention Award in 2017, and Technological Invention Award of Hebei province in 2012.

# 化学工程技术奖获得者

# 袁晴棠

袁晴棠，女，1938年5月出生于河南省南召县。教授级高工，石油化工专家。1961年毕业于天津大学。1985—1994年任中国石化总公司发展部副主任、主任，1994—2004年任中国石化总公司、中国石化集团公司兼中国石化股份公司总工程师、科技委常务副主任。曾任中国石油学会副理事长、中国化工学会常务理事、世界石油理事会中国国家委员会委员。1995年当选中国工程院院士。

袁晴棠长期致力于乙烯技术的研究与开发，为推进中国石化集团公司的科技进步和中国乙烯技术的发展作出了突出贡献。获得国家科技进步奖一等奖1项，省部级科技进步奖特等奖1项、一等奖2项、二等奖2项、三等奖1项。

## 一、主持乙烯技术研究与开发

经过近40年的研究开发，袁晴棠带领团队开发成功了复杂原料百万吨级乙烯成套技术。一是创新开发了以异形炉管为核心的超大型、长周期、高效系列裂解炉技术。针对重质原料裂解运行周期短、高含烯烃原料直接裂解易结焦、大型裂解炉操作灵活性差三大难题，开发了高选择性与长周期运行兼备的异形辐射段炉管裂解技术，炉子运转周期延长50%以上，攻克了重质原料运行周期短的难题；开发了高含烯烃原料裂解技术，拓宽了低成本原料来源；开发了复杂原料超大型分炉膛裂解/分炉膛烧焦裂解炉技术，实现了操作灵活性，投资降低10%。二是首创以分凝分馏塔为核心的低能耗、高乙烯回收率的高效分离新工艺。开发了传质传热高效协同的分凝分馏塔技术，尾气中乙烯损失减少70%；开发了低能耗的深冷分配分离技术，制冷机功耗降低5%～7%；开发了长周期新型高效急冷技术。三是创制乙烯全系列高性能催化剂。四是研制百万吨级乙烯重大装备压缩机组和冷箱。五是开发绿色高效系列专项技术。

工业运行数据表明，复杂原料百万吨级乙烯成套技术的裂解炉运行周期和热效率、乙烯回收率、加工损失率和能耗、全系列催化剂性能等关键技术指标均达到国际领先水平。该成套技术的开发和工业应用引领了我国乙烯工业的技术进步，支撑了我国乙烯工业的快速发展。截至2021年年底，复杂原料百万吨级乙烯成套技术已得到大量推广应用，采用该成套技术已投产和在建的乙烯装置共17套，乙烯总产能1542万吨/年，其中裂解炉推广177台，合计产能2107万吨/年，裂解炉、催化剂和冷箱已出口国外。

该成套技术获2020年度国家科技进步奖一等奖。

### 二、负责组织制定并实施中国石化科技发展规划、计划，组织"十条龙"等重大科技攻关

袁晴棠长期负责组织制定并实施中国石化科技发展规划、计划，曾主持编制了《中国石化总公司（1993—2000）八年科技进步规划》《中国石化集团公司"十五"科技发展计划及2015年规划》等，并于1991年与时任中国石化副总经理闫三忠共同首次提出并经党组批准创立了"十条龙"科技攻关制度，并由她负责具体组织实施"十条龙"攻关工作。通过"十条龙"科技攻关，固定床渣油加氢、丙烯腈、聚丙烯、组合床重整等数十项成套技术完成开发并实现工业化。至今，"十条龙"科技攻关制度仍充满活力，有力地推动了中国石化的科技进步。

### 三、完成一系列科技发展和产业发展的战略研究工作

袁晴棠长期承担中国石化集团公司的科技发展和产业发展战略研究，主持数十家企业技术咨询。完成中国工程院30余项国家层面和产业层面战略研究课题，为国家制定科技和产业规划提供依据。

# Awardee of Chemical Engineering Technology Prize, Yuan Qingtang

Yuan Qingtang, female, was born in Nanzhao County of Henan Province in May 1938. She graduated from Tianjin University in 1961 and served as Chief Engineer of China Petrochemical Corporation, Sinopec Group Corporation and Sinopec Corporation, Executive Deputy Director of Science and Technology Committee, and Executive Director of the Chinese Chemical Society. She was elected as an academician of the Chinese Academy of Engineering in 1995. She is currently a consultant of the Science and Technology Committee of Sinopec Group Corporation and a professorate senior engineer.

She has long been devoted to the research and development of ethylene technology. She chaired the technology development of new cracking furnace and made decisions to carry out industrial tests and first commercial applications, which has achieved great technological breakthrough. She timely proposed and decided to develop the large-scale cracking furnace technology. She organized and developed ethylene separation technology and a full range of catalysts. She made the decision to develop the relevant separation technology for the revamp of the ethylene plants and applied the technology to the revamp of small and medium-sized ethylene plants. She chaired the technology development of irregular radiation section furnace tube cracking with both high selectivity and long operating cycle, a new high-efficiency separation process with low energy consumption and high ethylene recovery, a series of green and high efficient specific technologies, a whole series of high performance catalysts for ethylene production, the equipment as compressor unit and cold box for million-ton ethylene production. The packaged million-ton ethylene production technology for processing complex feedstock was successfully developed and has supported the technical progress of Chinese ethylene industry. Its key technical indexes have reached international leading level. It also won the First Prize of State Science and Technology Advancement Award in 2020.

She has been responsible for formulating and implementing Sinopec science and technology development plans and programs for a long time and led technical consulting for dozens of enterprises. She has completed more than 30 national-level and industry-level strategic research projects of the Chinese Academy of Engineering.

She has won a first prize of State Science and Technology Advancement Award, one special prize, two first prizes, two second prizes, and one third prize for scientific and technological progress at provincial and ministerial level.

## 资源能源技术奖获得者

# 郭彤楼

郭彤楼，1965年10月出生于江苏省邳州市。2004年获同济大学海洋地质学专业博士学位。1990年至今先后在中国石化江苏石油勘探局、南方海相油气勘探项目经理部、南方勘探开发分公司、勘探分公司、华东油气分公司、西南油气分公司从事油气勘探开发与管理工作。现任中国石化西南石油局有限公司执行董事、西南油气分公司代表，中国石油学会天然气专业委员会副主任，四川石油学会副理事长。

郭彤楼长期从事天然气勘探开发研究与管理工作，先后主持承担了国家科技重大专项、国家示范工程等重点科研项目20余项，主持提出多旋回盆地"叠合－复合控藏"创新认识，指导了四川盆地油气勘探思路的转变。作为主要发现者或组织者之一，先后发现普光、元坝、涪陵等千亿立方米以上规模大气田7个，是中国石化在四川盆地"两万亿储量、两百亿产量"的主要贡献者，为中国石化四川盆地天然气年产量从2000年10亿立方米到2021年230亿立方米的跨越式发展作出了突出贡献。先后获国家科技进步奖一等奖3项、省部级科技进步奖一等奖6项以及李四光地质科学奖等奖项。

**一、研究提出四川盆地印支以来三期构造运动时空上的叠合决定了油气藏演化、空间上的复合决定了气藏分布，形成"叠合－复合控藏"创新认识，指导发现了普光、元坝、川西大气田**

针对四川盆地成藏复杂、勘探目标埋深大、预测难、钻探难等问题，重新审视未发现新区和失利地区，从多构造体系复合、多期构造运动叠加过程入手，以构造演化研究为主线，以不同构造时期、不同应力环境各成藏要素的耦合为重点，通过正、反演分析相互印证，形成"叠合－复合控藏"创新认识，助力推动勘探思路转变。作为主要组织者和主要贡献人之一，先后发现探明了普光、元坝和川西雷口坡组等海相大型碳酸盐岩气田，新增天然气探明储量8293亿立方米。"海相深层碳酸盐岩天然气成藏机理、勘探技术与普光大气田的发现"获得 2006 年国家科技进步奖一等奖,"元坝超深层生物礁大气田高效勘探及关键技术"获得 2014 年国家科技进步奖一等奖,"川西气田雷口坡组天然气勘探重大商业发现"获中国石化 2020 年规模储量商业发现特等奖。

### 二、创新提出中国式页岩气富集成藏关键因素,推动了中国首个页岩气田的发现和四川盆地页岩气的勘探开发进程

主持开展四川盆地首次全国页岩气资源评价,基于多旋回盆地多期叠加改造的特点,把"叠合－复合控藏"理论应用到海相页岩气,形成"构造－保存控富"创新认识,即"晚燕山期以来构造运动造成的构造和保存条件差异控制页岩气成藏富集程度,多期层滑和构造作用形成的网状裂缝是页岩气富集、高产、稳产的关键",优选川南、川东等地区为最有利勘探突破区,为国家页岩气规划制定提供了重要支撑。主持优选焦石坝构造为首钻目标,部署实施焦页 1 井,成功发现中国第一个大型页岩气田——涪陵页岩气田。海相页岩气研究和勘探开发成果获 2014 年省部级科技进步奖特等奖、2017 年国家科技进步奖一等奖。

主持常压页岩气国家科技示范工程,开展理论、技术攻关,初步实现了南川、武隆、丁山等常压页岩气的效益开发,2020 年提交中国首个常压页岩气探明储量 1918 亿立方米。常压页岩气勘探开发成果获 2020 年度省部级科技进步奖一等奖、2019 年中国石化天然气商业发现特等奖。

### 三、把"叠合－复合控藏"创新理念应用到新类型页岩气、致密砂岩气勘探开发,研究提出油气输导层(体)富集成藏新模式,实现了我国新层系、新类型页岩气和致密砂岩气勘探开发的重大突破

根据工作区页岩气地质特征,突破了国内外只在黑色富有机质页岩中寻找页岩气的传统观念,研究提出"在良好保存条件、有效烃源匹配条件下,低有机质丰度粉砂质页岩能够富集成藏"的新认识,组织实施钻探金石 103 井,获得高产稳产页岩气,这是我国首次在寒武系筇竹寺组地层取得页岩气勘探的重大突破。将为页岩气规模开发由龙马溪组单一层系向新区、新层系、新类型领域纵深推进川渝地区国家天然气(页岩气)千亿立方米级产能基地建设提供有力支撑。

2021 年以来,作为主要领导者和组织者,转变勘探开发思路,把页岩气、常规气的理念有机融合,改变过去只把输导体作为储层的传统思维,提出了有效烃源岩、有效输导体系和有效致密砂岩储层三位一体的输导体致密砂岩气富集成藏模式,多口井获得高产稳产天然气,落实又一个千亿立方米以上规模储量大气田。

## 四、构建复杂气藏"地质—工程一体化"开发模式,支撑了多个大气田的高产稳产和效益开发

针对超深层高含硫大气田、深层及常压页岩气地质条件复杂、工程技术难度大的问题,以油气藏认识为核心,通过一体化研究和一体化运行,不断深化油气藏认识、持续优化工程应用,提高作业效率和开发效益,实现了7000米超深层元坝大气田的高产稳产与中国第一个深层页岩气田——威荣页岩气田、第一个常压页岩气田——南川页岩气田的效益开发。"世界首个超深高含硫大气田实现绿色安全高效的一体化开发管理"获第二十八届全国企业管理现代化创新成果一等奖。

# Awardee of Resources and Energies Technology Prize, Guo Tonglou

Guo Tonglou was born in Pizhou City of Jiangsu Province in October 1965. And received his Ph.D. degree in Marine Geology from Tongji University in 2004. Since 1990, he has successively worked in Sinopec Jiangsu Petroleum Exploration Bureau, Southern Marine Oil & Gas Exploration Project Department, Southern Exploration & Development Branch, Exploration Branch, East China Oil & Gas Branch, and Sinopec Southwest Oil & Gas Branch. Currently, he is the Executive Director of Sinopec Southwest Petroleum Bureau Co., Ltd, and the representative of Southwest Oil&Gas Company, and the deputy director of the Natural Gas Professional Committee of the Chinese Petroleum Society, Vice President of Sichuan Petroleum Institute. It has won the first prize of the National Science and Technology Progress Award for 3 times and the first prize of the Provincial and Ministerial Science and Technology Progress Award for 6 times, Li Siguang Geological Science Award.

Guo Tonglou has been committed to the management of gas exploration and development in the front line of scientific research and production for more than 30 years. He has successively presided over and undertaken more than 20 key scientific research projects, such as Major National Science and Technology Projects and National Demonstration Projects. He has presided over and put forward the innovative understanding of "Superimposition-Compound Control of Natural Gas Accumulation" in multicycle basins, which has guided the transformation of oil and gas exploration thoughts in Sichuan Basin. As one of the major discoverers or organizers, he has successively discovered 7 gas fields with a scale of more than 100 billion cubic meters, such as Puguang, Yuanba, Fuling, etc. It has made major contributions to Sinopec's goal of "Two trillion Reserves and 20 billion Productions" in Sichuan Basin, and has made outstanding contributions to the leapfrog development of Sinopec's annual natural gas production from 1 billion cubic meters in 2000 to 23 billion cubic meters in 2021.

# 生态环保技术奖获得者

# 徐祖信

徐祖信，女，1956年4月出生于江西省萍乡市。1988年获河海大学工学博士学位。1993—1995年作为访问学者在意大利罗马大学工学院开展研究工作。1995年回国至今在同济大学工作，任同济大学环境科学与工程学院教授。第六届、第八届中国环境科学学会理事会常务理事，国家水体污染控制与治理科技重大专项技术副总师，海南省"六水共治"技术总师。中国工程院院士。

徐祖信长期致力于城市河流污染治理研究。坚持深入工程第一线，充分发挥环境、水力、市政三个学科的交叉优势，提出了城市重污染河流"全系统耦合调控治理"的技术思想，形成了系统性解决方案并取得显著成效。相继主持了福州、深圳、南京等30多个城市的水污染治理，主编多部技术规范，在全国获得广泛应用。曾获国家科技进步奖二等奖2项，省部级科技进步奖一等奖4项、二等奖4项。受联合国人居署邀请，编著城市水污染治理专题报告并向发展中国家推介，提升了我国在水污染治理领域的国际声望。

## 一、河网水系与排水管网综合控污技术

建立城市排水管网缺陷诊断分析技术。基于阵列分析，研究不同来源水量特征因子差异化表征手段，应用蒙特卡罗源解析模型，计算分析管网破损、混接和错接的特征水质水量，建立分区诊断模型反演分析，创新了管网缺陷诊断的数值化分析技术。

研发管网和河网耦合控污的综合设计方法。根据调蓄和排水性能概化河网，研发复杂河网污染"有限单元网格"分析模式，映射分析污染源、管网、河网关系，从而建立复杂河网污染排放清单；确立管网与河网耦合控污关系，解决了城市河网控污综合设计难题。

建立基于河网水质保障的厂网协同运行技术。基于河道水质控制和污水处理厂容量

约束，动态解析河道关键点位、源、管、厂水质水量全程实时变化，确定目标水量输送瓶颈和关键节点客水量，优化管网设计，实现厂网协同运行。

应用上述成果，调查分析建立了上海苏州河水系河网排放清单，截污率从44%提升到85%；通过耦合控污设计，巢湖市排水管网污水输送率提高到80%以上。

## 二、复杂河网流动与净化协同调控技术

研发潮汐河网流动与净化耦合调控方法。分析潮汐河流涨落潮生化反应、河网流速、大气复氧的响应关系，开发河口地区多维度嵌套的水动力水质模型。基于污染推移控制，耦合调控流动速率和复氧速率，开展河网水系推流计算分析；创建了顺应河网地势和潮汐规律的潮引潮排、蓄排结合的闸门体系调控方法，实现潮汐河网无外加动力扩增净化通量，攻克了河流阻滞、污染顶托的难题。

建立缓流水体水质生态净化技术。平原河流低碳高氮问题限制了流动净化能力，研发外挂玉米芯缓释碳源、提供生物膜载体，构建表层好氧、内层缺氧的生物净化环境；调查分析沉水植物种类与上覆水质的响应关系，确定了退化主控因子和恢复阈值；以外加碳源和恢复沉水植物为核心，构建缓流水体生态净化技术体系，成功应用于苏州河梦清园水质净化工程。

利用潮汐动能扩增净化通量，苏州河黑臭治理实现历史性突破，不同河段达到Ⅴ类和Ⅳ类水标准。

## 三、夏季高温多雨城市河流雨天黑臭控制技术

揭示南方城市河流雨天黑臭问题的主要成因是城市管网溢流和乡村河道漫流，沉积污染与农村污水直排是要害所在。突破雨天污染治理，才能稳定改善河道水质。

研发溢流污染晴天和雨天耦合控制技术。研究沉积污染对底泥剪切力的影响，分析蓄水位与冲刷力关系，发明了无动力翻转堰板，晴天实现管道沉积物自动冲刷；研究絮体高紊瞬态强度特性，发明短时絮凝强化分离技术，应用于溢流污染旋流分离，微细颗粒物分离效率同比提升50%以上；研发溢流污水在线和离线协同调蓄方法，实现溢流污染控制。

建立农村生活污水生态处理技术体系。创新人工湿地内部氧浓度自发调控技术，建立硝化与反硝化自然交替工艺，攻克高负荷潜流湿地无动力脱氮难题。筛选驯化适应人工湿地生境的蚓种，揭示代谢与孔隙疏通关系，研发蚓、菌耦合修复堵塞技术，解决了人工湿地堵塞自我修复难题。构建农村污水处理的简便、低碳、生态技术体系，与国际现有水平相比，氨氮去除速率提高1～5倍，总氮去除速率提高1～2倍，费用减少50%。

应用上述研究成果，苏州河水环境治理在国内首次开展雨天黑臭治理，单次降雨调蓄污水近10万吨；在巢湖市建设国内首个沉积污染溢流控制工程，中心城区溢流COD

负荷平均削减 20% 以上；在上海主持建设农村污水处理工程 106 个，其他地区推广建设 153 个，明显改善所在区域河道水质。

# Awardee of Ecology and Environmental Protection Technology Prize, Xu Zuxin

Xu Zuxin, female, was born in Pingxiang City of Jiangxi Province in April 1956. She is a fellow of the Chinese Academy of Engineering, and a professor in the College of Environmental Science and Engineering at Tongji University. After obtaining a Ph.D. degree from Hohai University in 1988, Prof. Xu has been dedicated to urban river pollution control for over 30 years.

Prof. Xu is an expert of international prestige who is committed to finding innovative and efficient solutions to urban river pollution control in a visionary, systematic and comprehensive manner. Prof. Xu has taken advantage of cross-disciplines of environmental engineering, hydraulics and municipal engineering to achieve urban river pollution control, and put forward the concept of "systemwide coupling regulation and control" for heavily polluted urban rivers, found a systematic solution, and made remarkable achievements. As the chief scientist for Suzhou Creek rehabilitation in Shanghai, Prof. Xu made a great contribution to getting rid of Suzhou Creek's black and odorous that had existed for over 70 years in Shanghai. She also serves as the deputy chief technical engineer of the National Water Pollution Control and Treatment Science and Technology Major Project and the chief technical engineer of comprehensive water environment governance in Hainan Province. Prof. Xu and her research group have innovated the technical system for the rehabilitation of heavily polluted urban rivers in China, which has an important impact in the field of water environment pollution control at home and abroad.

Prof. Xu successively took charge of river pollution rehabilitation in more than 30 cities, and edited several technical specifications, which have been widely applied in China. As the first accomplisher, Prof. Xu was awarded China's National Science and Technology Promotion Prize twice, and the Shanghai Science and Technology Promotion Prize eight times, including 4 first-grade prizes and 4 second-grade prizes. She was also invited by UN-Habitat to compile a special report on rehabilitation of heavily polluted urban rivers, which was released during the Fourth session of the UN Environment Assembly, and was introduced to developing countries by the UN, enhancing China's international reputation in the field of water pollution control.

# 工程建设技术奖获得者

# 龚晓南

龚晓南，1944年10月出生于浙江省金华市。1967年从清华大学土建系毕业后，先后在国防科委8601工程处、国防科委1405研究所工作。1981年、1984年分别获浙江大学岩土工程专业硕士学位和博士学位。1981年起在浙江大学任教，曾任浙江大学土木工程学系副主任、主任，浙江大学滨海和城市岩土工程研究中心主任。1986—1988年赴德国Karlsruhe大学土力学及地下工程研究所做研究工作。2002年被授予茅以升土力学及基础工程大奖，2011年当选中国工程院院士。

龚晓南长期从事土力学及岩土工程教学与科研工作，在理论研究、科研成果应用和工程教育方面作出了一系列开创性工作。

## 一、创建复合地基理论，推动形成复合地基技术工程应用体系

1992年出版复合地基领域的首部专著《复合地基》，首次构建了复合地基理论框架，被誉为复合地基发展的第一个里程碑，为复合地基理论和技术的发展奠定了基础，引领复合地基新技术的研发及工程应用。研究揭示了基础刚度对复合地基工作性状的影响机理，建立考虑桩土相对刚度和基础刚度影响的复合地基计算分析理论，并于2002年、2007年和2018年分别出版《复合地基理论及工程应用》第一版、第二版和第三版，不断发展和完善复合地基理论内涵。2003年主编出版《复合地基设计和施工指南》，2012年主持完成国标《复合地基技术规范》的制定，促进形成较完整的复合地基技术工程应用体系，促使我国复合地基理论和技术一直处于国际领先地位。领衔完成的项目"复合地基理论、关键技术及工程应用"获2018年国家科技进步奖一等奖。

## 二、研发地基处理新技术，发展地基处理理论，引领地基处理领域科技发展

龚晓南长期从事软黏土力学、地基处理理论和技术应用研究，在排水固结、深层搅

拌、强夯和强夯置换、电渗加固和软土固化等加固技术领域取得一系列成果，出版《地基处理新技术》（1997年）、主编《地基处理手册》、创办《地基处理》刊物，为工程建设服务，得到业界好评。2017年、2020年先后主编出版浙江省工程建设标准《静钻根植桩基础技术规程》《淤泥固化土地基技术规程》。参与、主持完成了十几个省市的交通工程、建筑工程、机场工程、围海工程等软土地基处理咨询与设计，主持绍兴和启东等地数十个基础工程事故处理，解决了许多技术难题。主持的多项重大工程的软土地基处理成为行业范例，是我国地基处理领域被高度认同的学术带头人。

### 三、开展基坑工程系列创新技术研究，引领基坑工程领域技术发展

长期从事基坑工程环境影响和控制方法研究，发展基坑工程按变形控制设计理论，研发基坑围护新技术和环境保护技术，不断解决基坑工程发展中遇到的技术难题。提出合理确定土钉支护临界高度并确定其适用范围的理念，发展了土钉支护设计理论和方法。在基坑工程空间效应、蠕变效应、环境影响控制和地下水控制等方面取得了一系列创新成果。1998年主编出版《深基坑工程设计施工手册》并于2018年出版第二版，2006年发起并主编系列《基坑工程实例》。发展了深埋重力-门架式围护结构、基坑围护桩兼作工程桩与地下室墙挡土结构和预压力钢拱基坑支护结构等多种围护新技术，主持杭州大剧院等数十项深、大基坑工程设计，促进了基坑围护设计水平的不断提高，引领基坑工程领域技术发展。领衔完成的项目"软弱地基深大基坑支护关键技术及工程应用"获2022年浙江省科技进步奖一等奖。

### 四、潜心岩土工程教育，教育教学成效斐然

自1981年留校任教以来，龚晓南长期潜心岩土工程教育，相继开设了高等土力学、土塑性力学、工程材料本构方程、计算土力学、地基处理技术和广义复合地基理论六门研究生课程，并编著和组织出版了相应教材，被许多高等学校采用，得到广泛应用和好评。1996年出版的《高等土力学》是我国出版的第一部高等土力学研究生教材，1990年出版《土塑性力学》，促进了塑性理论在岩土工程中的应用，成为许多高校研究生教材或参考书，1998年被译成韩文出版，1999年出版第二版。在担任土木工程学系系主任期间（1994—1999年），在全国率先组织制定"大土木"培养方案，领衔完成的《"大土木"教育理念下土木工程卓越人才"贯通融合"培养体系创建与实践》获2018年国家级教学成果二等奖。出版的大学教材《地基处理》获2022年国家教材委员会颁发的全国优秀教材二等奖。

# Awardee of Engineering and Construction Technology Prize, Gong Xiaonan

Gong Xiaonan was born in Jinhua City of Zhejiang Province in October 1944. He received his bachelor's degree in Civil Engineering from Tsinghua University in 1967, then worked at the 8601 Engineering Department of the Commission for Science, Technology, and Industry for National Defense. In 1978, he joined Zhejiang University for postgraduate study, earning his master's and Ph.D. degrees in 1981 and 1984, respectively. He became a faculty member at Zhejiang University in 1981. In the same year, he received a scholarship from the German Humboldt Foundation and went to Karlsruhe University (now Karlsruhe Institute of Technology) as a postdoctoral researcher in December. He was awarded the Mao Yisheng Soil Mechanics and Foundation Engineering Prize in 2002, elected as a fellow of the Chinese Academy of Engineering in 2011, and has been the director of the Research Center of Coastal and Urban Geotechnical Engineering at Zhejiang University since 2012.

Prof. Gong has been engaged in soil mechanics and geotechnical engineering education and research for over 40 years and has made a series of pioneering contributions to the field. The most outstanding contributions are: the establishment of the theory of composite foundation and its popularization in engineering practice, which won the State Science and Technology Progress Award (First Class) in 2018; the development of new technologies for ground improvement, the founding Editor of the Journal of Ground Improvement, and the "textbook" solutions to many key engineering problems, making him an undisputed leader in this area; the innovation in foundation pits design to reduce their environmental impacts and the initiative of the deformation-based design guideline.

Prof. Gong has also shown great passion and devoted enormous efforts to the education and training of the next generation of engineers. He has taught 6 graduate-level courses and published several well-received textbooks. He was awarded the National Teaching Achievement in 2018 and the National Excellent Textbook Award in 2022.

# 工程建设技术奖获得者

# 谭 永 华

谭永华，1963年6月出生于江苏省扬州市。1987年获西北工业大学固体力学专业硕士学位。1987—2002年在原航空航天工业部067基地从事液体火箭发动机研究设计工作，先后担任067基地十一所所长、067基地副主任。2002年—2016年8月任中国航天科技集团有限公司第六研究院副院长、院长。2016年8月至今任中国航天科技集团有限公司科学技术委员会副主任、航天六院科技委主任。其间曾担任长征二号E副总设计师、长征二号D运载火箭副总指挥、新一代运载火箭副总指挥、国防科工局某宇航动力子领域总设计师。

谭永华是我国航天液体动力领域的国家级领军人才，从事液体火箭发动机研究设计30余年，是新一代液体火箭发动机领域的主要开拓者之一，曾获国家科技进步奖特等奖、一等奖、二等奖各1项，国防科技进步奖特等奖1项、一等奖2项等。

**一、主持研制成功120吨高压补燃循环液氧煤油发动机，使我国成为世界上第二个掌握此核心技术的国家，将火箭近地轨道运载能力提高2倍以上**

攻克高压补燃循环发动机自身起动、点火重大技术瓶颈。针对起动过程强热力耦合、参数瞬时剧变的补燃循环系统特性，提出起动非稳态过程多参数耦合动力学仿真和多组件解耦控制试验方法，解决了起动控制元件时序匹配、热力组件起动能量控制及20兆瓦级涡轮起旋剩余功率控制难题，实现快速平稳自身起动。针对推进剂低温、非自燃特点，国际首创单点火导管系统，实现点火能量精准匹配控制，解决推力室、发生器10毫秒级协同可靠点火难题。

攻克大尺度燃烧组织和补燃燃烧稳定性控制难题。提出带二次喷注的液-液预混合式喷注方案，解决大流量高富氧发生器稳定燃烧问题；提出同轴直流离心内混喷注/隔板喷嘴分区方案，攻克了大尺度气-液燃烧稳定性控制难题，实现了当前国内最低的燃烧室压力脉动（低于 0.6%），成功解决了燃烧诱发结构大振动问题。

解决发动机结构动力学设计难题。针对发动机异形组件多、力学特征差异大、高（低）温高压、多源激励等复杂力热环境，建立力热耦合结构动力学模型，创造性提出了常平座－机架结构动力学特性一体化设计方案，颠覆了传统封闭式机架传力模式，将发动机一阶频率从 6 赫兹提高到 9.5 赫兹以上，解决了火箭动力系统低频谐振重大工程技术难题。

提出并主持研制发动机故障诊断系统。揭示了富氧高压补燃循环发动机典型故障模式和故障特征提取方法，提出故障诊断算法，研制了发动机故障诊断系统，实现全过程监控、故障预警和应急关机，有效防止灾难性故障发生，并为重复使用液体火箭发动机健康管理系统的工程研究奠定基础。

120 吨液氧煤油发动机获国家科技进步奖一等奖，并应用于长征五号、长征六号、长征七号、长征八号系列运载火箭，支撑火箭成功发射空间站各舱段、嫦娥五号探测器、火星探测器等重大载荷。

### 二、主持载人航天工程火箭发动机研制，将可靠性提升到国际先进水平，支撑载人火箭成为中国最可靠和安全的火箭，确保历次载人航天任务圆满成功

提出发动机可靠性增长方法。提出基于边缘工况组合的加速可靠性增长试验方法，采用基于数据分析的敏感度辨识等技术，用较少子样暴露发动机隐患，采取 15 项重大措施提高发动机固有可靠性。

攻克燃烧振荡破坏难题。建立常温推进剂雾化、掺混、燃烧模型，揭示了推力室燃烧振荡与发动机结构耦合机理，提出结构优化方案，解决了承力结构断裂、导管开裂等难题。

揭示涡轮热疲劳开裂机理。针对涡轮热疲劳裂纹导致试验失败重大故障，提出并建立大比功率转子轴系多点耦合振动模型，掌握了涡轮热疲劳裂纹产生和发展规律，并优化结构和工艺设计、制定设计规范，解决了涡轮开裂重大隐患。

上述研究成果将发动机单机可靠性提高近 1%，成功应用于长征二号、长征三号、长征四号系列火箭，为运载火箭高密度发射且成功率居世界前列作出重要贡献。相关成果获国家科技进步奖特等奖。

### 三、主持某二级发动机性能提升研制和液体亚燃冲压发动机关键技术攻关

主持某二级发动机性能提升研制。攻克了大尺寸轻质薄壁喷管全再生冷却技术难题，使推力和比冲分别提高 3% 和 4%；突破了大型泵压式发动机在挤压供应模式下二次点火关键技术。相关成果获国家科技进步奖二等奖。

主持液体亚燃冲压发动机关键技术攻关。应用液体火箭发动机高效燃烧和推进剂供应等技术，提出大空域、宽包线整体式冲压发动机方案，研制出燃烧效率高、结构紧凑、

调节精度高的液体亚燃冲压发动机。相关成果获国防科技进步奖一等奖。

**四、国内首次提出可变截面气蚀管与针栓式喷注器相结合的高可靠双调节变推力技术方案，主持研制成功7500N大范围变推力发动机，攻克了探月工程月面下降发动机5∶1推力精确调节技术瓶颈**

开辟了我国液体火箭发动机技术新领域，保障了嫦娥三号、嫦娥四号、嫦娥五号探测器及天问一号火星探测器精准着陆，为后续地外天体软着陆奠定了基础。相关成果获国防科技进步奖一等奖。

# Awardee of Engineering and Construction Technology Prize, Tan Yonghua

Tan Yonghua was born in Yangzhou City of Jiangsu Province in June 1963. In 1987, he received his master of solid mechanics from Northwest Polytechnic University. From 1987 to 2002, he was engaged in the design and research of liquid rocket engine (LRE) in 067 Base of the former Ministry of Aerospace Industry, and successively served as the director of the 11th Institute of 067 Base and the deputy director of 067 Base. From 2002, he served as the vice president and president of the Sixth Research Institute of China Aerospace Science and Technology Corporation (CASC). The deputy director of the Science and Technology Committee (STC) of CASC. During this period, he served as the deputy chief designer of Long March-2E, the deputy chief commander of Long March-2D launch vehicle and the new generation launch vehicle.

Tan Yonghua is a national-level leading talent in aerospace liquid power in China. He has won one special prize, one first prize, and two second prizes each for the National Science and Technology Progress, one special prize, and two first prizes for the National Defense Science and Technology Progress. He led the successful development of a 120t high-pressure staged combustion circulating liquid oxygen kerosene engine, and increased the launch capacity of the rocket in low earth orbit to more than twice. He directed the development of rocket engines for the manned spaceflight project, raised the reliability to support the manned rocket to become the most reliable and safe rocket in China, and ensured the complete success of previous manned spaceflight missions. For the first time in China, he proposed a high-reliability dual-control variable thrust technology scheme combining variable geometry cavitating venturi and pintle injectors. He led the successful development of the 7500N large-scale variable thrust engine, which overcame the 5∶1 thrust precision control technology bottleneck of the lunar surface descent engine for the lunar exploration project.

# 工程建设技术奖获得者

# 吴宏伟

吴宏伟，1962年出生于福建省福州市。1993年获英国布里斯托大学博士学位，1993—1995年在英国剑桥大学开展博士后研究。1995年加入香港科技大学工作至今，现任土木及环境工程学系讲席教授、中电控股可持续发展学冠名教授、研究生院院长兼广州校区副校长，兼任中国力学学会岩土力学专业委员会副主任。香港工程科学院院士、英国皇家工程院院士，英国土木工程师学会、美国土木工程师学会及香港工程师学会资深会员。曾担任国际土力学及岩土工程学会主席（2017—2022年），为该学会1936年成立以来首位中国籍主席。

吴宏伟是土力学与岩土工程领域公认的世界领军学者，长期从事非饱和土力学与生态岩土工程方面的研究工作。曾获2020年国家自然科学奖、2015年国家科技进步奖、2013年教育部科技进步奖、2002年中国土力学与岩土工程学会茅以升青年奖等重要奖项。在国际上，他获得了2022年国际滑坡学会Varnes Medal、2017年英国土木工程师学会Telford Premium Prize、2001东南亚岩土工程技术学会首个Tan Swan Beng奖、1990年英国结构工程师学会Henry Adams Award，并于2007年、2012年和2016年3次获得加拿大岩土工程学会R. M. Quigley Award。

## 一、建立状态相关非饱和土本构理论，开创了生态岩土工程新方向

传统非饱和土力学理论难以解决气候变化与工程活动作用下普遍存在的渗流-变形-强度耦合问题，也无法考虑非饱和土状态与植物间的相互作用。针对这些重大问题，吴宏伟团队经过20多年的科技攻关，取得了系统性创新成果。

在理论方面，发现了吸力和应力状态耦合影响非饱和土渗流-变形-强度的规律，建立了状态相关非饱和土本构理论，解决了气候变化和工程活动作用下普遍存在的渗流-变形-强度耦合问题。出版专著 *Advanced Unsaturated Soil Mechanics and Engineering*，被

全球 30 多所大学作为研究生课程教材和参考书籍。相关成果获 2020 年国家自然科学奖。

在学科方向上，基于上述新理论揭示了大气－植被－土体相互作用的机理，发现了不同形状根系的植被对非饱和土水力与力学耦合作用规律，建立了植被边坡的稳定性分析理论，开创了生态岩土工程新研究方向，为生态建设提供了科技支撑。撰写了全球首部生态岩土工程专著 Plant-soil Slope Interaction，相关成果获加拿大岩土工程学会 R. M. Quigley Award，为大中华区首位获奖者。

在应用方面，自主研发的仪器被全球 300 多家科研单位采购与应用，其中非饱和土体变测量系统被公认为精度最高，成为国际标准方法。攻克了边坡渗流－变形－强度耦合分析难题，成果被全球首部松散土边坡加固设计指南采纳。研发了生态型三层土质覆盖系统，无须使用土工膜，解决了传统系统的失稳和老化问题，防渗性能优于美国环保局标准 27%，成功应用于深圳最大垃圾填埋场等，被国标推荐使用。

**二、解决了连续墙施工过程三维应力和应变分析的难题，建立了深基坑开挖影响桩基础的计算方法，为工程安全提供科学依据**

城市地下空间开发的核心问题在于深基坑工程安全开挖和支护，精准预测土体应力场变化及其对周边建筑的影响是国内外公认的重要科学难题。吴宏伟团队揭示了连续墙开挖过程竖向荷载传递和水平成拱效应的三维应力场变化控制机理，推导了应力状态释放和重分布的计算公式，建立了连续墙开挖及支护的理论分析方法。相关成果获英国土木工程师学会 Miller Prize 和英国结构工程师学会 Henry Adams Award。

发现了坑底桩对基坑抗突涌的影响规律，揭示了基坑开挖影响桩基础承载力和沉降的机理，建立了准确的计算方法。相关成果荣获加拿大岩土工程学会 R. M. Quigley Award。

上述研究成果作为项目"深大长基坑安全精细控制与节约型基坑支护新技术及应用"的重要部分，获得 2015 年国家科技进步奖。

# Awardee of Engineering and Construction Technology Prize, Ng Wang Wai

Ng Wang Wai was born in Fuzhou City of Fujian Province in 1962. He is the Vice-President of the Hong Kong University of Science and Technology (HKUST) in the Guangzhou campus. He is also the Dean of HKUST Fok Ying Tung Graduate School, CLP Holdings Professor of Sustainability and a Chair Professor in the Department of Civil and Environmental Engineering at HKUST.

Professor Ng earned his PhD degree from the University of Bristol in 1993. After carrying out post-doctoral research at the University of Cambridge between 1993 and 1995, he returned to Hong Kong and joined HKUST as Assistant Professor in 1995 and rose through the ranks to become

Chair Professor in 2011.

As a world authority on unsaturated soil mechanics, eco-geotechnical engineering and landslides, Professor Ng is Fellow of the Royal Academy of Engineering, Fellow of the Hong Kong Academy of Engineering Sciences. He is the immediate Past President of the International Society for Soil Mechanics and Geotechnical Engineering (2017–2022). He is also Fellow of the Institution of Civil Engineers, the American Society of Civil Engineers, and the Hong Kong Institution of Engineers. Currently.

Professor Ng has received many prestigious awards, including the 2020 State Natural Science Award and the 2015 State Scientific Technological Advancement Award, the 2013 Scientific Advancement Technological Award by the Ministry of Education, and the Mao Yisheng Youth Award in 2002.

Internationally, Professor Ng is the recipient of the 2022 Varnes Medal from the UNESCO-International Consortium on Landslides, the 2017 Telford Premium Prize from the Institution of Civil Engineers (UK), the R. M. Quigley Award from the Canadian Geotechnical Society three times in 2016, 2012 & 2007, the first Tan Swan Beng Award from the Southeast Asian Geotechnical Society in 2001. Moreover, he received the Henry Adams Award from the Institution of Structural Engineers (UK) and the Miller Prize from the Institution of Civil Engineers (UK) in the 1990s.

# 工程建设技术奖获得者

# 张 锦 岚

张锦岚，1963年12月出生于山东省曹县。现为中国船舶集团有限公司首席专家，研究员。30余年来始终扎根在核潜艇研制一线，带领团队主持攻克了舰船结构、减振降噪、高速机动、武器集成等系列重大技术难题，实现了我国核潜艇技术的跨越发展，为保卫海洋核心利益、震慑强敌发挥了重要作用，为构建可信可靠的远程海基核力量作出了重大贡献。获国家科技进步奖一等奖1项、国防科技进步奖特等奖、国防科技创新团队奖（团队带头人）等国家级科技奖励5项，获首届全国创新争先奖状，被授予中国"船舶设计大师"等荣誉称号。

1985年，张锦岚毕业后进入七一九所时，我国核潜艇研制事业正处于窘境：型号断线，人才断档，人员流失。在同学或身边同事纷纷离职经商时，他不为所动、矢志不移，坚守核潜艇研制事业，全身心投入工作和学习中。在研制任务不太饱满的情况下，他不放过任何一个提高业务水平和拓宽知识面的机会，主动争取和参与预研课题，自学有关电子、电气等本专业外的书籍以及电脑知识，掌握最新的设计手段。作为当时中国核潜艇研制史上最年轻的技术人员，他争取到与黄旭华院士一起参加中国核潜艇首次深潜试验的机会，冒着生命危险，两次随船出海下潜到极限深度，为试验的圆满成功作出了重大贡献。他还率先掌握并推广应用当时最先进的计算机技术，使核潜艇设计由手工转向CAD，实现核潜艇研制的一次重大变革。通过不懈努力，张锦岚为创新核潜艇研制工作打下了良好基础，荣获"全国讲理想、比贡献"科技标兵称号。

任核潜艇型号副总设计师时，时逢核潜艇研制工作断线20多年后重新上马，技术断层，产品设计、建造工艺、生产组织及管理水平等方面面临巨大挑战，可供借鉴的东西不多，张锦岚与同事们一起协力攻关，攻克了大量技术难题。在技术攻关项目"建造原则工艺研究"中，他组织相关专业人员经过广泛调研、充分论证，提出了既满足设计要求，又符合总装厂实际的建造方案、主要建造工艺措施，为核潜艇顺利研制奠定了基础；

在核潜艇建造中，时任型号副总师和现场行政负责人的张锦岚，与型号总师一起向未知领域挑战，攻克了大量技术难题，并首创大型舱段结构型式、首创大面积采用新型船体材料、首创减振降噪新方法，使我国核潜艇在总体性能、核安全和系统集成技术等方面均实现了重大跨越。为解决"卡脖子"问题，他带领团队成员持续攻关，为构建可信的远程海基核力量作出了重大贡献，获首届全国创新争先奖状。

多年来，为了中国核潜艇研制事业的发展，为了打造一流产品，张锦岚一直将"小我"置身度外。在任务面前，在考验面前，他总是拼字在前、干字在前。参加深潜试验时，有人担心重蹈美国"长尾鲨号"覆辙，葬身海底，25岁的他却为有机会参与试验而感到荣幸。在主持技术攻关时，为按时保质完成任务，为拿出最佳方案，他经常加班加点、通宵达旦地工作。为推动核潜艇研制进度，他长期驻守条件艰苦的配建现场，稳定军心，现场解决技术问题，在配建现场做到了哪里困难突出、哪里矛盾多、哪里任务重，他的身影就出现在哪里。近几年，核潜艇总体所现场配建、试验任务空前繁重，张锦岚克服重重困难，常年奔波于武汉、配建配试现场和全国各协作单位，每年出差的天数超过200天，成为哪里有需要就立马飞哪里的"空中飞人"。

# Awardee of Engineering and Construction Technology Prize, Zhang Jinlan

Zhang Jinlan was born in Caoxian County of Shandong Province in December 1963. He is the chief expert in the field of nuclear submarine of China Shipping Group. He has been rooted in the research line of nuclear submarine for more than 30 years. He led the team to overcome a series of major technical problems, such as ship structure, vibration and noise reduction, high-speed maneuvering, weapon integration, and so on, realized the leapfrogging development of China's nuclear submarine technology, played an important role in defending the core interests of the ocean, deterred the strong enemy, and made great contributions to the construction of a credible and reliable long-range sea-based nuclear force.

Won the national science and technology progress first prize 1 ( ranking 1 ), national defense science and technology progress special prize, national defense science and technology innovation team award ( team leader ) and so on 5 national science and technology awards, won the first national innovation first prize, "ship design master" and other honorary titles.

Comrade Zhang Jinlan took part in his work in 1985 and is now the chief expert and researcher of China Shipping Group Co., Ltd. He has always kept his original heart in mind, devoted all his efforts to building a national important instrument, committed himself to providing first-class equipment for the first-class navy, and made great contributions to the development of naval equipment research and development. Has been awarded the first prize of national scientific and technological progress 1 (row 1) and other provincial and ministerial level and above 5 scientific and technological awards, has been awarded the title of master of Chinese ship design.

**Ideal, more contribution, he is the standard soldier**

In order to improve the development level of naval equipment in our country, Zhang Jinlan youth is determined to choose maritime engineering specialty. When he was in college, he joined Communist Party of China at the age of 21 because of his excellent qualities and studies. In 1985, when he entered the 719 institute after graduation, the nuclear submarine research and development career was in a quandary: the model was disconnected, the talent was cut off, and the personnel were lost. In the students or colleagues have left the sea to look for gold, he is unmoved, determined, adhere to the nuclear submarine research and development career, will devote their whole body and soul to work and study. Under the condition that the research task is not full, he does not miss any opportunity to improve his business level and broaden his knowledge: take the initiative to strive for and participate in pre-research projects; self-study books other than electronics, electrical and other major; self-study computer knowledge, master the latest design means As the youngest technician in the history of nuclear submarine development in China at that time, he won the opportunity to participate in the first deep diving test of nuclear submarine in China with academician Huang Xuhua, risked his life, and dived to the limit depth twice with the ship, which made great contributions to the complete success of the experiment. He also took the lead in mastering and popularizing the most advanced computer technology at that time, so that nuclear submarine design was changed from manual to CAD, and a major change in nuclear submarine development was realized. Through unremitting efforts, Zhang Jinlan laid a good foundation for innovating nuclear submarine research and development and realizing his ideal ambition, and won the title of "national ideal, comparative contribution" scientific and technological standard.

**Conquer the key core technology, he is a pioneer**

General Secretary Xi pointed out: key core technologies cannot be bought, bought, or obtained. Only by holding the key core technologies in their own hands can we fundamentally ensure national economic security, national defense security, and other security. For many years engaged in the development of heavy weapons in large countries, Zhang Jinlan has deep feelings for this, and has been on the road to innovation bravely forward, strive to be a pioneer. When he was deputy chief designer of nuclear submarine model, when nuclear submarine was cut off for more than 20 years, the technical fault, product design, construction technology, production organization and management level were faced with great challenges, and there were not many ready-made things to be used for reference. Comrade Zhang Jinlan and his colleagues worked together to overcome key problems and overcome a large number of technical problems. In the technical research project "Construction principle and Technology Research", he organized the relevant professional personnel, after extensive investigation and full demonstration, put forward the construction scheme and main construction technology measures which not only meet the design requirements, but also meet the actual construction requirements of the assembly plant, which laid the foundation for the smooth development of nuclear submarine. In the construction of nuclear submarine, Zhang Jinlan, then deputy master of model and administrative person in charge of the site, together with the chief of model, challenged to unknown fields, conquered a large number of technical problems, and pioneered the structural types of large segments, the first to adopt new hull materials in large areas, and the first new methods to reduce vibration and noise, so that nuclear submarine in China has achieved great leapfrogging in the aspects of coupled vibration between hull and local structures performance, nuclear safety and system integration technology. In order to solve the problem of "sticking neck", he led team members to continue to address key problems, made great contributions to the construction of a credible long-range sea-based nuclear force, and won the National Innovation Award.

### In front of "Big self", he is "fighting for the third Lang."

For many years, for the development of nuclear submarine research and development in China, in order to create first-class products, Zhang Jinlan has been putting the "ego" out of the way. In front of the task, in front of the test, he always spelled in front, dry in front of. When he took part in the deep dive test, some people worried that he would repeat the mistakes of the long tail Shark in the United States and die at the bottom of the sea, but the 25-year-old was honored to have the opportunity to participate in the experiment. When presiding over technical key problems, in order to ensure the quality of the task on time, in order to come up with the best plan, he often works overtime and works all night. In order to promote the development progress of nuclear submarine, he has been stationed at the site with difficult conditions for a long time, stabilized the military mind, and solved technical problems on the spot. Where the difficulty is prominent, where the contradiction is many, where the task is heavy, his figure appears where the construction site is difficult. In recent years, nuclear submarine coupled vibration between hull and local structures site allocation, experimental tasks unprecedented heavy, Zhang Jinlan overcome many difficulties, all the year round Wuhan, with the construction of test sites and national cooperation units, the number of travel days per year more than 200 days, become where there is a need, immediately fly where the "flying people."

# 何梁何利基金科学与技术创新奖获得者传略

PROFILES OF THE AWARDEES OF PRIZE FOR
SCIENTIFIC AND TECHNOLOGICAL INNOVATION OF
HO LEUNG HO LEE FOUNDATION

# 青年创新奖获得者

# 戴 庆

戴庆,1985年10月出生于江苏省淮安市。2011年获剑桥大学材料工程专业博士学位,2011—2012年在英国剑桥大学从事博士后研究。2012年回国至今在国家纳米科学中心工作,2019年起任国家纳米科学中心所务委员、科技处处长。曾获中国青年科技奖、北京市自然科学二等奖;入选美国光学学会会士、英国皇家化学会会士和发展中国家科学院青年通讯会士。

戴庆从事纳米光子材料与器件研究工作,在新型极化激元的激发机制、调控规律、器件设计和测试方法等方面取得了系列原创性学术成果,推动了纳米光子学领域的发展。

## 一、探索多种极化激元新模式的激发机制,为纳米尺度光电互联提供全新的物理思路

极性材料中声子极化激元(半光子-半声子)由于在中红外频段具有高压缩、低损耗和奇异的双曲特性,因此成为一种在纳米尺度光电互联信息传输过程中具有前景的新载体,而如何高效地激发并深入探索其中的物理机制成为该方向的巨大挑战之一。近年来,研究团队深入开展高能量分辨的近场光学金属探针激发和高空间分辨的电子激发在声子极化激元全新模式上的探索,并揭示了更多双曲特性背后的深层次物理机制,为声子激元的表征和调控研究带来了新机遇;并进一步结合理论分析揭示了一种集高光场限域和易激发优势于一身的新型声子激元"幽灵"模式的存在,革新了极化激元领域的教科书定义;电子激发实验测量了单层氮化硼声子极化激元(500倍波长压缩能力),结束了关于单层氮化硼声子极化激元频段和性能的理论争论。上述成果获得两次中国光学十大进展。

**二、阐明极化激元在多界面结构中的性能调控规律，为光电互联关键功能器件在复杂界面环境中的设计奠定了全新材料基础**

随着光电互联器件的高集成度需求，极化激元在未来应用过程中的界面设计将成为面临的核心挑战。研究团队对异质界面进行了深入探索：设计石墨烯/氮化硼异质结，屏蔽介电环境干扰，成功将入射光波长压缩近500倍（接近理论预测极限），解决了光子器件与电子器件尺寸失配的问题；通过悬空结构提供纯净的介电环境，获得室温下目前报道的石墨烯等离激元具有的最高传输性能纪录，对比同等条件下氧化硅基底上的石墨烯等离激元性能提升一个数量级以上；设计石墨烯/氧化钼异质结，并结合独特的化学掺杂手段，首次在实验上证明了杂化极化激元的等频轮廓发生拓扑转变，不仅使其传播方向突破了原有晶向的限制，还能够将能量高效汇聚进行定向低损传输。

**三、自主研制低温近场光学显微镜，为光电互联关键功能器件提供全新的表征技术**

鉴于研究团队长期在极化激元新物理和新材料的探索，深刻意识到在提高光电互联关键功能器件性能方面需要更全面的先进的表征技术。率领研究团队自主搭建了国内首台低温（70 K）近场光学显微镜，突破光学衍射极限，实现了纳米样品的光学参数精确测量；提出介电环境设计调控极化激元的新思路，实现激元片上定向、低损传输。

**四、发展冷阴极 X 射线成像测试技术，为深海载人潜水器焊缝缺陷提供高精度、三维检测方案**

深海潜水器是陆地和海底之间的重要运载工具，其结构力学安全性能要求极高。特别是钛合金焊缝作为球壳的重要部位，其力学性能评估尤为关键。针对前期研究中利用 X 射线对焊缝检测已形成卓有成效的方法和标准，但毫米级缺陷检测精度尚不足以支持建立焊缝静强度力学模型、也难以准确获得缺陷在长期服役条件下的动态信息这一问题，戴庆团队提出了基于冷阴极 X 射线源高分辨"适形"检测技术方法，实现阳极电压 200 kV、空间分辨能力 10 μm 的钛合金球壳缺陷三维信息重构功能，为"蛟龙号""深海勇士号"和"奋斗者号"服役过程提供质量安全检测，并为发展先进球壳制造技术提供原始数据，支持国家深海战略发展规划。

# Awardee of Youth Innovation Prize, Dai Qing

Dai Qing was born in Huai'an City of Jiangsu Province in October 1985. He graduated from Cambridge University with a Ph.D. in Materials Engineering in 2011. After one year of postdoctoral research at Cambridge, he joined the National Center of Nanoscience and Technology in 2012.

All along, Prof. Dai has been devoted to the research of nanophotonic materials and devices. A series of original academic achievements have been made in the field of new polaritons, including excitation mechanisms, multifunctional tunability, device design, and characterization techniques. In addition, Prof. Dai has also won many academic awards and honors. Typical examples include winning the China Youth Science and Technology Award and the second prize of the Beijing Natural Science Award and being elected as a Fellow of the American Optical Society, a Fellow of the Royal Society of Chemistry, and the Youth Communication Society of the Academy of Sciences of Developing Countries.

First, they explored the excitation mechanism of many novel modes of polaritons, providing a new physical idea for nano-scale photoelectric integration. Prof. Andrea Alù, a pioneer in the field of nano-optics in the United States, commented in Nature: the establishment of a new polaritonic excitation method, which will be used in the future development of a variety of polaritons. Second, they elucidated the performance regulation laws of polaritons in the multi-interface structure, laying a new material foundation for the design of key devices in the complex interface environment of photoelectric integration. Third, the team independently developed the first domestic cryogenic near-field optical microscope that can break through the optical diffraction limit and realize the accurate measurement of the optical parameters of nano-samples, providing a new characterization technology for key functional devices of optoelectronic integration. Finally, they developed cold cathode X-ray imaging testing technology to provide a high-precision and three-dimensional detection scheme for weld defects of deep-sea manned submersibles.

# 青年创新奖获得者

# 冯 雪

冯雪，1977 年出生。2003 年获清华大学博士学位。2004—2007 年分别在美国伊利诺伊大学厄巴纳－香槟分校机械工程系、美国加州理工学院航空系从事博士后研究。2007 年回国至今在清华大学航天航空学院工作，现为清华大学长聘教授，柔性电子技术国家级重点实验室主任、应用力学教育部重点实验室主任。授权国家发明专利 190 余项、自主软件著作权 9 项等；先后获得第十五届中国青年科技奖、第七届全国优秀科技工作者、教育部技术发明奖一等奖、中国机械工业科学技术一等奖、中国电子学会自然科学一等奖等荣誉和奖项。

冯雪主要从事固体力学与柔性电子技术研究，坚持基础前沿探索与国家需求牵引双轮驱动，基于力学原理发展了柔性集成器件的设计基础理论、核心制造技术及结构载荷一体化应用方法。

## 一、基于力学原理的柔性集成器件设计理论及异质界面调控方法

基于硅等无机半导体材料的集成器件是现代信息工业的基石。柔性集成器件实现了形态柔性并兼顾无机半导体器件的高性能，为集成电路发展提供了一个新维度并带来变革性应用。

在保持无机半导体材料体系不变的前提下，实现集成器件从刚到柔的转化，其核心难点在于设计柔性集成器件的拓扑形态，使材料变形向结构变形转化。冯雪团队建立了可延展互连结构有限变形理论框架，给出了屈曲结构、蛇形互连、分形互连、三维螺旋结构等系列可延展结构变形后的应力分布规律，阐明了其可延展展开机制，澄清了材料变形向结构变形转化的内在关系，实现了柔性集成器件弯曲、扭转、拉伸等变形，为柔性电子设计提供理论指导。

柔性基底无法为硬质无机功能薄膜提供高温生长环境并保证加工精度，需要通过转

印技术实现柔性集成器件的构筑，其核心难点在于调控转印过程中印章异质界面的黏附强度。冯雪团队建立了粘弹性率相关效应的异质界面黏附解析模型，阐明了应变率对界面能量释放率的调控机制，揭示了印章–薄膜–基底双界面间"竞争断裂"的力学本质，奠定了柔性集成器件转印集成的理论基础，并基于动力学转印方法实现了光子、电子、传感单元的混合集成，已成为柔性膜–基结构集成的通用方法。所发展的动力学转印方法被近百个美国专利引用，解决了MicroLED器件巨量转移过程中所遇到的LED芯片误黏附以及边缘对准偏差问题，LED芯片转移良率提升近一个量级。相关成果获北京市自然科学一等奖与中国电子学会自然科学一等奖。

## 二、柔性集成器件大规模制造技术

实现柔性器件单元的晶圆尺寸微米级薄化是柔性集成器件大规模制造的基础，其核心难点是在减薄过程中对晶圆尺寸范围内的缺陷、残余应力及损伤引入及演化进行调控。冯雪团队揭示了外应力场和电场共同作用下局域态向系统吉布斯函数减小方向的扩散机制，建立了基于应力局域态与半导体能带耦合的载流子输运自洽模型与器件性能变化规律；在此基础上提出了柔性芯片磨削力控制理论与渐进式晶圆级纳米金刚石减薄方法，实现了对晶圆尺寸柔性器件单元减薄过程中残余应力、缺陷等的有效调控；基于上述理论与技术突破，率先实现流片后4寸、6寸、8寸、12寸不同大小和硅基、碳化硅等不同类型的柔性晶圆和系列超薄芯片/器件，解决了大尺寸晶圆减薄过程中结构易损坏与性能易衰减等制造难题。建成了国际首条柔性集成器件制造小试线，打造了国内首个面向柔性集成器件的检测体系及平台，获得CMA与CNAS认证。相关成果获日内瓦国际发明展金奖与全国发明展览会发明创业奖金奖。

## 三、高温固体力学

热防护系统是决定高速飞行器设计成败的关键要素，服役环境下的高速飞行器热防护系统具有尺寸大、温度高、变化快等突出特点，其气动外形演化规律不明确、失效机理不清晰严重制约了高速飞行器性能指标的进一步提升，亟须发展基于高温柔性视觉的飞行器在线测试一体化设计与集成，实现大视野、宽温域、高动态的过程数据精细化测量和定量表征。

冯雪团队建立了高温光学竞争成像模型，发展了基于谱段筛选的光学窗口选择与匹配方法，发明了强干扰条件下热防护结构精细化成像技术；基于柔性电子技术，发明了自适应柔性光学成像与测量系统，实现了测量系统的结构自主可调、参数动态可控、目标多源可辨，解决了复杂服役环境下高超热防护系统性能参数的全局化、全过程测量难题；研发了高温风洞和机载柔性一体化光学测量系统与装备，实现了强干扰风洞环境与复杂空间、异形曲面环境的高可靠集成。

相关技术与装备成功应用于中国航天空气动力技术研究院、中国空气动力研究与发展中心、航天一院等单位的飞行器考核测试中，完成近千项科学试验，实现了飞行器设计和考核能力的跃升。相关成果获教育部技术发明奖一等奖与中国机械工业科学技术奖一等奖。

# Awardee of Youth Innovation Prize, Feng Xue

Feng Xue was born in 1977. He obtained his doctor's degree from the Department of Engineering Mechanics of Tsinghua University in 2003. From 2004 to 2007, he pursued postdoctoral research in the Department of Mechanical Engineering of the University of Illinois at Urbana Champaign and the Department of Aeronautics of the California Institute of Technology. He went back to China in 2007 and has been working in the School of Aerospace Engineering of Tsinghua University since then. He is now a tenured professor of Tsinghua University and the director of the National Key Laboratory of Flexible Electronic Technology and the Key Laboratory of Applied Mechanics of the Ministry of Education. More than 190 national invention patents and 9 proprietary software Copyrights have been granted to the technologies developed by him. He was granted with the 15th China Youth Science and Technology Award, the 7th National Outstanding Scientific and Technological Workers, the first prize of the Technology Invention Award of Ministry of Education, the first prize of Science and Technology Award of China Machinery Industry, and the first prize of Natural Science Award of Chinese Society of Electronics.

Professor Feng Xue is engaged in the research of solid mechanics and flexible electronic technology. He adheres to the double-wheel drive mode that closely combines the fundamental research to explore frontier area and the application research to meet national demands. Based on the principles of mechanics, he developed the basic design theory, core manufacturing technology and structural –load integration application method of flexible integrated devices.

# 青年创新奖获得者

# 刘 建 锋

刘建锋，1979年8月出生于河南省新乡市。2002年毕业于山东科技大学土木与建筑学院获工学学士学位；2005年毕业于四川大学水利水电学院获工学硕士学位；2009年毕业于四川大学水利水电学院获工学博士学位，同年留校从事教学和科研工作至今。担任中国岩石力学与工程学会岩土多场耦合专业委员会、低碳能源岩石力学与工程专业委员会、测试专业委员会等副主任委员；国家原子能机构高放废物地质处置创新中心、中国力学学会MTS材料试验协作专业委员会、中国岩石力学与工程学会采矿岩石力学分会、中国岩石力学与工程学会工程设计方法分会、四川省石油协会地质勘探专业委员会、四川省岩石力学与工程学会等委员/常务理事。

刘建锋从事能源、水电、交通、地质碳封存及高放废物地质处置等工程领域的深地岩体力学基础理论与工程实践研究。工程岩体是非透明的天然地质体，其内部本身很复杂，而且深部地下处于温度场、应力场、渗流场等复杂赋存环境状态和工程建设的人为扰动作用等耦合条件之中，地下越深，这种耦合作用对岩体工程安全和灾变的影响也越复杂，深部工程建设比浅部面临更多、更复杂、更难的灾害问题，对工程建设安全的制约和影响也更大，对其研究和防灾治理也比浅部条件下更为困难。在深部条件下，不仅浅部的传统技术不能很好适用，而且相关理论研究也更为复杂。结合我国大工程建设实际，刘建锋围绕深地工程安全和灾害防治，从试验测试、理论分析和评价方法等方面开展了系统的研究工作。针对深部条件下岩体力学响应条件是深地复杂赋存环境与工程扰动状态的耦合条件影响，探索了获取深地耦合条件下岩体损伤力学演化的测试方法与设备，获得了多项发明专利授权，形成了系统的测试平台与方法；针对深地复杂耦合条件下的岩体损伤行为，考虑不同尺度下的损伤状态，对深地复杂环境下岩体损伤力学行为进行理论分析，并以能量理论为纽带，对深部条件下岩块到岩体损伤力学响应进行统一描述；针对深部条件下岩体稳定状态分析，以对工程变形和破坏具有决定影响的损伤应力与临界应变作为评判标准，实现了稳定状态评价及优化调控的分析。从解答工程问题的测试难题入手，再到回归工程实践，丰富了深地工程建设中岩体力学的理论和应用研究。刘建锋共申请发明专利 100 余件，已获授权发明专利 60 余件，其中美国发明 26 件，获软件著作权 15 项；获授权的专利技术得到了成功转化和应用；主持国家自然科学基金重点项目及面上项目、国防科技计划等国家级与省部级科技攻关 10 余项，获国家科技进步奖二等奖 1 项、教育部科技进步奖一等奖 1 项、中国岩石力学与工程学会技术发明奖一等奖 1 项、工业和信息化部科技进步奖二等奖 1 项、中国石油和化工自动化应用协会科技进步奖一等奖和技术发明奖二等奖各 1 项、中国发明学会发明创新二等奖 1 项、中国水土保持学会科技进步奖二等奖 1 项等多个省部级奖项。其个人获中国产学研合作创新奖、中国岩石力学与工程学会青年科技奖、中青年科技领军人才等多项荣誉。

# Awardee of Youth Innovation Prize, Liu Jianfeng

Liu Jianfeng was born in Xinxiang City of Henan Province in August 1979. In 2002, he graduated from the School of Civil Engineering and Architecture of Shandong University of Science and Technology with a bachelor's degree in engineering. In 2005, he received the master degree in engineering from the College of Water Resources and Hydropower of Sichuan University. In 2009, he received the doctorate degree in engineering from the College of Water Resources and Hydropower of Sichuan University. In the same year, he was hired by Sichuan University, and has been engaged in the teaching and scientific research so far. Prof. Liu has served as vice-chairman of Geotechnical Multi-field Coupling Committee of Chinese Society for Rock Mechanics and Engineering, Rock Mechanics and Engineering Committee of Low Carbon Energy, Testing Committee and other committees. He also has served as a member or executive director in the Innovation Center for High-level Radioactive Waste Geological Disposal of the National Atomic Energy Agency, in the MTS Material Testing Co-operation Committee of the Chinese Society of Mechanics, in the Mining Rock Mechanics Committee and the Engineering Design Method Committee of Chinese Society for Rock Mechanics and Engineering, in the Professional Committee for Geological Exploration of the Sichuan Petroleum Association, and in the Institute of Rock Mechanics and Engineering of Sichuan Province.

Prof. Liu is engaged in the basic theory and engineering practice research on deep rock mass mechanics in the fields of energy, hydropower, transportation, geological carbon storage and geological disposal of high-level radioactive waste. Engineering rock mass is a non-transparent natural geological body with complex internal space, which is invisible and intangible. Engineering problems in the deep underground are subjected to coupling conditions of complex temperature field, stress field, seepage field, and artificial disturbance of Engineering construction. The deeper the underground, the more complex the coupling influence on the safety and catastrophe of rock mass engineering. Deep engineering construction faces much more complicated disaster problems than shallow engineering construction. It also has greater restriction and influence on the safety of engineering construction, which makes it more difficult to be studied and prevented. Under deep conditions, not only the shallow traditional technology can not be well applied, but also the related theoretical research is more complex. In combination with the actual construction of major projects in China, the systematic research work is carried out from the testing aspects, theoretical analysis and evaluation methods around the safety of deep engineering and disaster prevention. In view of the influence of coupling condition between deep complex occurrence environment and engineering disturbance state on rock mass mechanical response condition in deep condition, the testing method and equipment to obtain the mechanical evolution of rock mass damage under deep coupling condition are explored, and several invention patents are granted, thereby forming a systematic test platform and method. Based on the damage behavior of rock mass under deep and complex coupling conditions and considering damage status at different scales, the damage mechanical behavior of rock mass in deep and complex environment is analyzed theoretically, and the damage mechanical response is described uniformly with energy theory. Based on the stability state analysis of rock mass under deep conditions, the damage stress and critical strain, which have decisive influence on engineering deformation and failure, are taken as the evaluation criteria to realize the analysis of stability state evaluation and optimal regulation. Starting with solving the engineering testing problems and then going back to the engineering practice, it enriches the theory and application research of rock mechanics in deep engineering construction. Prof. Liu has applied for more than 100 invention patents, of which over 60 patents are authorized, including 26 in the United States and 15 in software copyright. The authorized patented technology has been successfully transformed and applied. He presided more than 10 national and provincial science and technology key projects including NSFC key projects and general projects, and National Defense Science and Technology Program.

Prof. Liu has won the second prize of National Science and Technology Progress Award, the first prize of Science and Technology Progress of Ministry of Education, the first prize of Technological Invention of Chinese Society for Rock Mechanics and Engineering, the second prize of Science and Technology Progress of Ministry of Industry and Information Technology, the first prize of Science and Technology Progress of China Association for Petroleum and Chemical Automation Applications, the second prize of Technological Invention of China, Second Prize of Invention and Innovation of Chinese Invention Society, Second Prize of Science and Technology Progress of Chinese Society of Water and Soil Conservation. Prof. Liu has won many honors, such as China Industry-University-Research Cooperation Innovation Award, Chinese Society for Rock Mechanics and Engineering Youth Science and Technology Award, Middle-aged and Young Science and Technology Leading Talents, etc.

# 青年创新奖获得者

# 林 学 春

林学春，1978年4月出生于湖北省仙桃市。2004年毕业于中国科学院物理研究所获理学博士学位，同年进入中国科学院半导体研究所工作。国家科技部重点专项"增材制造与激光制造"总体组专家，中国光学工程学会副秘书长、北京光学学会副理事长。

林学春长期从事高功率固体激光技术及应用研究，研究成果具有从激光物理、激光器、激光制造工艺到产业应用的全链条特色。获授权发明专利百余项，其中美国专利3项；以第一完成人获得2017年国家技术发明奖二等奖和2020年中国光学工程学会技术发明奖一等奖，并获得2019年中国青年科技奖。

## 一、高功率连续固体激光器关键技术与激光焊接应用

针对高功率连续固体激光器面临的高可靠性、高光束质量技术瓶颈，提出互注入锁定复合谐振腔方法，实现多模块的功率扩展，在高功率激光条件下获得了长时间稳定输出，为高可靠性千瓦级激光器的研制开辟了新途径；提出增益空间约束软边光阑谐振腔方法，匀化了种子源全功率段的光束质量，为激光放大奠定了基础，解决了高功率固体激光器稳定性与光束质量差的共性技术难题。在国内首次建成千瓦级固体激光器生产线，研制出具有自主知识产权的1～7kW系列化产品，5kW激光器的光束质量达33.4mm·mrad，8小时功率不稳定度为±0.77%，为我国激光先进制造业提供了核心激光源，打破了该类核心器件全部依赖进口的被动局面。该成果入选"十二五"国家重大科技创新成就展。

基于自主创新研发的激光器，开发出成套激光零部件精密焊接工艺，用于国内首款无级自动变速箱轮毂（奇瑞汽车）焊接，速度达150件/小时，是传统电子束焊的3倍，形变达±0.07mm（优于设计值：<±0.1mm），扭力强度达1530N·m（是设计值450N·m的3倍以上），优于国内外公开文献报道。该激光焊接技术已经生产160万套，良率达

99.95%，已应用于奇瑞汽车瑞虎、艾瑞泽全部新款车型；为北京奔驰焊接了400万余件天窗滑轨，百万件良率达99.98%，其中76万件返销德国，供应总部奔驰汽车生产，系德国奔驰按欧洲标准首次采用中国该类配件。该成果推动了国产汽车核心部件精密焊接工艺的升级换代，获2017年度国家技术发明奖二等奖。

### 二、大能量高重频固体激光器关键技术与激光清洗应用

针对高功率（大能量高重频）脉冲固体激光器温度梯度导致的热畸变、高峰值功率引起的器件损伤等技术瓶颈，提出错位排列半导体均匀泵浦方法，降低了增益介质的径向温度梯度与热应力，提升了脉冲能量负载能力，为大能量高重频固体激光器研制开辟了新思路。通过错位排列均匀泵浦方法，抑制了大能量脉冲放大的波前畸变，实现了单脉冲能量1.05J、重复频率3kHz、平均功率3.17kW、脉冲宽度78.2ns的大能量、高重频纳秒脉冲激光输出，为千赫兹纳秒激光器的国际最高指标。

开发出千瓦级脉冲固体激光清洗设备，1000W@24h不稳定度≤±1.09%，实现小批量生产与销售。深入研究大能量高重频脉冲激光作用下的烧蚀气化机理，提出了高强钢、热轧钢、铝合金等表面氧化层清洗工艺优化方案以及激光逐层定量除漆工艺方法，成功用于中策橡胶集团轮胎模具清洗、中船713所舰船某发射筒表面沉积物清洗、中船716舰船高强钢焊前清洗、沈飞某飞机电搭接件绝缘氧化膜清洗、中国石油集团西部钻探工程公司高压管汇防腐漆层清洗等，促进了我国传统工业清洗技术的升级换代。该成果获2020年中国光学工程学会技术发明奖一等奖。

### 三、多声子吸收辅助宽带辐射发光机制

传统频域调谐采用激光非线性频率变换，对激光能量或峰值功率密度有高度依赖性。提出多声子吸收辅助宽带辐射产生激光新理论，实现无阈值波长转换与调谐。在共熔盐体系内，通过无序掺杂多种（$Nd^{3+}$、$Si^{4+}$、$P^{5+}$、$S^{6+}$、$Li^+$、$Zn^{2+}$）离子，实现基质材料的有效高熵化，引入声子能级参与实能级的电子跃迁过程，电子跃迁能级区域被大幅拓宽，获得了大于100THz的超宽声子谱均匀分布展宽，实现了频域分布精确调制的无阈值频率转换及调谐。利用高熵玻璃频谱剪辑获得任意波长输出，打破了传统激光材料跃迁规则，是激光物理领域的重大突破。

# Awardee of Youth Innovation Prize, Lin Xuechun

Lin Xuechun was born in Xiantao City of Hubei Province in April 1978. He obtained a doctorate in laser physics from the Institute of Physics of the Chinese Academy of Sciences in 2004. In the same year, he worked in the Institute of Semiconductors of the Chinese Academy of

Sciences. In 2005, he established the All-solid State Laser Laboratory. In 2007, he was promoted to a professor, and served as the laboratory director. He focuses on high power solid-state laser and applications. In 2022, he was selected into the list of the National Science Fund for Distinguished Young Scholars. He served as a professor of the University of Chinese Academy of Sciences, director of Beijing All Solid State Laser Advanced Manufacturing Engineering Technology Research Center, part-time professors of Harbin University of Technology, Wuhan University, etc., and senior visiting scholar of the University of California, Los Angeles. He is the deputy secretary general of China Optical Engineering Society, the deputy director general of Beijing Optical Engineering Society, and the editorial board member of Chinese Journal of Lasers and Infrared and Laser Engineering. He published 146 academic papers in journal Light Sci Appl., Laser Photonics Rev., Opt. Express etc. He has obtained 106 authorized invention patents (including 3 American patents), and supervised 25 postdoctoral, doctoral and master's students. He won the second prize of National Technological Invention Award in 2017, China Youth Science and Technology Award in 2019, the first prize of China Optical Engineering Society Technological Invention Award in 2020, and Qiushi Outstanding Youth Achievement Transformation Award. in 2021.

Lin Xuechun has long been engaged in research on high power solid-state laser technology and application, and his research achievements have the characteristics of a full chain from laser physics, lasers sources, laser manufacturing processes to industrial applications.

# 青年创新奖获得者

# 彭 艳

彭艳，女，1982年6月出生于山东省临沂市。2009年毕业于中国科学院沈阳自动化研究所获工学博士学位。2009年至今在上海大学工作，任无人艇工程研究院、人工智能研究院研究员。2014—2017年先后任上海大学无人艇工程研究院执行院长、院长，2020年10月起任上海大学人工智能研究院执行院长，2021年8月起任上海市海洋人工智能协同创新中心主任。俄罗斯自然科学院外籍院士。

彭艳长期从事海洋无人艇研究，在海能海用能量收集、智能决策等方面作出一系列开创性研究工作，推动了我国智能无人艇技术和装备进程。

## 一、海洋无人系统基于环境动能自俘能科学问题重要突破

针对海上任务作业区域、时长严重受限于所携带的能源补给难、海能海用海洋环境动能自俘能能量密度极低等国际性难题带来的"探不久"问题，发现单位体积内磁通密度突变构建可极大提升功率密度，且上调频效应可极大提升压电叠堆机电转化效率，解决了高功率密度自俘能两个科学问题：①超低频无规则环境能量高效转化物理机理；②超低频环境动能与俘能器件高效耦合机制。所发现的单位体积内电磁突变现象所产生的能量密度是目前国际电磁自供能主流构型的47.4倍，实现5Hz超低频激励下最大功率密度40 mW/cm$^3$、平均功率密度12.53 mW/cm$^3$的自供能突破，实现了能量收集器从无法充电到直接给系统供能的转变，为利用海洋环境实现超长续航提供重要支撑。

## 二、海洋无人艇广域探测

针对海洋区域广、探测节点有限带来的海域"探不广"难题，突破最大能效增益海洋探测节点配置等关键技术，探测覆盖效率较国际主流算法提高20%、能量效率提高40%。

### 三、海洋动态弱小目标探测与识别

针对分类歧义性大造成置信度与定位精度不匹配的问题，提出定位－分类序列目标检测算法，降低了分类/置信度的歧义性，与国际主流相比精度提升了7.89%。针对跨层语义信息丢失带来分割精度低和深度特征学习黑箱效应的问题，提出语义结构约束和语义注意力提升模式，引导语义跨层保持，构建了感知模型中语义信息跨层传递的机制。所提出的方法在跨层传递过程中实现了对语义信息的保持，并可用张量进行解构；与国际主流算法相比，在保留了分割物体特征的同时，平均精度提升了5%。复杂海况下无人艇颠簸晃动严重，给空间约束混合模型的初始化带来挑战，基于此提出先验估计网络和空间约束混合模型的实时目标检测方法，实现了模型初始先验信息的实时动态更新，与基于概率图模型的语义分割模型相比，海天线和障碍物检测精度分别提升69.5%和23.9%。

### 四、创新性成果应用

研制"精海"15个系列无人艇，服务南海探测、桑吉轮重大撞船事故应急探测、极地科考和水下考古等；智能化水下考古探测到清代同治年间沉船，被评价为"树立了世界浑水水下考古技术的新标杆，是中国水下考古迈入世界一流水平的重要标志之一"；在我国小型无人艇竞优组队多次获得第一。研究成果获国家科技进步奖二等奖1项、国家技术发明奖二等奖1项、教育部科学技术进步奖一等奖1项等。

# Awardee of Youth Innovation Prize, Peng Yan

Peng Yan, female, was born in Linyi City of Shandong Province in June 1982. She received her Ph.D. degree from Shenyang Institute of Automation, Chinese Academy of Sciences. Since 2009, she has been working as a researcher at the Research Institute of Unmanned Surface Vehicles (USV) Engineering and the School of Artificial Intelligence at Shanghai University. From October 2014 to November 2017, she served as the Executive Dean of the Institute of USV at Shanghai University. Since December 2017, she has served as the Dean of the Institute of USV at Shanghai University. Since October 2020, she has served as the Executive Dean of the School of Artificial Intelligence at Shanghai University. Since August 2021, she has served as the Director of the Shanghai Ocean Artificial Intelligence Collaborative Innovation Center. She has won honorary titles such as foreign academician of the Russian Academy of Natural Sciences.

Yan Peng has been devoted to the research of marine USV for a long time, and has done a series of pioneering research work in the fields of marine energy collection and intelligent decision-making, which has promoted the process of our country's intelligent USV technology and equipment.

## 1. An important breakthrough in self-capturing energy for marine unmanned systems based on environmental kinetic energy

In view of the international problems that the operating area and duration of offshore missions are severely limited by the energy supplies, and the energy density of kinetic energy self-harvesting energy in the Marine environment is extremely low, those bring the problem of "short exploration". She found that the phenomenon that building the abrupt change of magnetic flux density dramatically increased volumetric power density, and frequency-up conversion improved the electromechanical conversion efficiency of piezoelectric stack significantly. The energy density reached 47.4 times that of the current international electromagnetic self-powered mainstream configuration due to the phenomenon of abrupt change of magnetic flux density. The maximum power density of 40 mW/cm$^3$ and the average power density of 12.53 mW/cm$^3$ under 5Hz ultra-low frequency excitation were achieved, and the transformation of the energy collector from being unable to charge to directly supplying energy to the system were completed. Those provide important support for realizing ultra-long endurance via the use of marine environment.

## 2. Wide-area environmental monitoring of marine USV

The wide ocean area and a limited number of monitoring nodes bring the problem of "limited monitoring". She has made breakthroughs in key technologies including ocean monitoring node configuration regarding maximum energy efficiency gain. The monitoring coverage efficiency was increased by 20%, and the energy efficiency by 40% compared with international mainstream algorithms.

## 3. Detection and recognition of weak and small targets in the ocean

To solve the problem of the mismatch between confidence and positioning accuracy caused by the large classification ambiguity, she proposed a positioning-classification sequence target detection algorithm, which reduces the classification/confidence degree ambiguity, and improved the accuracy by 7.89% compared with the international mainstream algorithms. In order to solve the problems of low segmentation accuracy and the black-box effect of deep feature learning caused by the loss of cross-layer semantic information, a semantic structure constraint and semantic attention enhancement model were proposed to guide semantic cross-layer retention, and a mechanism for cross-layer semantic information transfer in the perception model was constructed. The results show that the proposed method can preserve the semantic information in the process of cross-layer transmission and can be deconstructed by tensors. Compared with the international mainstream algorithm, the average accuracy is still improved by 5% while retaining the feature of the segmented object. The severe turbulence and shaking of the USV under complex sea conditions bring challenges to the initialization of the hybrid model with spatial constraints. Based on this fact, a real-time target detection method based on the prior estimation network and the hybrid model with spatial constraints was proposed, which realized the real-time dynamic update of the initial prior information of the model. Compared with the semantic segmentation model based on probability graph model, the accuracy of sea antenna and obstacle detection were increased by 69.5% and 23.9%, respectively.

**4. Application of innovative achievements**

The team has developed 15 series of "JingHai" USV, and served for South China Sea exploration, emergency detection of major ship collision accidents of the oil tanker Sanchi, polar research and underwater archaeology, etc.; intelligent underwater archaeology detected the sunken ship in the reign of Tongzhi of Qing, which is evaluated as "setting a new benchmark for underwater archaeological technology in muddy waters in the world, and one of the important symbols that China's underwater archaeology has entered the world's first-class level." In small-scale USV competitions, the team has won the first place many times. The research results have won the second prize from the National Science and Technology Progress Award, the second prize from the National Technology Invention Award, the first prize from the Ministry of Education Science and Technology Progress Award for one time, respectively.

# 青年创新奖获得者

# 杨 元 合

杨元合，1981年8月出生于青海省乐都县。2008年毕业于北京大学自然地理系获理学博士学位。2008—2012年先后赴美国俄克拉荷马大学和英国阿伯丁大学进行合作研究。2012年至今在中国科学院植物研究所工作，现任研究员、博士生导师，植被与环境变化国家重点实验室副主任。并在国际冻土碳评估工作组、中国植物学会、中国生态学学会、中国青藏高原研究会等多个学术组织任职。主持中国科学院先导项目、国家自然科学基金等项目，曾获科学探索奖、中国青年科技奖、美国生态学会亚洲分会青年科学家奖等荣誉。

杨元合主要从事全球变化生态学和草地生态学研究，近年来在土壤与全球变化、生态系统碳-氮交互作用等方面取得重要进展。

解析了冻土碳循环对气候变暖的响应机制，相关结果促进了对极端环境下碳循环特征的认识。部分成果发表在 *Science Advances*、*Nature Geoscience*、*Nature Communications*，被 *Nature Asia* 选为 Research Highlight，并被 Faculty Opinions 推荐，被 *Global Change Biology* 专文评述。

阐明了土壤有机碳动态及其调控机制，相关结果为预测气候变暖背景下的土壤碳动态以及碳循环与气候变暖之间的反馈关系奠定了理论基础。部分成果发表在 *Science Advances*、*Nature Communications*、*Ecology Letters*。入选 *Ecology Letters* 封面文章以及 *Nature Communications* 杂志 2019 年度最受关注的 50 篇地球科学领域文章，被 *Nature Climate Change* 选为 Research Highlight，并被 Faculty1000 多次推荐。

揭示了生态系统碳-氮循环间的交互作用，相关结果为发展碳氮耦合模型提供了理论依据。部分成果发表在 *Nature Communications*、*Ecology*、*Global Change Biology*，并被写入美国科学院院士主编的教科书，同时入选 *Global Change Biology* 封面文章。

# Awardee of Youth Innovation Prize, Yang Yuanhe

Yang Yuanhe was born in Ledu County of Qinghai Province in August 1981. 2008, PhD, Peking University, P. R. China. 2008–2012, Postdoctoral Research Fellow, University of Oklahoma, USA and Honorary Research Fellow, University of Aberdeen, UK; 2012–present, Principle Investigator, PhD supervisor, 2016–present, Deputy Director of State Key Laboratory of Vegetation and Environmental Change. He received several prestigious awards such as Explorer prize, China Youth Science and Technology Award, Early-career Ecologist Award by Ecological Society of America-Asian Ecology Section. He has served in many academic organizations such as The IPA Permafrost and Carbon Budgets Interest Group, Botanical Society of China, Ecological Society of China, The China Society on the Tibetan Plateau, and presided over Strategic Priority Research Program of Chinese Academy of Sciences and National Natural Science Foundation of China.

Prof. Yuanhe Yang is mainly engaged in the research of global change ecology and grassland ecology. In recent years, he has made considerable progress in the research of soil and global change, terrestrial carbon-nitrogen interactions.

He analyzed response patterns and potential mechanisms of permafrost carbon cycle to global warming, and the relevant results promoted the understanding of the characteristics of carbon cycle in extreme environment. Some research achievements have been published in international journals such as *Science Advances*, *Nature Geoscience*, *Nature Communications*. Also, these achievements were selected as Research Highlight by *Nature Asia*, recommended by Faculty Opinions, and commented by *Global Change Biology*.

He elucidated soil organic carbon dynamics and its regulatory mechanisms. These findings lay a theoretical foundation for accurately predicting soil carbon dynamics and its feedback to climate warming, which have been published in international journals such as *Science Advances*, *Nature Communications*, *Ecology Letters*, and selected as the cover story of *Ecology Letters*, selected as the most concerned 50 geoscience papers of *Nature Communications* in 2019, chosen as Research Highlight by *Nature Climate Change*, received multiple recommendations by Faculty1000.

He revealed the interactions between carbon and nitrogen cycle in terrestrial ecosystems, which provided theoretical underpinnings for the development of carbon – nitrogen coupling model. Some representative results have been published in *Nature Communications*, *Ecology* and *Global Change Biology*. Selected publications were written into two textbooks edited by academicians of the American Academy of Sciences and chosen as the cover story of *Global Change Biology*.

# 青年创新奖获得者

# 詹祥江

詹祥江，1979年4月出生于河南省光山县。2006年博士毕业于中国科学院动物研究所，2008年起在英国Cardiff大学进行博士后研究。2014年回国后在中国科学院动物所工作，组建种群和进化遗传学研究组，并先后担任中英生物复杂性研究联合实验室主任、所长助理、副所长，兼任英国皇家学会"牛顿高级学者"、中华人民共和国濒危物种科学委员会委员等。

詹祥江主要从事动物学与进化生物学研究，在鸟类迁徙、飞行和极端环境适应等领域取得了系列原创性成果，入选2021年度中国科学十大进展、2021年度中国生命科学十大进展。

### 一、揭示鸟类迁徙路线的主要成因及长距离迁徙的关键基因

创新性地交叉整合遥感卫星追踪、基因组学、神经生物学等多学科研究手段，从行为、进化、遗传、生态及气候变化等多维度揭示了气候变化是鸟类迁徙路线和迁徙方向形成的主要原因，首次发现了鸟类长距离迁徙的关键基因 *ADCY8*。该工作入选2021年度中国生命科学十大进展和2021年度中国科学十大进展。

### 二、揭示动物高原适应性进化的一系列遗传学机制

首次发现北极近缘物种对于青藏高原动物适应性进化的遗传贡献，并系统性地解析了高原动物适应低温、低氧、强UV胁迫的遗传机制。阐明了猎隼快速拓殖青藏高原的过程，发现了由北极姊妹种矛隼渗入的2个低温适应关键基因 *SCMH1* 和 *SCARB1*，并揭示了非编码区突变在低氧、强UV适应相关基因表达调控中的重要作用，为动物适应高原极端生境提供了新的见解。在青藏高原野生动物（猎隼）研究中，建立了种群转录组学的研究方法，揭示了RNA转录在高原低氧反应中的重要作用，并证实DNA多态性与RNA

表达多样性在应对压力上表现出协同效应；揭示了转录本多样性产生的新机制，发现表达量越高的基因在转录过程中倾向于产生更多的体细胞突变，从而产生更多的剪切位点和新的转录本。在对各自进化出相似高原适应特性的四种高原哺乳动物的研究中，发现它们的基因组上存在一系列平行进化的基因，功能实验证实单个位点的突变能够引起青藏高原低氧适应表型的趋同；发现驯化动物羊驼的 *FGF5/ANTXR2/C4orf22* 基因在其对安第斯高原环境的低氧适应性进化中起重要作用，其 *PRDM8* 基因在低氧适应过程中承担着与低氧诱导因子相类似的功能。

### 三、首次阐明多种现生鸟类飞行能力丢失的共同遗传基础

基于 48 种鸟类全基因组比较，发现 *ATGL* 和 *ACOT7* 的基因突变导致飞行能力退化鸟种的主要能量来源由脂肪转变为碳水化合物，从而能更快速地产生能量，以适应其独特的运动方式（奔跑或短时间爆发性飞行）。该发现改变了"鸟类飞行能力退化是由于形态学变异，特别是翅膀变短"这一自达尔文时代以来的流行观点。

### 四、发表世界首例猛禽基因组

通过测定游隼和猎隼的基因组，发现与其他鸟类相比，隼类基因组中的重复 DNA、大片段重复、特有的插入缺失以及物种特有基因都更少；且隼类基因组具有显著的快速进化，这为隼类进化为成功的捕食者奠定了遗传基础。

# Awardee of Youth Innovation Prize, Zhan Xiangjiang

Zhan Xiangjiang was born in Guangshan County of Henan Province in April 1979. He got his PhD degree from the Institute of Zoology, Chinese Academy of Sciences (CAS) in 2006. He had worked at Cardiff University, UK as a research associate and lecturer since 2008. After returning to China in 2014, he established his own research team and served as the director of the CU-IoZ Joint Laboratory for Biocomplexity Research at the Institute of Zoology, CAS. He served as Assistant Director and now Deputy Director of Institute of Zoology, CAS. He is a member of the Endangered Species Scientific Committee of the People's Republic of China. He focuses on zoology and evolutionary biology, and has made a series of achievements in bird migration, flight and adaptation to extreme environments, one of which has been selected as "Top 10 Scientific Advances of 2021, China" and "2021 Top 10 Scientific Advances in Life Sciences of China".

**1. Decoding spatio-temporal dynamics of bird migration routes and the genetics basis of long-distance migration**

This work is the first study elucidating the main factors shaping the Arctic migration routes and identifying the key genes which may play an important role in determining the migration route length. It highlights the significance of integration of satellite telemetry, NGS genome sequencing and functional genomics with classical analyses (species distribution modeling and paleo vegetation reconstruction) in untangling an intriguing scientific question (formation and maintenance of migration route). The study was selected as "Top 10 Scientific Advances of 2021, China" and "2021 Top 10 Scientific Advances in Life Sciences of China", respectively.

## 2. Revealing genetic mechanisms underlying adaptations of highland animals

His research team found key roles of gene flow from Arctic relatives in hypothermia adaptation, and *cis*-regulatory elements in hypoxic response and ultraviolet (UV) protection of saker falcons (*Falco cherrug*) living on the Qinghai-Tibetan Plateau (QTP). They described how a predatory bird species had rapidly conquered the QTP, identifying two key genes, *SCMH1* and *SCARB1*, for cold adaptation from Arctic introgression, and highlighted non-coding genomic mutations on the regulation of hypoxia and UV resistance relevant genes. This study provides new insights into adaptation or response of animals to the extreme environmental pressures associated with high altitude on the QTP.

His research team applied population transcriptome approaches to the study of QTP adaptation or response in saker falcons for the first time, resulting in findings of an important role of RNA transcription in response to hypoxia and hypothermia, and exemplified the synergistic responses of DNA polymorphism and RNA expression diversity in coping with common stresses. Moreover, a new mechanism of transcription diversity was revealed. They found that alternative splicing occurs more frequently, yielding more isoforms, in highly expressed genes. These isoforms were produced mainly by alternative use of *de novo* splice sites generated by transcription-associated mutation, not by the RNA editing mechanism normally invoked. They also found that high expression of genes increases mutation frequencies during transcription, especially on non-transcribed DNA strands. After DNA replication, transcribed strands inherit these somatic mutations, creating *de novo* splice sites and generating multiple distinct isoforms in the cell clone.

In their collaboration study on mammals living on the QTP, the team found a series of parallel evolution genes in the genomes of four species, plateau pika (*Ochotona curzoniae*), plateau zokor (*Myospalax baileyi*), yak (*Bos grunniens*) and Tibetan antelope (*Pantholops hodgsonii*), that have developed similar plateau adaptation traits. They found and confirmed that a single mutation can lead to phenotypic convergence for hypoxia adaptation on the QTP by both *in vitro* and *in vivo* experiments. In another study on mammals living in the Andes, they found that genomic signatures of domestication in the alpaca (*Vicugna pacos*) feature hypoxic adaptation traits. *FGF5*, *ANTXR2* and *C4orf22* genes play key roles in regulating hypoxia stress, while *PRDM8* is a novel gene associated with hypoxic adaptation, the expression of which may be mirrored by decreased expression of *SOX6* and *HIF1α*.

### 3. Elucidating the common genetic basis of flight loss in modern birds

In an analysis of 295 million nucleotides from 48 bird genomes, his research team identified two convergent sites causing amino acid changes in ATGL$^{Ser321Gly}$ and ACOT7$^{Ala197Val}$ in flight-degenerate birds, which have not previously been implicated in loss of flight. These findings suggest that physiological convergence plays an important role in flight degeneration, while anatomical convergence, especially wing reduction often invoked, may not.

### 4. Publishing the world's first raptor genome

His research team had sequenced the genomes of peregrine and saker falcon and presented parallel, genome-wide evidence for evolutionary innovation and selection for a predatory lifestyle. Analysis of 8,424 orthologs in the falcons, chicken, zebra finch and turkey identified consistent evidence for genome-wide rapid evolution in these raptors. SNP-based inference showed contrasting recent demographic trajectories for the two falcon species, and gene-based analysis highlighted falcon-specific evolutionary novelties for beak development and olfaction and specifically for homeostasis-related genes in the arid environment-adapted saker.

# 区域创新奖获得者

# 方 创 琳

方创琳，1966 年 9 月出生于甘肃省庆阳市。1998 年毕业于中国科学院地理研究所获理学博士学位。1998—2000 年在北京大学城市与环境学系博士后流动站工作。2000 年 6 月至今在中国科学院地理科学与资源研究所工作。先后任新疆大学教育部长江学者特聘教授、丝绸之路经济带城乡发展研究院院长、中国科学院区域可持续发展分析与模拟重点实验室副主任、中国科学院地理资源所区域与城市规划研究中心主任、中国科学院大学教授、北京师范大学教授等。自然资源部全国国土空间规划编制专家，住房城乡建设部人居环境科技专委会委员。中国城市群研究基地联盟理事长，中国区域科学协会副理事长，中国地理学会人文地理专业委员会主任，中国城市经济学会城市群都市圈专业委员会主任。国际欧亚科学院院士。

方创琳主要从事城市地理学与城市发展的系统研究，在城镇化与生态环境耦合机理、城市群形成发育规律及格局、城市空间优化与决策支持、美丽中国建设评估等方面作出了一系列开创性工作。

## 一、创建城镇化与生态环境耦合理论及耦合器调控方法

在揭示城镇化与生态环境交互胁迫关系及拐点这一科学难题中，方创琳通过构建系统动力学模型验证发现，西方发达国家城市化发展的三阶段规律无法解决中国城镇化面临的现实问题，进而将 1975 年美国 Northam 提出的城镇化 S 形曲线三阶段修正为四阶段（初期为城镇化率小于 30%、成长期为城镇化率达 30%～60%、成熟期为城镇化率达 60%～80%、顶级期为城镇化率达 80% 以上），实现了与经济增长与发展四阶段的一一对应，为我国城镇化与工业化同步发展提供了科学依据；创建耦合圈理论，发现城镇化与生态环境之间存在近远程耦合关系，首次引入库兹涅茨曲线揭示了二者耦合机理是由幂函数和指数函数叠加成的双指数曲线，建立了动态耦合度模型并找到耦合拐点，算出

中国城镇化与生态环境耦合拐点为城镇化率达到47.1%，为我国城镇化高质量发展和生态环境高水平保护提供了科学依据。在此基础上，进一步提出了由11个自然人文要素和200个变量构成的耦合器调控方法，实现了城市人地系统研究由近程到近远程、由定性到定量的转变。成果应用于《首都水源涵养功能区和生态环境支撑区建设方案》研制并提出伞形保护格局，由国家发改委向27个部委发文实施。

### 二、揭示城市群形成发育机理、有机成长规律与空间组织格局

研发了城市群空间范围精准识别方法，首次将1957年J. Gottman提出的城市群识别5大定性标准拓展为10大定量标准，新增了全球化、文化等质量标准；建立城市群发育程度、空间联系强度模型，揭示了其形成发育的阶段性规律、多中心组合规律和联合爬升规律，为培育不同发育程度的城市群提供理论支撑；采用空间功能分区方法划定了与生态环境格局相匹配的由5个国家级、9个区域级和6个地区级城市群组成的中国城市群三级配置格局，填补了全球城市群无分类的国际空白，成果被《国家"十三五"规划纲要》《全国国土空间规划纲要2020—2035》采用，推动城市群成为国家新型城镇化的空间主体。成果被联合国大会确定的世界城市日发布并纳入2019年成果集萃，并被美国科学促进会转载。

### 三、研制城市空间格局优化决策支持系统并得到广泛应用

在对西方城市发展机理综述的基础上，结合中国特色分析了城市规模由小—中—大—特大—超大演化的五级拓展过程与演化机理，创建了城市空间格局均衡优化理论，研发了城市空间格局多层级优化决策支持系统方法，诊断出中国城市空间格局合理度为78.3%，优化生成了由770个城市构成的中国城市规模金字塔格局，支撑国务院发文调整了城市规模标准，城市规模划分五级方案被国务院〔2014〕51号文件全部采用。参与完成联合国人居署《国际城市与区域规划准则》与《新城市议程》，成为联合国首次就该领域发布的文件。

先后获第二届全国创新争先奖、国家哲学社会科学优秀成果最高奖、教育部科技进步奖一等奖等省部级科技进步奖一等奖11项、二等奖5项。

# Awardee of Region Innovation Prize, Fang Chuanglin

Fang Chuanglin was born in Qingyang City of Gansu Province in September 1966, received his Ph.D. degree from the Institute of Geographic Sciences and Natural Resources Research, Chinese Academy of Sciences (CAS) in 1998. He then conducted his post-doctoral research from June 1998 to June 2000 in the Department of Urban and Environmental Sciences, Peking

University. Since June 2000, he has been working at the Institute of Geographic Sciences and Natural Resources Research, CAS. He occupies various posts in academia, including Cheung Kong Scholar Chair Professor of Xinjiang University awarded by the Ministry of Education of the People's Republic of China, director of the Institute of Urban and Rural Development of the Silk Road Economic Belt, associate director of the Key Laboratory of Regional Sustainable Development Modeling, CAS, director of the Center for Regional and Urban Planning and Design Research of Geographic Sciences and Natural Resources Research, CAS, professor of the University of Chinese Academy of Sciences (UCAS), professor of Beijing Normal University, expert in the preparation of National Spatial Planning of the Ministry of Natural Resources of the People's Republic of China, member of the Habitat Science and Technology Special Committee of the Ministry of Housing and Urban-Rural Development of the People's Republic of China, chairman of the China Urban Cluster Research Base Alliance, vice chairman of the Regional Science Association of China, director of the Human Geography Specialty Committee of the Geographical Society of China, director of the Urban agglomeration Metropolitan Area Professional Committee of the China Society of Urban Economy, academician of International Eurasian Academy of Sciences (IEAS).

Chuanglin Fang, with well-established expertise in the domain of urban geography and urban development, has made a series of pioneering research works on the coupling mechanism between urbanization and ecological environment, the formation and development pattern of urban agglomerations, the decision-support of urban spatial pattern optimization, and the progress assessment of Beautiful China program. His main scientific and technological achievements are as follows. He established the coupling coil theory and coupler control method of urbanization and eco-environment. He revealed the formation and development mechanisms, the laws of organic growth, and spatial organization patterns of urban agglomerations. He also developed a decision-support system for optimizing urban spatial patterns, which has been widely referenced.

Chuanglin Fang has won 11 first prizes and 5 second prizes for scientific and technological progress at the provincial and ministerial levels, including the Second National Innovation Award, the National Top Prize for Outstanding Achievements in Philosophy and Social Sciences, and the First Prize of Science and Technology Progress of the Ministry of Education.

# 区域创新奖获得者

# 李　星

李星，1964年5月出生。1999年获德国柏林自由大学应用数学专业博士学位。2002年在英国巴斯大学担任皇家学会高级访问学者，2008年在美国哈佛大学担任高级研究学者。历任宁夏大学数学系主任、宁夏大学副校长、宁夏师范学院院长、宁夏师范学院党委书记等职务，现任宁夏大学党委书记。兼任第十一届中国数学会副理事长，首届中国数学会女数学家委员会和西部数学发展工作委员会主任，第六、七届教育部科技委数理学部委员，高等学校数学类教学指导委员会委员等。先后获"全国五一劳动奖章"，全国先进工作者（全国劳模）、全国高等学校优秀骨干教师、全国优秀科技工作者等荣誉称号。

李星主要研究复分析、积分法方程理论及其应用，在双周期弹性数学理论、多场耦合材料及结构的接触和断裂力学分析等方面作出了一系列开创性工作。

## 一、解析函数边值理论及双（准）周期弹性数学理论

首次提出并求解了一类解析函数边值逆问题，形成了新的研究方向；构造了既能分出多值部分又能保证双准周期性的复应力函数，引入满足特定要求的双周期椭圆函数进行双准周期核的Sherman变换，实现了双周期弹性断裂问题的双准周期核奇异积分方程构造求解；严格证明了当应力是双周期分布时，位移是双准周期分布的，澄清了长期以来同行专家的误区；开拓运用解析函数边值问题和奇异积分方程的理论，成功获得几类全平面应变问题的解析解，尤其是借助解析函数边值理论十分简明地给出了几类超奇异积分方程的解析解。相关研究成果获宁夏科技进步奖二等奖2项。

## 二、准晶、功能梯度、磁电、热电等多场耦合材料的接触力学

李星等在恒温、温变环境下的无摩擦、滑动摩擦接触条件下，建立和求解了多种典

型压头下材料的周期、轴对称、三维滑动摩擦热接触以及退让等一系列接触力学模型，对于特殊接触力学问题获得了载荷 – 位移曲线的解析表达式；针对接触力学的积分方程分析方法，采用多项式、样条函数、小波等逼近，结合离散卷积快速傅里叶变换和共轭梯度等方法，发展了超奇异积分方程组的收敛算法、时域内逆 Laplace 变化算法和非线性退让接触迭代算法；求解热、磁、电、弹多场耦合下的压痕特征，分析了各物理场对压痕行为的贡献，相关成果推动了多场耦合材料压痕检测技术的理论基础。相关研究成果获宁夏科技进步奖二等奖 1 项。

### 三、压电、准晶、铌铍复合材料等热点材料的断裂力学

给出了压电、准晶、铌铍复合材料等热点材料断裂力学问题的数学提法，求解了非均匀复合材料静态和动态载荷下的断裂力学问题，特别是在单周期和双周期的孔洞、裂纹群对功能材料断裂性能影响的研究方面形成特色；开展裂尖区域多物理场的定量分析，分析了材料在多场耦合作用下的多尺度断裂力学行为和损伤演化机制，为材料断裂失效机理和结构服役安全评价提供了理论支撑；同时针对复连通域材料的多场耦合问题的复变函数解法开展理论研究，拓宽了复变函数理论的应用范围。相关研究成果获宁夏科技进步奖二等奖 1 项。

# Awardee of Region Innovation Prize, Li Xing

Li Xing was born in May 1964. In 1999, he was awarded the degree of PhD in Applied Mathematics from the Free University of Berlin, Germany. Currently he is secretary of the party committee of Ningxia University, serving concurrently as associated editor of China Mathematical Abstract, vice-chairman of Ningxia Hui Autonomous Region Science Association, president of Ningxia Council of Mathematics. His most outstanding scientific contributions include the following three aspects.

He initiated new research orientation by proposing and solving inverse boundary value problems for analytic functions. His research claims that the displacement is bi-quasi-periodically distributed when stress is in double periodic array. That clarifies the prolonged incorrect recognition of the issue among experts in this field. His monograph Theory of Double Period Elastic Fracture and other achievements were highly recognized by Professor Heinrich Begehr, Professor Guochun Wen and other renowned mathematicians at home and abroad. They reviewed and commented his studies as being "innovative work" and "significant contribution made by a Chinese scholar".

He established and solved a series of contact mechanics models of periodic, three-dimensional sliding friction thermal contact and receding contact under various typical indenters.

All the achievements relevant reinforced the theoretical basis underpinning the indentation detection technology for the multi-field coupling materials.

He examined and solved the fracture mechanics problems of heterogeneous composites under static and dynamic loads in piezoelectric, quasicrystal, and other advanced materials. He performed quantitative analysis of multiple physical fields in the crack field and exploited the multi-scale fracture mechanical behavior and damage evolution mechanism of materials under the coupling action of multiple fields, providing theoretical basis for fracture failure mechanism of materials and safety evaluation of structures in service.

Li Xing was selected as both tier 1 and tier 2 candidates of the first National Talents Project, and awarded Leading Talent of National Special Support Program for High-Level Talents. Apart from the National Labor Medal, he has been conferred dozens of honorary tiles, including National Outstanding Worker, National Excellent Teacher of Institutions of Higher Education and National Excellent Worker in Science and Technology.

# 区域创新奖获得者

# 欧 珠

欧珠，1961年6月出生。1986年毕业于西藏大学数理系数学专业并留校任教，2000年获挪威卑尔根大学计算机软件与理论专业硕士学位。2000年1月回国后先后任西藏大学计算机科学系副主任、计算机科学系主任、工学院筹备组副组长、工学院院长、藏文信息技术研究中心主任（兼）。其间，2003年7月—2004年7月在中国科学院软件研究所挂职。2012年7月任西藏大学党委委员、副校长。2016年8月—2021年9月历任西藏民族大学党委副书记、副校长，党委书记、副校长。2021年10月至今任西藏自治区政协教科卫体专委会副主任。先后担任全国术语标准化技术委员会少数民族语分会藏语工作委员会委员、中国计算机学会专业委员会委员、中文信息学会第七届理事会常务理事等社会职务。其科研成果荣获国家科技进步奖二等奖、中国标准创新贡献奖一等奖、钱伟长中文信息处理科学技术三等奖等。

欧珠长期从事少数民族信息技术研究，在藏文信息处理、藏语人工智能和大数据应用等教学科研方面作出了一系列开创性工作。

## 一、建立藏文信息处理基础标准

欧珠及其团队主持编制了9项藏文信息技术国家标准，解决了藏语言文字的字、音、形、义等信息处理核心技术，为藏文信息处理技术建基立标，填补了多项国内外技术空白，同时有效促进了国际软件企业产品对藏文的支持。其中，《GB/T 20542—2006 信息技术 藏文编码字符集 扩充集A》获得中国标准创新贡献奖一等奖。

## 二、提速藏文信息技术工程

欧珠先后突破藏文输入技术、藏文办公系统、藏文操作系统、藏文文字识别技术等多项核心技术，构建了藏文信息处理理论体系，有力维护了我国藏语言文字主权，有效提升了我国藏族地区信息化水平。"藏文软件研发与推广应用"项目荣获国家科学技术进步奖二等奖、西藏自治区科学技术奖一等奖。

### 三、拓荒藏语人工智能和大数据应用领域

欧珠及其团队在藏语人工智能和大数据应用领域建立了庞大而完善的藏语语言资源库，建设了全智能能力平台，提出了基于神经网络的深度学习藏语智能语音技术完整解决方案。在藏语语音识别、藏语语音合成、藏汉文本翻译、藏文文字识别、藏文手写识别、藏语自然语言理解等方面实现了技术突破，形成了覆盖智能语音、智能语义、智能视觉和大数据分析四个方面的核心技术，构建了由资源层、技术层、平台层、应用层全覆盖的人工智能产品生态体系，研发了藏语智能输入法（TIIM）、藏语语音识别系统（TASR）、藏语语音合成系统（TTTS）、藏汉文本翻译系统（MT）、藏文光字符识别系统（TOCR）、藏文手写识别（THWR）以及集成以上技术的面向行业的慧言一体机、国家通用语言文字智能学习系统、基于地理信息平台的藏语方言数据库等产品。

# Awardee of Region Innovation Prize, Ngodrup

Ngodrup was born in June 1961. After graduating from Tibet University with a major in mathematics in 1986, he took up the position as a teacher in the same university. He pursued postgraduate studies at University of Bergen in Norway, majoring Computer Software and Theory and received a master degree of science. He returned to Tibet University in January 2000 and served, successively, as Deputy Director in the Department of Computer Science, Director in the Department of Computer Science, Deputy Chief of Preparatory Group in the Department of Engineering, Dean of the Department of Engineering, Director (concurrently) of Tibetan Information Technology Research Center. During this time, he assumed a temporary post in the Institute for Software Research of Chinese Academy of Sciences between July 2003 and July 2004. In July 2012, he served as the member of the party committee and Vice-Principal in Tibet University. From August 2016 to September 2021, he served first as Deputy Secretary of CPC as well as Vice-Principal, and later as Secretary of CPC as well as Vice-Principal in Xizang Minzu University. Since October 2021, he served as Deputy Director of Education, Science, Health and Sports Committee of Tibet Autonomous Region's political consultative conference. He held a number of social positions, including member of the Tibetan Language Working Committee, Ethnic Minority Language Branch, National Technical Committee for Terminology Standardization; member of Professional Committee, China Computer Society; standing member of 7th council of Chinese Information Society. He has also received multiple awards, including second prize for National Award of Science and Technology Progress, first prize for Innovation Contribution Award of Chinese Standard, third prize for Qian Weichang Science and Technology Award in Chinese information processing, to name just a few.

Ngodrup has been committed to the study of information technology for ethnic minorities and has pushed back the frontier of a series of research and teaching, from Tibetan language information processing and Tibetan language artificial intelligence to big data application.

### 1. Establish the basic standard for Tibetan language information processing

Ngodrup, together with his team, compiled nine national standards for Tibetan language information technology. These standards provided core techniques needed to process the characters, phonetics, morphology and semantics of Tibetan language, established criterion for Tibetan language information processing technology, and filled in multiple domestic and international technical gaps. Among those achievements, 《Information technology—Tibetan coded character set—Extension A ( GB/T 20542-2006 )》 won the first prize for Innovation Contribution Award of Chinese Standard.

### 2. Speed up the Tibetan language information technology projects

Breakthroughs have been made in multiple core technologies, including Tibetan input technique, Tibetan office system, Tibetan operation system, Tibetan language recognition technique, etc. These technologies have not only allowed China to uphold its sovereignty on Tibetan language and Tibetan language information processing, created theoretical system for Tibetan language information processing, but also effectively improved informatization in the Tibetan region. 《Research and Application of Tibetan Software》 has won second prize of National Science and Technology Progress Award, as well as first prize of Science and Technology Award in Tibet Autonomous Region.

### 3. Pioneer Tibetan language AI and big data application

Technical breakthroughs have been made in Tibetan speech recognition and synthesis, Tibetan-Chinese bilingualism Machine translation, Tibetan character and handwriting recognition, Tibetan natural language comprehension, etc. The team have developed core technologies in intelligent speech, semantics and vision as well as big data analysis, and constructed an AI product ecological system covering resources, techniques, platforms and application. Products developed by the team include TIIM, TASR, TTTS, MT, TOCR and THWR, as well as products like All-in-One Multifunctional Intelligent Machine, Intelligent learning system of standard spoken and written Chinese language and Tibetan Dialect Database Based on Geographic Information Platform. All those above-mentioned research results have been transformed into products of Tibetan intelligent speech information technology in real practice, and benefited people of different ethnic groups.

# 区域创新奖获得者

# 赵永祥

赵永祥，1965年9月出生于湖北省石首市。1999年获中南大学湘雅医学院心胸外科博士学位。1999—2000年在德国雷根斯堡大学血液肿瘤研究所进行博士后研究。2000—2003年在哈佛大学Dana-Farber肿瘤研究所从事博士后研究。2003—2007年任中南大学湘雅三医院国家卫生部移植医学工程技术中心教授/主任医师。2007—2010年任厦门大学附属中山医院心胸外科兼职教授/主任医师。2009年至今任广西医科大学党委常委、副校长，国家生物靶向诊治国际联合研究中心主任。国际欧亚科学院院士。全国科技领军人才联盟副理事长，中国生物医药整合联盟常务副理事长，中国医药生物技术协会基因编辑分会理事长，中国抗癌协会合成生物医药专业委员会主任。

赵永祥长期从事生物反应器靶向诊治肿瘤研究，取得了一系列开创性成果。

创建国际首个基因编辑原发并转移肝癌猴模型，为深入研究肝癌等恶性肿瘤发病机制、探索有效靶向诊治新技术、新药物研发提供了优良的技术平台。成果入选"2021年中国医药生物技术十大进展"。

运用肝癌猴模型，成功开发出全身静脉注射体液免疫过敏反应高效溶瘤病毒，临床多中心证实具有突破性疗效，此方向已成为国际上该领域的重要研究分支；研发出静脉注射细胞免疫过敏反应癌/DC高效融合细胞疫苗，正在开展Ⅱ期临床试验；创建了触发式生物靶向反应器诊断AFP阴性早期肝癌试剂盒，已检测1000多例恶性肿瘤患者，显著提高了AFP阴性肝癌检出率。相关成果获教育部自然科学奖一等奖、中国专利优秀奖。

运用肝癌猴模型，在国际上首次发现了还原型氧化石墨烯的超强催化特性，据此成功研制了世界首个肿瘤原位溶瘤反应器，解决了目前纳米制剂体内靶向传送效率低、疗效不理想的关键技术瓶颈，为恶性肿瘤的有效防治提供了新策略。研究处于原位溶瘤研究领域前沿。

# Awardee of Region Innovation Prize, Zhao Yongxiang

Zhao Yongxiang was born in Shishou City of Hubei Province in September 1965. In 1988, he graduated from Xiangya Medical College of Central South University with a Doctor's degree in cardiothoracic surgery. From 1999 to 2000, he was supported by DAAD scholarship for postdoctoral research at the Institute of Hematologic Oncology, University of Regensburg, Germany. He was a postdoctoral fellow at the Dana-Farber Cancer Institute at Harvard University from 2000 to 2003. From 2003 to 2007, he was a professor/chief physician at the Engineering and Technology Center of Transplant Medicine, Ministry of Health, the Third Xiangya Hospital, Central South University. From 2007 to 2010, he was an adjunct professor/chief physician of cardiothoracic Surgery Department, Zhongshan Hospital of Xiamen University. Since 2009, he has been a member of the Standing Committee of the Party Committee and Vice President of Guangxi Medical University, and director of the National International Joint Research Center for Biological Targeted Diagnosis and Therapy.

He is also a Academician of International Eurasian Academy of Sciences, Vice-Chairman of the National Alliance of Leading Scientific and Technological Talents, Executive Vice chairman of the Chinese Biomedical Integration Alliance, chairman of the Gene Editing Branch of the Chinese Medical Biotechnology Association, the director of the Synthetic Biomedical Committee of the Chinese Anti-Cancer Association.

Yongxiang Zhao has been engaged in the targeted diagnosis and therapy for tumor using bioreactor for a long time, and has made a series of pioneering achievements. The world's first gene-edited monkey model of primary and metastatic liver cancer was selected as one of the "Top 10 Advances in Chinese Medical Biotechnology in 2021" as a breakthrough in key technologies, providing an excellent technical platform for in-depth research on the pathogenesis of liver cancer and other malignant tumors, exploration of new effective targeted diagnosis and treatment technologies, and research and development of new drugs.

Using this model, we have successfully developed the highly effective oncolytic virus of systemic intravenous humoral immune hypersensitivity reaction, which has been proved to have a breakthrough effect in clinical multi-centers. This direction has become an important branch of research in this field internationally. We also have developed the highly effective fusion cell vaccine of intravenous cell immune allergic reaction cancer /DC, and are carrying out phase II clinical trials. Moreover, the triggered biological targeting reactor for the diagnosis of AFP negative early liver cancer kit was created, which detected more than 1000 cases of malignant tumor patients, significantly improving the detection rate of AFP negative liver cancer. These achievements won the first prize of Natural science of the Ministry of Education and the China Patent Excellence Award.

Using the monkey model of liver cancer, the super-powerful catalytic properties of reduced graphene oxide had been discovered for the first time in the world, and the world's first tumor in situ oncolysis reactor had been successfully developed, which solve the key technical bottlenecks of the low efficiency and unsatisfactory efficacy of the targeted delivery of nano-agents in vivo, and provides a new strategy for the effective prevention and treatment of malignant tumors.

# 产业创新奖获得者

# 丁建宁

丁建宁，1966年3月出生于江苏省丹徒。2001年获清华大学工学博士学位。1991—2002年在江苏大学（原江苏工学院、江苏理工大学）工作，2002—2003年在香港城市大学做Research Fellow，2003—2007年任江苏大学科学研究院常务副院长，2007—2018年任常州大学副校长、江苏省光伏科学与工程协同创新中心主任，2018年10月—2022年1月任江苏大学副校长、智能柔性机械电子研究院院长，2022年1月至今任扬州大学校长、碳中和技术研究院院长。兼任中国微米纳米技术学会常务理事，中国仪器仪表学会微纳器件与系统分会副理事长，中国宇航学会空间太阳能电站专业委员会副主任委员，中国机械工程学会摩擦学分会常务委员等职。中国微米纳米技术学会会士。

丁建宁从事微纳制造、新能源制造技术及装备、智能柔性机械电子研究，在光伏材料绿色制造和光伏电池产业化制造技术及装备等方面作出了一系列开创性研究工作。

**一、突破太阳能电池多晶硅材料冷氢化制造工艺装备，实现清洁、低能耗生产**

研制出多晶硅冷氢化生产核心专用加热合成反应器成套工艺装备，为我国光伏产业发展奠定基础。成果实施产业化，应用于我国首套多晶硅冷氢化工业装置，改变了我国多晶硅生产技术落后、高能耗、高污染状况，进入世界先进水平。获2012年国家科技进步奖二等奖。

**二、突破高效低成本晶硅太阳能电池片制造技术与装备，建成国际领先的制造产线**

发明易钝化的表面微纳结构及其制造技术，创制催化刻蚀装备，实现低成本制造和宽光谱高效光吸收；发明电池片表界面掺杂、钝化制造技术，实现载流子高效传输；发明双层栅线叠加浮金属化结构和高精度全自动二次丝网印刷技术，实现载流子高效收集。使电池量产效率从18%提高至23.8%以上，组件价格下降94%，发电成本低于煤电；成果实施产业化,创电池效率和组件输出功率世界纪录,助推光伏电力平价上网。相关成果获 2020 年国家技术发明奖二等奖、2018 年中国专利银奖。

**三、突破超薄柔性电池组件技术及制造装备,拓展光伏发电系统应用**

提出多场耦合射流换热理论,突破厚度 1.1～2mm 超薄玻璃物理钢化技术及装备,建立国际首条量产线,组件世界最薄(4mm)。成果实施产业化,全球市场占有率达 60%。针对空间太阳电站,提出解决反渗透膜选择性和渗透性相互制约的途径,发明零下 80℃超低温储能电池制造技术,首创可拉伸柔性电池电极材料;首创电化学人工肌肉,可为空间电站提供轻质、柔性的驱动机构。

# Awardee of Industrial Innovation Prize, Ding Jianning

Ding Jianning was born in Dantu District of Jiangsu Province in March 1966. He received his Ph.D. degree in engineering from the Department of Precision Instruments and Mechanics, Tsinghua University in 2001. From 1991 to 2002, Ding worked at Jiangsu University. From 2002 to 2003, he was a research fellow at City University of Hong Kong. From 2003 to 2007, he was the executive deputy director of the Institute of Science at Jiangsu University. From 2007 to 2018, he was the vice president of Changzhou University and the director of Jiangsu Collaborative Innovation Center of Photovoltaic Science and Engineering. From Oct, 2018 to Jan, 2022, he was the vice president of Jiangsu University and the director of the Institute of Intelligent Flexible Mechatronics. Since Jan, 2022, he is the president of Yangzhou University and the director of the Institute for Carbon Neutrality Technologies. He is also the executive director of Chinese Society of Micro-Nano Technology (CSMNT), vice chairman of Micro-Nano Devices and Systems Branch of Chinese Society of Instrumentation, deputy director of Space Solar Power Plant Committee of Chinese Aerospace Society, executive member of Tribology Branch of Chinese Mechanical Engineering Society, and a member of CSMNT.

Ding Jianning is engaged in researches on micro-nano manufacturing, new energy manufacturing technologies and equipment and intelligent flexible mechatronics, and has made pioneering achievements in green manufacturing of photovoltaic materials and industrialized manufacturing technology and equipment of photovoltaic cells.

**1. He makes breakthrough in the cold hydrogenation process and equipment of solar cell polysilicon materials which enables their clean production with low energy consumption.**

Ding developed a complete set of process equipment for the heating synthesis reactor dedicated to the cold hydrogenation production of polysilicon. This lays a solid foundation for the development of China's photovoltaic industry. After his research achievements were industrialized and applied in the first set of polysilicon cold hydrogenation plant in the country, China's technological backwardness of high energy consumption and high pollution in the polysilicon production was altered and the country entered into the advanced level in the world. For that, Ding won the second prize of National Award for Science and Technology Progress in 2012.

## 2. He makes breakthrough in the manufacturing technology and equipment of high-efficiency and low-cost crystalline silicon solar cells which leads to the building of an internationally leading manufacturing line.

Ding invented the easy-to-passivate surface micro-nanostructure and its manufacturing technology, and created the catalytic etching equipment help to realize low-cost manufacturing and efficient broad-spectrum light absorption. He invented the interface doping and passivation manufacturing technology of the cells which enables efficient carrier transmission. In addition, the double-layer grid superimposed floating metallization structure and high-precision automatic secondary screen printing technology were invented to realize efficient carrier collection. As a result, the efficiency of the mass production of cell has increased from 18% to more than 23.8%, and its module price has fallen by 94%, bringing the generation cost down to lower than that of coal. These technologies set world records for cell efficiency and module output power after being industrialized, and have promoted photovoltaic power parity on the grid. Ding won the second prize of the National Award for Technological Invention in 2020 and China Patent Silver Award in 2018.

## 3. He makes breakthrough in ultra-thin flexible cell module technology and manufacturing equipment which expands the usage of photovoltaic power generation system.

Ding proposed the theory of multi-field coupling jet heat transfer, and pushed the physical tempering technology and equipment of ultra-thin glass to the thickness of 1.1-2mm. And then the world's first mass production line of the thinnest 4mm module was established. Consequently, China's global market share in related sector reaches 60%. For the space solar power station, he proposed a way to solve the mutual constraints of selectivity and permeability of reverse osmosis membranes, invented the manufacturing technology for ultra-low temperature energy storage cell at minus 80℃, and created the first stretchable flexible cell electrode material. His pioneer work in electrochemical artificial muscle provides a lightweight and flexible drive mechanism for space power stations.

# 产业创新奖获得者

# 董书宁

董书宁，1961年2月出生于陕西省西安市。1984年本科毕业于兰州大学水文地质及工程地质专业，2010年获长安大学地质工程专业工学博士学位。1984年至今在中煤科工集团西安研究院（原煤炭科学研究总院西安分院）工作，从事矿山水害防治理论、技术研究与工程实践。先后担任煤炭科学研究总院西安分院水文地质研究所助理工程师、工程师，副所长、岩土工程公司经理、高级工程师，西安分院副院长，中煤科工集团西安研究院院长（董事长）、研究员，2013年9月起至今任中煤科工集团首席科学家。兼任国家安全生产专家组煤矿地质灾害组组长、中国矿山安全学会水害防治专业委员会主任委员、国际矿井水协会中国国家委员会副主席等职。

董书宁从事矿山水害防治理论技术研究和工程实践，在煤层顶、底板水害精准预防与矿山突水灾害高效治理等方面取得了多项创新性成果。曾获国家科技进步奖二等奖2项、省部级科技进步奖一等奖17项及中国专利优秀奖，以及孙越崎能源大奖、杰出工程师奖等多项荣誉。

**一、攻克矿井突水控制注浆高效封堵关键技术，主持/组织完成全国20余项矿山重（特）大突水抢险治理工程，创造了世界采矿史上同等条件下抢险堵水用时最短纪录，为挽救矿工生命及矿山财产损失作出了突出贡献**

创新提出利用保浆袋控制注浆快速封堵过水巷道的技术思路。通过研究得出动水条件下过水巷道保浆袋固结体运移与堆积力学机制，研发出可在钻具中内置高强度柔性保浆袋的钻－注一体化控制注浆装备，解决了动水条件下浆液流失、无法快速封堵的难题；研发封堵体底部淤积层"一步法"置换技术，使封堵体根植于巷道围岩中，避免了"溃坝"风险；基于突水通道内特殊水动力条件，开发了"浆液－骨料反过滤"快速封堵技术，最终实现了突水通道的高效可靠治理。

技术成果被列入《安全生产先进适用技术与产品指导目录》，在神华骆驼山矿等 20 余座煤矿及非煤矿山抢险堵水中成功应用，堵水率达到 95% 以上。其中，骆驼山煤矿"3·1"特大突水灾害抢险堵水工程创造了世界采矿史上同等条件下注浆堵水用时的最短纪录。

**二、创建煤层底板水患超前区域探查治理技术体系，实现了底板水害防治由被动治理向主动预防、局部治理向区域治理的重大转变，解决了我国中东部矿区煤层底板岩溶含水层水灾隐患治理难题**

提出基于顺层近水平定向钻进技术的煤层底板水患主动超前区域治理新方法，揭示了煤层底板应力扰动－水压导升耦合致灾机理，形成了底板突水预测的突水临界指数法，划分出奥灰含水层上部垂向富水性差异"三带"结构，建立了注浆治理层位与靶区选择准则，模拟计算并揭示了裂隙介质中水平钻孔注浆浆液扩散与运移规律，构建了适用于我国中东部煤田的超前区域治理模式。组织研发了煤矿井下定向钻进配套装备及灰岩地层水平钻孔施工工艺，建立了隐伏导水通道多分支水平孔超前精准探查技术，开发出定向钻孔群外缘孔约束注浆、中间孔分序跳孔注浆、相邻孔错位注浆新工艺，提出了"孔间透视－关联分析－量化评价"的注浆效果检验技术，形成了集"定向钻进、超前探查、高效注浆、效果检验"于一体的超前区域探查治理综合技术体系，使钻孔有效孔段率提高 5 倍以上，实现了水灾隐患的无盲区全覆盖精准治理，从根本上改变了煤层底板水害防治的技术与方法。

该成果广泛应用于焦作、淮北、邯邢等 12 个大水矿区，解放了大量受煤层底板岩溶水害威胁的煤炭资源，支撑煤炭安全产能 3500 万吨／年，已列入《煤矿防治水细则》等行业规范性文件，并主持制定了首部行业标准。

**三、开发煤层顶板水"控制疏放、截流减排"防控技术，实现了顶板水防治由治理为主向治保结合的重大转变，促进了我国西部矿井安全高效绿色开发**

提出煤层顶板水治保结合技术思路，系统研究了鄂尔多斯盆地煤炭开采与地下水系统的相互影响关系，提出了基于含水层结构、采掘扰动强度、水动力条件的顶板水害类型及危险性判识方法；揭示了含水层卸压涌水过程的动力学机制，形成了多尺度扰动程度定量评价方法；研发出基于多阶系统动力学的矿井涌水动态预测技术，构建了煤层顶板水疏放钻孔布设、疏放水量、疏放时间非线性优化模型，结合水害分区评价确定疏放标准，进行工作面、采区多尺度疏放水工程总体优化布局，形成了基于安全水头约束的顶板水控制疏放技术。针对侧向补给强、难以有效疏放的含水层，提出"三维孔序优选，双位双向引流，一带两区检验"的注浆帷幕截流减排技术，可消减矿井涌水量 90% 以上。成果有力支撑了神东、宁东、陕北等大型煤炭基地的煤炭资源安全绿色开发。

# Awardee of Industrial Innovation Prize, Dong Shuning

Dong Shuning was born in Xi 'an City of Shaanxi Province in February 1961. He received his bachelor degree in hydrogeology and engineering geology from Lanzhou University in 1984 and got his doctor degree of geological engineering from Chang 'an University in 2010. Since 1984, he has been working in Xi 'an Research Institute of China Coal Technology & Engineering Group ( formerly Xi 'an Branch of China Coal Research Institute ). He has been the chief scientist of China Coal Technology & Engineering Group since September 2013. He is also an adjunct professor in many universities, Leader for The Coal Mine Geological Disaster Group of The National Safety Production Expert Group, Vice Chairman of The Chinese National Committee for The International Mine Water Association.

Dong Shuning is engaged in the theoretical, technical research and engineering practice of mine water disaster prevention and control, and achieved some innovative results. Dong Shuning has obtained two Second Class Prizes of National Science and Technology Progress, 17 First Class Prizes of Provincial and Ministerial Science and Technology Progress. He has been awarded Sun Yueqi Energy Award and Outstanding Engineer Award.

Firstly, it has conquered the key technology of efficient grouting plugging for mine water inrush control, completed more than 20 major water inrush rescue and treatment projects in mines nationwide, and created the record of the shortest time for water rescue and plugging under the same conditions in the world mining history, making outstanding contributions to save the lives of miners and the loss of mine property.

Secondly, the area exploration and preact grouting technology of seam floor water disaster was established, which realized the great transformation from passive control to active prevention and local governance to regional governance of water disaster of coal seam floor, and solved the problem of water disaster treatment of coal floor karst aquifer in the middle and the east of China.

Thirdly, the control and protection technology of "control and discharge, water flow interception and emission reduction" of coal seam roof water has been developed, which has realized the major transformation of roof water control from the governance-oriented to the combined governance and protection, and promoted the safe, efficient and green development of mine in western China.

# 产业创新奖获得者

# 蒋官澄

蒋官澄，1966年2月出生于重庆市大足区。2005年获中国海洋大学理学博士学位。1987—2008年在中国石油大学（华东）工作，2009年至今在中国石油大学（北京）工作。兼任中国石油学会青年工作委员会常委副主任（2017—）、石油石化污染物控制与处理国家重点实验室"固体废物处理与资源化"方向学术带头人、中国地质学会探矿工程专业委员会委员（2018.11—）。

蒋官澄主要从事油田化学研究，在储层保护与钻井液方面作出了系列开创性研究工作。曾获中华国际科学交流基金会杰出工程师奖（2020年）、孙越崎能源大奖（2022年）。

## 一、常规油气储层保护

建立了油气井全过程储层损害定量"预测、诊断、保护与解堵"技术，使其智能化：①预知储层可能将发生的损害机理、类型和程度等，指导储层保护措施的建立；②如果储层已被损害，准确诊断发生损害的机理、类型、范围和程度，为解除储层损害奠定基础；③基于预测技术，为不同类型油气藏的勘探开发各作业环节提供储层保护技术，避免储层损害发生；④基于诊断技术，为已损害的储层提供解堵措施，恢复甚至提高油气井产量。该技术三年内在12个国家规模应用1.16万多口井、产量提高1.5倍以上；理论成果入编美国大学教材，相关成果获2007年国家科技进步奖二等奖。

## 二、复杂结构井的储层损害与钻井复杂

首次引入仿生学理论，揭示海洋贻贝、蚯蚓强胶结岩石、强润滑土壤表面的原理，剖析贻贝、蚯蚓分泌物的组成与结构，发明了仿生固壁剂和键合型润滑剂，创建了超低摩阻随钻井壁强化仿生理论与技术，解决了复杂结构井常遭遇的井壁失稳、高摩阻等国际重大难题，并为"储层损害与钻井复杂"防控原创性技术的研发开辟了新的研究思路

和方向。该技术三年内在 12 个国家规模应用 1142 口井。相关成果获 2016 年国家技术发明奖二等奖。

### 三、非常规等复杂油气的储层损害与钻井复杂

针对非常规等复杂油气储层特征，创建了岩石表面既疏水又疏油的双疏理论，分别指导发明了"强胶结－抗温抗压－恒流变"型无土相油基钻井液，攻克了近 20 年未攻克的无土相油基钻井液抗温与抗压能力低、低温增稠、漏失严重的国际重大难题，使抗压、抗温、恒流变范围分别较国外领先技术提高 35%、44.4% 和 82.4%；"减阻提速－安全提产－生态环保"型高效能水基钻井液攻克了国内外 15 余年无法将油基钻井液"抑制、润滑、保护储层"优点融入水基钻井液中的国际难题，并首次使水基钻井液升级为生态环保型；"聚膜－解吸"型无固相水基钻井液攻克了 20 余年未攻克的"无土相水基钻井液不能形成滤饼，致使无法封堵、摩阻等钻井复杂与储层损害严重"的国际重大难题，并首次通过钻井液解吸吸附气而提高产量。继而实现了非常规、深层等复杂油气的高效勘探开发，并在我国 80% 以上高难度井和海外 10 个国家规模应用 2270 口井。相关成果获 2012 年国家科技进步奖二等奖、2020 年中国专利金奖、2017 年部级科技进步奖特等奖等。

上述成果形成了集研发、工业生产与现场技术服务为一体的原创性成果产业链，解决了"储层损害与钻井复杂"的国际重大瓶颈难题，支撑了我国多个大型油气田建设；与国际一流公司同台竞标且全部中标，实现了技术反超，并被世界排名第一的斯伦贝谢油服公司引进成为主流技术；相关成果荣获部级创新团队奖，获授权发明专利 109 件、计算机软件著作权 7 项。

# Awardee of Industrial Innovation Prize, Jiang Guancheng

Jiang Guancheng was born in Dazu District of Chongqing City in February 1966. In 2005, he graduated from the School of Chemistry and Chemical Engineering of Ocean University of China and awarded a doctor's degree in science. He has won the "Outstanding Engineer Award" of the China International Science Exchange Foundation, and the Sun Yueqi Energy Award.

Professor Guancheng Jiang is engaged in oilfield chemistry research, has made a series of pioneering research work in reservoir protection and drilling fluid, and has made three major original achievements: quantitative "prediction, diagnosis, protection and plug removal" technology of reservoir damage in the whole process of oil and gas wells, bionic theory and technology of ultra-low friction and enhanced borehole wall while drilling, and theory and technology of amphiphobic drilling fluid. Then an industrial chain integrating "R&D, industrial production and on-site technical services" was formed, which pushed foreign companies out of the Chinese market, applied nearly 30000 wells in more than 60% of China's oil and gas fields, supported the construction of several large oil and gas fields. It has seized the international market and has been successfully applied in 11 overseas countries, changing from technology blockade to technology domination.

Some of the achievements have been incorporated into the textbooks of American universities and have been highly praised by academicians of the same industry at home and abroad; Jiang has won 3 National Science and Technology Awards, 1 China Patent Gold Award, authorized 109 invention patents (including 32 in Europe and America) and 7 software copyrights.

# 产业创新奖获得者

# 骆建军

骆建军，1970年1月出生于浙江省诸暨市。1991年毕业于上海交通大学电子工程系，此后在杭州电子科技大学和浙江大学分别获得硕士和博士学位。1997年进入杭州东方通信股份有限公司国家级技术中心担任芯片设计技术带头人；2001年去美国硅谷工作，参与创立了美国 Baleen System 公司。2011年回国创立了华澜微电子股份有限公司，现任华澜微电子股份有限公司董事长、总经理，兼任杭州电子科技大学微电子研究院院长、教授。

骆建军长期从事集成电路芯片设计，在计算机高速总线、数据通信、数据存储和信息安全方面作出了一系列开创性研究工作。他抓住"传统胶卷、磁盘和机械硬盘（HDD）被半导体（固态）存储替代"这一产业更新换代的良机，立足基础理论演化出核心工程技术架构，积极投身产业界，实现了一系列片上系统芯片和数据存储产品的产业化，结束了中国没有自己硬盘产业的历史。

一、探索核心算法和芯片架构，设计并积累了经过硅实体验证的、国内完整系列的存储控制器芯片知识产权核，填补了国内空白

设计并积累起了完整系列的计算机高速总线接口 IP，覆盖①SD/eMMC、USB、PATA/IDE、SATA、SAS、PCIe 总线，包括其物理层和协议层；②丰富的数据加解密硬件电路 IP，包括中国商用密码局制定的 SM2、SM3、SM4、SM9，以及国际领域的 AES、椭圆曲线（ECC）、RSA、DES/3DES 等；③闪存纠错和控制算法，包括 BCH、LDPC、TPC 和闪存均衡算法等。这些 IP 核是我国在高性能计算、计算机总线、信息安全领域核心芯片开发的宝贵基础积累。

二、打通从基础科研到产业落地的道路，率先引领打造了一系列存储控制器芯片和存储产品，逐渐形成了我国完整的数据存储产业

骆建军研发出中国的第一颗固态硬盘（SSD）控制器芯片、第一颗 SD/eMMC 主控芯片、第一颗 SAS 主控芯片；发展出全系列存储控制器芯片，包括存储卡/U 盘控制器芯片、移动硬盘控制器芯片、固态硬盘控制器芯片、硬盘阵列控制器芯片，并以此发展出全系列存储产品，使我国的数据存储产业迅速成长起来。该方面的创业创新成果，配合上长江存储的闪存，正在形成我国完整存储产品的家族"移动存储卡→移动硬盘/U 盘→固态硬盘→硬盘阵列→大数据存储系统"。

三、提出独创的专利芯片架构和电路构造，在高密度硬盘、数据加密、可控自毁硬盘等细分领域国际领先

骆建军带领团队以基础芯片和算法为核心技术，开发出各种系列特色电脑硬盘、加密存储产品。例如，全球最高密度硬盘——2.5 英寸标准 SSD 容量达到 5TB（市场同比最高容量 1TB）；2021 年已经提高到 20TB（市场同比最高容量 8TB）；芯片加密/可控自毁硬盘此类高密度高可靠性固态硬盘已经应用在航天工程的工作站、各种高端装备。该团队在这些细分领域国际领先。

# Awardee of Industrial Innovation Prize, Luo Jianjun

Luo Jianjun was born in Zhuji City of Zhejiang Province in January 1970. He graduated from Electronic Engineering Department of Shanghai Jiaotong University in 1991, and then received his Master and Ph.D degrees from Hangzhou Dianzi University and Zhejiang University respectively. He joined Hangzhou Eastern Communication Corporation as the leader of integrated circuit (IC) design team in 1997. He moved to Silicon Valley in the United States in 2001, and then started his venture as the co-founder of Baleen System, a fabless IC design house. After returning back China in 2001, he established Sage Microelectronics Corporation (SageMicro) in Hangzhou. Now Professor Jianjun is the Chairman of SageMicro as well as the director & professor of Microelectronics Research Institute (MERI) of Hangzhou Dianzi University.

Jianjun Luo devoted to Integrated Circuit (IC) design for years. He made progress in the field of computer high speed interfaces (buses), data communication, data storage and information security. While the traditional storage mediums such as film, floppy disk and hard disk drive (HDD) being replaced by solid-state storage, Jianjun seized this opportunity to build a series of algorithms and architectures based on theoretical research work, and threw himself into developing a series of System-On-Chips (SOCs) as well as putting the corresponding storage products into mass-production. It is he who accelerated the commercialization and industrialization of solid-state storage technology. Finally, the localized storage industry grown up rapidly in the mainland of China.

**1. With basic theoretical research work on core algorithms and IC architectures for years, implemented and accumulated a whole set of silicon-proven Intellectual Property (IP) cores. It filled the domestic blank.**

Professor Jianjun accumulated a whole set of Intellectual Property (IP) cores, which covered ① high speed computer interfaces including SD/eMMC, USB, PATA/IDE, SATA, SAS, PCIe with both physical layer and protocol layer; ② rich circuit modules of encryption and decryption for SM2, SM3, SM4, SM9 which defined by Office of Security Commercial Code Administration (OSCCA, China) as well as AES, ECC, RSA, DES/3DES, HASH algorithms deigned by National Institute of Standards and Technology (NIST, US); ③ flash management and error correction algorithm, etc. These IP cores are valuable for developing ICs in the field of high-performance computing (HPC), computer buses and information security.

**2. Broke through the bottleneck from basic scientific research to industry landing by designing and putting into mass production of a series of storage controller ICs as well as the corresponding storage products. A complete storage industry has been formed gradually in China.**

Professor Jianjun designed China's first SSD controller, SD/eMMC controller, SATA controller. After constant hard work for a decade, his team incubated a while storage controller family, including memory card & USB flash controller, mobile hard drive controller, SSD controller, hard drive array controller. Furthermore, a complete storage industry with these local developed controller chips has been growing to maturity. Professor Jianjun's creative work stimulated Chinese local storage industry growth, is leading to a complete storage family: memory card → mobile hard drive/USB flash Drive → SSD → hard drive array → big-data storage system.

**3. Proposed the patented chip architectures and circuit structures, and leading the industry in some segments such as high-density drive, data security and controllable self-destructive drive, etc.**

Professor Jianjun's team developed a series of unique products in computer hard drive and security storage field. For example, the world's top density SSD unit was announced 5TB capacity with standard 2.5-inch form-factor by his company SageMicro®, compared with 1TB as the highest capacity in the market; And upgrade to 20TB in 2021 compared with 8TB as the top capacity in the market. For example, high reliability SSD dedicated for Aerospace Applications was applied in the space station successfully, data encrypted drive & controllable destructive drives were implemented for high-end equipment. The team is leading the global research and development directions in these kinds of unique storage products.

# 产业创新奖获得者

# 廉玉波

廉玉波，1964年4月出生于江苏省仪征市。1987年获南京航空航天大学学士学位，2000年获南京大学硕士学位。1987—1991年进入中国汽车技术研究中心从事汽车设计与制造研究。1991年10月—2000年11月担任上汽集团仪征汽车有限公司副总工程师，作为主设计师，自主完成7座MPV等车型设计，负责动力系统核心技术研究。2000年11月—2003年12月任上海同济同捷汽车设计公司常务副总经理，负责公司整车及系统的设计开发工作。2004年2月至今担任比亚迪汽车工业有限公司执行副总裁、总工程师，全面负责动力系统核心技术攻关和电动汽车整车研发工作，提出高比能、高安全、耐低温动力电池设计方法，研制出高性能、高效率、高集成混合动力/纯电驱动系统，打造了全新的高性能电动汽车整车专属平台，搭载于系列化高性能电动汽车。先后担任全国汽车标准化技术委员会电动车辆分技术委员会主任委员、国家重点研发计划"新能源汽车"重点专项总体专家、中国汽车工程学会常务理事。曾荣获国家科学技术进步奖二等奖、广东省科学技术进步奖特等奖、中国汽车工业科学技术进步奖特等奖、杰出工程师奖、中国汽车工业优秀科技人才奖、第二十一届及第二十二届中国外观设计奖金奖。

廉玉波从事一线研发工作34年，在电动汽车动力电池系统、驱动系统和整车一体化集成设计等方面作出了原创性、开拓性工作。

## 一、高安全动力电池技术

针对高端纯电动汽车动力电池高安全与高能量密度协同提升难的问题，构建了以稳定材料、可靠结构和智慧管理为目标的全层级电池安全设计体系，采用超大长宽比刀片电芯设计技术和高速高精度制造工艺，刀片电池极芯体积利用率提升到98%；采用电芯到整包无模组集成技术，以超长刀片电芯阵列为骨架，将电芯与上盖、底板直接粘连，整包空间利用率大幅提升，系统体积能量密度达 240Wh/L（特斯拉 206Wh/L），实现电池包直接碰撞不起火爆炸，彻底解决了动力电池热失控痛点。应用上述技术的高安全电池通过了美国最严苛安全标准 UL2580 认证，搭载的高安全电池整车累计运行超 300 亿千米未出现由电池引发的安全事故。

## 二、自主高可靠汽车级 IGBT 芯片技术

针对汽车级 IGBT 在瞬态电流冲击和长期高低温循环下可靠性低的问题，首创精细化平面栅复合场终层高耐流 IGBT 结构，提出了基于载流子局域寿命控制的均温方法，发明了基于相容原理的 AISC（铝碳化硅）扰流散热技术，构建了精细多维 + 相容的高可靠 IGBT 设计体系，自主建成了全国首条汽车级 IGBT 全产业链生产线，并实现大规模产业化应用，打破国外技术封锁和垄断。与德国英飞凌同类产品相比，自主高可靠汽车级 IGBT 芯片极限电流能力提升 37%、高低温循环寿命提高一倍。

## 三、高效率一体化驱动总成技术

针对驱动总成耦合部件多、在整车复杂运行工况下效率低的问题，建立了高性能电动汽车动力系统设计、研发与制造体系，主持研制出高安全–高可靠–高效率电动汽车动力系统和具有完全自主知识产权的高性能电动汽车专属整车平台，输出至丰田、戴姆勒（奔驰）等国际一流汽车厂商，推动了我国电动汽车核心技术从依赖进口到国产替代、再到批量出口的跨越式进步。

## 四、高性能纯电 e 平台 3.0 关键技术

纯电 e 平台 3.0 基于高阶智能辅助驾驶、优化资源综合利用率、提升整车安全的开发逻辑，构建了涵盖整车、系统到零部件的全层级高效设计开发体系，打破了驱动、充电、热管理等系统分立的边界。纯电 e 平台 3.0 集成了多项先进技术，其中刀片电池和车身融合形成完整的整车传力结构，打造全球法规超五星安全标准；驱动电机升压充电拓扑架构，复用大功率驱动系统实现宽域大功率充电；宽温域高效热泵系统打破系统边界，开发多模式热量补偿技术，实现 –25～60℃ 的工作温度。纯电 e 平台 3.0 具有高度扩展性，全面覆盖 A0—D 级车型兼容轿车、SUV、MPV 等，车型百公里加速快至 2.9S。

廉玉波主持研发了具有完全自主知识产权的电动汽车动力系统和整车平台，相关创新成果搭载于王朝、海洋等系列化高端电动乘用车产品，并带动比亚迪电动汽车销量快速增长，出口至包括美日欧等传统汽车强国在内的 50 多个国家和地区，为我国电动汽车技术和产业化发展作出了突出贡献。

廉玉波作为标准主要起草人，承担了包括电动汽车"三大强标"在内的 6 项国家标准的制定工作，并带领比亚迪以组长单位身份主导制定了全球第一个电动汽车安全技术法规。获授权专利 358 项，以第一发明人获授权发明专利 121 项。

# Awardee of Industrial Innovation Prize, Lian Yubo

Lian Yubo was born in Yizheng City of Jiangsu Province in April 1964. He graduated from Nanjing University of Aeronautics and Astronautics with a bachelor's degree in 1987 and received a master's degree from Nanjing University in 1998—2000. From 1987 to 1991, he joined the China Automotive Technology and Research Center to conduct research on automotive design and manufacturing. From October 1991 to November 2000, he served as Vice-Chief Engineer of SAIC Yizheng Automobile Co., Ltd. As the Chief Designer, he completed the design of 7-seat MPV and other models independently, and was responsible for the core technology research of power system. From November 2000 to December 2003, he served as Deputy President of Shanghai Tongji Tongjie Automobile Design Company, and was responsible for the design and development of the company's entire vehicle and system. From February 2004 to present, he served as Executive Vice President and Chief Engineer of BYD Automobile Industry Co., Ltd. He is comprehensively responsible for the key technology research of the power system and the development of the electric vehicle; Proposed a new design method of power battery to obtain high specific performance, high safety and low temperature resistant. He has developed a high-performance, high-efficiency, highly integrated hybrid/electric driving system to create a new exclusive platform for high-performance electric vehicles, which is equipped on a series of high-performance electric vehicles. Yubo has successively served as the chairman of NTCAS Electric Vehicle Sub-Technical Committee, the Head Expert of "New Energy Vehicle" Key Special Project in the National Key R&D Program, and the Executive Director of China-SAE. He won the second prize of National Science and Technology Progress Award, the special prize of Guangdong Province Science and Technology Progress Award, the special prize of China Automotive Industry Science and Technology Progress Award, Outstanding Engineer Award, China Automotive Industry Excellent Science and Technology Talent Award, And the 21st and 22nd China Appearance Design Award.

Yubo Lian has been engaged in primary research and development work for 34 years and has made original and pioneering work in the filed of electric vehicle power battery system, driving system and integrated design of the whole vehicle, etc.

Yubo Lian as the main drafter of the standard, has undertaken the formulation of 6 national standards, including the "three strong standards" for electric vehicles, and led BYD to lead the formulation of the world's first technical regulations for electric vehicle safety as the team leader. He also authorized 358 patents, 121 patents as the first inventor.

# 产业创新奖获得者

# 石　碧

石碧，1958年6月出生于四川省成都市。1992年获四川大学工学博士学位。2000—2008年任四川大学皮革化学与工程教育部重点实验室主任，2008年至今任四川大学制革清洁技术国家工程实验室主任。2009年当选中国工程院院士，同年当选国际皮革化学师及工艺师协会联合会主席，成为该联合会100余年历史中首位华人主席。曾获全国先进工作者称号以及国际皮革联合会卓越贡献奖（迄今中国唯一获奖人）。

石碧主要从事制革化学、制革清洁技术研究，带领团队开发和推广应用了多项制革清洁生产关键技术，对我国制革工业的绿色持续发展产生了引领作用。

## 一、制革染整工段清洁生产关键材料的开发及工程应用

制革染整过程残余在废液中的染料、加脂剂、复鞣剂等是产生高色度、高COD废水的主要原因。针对这些问题，石碧利用植物多酚与铬的氧化还原-原位络合反应，开发了第一种可以同时强化染整材料在皮革中的渗透和结合，并具有很好填充作用的栲胶型金属络合鞣剂（即在我国皮革领域产生了较大影响的HS鞣剂）。通过工程转化，使我国上千个制革企业采用了以这一关键材料为基础的复鞣-高吸收一体化技术，不仅使制革染整工段污染物排放量大幅降低，也对提高我国深色皮革的质量、促进产品出口产生了重要影响。该成果获1993年国家技术发明奖二等奖。

## 二、制革制备工段污染物源头控制技术的开发与应用

准备工段的污染物产生量占制革全过程总污染物产量的70%以上，主要包括采用化学毛脱工艺产生的高浓度硫化物、COD废水，采用铵盐脱灰工艺及铵盐-胰酶软化工艺产生的高浓度氨氮（$NH_3-N$）废水。针对该问题，石碧带领团队开发了以酶处理技术为基础的制革准备工段污染物源头控制关键技术，包括：①研制基于多酶协同作用的"保

毛脱毛"技术,实现了源头削减 COD、硫化物等污染物的目的;②发明基于多酶协同作用的无铵盐复合酶软化技术,从源头消除了制革准备工段氨氮的产生。同时带领团队与企业合作,首先实现了系列酶制剂产品的产业化,进而在我国制革企业广泛推广应用了基于生物酶的制革准备工段污染物源头控制技术。实践证明,采用这些技术后,废水中硫化物、氨氮和 COD 分别减少 90%、80% 和 60%,污泥减少 60%,节水 20%,污水处理费用降低 35% ~ 50%,综合经济效益提高 5% ~ 8%。成果"基于酶作用的制革污染物源头控制技术及关键酶制剂创制"获得 2015 年国家技术发明奖二等奖。

### 三、制革鞣制工段生态环保技术的开发与应用

近 170 年来,国内外皮革生产主要采用铬鞣技术,由此产生的含铬废水、含铬固废和含铬废弃皮革制品导致了潜在的生态环境风险。无铬生态皮革制造技术的开发成为近 20 多年来国际皮革领域科技竞争的焦点。

1. 在我国率先研究和开发无铬、少铬鞣制技术

石碧首先从理论上证实了以棓儿茶素为基本结构的植物鞣剂与醛类化合物具有显著的交联协同效应,能使皮革的湿热稳定性达到 90℃以上,并据此成功开发了以这两类材料为基础的无铬结合鞣制技术,可以在山羊皮等薄型原料皮的制革过程中取代沿用了 100 多年的铬鞣技术。同时,开发少铬 – 改性戊二醛结合鞣制技术,使铬的用量降低 75%。成果"无铬、少铬鞣法生产高档山羊服装革"获 2000 年国家科技进步奖二等奖。

2. 持续开展无铬生态皮革制造技术开发

在国家重点研发计划项目"生态皮革鞣制染整关键材料及技术"的支持下,石碧带领团队以天然多糖为基础原料,通过分子设计、合成方法研究,成功开发了两类能满足各类皮革生产需要的新型无铬鞣制材料;通过这些材料的应用工艺研究,成功构建了无铬生态皮革制造技术。2019 年上半年,无铬鞣制材料在我国规模最大的皮革化工企业四川亭江新材料股份有限公司(上市公司)成功投产。之后,基于新型无铬鞣制材料的无铬生态皮革制造技术在我国河北、福建、山东、甘肃等地的重要制革基地投入应用,在铬鞣剂的替代中发挥了重要作用。

在 2019 年的第二十届中国国际皮革展览会上,多家中国制革企业展出了采用四川大学技术制造的生态皮革产品,引起国际同行的广泛关注,使得在我国推广相关技术的国外大公司逐渐退出中国市场,标志着我国在无铬生态皮革制造技术方面率先取得系统性突破。研究成果对引领我国皮革工业绿色发展、提升我国皮革产业的国际竞争力具有深远意义。

# Awardee of Industrial Innovation Prize, Shi Bi

Shi Bi was born in Chengdu City of Sichuan Province in June 1958. He received his Ph.D. degree in engineering from Sichuan University in 1992. Now, he is the director of National Engineering Laboratory for Clean Technology of Leather Manufacturing at Sichuan University. In 2009, he was elected as the president of the International Union of Leather Technologists and Chemists Societies (IULTCS), the first Chinese president in over 100-year history of this organization. In 2009, he was elected as Academician of Chinese Academy of Engineering.

Shi Bi is mainly engaged in the research of tanning chemistry and clean technologies for leather manufacturing. During the past 30 years, numerous key technologies for clean production of leather were developed and widely applied by his team, which played a leading role in the green and sustainable development of leather industry in China.

In 1990s, he developed the first vegetable tannin-based metal complex tanning agent by using the redox and in-situ complexation reactions of plant polyphenols and chromium. The product can enhance the penetration and binding of post-tanning chemicals in leather, and thus reduce the emission of pollutants significantly in the post-tanning process. This key technology was adopted in over 1000 tanning companies in China, and largely reduced pollution of leather industry. As for beamhouse process, He developed "hair saving unhairing" technology and ammonium-free bating technology based on the synergistic effect of multi-enzymes, which reduce sulfide, ammonia nitrogen and COD contents in wastewater by 90%, 80%, and 60% respectively. In order to eliminate chromium pollution in the leather industry, he begun his research on chrome-free tanning technology since 1994. Now, the eco-friendly chrome-free tanning technology developed by his team is more and more applied in Chinese tanneries, being changing the history of chrome tanning lasted for over 100 years.

# 产业创新奖获得者

# 王爱杰

王爱杰，女，1971年12月出生。2000年获哈尔滨工业大学环境工程专业工学博士学位。现为哈尔滨工业大学教授，城市水资源与水环境国家重点实验室（深圳）主任，中国发明协会会士（2018—），国际水协会杰出会士，美国俄克拉荷马大学兼职教授。兼任中国发明协会副监事长、中国传感器与物联网产业联盟副理事长、工信部非常规水利用标准化委员会副主任、中国化工学会工业水处理专委会副主任、中国生态学会微生物生态专委会副主任等职务。

王爱杰长期从事污水资源化工程科技研究，发展了生物调控理论，在低碳再生、安全再生和精准管控方面作出系列开创性研究工作，创建的多污染物及风险因子协同控制技术系统推广应用于107项工程，支撑7项国家/行业标准编制，创建11个产学研创新平台；申请和授权专利100余件；获国家技术发明奖和国家科技进步奖二等奖4项、省部级一等奖4项、中国专利优秀奖1项、产学研合作创新奖1项等，为我国污水安全再生利用作出重要贡献。

**一、揭示污水再生处理过程碳循环利用机制，开辟非碳源依赖生物脱氮新途径，创建自主品牌技术系统，解决了低碳氮比污水低碳再生工程科技难题**

研究揭示了污水再生处理过程碳循环利用机制，发明了"控碳脱氮"新原理，通过优化碳源的分配路径和利用方式，使水中有限的碳源能够最大限度地被用于脱氮。针对污泥碳源的定向转化利用，还发明了污泥快速发酵释放小分子碳源新方法，并精确控制碳源定向"反哺"脱氮工艺，创建了低碳耗污水深度净化技术系统，实现了外碳源和污泥的同步减量。工程应用表明，采用控碳脱氮途径，可以在少投碳甚至不投碳的情况下使大多数污水处理过程达到国家一级A排放标准。

通过揭示硫和铁介导微生物代谢偶联、加速生物脱氮的作用机制，提出利用无机电子供体替代有机碳源的自养生物脱氮新原理，发明了结构与尺寸可控、自驱动脱氮过程的高活性生物载体及制备方法，自行设计和研制了系列高负荷脱氮活性生物载体ThiocreF®（注册商标），建成全球首条生产线和量产设备，可满足年处理污水量2亿吨，创建了以ThiocreF®为核心的自主品牌——珊氮®技术（注册商标），形成了菌剂、载体、装备三类核心产品；在宁晋建成国际首例零碳耗深度脱氮处理工程，运行成本降低50%，温室气体$N_2O$减排显著，入选2020年工业园区第三方治理典型案例；作为中国首座"城市污水资源概念厂"的主体工艺，珊氮®技术突破了污水低碳再生与水质安全保障难以有效协同的"卡脖子"问题，已在长江、黄河等流域市政污水、工业污水、分散源污水、污染水体大规模推广应用，引领了我国水处理行业的低碳发展。

**二、提出内、外源生物强化新原理，突破污染物无害化和定向转化关键技术，创建风险阻控绿色工艺系统，攻克了污水安全再生的工程科技难题**

针对常规工艺难以深度去除水中硝基、偶氮、卤代等毒害有机物（及新污染物）的问题，率先报道并揭示了小幅外电压（0.5—1.0V）加速硝基芳烃定向生物转化的脱毒机制，发明了定向调控微生物功能酶活性的弱电和微氧（0.1—0.5mg/L）方法，大幅提升了有机物解构、脱毒、脱卤、脱色速率（2～6倍），从而提出内源生物增强和外源生物激活新原理，开辟了工程系统微生物活性快速调控新途径，丰富和发展了生物调控理论。基于此，创制了系列生物催化材料和弱电、微氧介入型增效处理加速器，建成全球首条加速器生产线，实现大规模量产；研发出以加速器为核心功能部件的系列复合水解酸化工艺、装备及智能调控系统，获大规模推广应用，攻克了水中占比超过70%的三类典型毒害有机物（硝基、偶氮和卤代物）高效去除和制约污水深度净化的工程难题，入选国家先进污染防治技术目录（2019年），淮安经济开发区工程案例入选国家水重大专项"百项优秀示范工程"。

针对硫系毒害物质的深度去除，发现并在国际上率先报道了微生物的超常规快速脱硫代谢方式，提出硫与碳、氮污染物之间电子转移生成单质硫的调控方法以及多污染物协同去除工艺原理，创建了硫资源化实现无害化的多污染物协同去除低耗技术系统，发明了从气、水和污泥中高效提取单质硫的方法及回收装备，单质硫转化率从常规工艺不足30%提升到90%以上，被列为国家鼓励发展的环境保护技术；编制国家标准，填补行业空白，被国际水协会推荐为"城市可持续水处理系统的代表性成果之一"，与荷兰公司合作，在"一带一路"沿线国家推广应用，实现了污水由单纯处理向资源转化的跨越。

基于上述成果，创建了系列绿色阻控工艺系统，推广应用于海河、淮河等流域，取得了降成本、稳达标、控风险的显著效果。

## 三、突破智能模拟和精准调控关键技术，创建控风险－控碳排－控效应的多目标管控方法体系，解决了再生处理过程低碳与安全的协控难题

针对再生处理过程低碳与安全协控难题，提出控风险和控碳减排多目标协同的技术路径，建立了"算碳－控碳－管碳"方法体系，创建了专有数据库和信息平台，可实现碳排放过程的分钟级计量；自主研发出机理模型和数据模型驱动的水处理工艺数字孪生技术、在线仿真精准控制系统及算力最小化的多源异构数据挖掘算法，实现了溶解氧、污泥回流等关键参数的在线控制；研制出智能水桩等新一代信息化设施，创建了污水处理厂泛在感知网络和运行状态智能调控体系，建立了控风险－控碳排－控效应的多目标管控方法，应用于长江、黄河流域再生水厂，实现了再生处理过程碳减排 20% 以上、设备运行故障率降低 30% 的综合效果。其中，全国第一座基于工业 4.0 的智慧水厂（河南博爱第二污水处理厂）入选 2020 年中国自动化领域最具影响力工程。

# Awardee of Industrial Innovation Prize, Wang Aijie

Wang Aijie, female, was born in December 1971. She obtained her Ph.D. degree from Harbin Institute of Technology (HIT) in environmental engineering in 2000. Currently, she is a Professor at Harbin Institute of Technology (HIT) and serves as the Director of State Key Laboratory of Urban Water Resources and Environment (Shenzhen), Vice Chairperson of the China Invention Association, Vice Director of China Sensor and IOT Industry Alliance, Vice Chairperson of Microbial Ecology Committee of Ecological Society of China. In 2022, she was elected as a Distinguished Fellows of the IWA. She also serves as Adjunct Professor of University of Oklahoma.

Prof. Wang has focused her research on wastewater reclamation and resource recovery for over 20 years. During her career, she extended the biological water treatment theories and engineering, and made pioneering contributions in areas of low-carbon water reclamation, safe water reclamation and intelligent system management. The synergistic mitigation process system for multiple pollutants and risk factor had been applied in 107 full-scale wastewater treatment plants across mainland China, supported the draft of 7 national/trade standard, and led the establishment of 11 platforms for industry-university-research cooperation. She has been awarded more than 100 national patents, been awardee of 2 National Science & Technology Progress Awards, 2 National Technology Innovation Awards, 4 Provincial-level Awards, the Golden Patent Award of China Association of Inventions. Her research had made critical contributions to the water reclamation in China.

# 产业创新奖获得者

# 王 军

王军，1963年11月出生于湖南省衡阳市。2020年获中南大学交通运输工程专业工学博士学位。1985年本科毕业后到铁道部四方机车车辆厂工作，历任设计师、客车设计处副处长/处长、副总工程师、动车本部副总经理。2001年4月起历任南车青岛四方机车车辆股份有限公司总工程师、副总经理兼总工程师、副董事长、总经理、董事长，2012起任中国南车股份有限公司副总裁（技术），2015年任中国中车股份有限公司副总裁（技术），现为中国中车集团党委常委、总工程师、科技创新委员会主任、首席科学家，兼任轨道交通车辆系统集成国家工程实验室主任、中国铁道学会常务理事、国家铁路局专家委员会委员、国家知识产权局专家咨询委员会委员等。

王军长期奋战在中国铁路机车车辆技术研发、制造及管理一线，在高速列车技术创新与产业化等方面作出了一系列开创性研究工作。

## 一、主持构建 CRH2 型国产化高速列车平台，支撑我国进入高铁时代

主持攻克高速列车转向架关键技术，创建我国第一个250km/h等级高速列车转向架技术体系，建立耦合跨线运营条件的部件－滚动－线路－服役跟踪试验体系及评价标准，奠定后续更高速度等级转向架技术平台。研制第一列国产化CRH2型高速列车，基于此研制了长编组高速列车、首创卧铺高速列车，快速构建产品平台与国产化能力，仅3年实现规模量产。支撑了铁路第六次大提速实施；运用于京广、京沪等9条普速干线，平均缩短旅行时间30%～40%；保障了京津、郑西高铁，合武、客专等40条线路开通运营。该成果获国家科技进步奖一等奖。

## 二、主持建成自主知识产权 CRH380A 高速列车平台，跻身世界先进行列

针对车－线－网－环境复杂大系统，提出高速列车顶层设计、系统匹配、指标分解、

性能优化全链条开发方法，建立列车集成架构与产品标准；提出等强度轻量化设计理念，攻克轻量化车体材料、结构、复杂工艺与车体气动/振动性能协同设计及优化技术，解决了轻质材料高强高模、结构模态、结构等寿命与整车系统匹配难题，组织开发出大断面、复杂曲面构型车体结构；提出高速列车健康管理要求并工程化，解决350km/h等级列车安全性、平稳性、舒适性难题。成功研制350km/h等级CRH380A型高速列车，2010年投入沪杭高铁、次年投入京沪高铁运营，创造486.1km/h运营线运营列车世界最高试验速度。该成果获省部级特等奖2项以及全国创新争先团队奖。

### 三、主持构建高速列车产业持续自主创新能力与规模，实现全球领跑

提出"技术+产业"双元驱动创新管理模式，确定技术/工程/人才等多要素动态匹配关系，需求牵引，拉动技术与工程等复杂要素融合互促、高效发展，快速形成高速列车产业自主能力。①主持建成高速列车设计-制造-产品三大技术融合平台，打造精益生产、全程管控的平台化制造模式，实现单一产品研发向产品平台转变；②首创"按需定制、高效设计、柔性制造"高速列车谱系化方法，开发周期由原3—5年缩短至2—3年，并研制了涵盖不同速度等级，满足高原、高寒、高湿、高风沙等不同运用环境的高速列车18种，快速形成满足市场需求的产品谱系；③组织建立中车Q质量标准体系，动车组百万公里故障率逐年下降，2020年仅0.40件（国际参考标准2件）；④创建高速列车在线监测与远程诊断系统，构筑大数据平台，保障复杂环境运营安全。

打造了国际领先、规模最大的高速列车持续创新能力、产品平台和完整产业链；所管理的四方股份公司自2006年首列国产化CRH2型列车下线，到2011年实现产能200列，居世界第一。全面支撑"复兴号"量产，支撑了400km/h高速列车、500km/h试验列车等高端装备持续产出。该成果获国家科技进步奖二等奖、国家级企业管理现代化创新成果一等奖与二等奖各1项、省部级特等奖项。

### 四、主持研制青藏铁路高原客车，解决世界最高海拔铁路复杂服役环境行车难题

作为青藏铁路工程中高原铁路客车的负责人，针对高原环境下恶劣复杂气候，提出客车总体技术方案，首创列车供氧系统，在世界上率先攻克铁路客车在高原环境下补氧难题；制订高原客车电气技术条件，首创避雷暴装置，保证了电气系统的高可靠性，有效防范高原频繁雷暴威胁。该成果是2008年"青藏铁路工程"国家科技进步奖特等奖的重要内容，填补了我国高原客车技术空白。

# Awardee of Industrial Innovation Prize, Wang Jun

Wang Jun was born in Hengyang City of Hunan Province in November 1963. He has been engaged in the research and development of rail transit equipment technology, system construction and engineering management, and is the main developer and leader of China's high-speed train technology innovation and industrialization. Now, he serves as a member of the Standing Committee of the Party Committee, the Chief Engineer, the Director of Science and Technology Innovation Committee and the Chief Scientist of CRRC. Wang Jun has achieved numerous awards, including one special prize, one first prize and one second prize of the National Science and Technology Progress Award, one first and one second prize of the National Enterprise Management Modernization Innovation Achievement Award, one first prize of the National State-owned Enterprise Management Innovation Achievement Award, National Innovation Team Award, China's Outstanding Engineer Award, Jemez Tien Yow Railway Science and Technology Award and Locomotive Medal, COTA Lifetime Achievement Award, etc. He has been selected into the National Numerous Talents Project and enjoys the special allowance of the State Council. Moreover, he cultivated a large number of outstanding scientific and management talents in the field of railway equipment.

He has presided over the creation of the first technology system for high-speed train bogie of 250km/h class in China and developed the first domestically-produced CRH2 high-speed train. On this basis, he developed the long composition high-speed train and first developed the sleeper high-speed train, established the product platform and domestically-produced capability, which support the implementation of the sixth speed increase of railway in China.

He proposed the full chain development method of the roof design, system matching, index decomposition and performance optimization for high-speed train. He made a breakthrough on the core problems of 350km/h class train system integration, light weight, high-speed travel, etc, and presided over the development of China's first 350km/h class high-speed train with independent intellectual property rights.

He proposed the dual driven innovation management mode of "technology + industry", presided over the establishment of the integration platform of design-manufacturing-product technologies and first created the pedigree method for high-speed train. He also promoted the cultivation of independent industrial capability over world-leading "Harmony" and "Fuxing" high-speed trains, which advances our high-speed train technology and industry to a fully leading position.

Facing the inclement and complex weather in plateau environment, he pioneered the train oxygen supply system, which took the lead in solving the difficult problem of oxygen supplement for railway passenger car in plateau environment in the world. He first created the lightning protection device, which ensured the high reliability of electrical system, and filled in the technology gap of passenger car on plateau in China.

# 产业创新奖获得者

# 王 如 竹

　　王如竹，1964年12月出生于江苏省张家港市。1990年获上海交通大学工学博士学位，同年开始在上海交通大学制冷与低温工程研究所工作至今，先后担任上海交通大学动力与能源工程学院、机械与动力工程学院副院长，教育部太阳能发电与制冷工程研究中心副主任、主任。先后兼任中国制冷学会副理事长、国际制冷学会B2委员会副主席、中国工程热物理学会常务理事。主持成果曾获国家自然科学奖二等奖和国家技术发明奖二等奖，同时是J&E Hall 国际制冷金牌、国际热科学 Nukiyama 纪念奖、国际制冷学会最高学术奖 Gustav Lorentzen Medal、国际能源署 Rittinger Heat Pump Award 等7个国际学术重要奖项的首位中国获奖学者。

　　王如竹在制冷、热泵与热调控领域作出了系统创新成果，显著推动了产业发展，为节能减排作出了重大贡献。

## 一、建立了完整的吸附制冷理论体系

　　发现压力势回收可显著提高吸附制冷浓度差，首创回热回质循环，将低驱动温度下的制冷系数提升近100%；提出物理与化学吸附相嵌的复合吸附，实现了高效稳定的吸附与解吸；高导热多孔基质复合吸附剂使导热系数提高20倍、渗透率提升近千倍，实现了吸附床的小温差换热。

## 二、构建了太阳能供热和制冷系列新方法

　　提出回热回质硅胶-水吸附制冷、变效溴化锂-水吸收制冷及精馏热利用的氨水吸收冷冻等方法，实现了60～150℃温域太阳能制冷效率的最大化。提出太阳集热-空气吸热结合的热泵热力循环和供热新方法，实现了太阳能高效稳定供热。

### 三、发明了系列空气源热泵热水和供热系统

率先实现空气源热泵热水器产业化，提出结合小温差末端供热的空气源热泵系统，并服务于北方清洁供热和南方舒适性供热。基于上述技术，进一步创制了替代工业锅炉的空气源热泵水蒸气发生系统，建立产业化科技型企业，成功应用于燃煤/燃气/电锅炉的清洁高效替代。

### 四、首创了储湿换热空调循环

揭示了储湿换热器热湿传递机理，可通过回收冷凝废热驱动空调除湿，结合温湿度弱关联控制新方法，实现了空调能效提高近100%。获欧美近十个国家专利，相关成果转化给中德合资企业用于提升轨道交通空调能效。

### 五、建立了开展变革性科学研究的能源-水-空气跨学科交叉平台

将吸附空气储湿应用于电子器件发汗冷却、空气取水、吸附储热等新兴技术，由他首创的仿生换热方法解决了通信基站从4G向5G演进的高密度散热问题，用于华为上百万5G基站；提出基于温度场重构技术和热容-热阻网络化快速计算的Soft Cooling冷却方法，解决了手机的瞬态散热调控问题，用于华为P20以后的超千万智能手机。

## Awardee of Industrial Innovation Prize, Wang Ruzhu

Wang Ruzhu was born in Zhangjiagang City of Jiangsu Province in December 1964. In 1990, he graduated from Shanghai Jiao Tong University with a doctor's degree in engineering. He has worked in the Institute of Refrigeration and Cryogenics of Shanghai Jiao Tong University since 1990. From 1997 to 2008, he served as the vice dean of the School of Power and Energy Engineering and the School of Mechanical Engineering of Shanghai Jiao Tong University. Since 2001, he has served as the deputy-director and director of the Engineering Research Center for Solar Power and Refrigeration of the Ministry of Education. He won the second prize of the National Natural Science Award and the second prize of the National Technological Invention Award, and was the first Chinese winner of seven important international academic awards, including the J&E Hall Gold Medal, Nukiyama Memorial Award, Gustav Lorentzen Medal-the highest academic award of International Institute of Refrigeration, and the Heat Pump Award of International Energy Agency. He has served as the vice president of the Chinese Association of Refrigeration, the vice president of the B2 Commission of the International Institute of Refrigeration, the executive director of the Chinese Society of Engineering Thermophysics.

He has made systematic achievements in the fields of refrigeration, heat pump and thermal energy regulation, which significantly promoted the industrial development and made significant contributions to energy conservation and emission reduction. Representative contributions include:

**1. He established a complete theoretical system of adsorption refrigeration**

He found that the pressure potential recovery can significantly improve the concentration difference of adsorption refrigeration, and proposed the heat and mass recovery cycle, which can increase the COP (coefficient of performance) by nearly 100% at low driving temperature. He proposed the combination of physical and chemical adsorption, to achieve efficient and stable adsorption and desorption. The composite adsorbent with high thermal conductivity porous matrix can increase the thermal conductivity by 20 times and the permeability by nearly a thousand times, thus realizing the small temperature difference heat transfer of the adsorption bed.

**2. He constructed a series of new technology for solar heating and cooling**

To maximize the solar cooling efficiency in the temperature range of 60~150℃, he invented the silica gel-water adsorption refrigeration cycle with heat and mass recovery, variable effect LiBr-water absorption refrigeration cycle and ammonia-water absorption freezing cycle with rectification heat recovery. To achieve efficient and stable heating by solar energy, he proposed the heat pump cycle and heating systems combining solar heat collection and air heat absorption.

**3. He invented a series of air source heat pump hot water and heating systems**

In 2003, he took the lead in realizing the industrialization of air source heat pump water heater. In 2012, he proposed the small temperature difference fan coil unit for air source heat pump, to serve the clean heating in the north and comfort heating in the south. Based on these technologies, he further created the air source heat pump steam generation system to replace industrial boilers. This was successfully demonstrated in an industrialized enterprise, for the clean and efficient replacement of coal-fired/gas/electric boilers.

**4. He proposed and realized high efficiency air conditioning system based on heat pump with water-sorbing heat exchangers**

He revealed the heat and moisture transfer mechanisms of the water-sorbing heat exchanger. By recovering the condensation waste heat to drive the dehumidification of the air conditioner, the proposed new method of temperature and humidity weak correlation control realized the energy efficiency improvement of the air conditioner by nearly 100%, which was patented by nearly 10 countries in Europe and the United States, and was transferred to Sino-German company to improve the energy efficiency of the air conditioner for rail transit.

**5. He established an interdisciplinary platform of energy, water and air for transformative scientific research**

He proposed atmospheric water adsorption storage technology, which was applied to transpiration cooling of electronic devices, atmospheric water harvesting, adsorption heat storage and other emerging technologies. He invented the first bionic heat transfer method, which solved the high-density heat dissipation problem of communication base stations evolution from 4G to 5G. This has been used in Huawei's millions of 5G base stations. He proposed the soft cooling method based on temperature field reconstruction technology and fast calculation of heat capacity thermal resistance networking, to solve the problem of transient heat dissipation regulation of mobile phones. It has been used for more than 10 million smart phones after Huawei P20.

# 产业创新奖获得者

# 徐文伟

徐文伟，1963年出生于江苏省常州市。1980年考入南京工学院自动控制系，先后获南京工学院学士和东南大学硕士学位。1991年加入华为研发部，历任华为总体技术办主任、无线研发总经理、预研部创始总裁、首任欧洲片区总裁、全球销售与服务总裁，海思创始总裁、企业业务集团创始CEO、IRB（产品投资评审委员会）主任，战略研究院院长等。现任华为公司董事、科学家咨询委员会主任。先后兼任国家集成电路产业咨询委员会委员，中国通信学会副理事长，中国光学工程学会副理事长，国家"十四五"信息光子重点专项专家组成员，国家"十四五"数学重点专项实施方案和2021年指南编制专家，科技部基础司基础研究中长期发展规划专家成员等。

徐文伟长期致力于通信产品研发和产业拓展，先后主持并参与了华为第一代局用程控交换机、第一颗芯片、第一套GSM系统、第一台云数据中心核心交换机等系列重大核心技术攻关和产品研发，是华为从小到大、从大到强、从国内走向国际以及全球化的重要参与者和推动者，为我国通信产业从自立到自强再到引领和卓越作出了重要贡献。

## 一、创立华为芯片设计中心（海思半导体），主持设计国内首款规模商用的数字交换芯片，创建"系统创新+芯片设计一体化"的产品研发模式

20世纪90年代初，电路交换规模是PSTN交换机的核心指标，常规"时－空－时"三级交换矩阵内部互联随端口数增长而指数增长，成为交换规模增长的瓶颈。为解决这个挑战，徐文伟提出多级流水线时分交换矩阵架构，发明一种大容量数字交换网架构，突破交换芯片复杂度随容量增加而指数增长的关键技术，1995年成为华为首个获得的国家技术发明专利。主持设计国内首款规模化商用数字交换芯片，是华为C&C08数字程控交换机的核心技术之一，为华为成功进入数字交换通信市场并逐步打开国际市场奠定了重要的工程技术基础。

徐文伟1991年主持开发华为第一代程控交换机时，设计了华为第一颗芯片并创立芯片设计中心，建立自研芯片的设计体系和流程方法。华为芯片设计中心于2004年更名为海思半导体，为海思半导体支撑华为核心业务、保障产品和技术的持续领先奠定了基础。基于自研芯片的成功实践，徐文伟创建了"系统创新+芯片设计一体化"的产品研发模式，从第一阶段替代进口芯片降低成本，到第二阶段通过自研芯片领先对手快速推出产品，发展到第三阶段围绕核心技术自研芯片实现产品创新和领先，实现了产品功能强、速度快、性能好、成本省的独特优势。

**二、提出云数据中心核心交换机的正交交换架构，突破网络实现超大规模、超低时延的技术和工程瓶颈，研制成功全球最大容量的云数据中心核心交换机**

2010年云计算兴起，分布式计算的集群规模从百台扩展到万台服务器，要求云数据中心网络具备超大容量、无阻塞和超低时延等极致性能，远超当时的交换架构、高速互联、功耗散热等工程能力瓶颈。

徐文伟主持华为云数据中心核心交换机的研发，制定了"以网络架构创新和跨学科集成创新突破工程瓶颈"的技术路线。

一是应用无阻塞CLOS交换网络理论，率先建立Leaf-Spine拓扑架构和集中流量均衡控制协议的融合架构，替代传统的接入－汇聚－核心三级收敛网络架构，实现了理论上无阻塞的数据中心网络，创造了业界最低的2～5μs超低时延。整网容量可以平滑扩容百倍，解决云计算业务弹性部署和算力平滑提升的难题。

二是针对背板架构下的电、热、力的耦合复杂工程难题，提出核心交换机的正交交换架构，组织研制电、热、力综合性能仿真平台，引入风洞建模、力学模型、电磁模型，有效解决了先进风道设计、高速链路异质阻抗匹配、接插件应力形变等，并在2013年日本最大的ICT展览会InterOP实现中国厂商首次获得大奖。该数据中心核心交换机属业界首创正交架构，上市容量是同代业界标杆的3.6倍，持续领先业界，突破高速光/电芯片等多项关键技术并打破国外垄断。

该项目成果累计获得授权发明专利上千项，其中国际发明专利超过40%；2016年后连续获国内第一、全球第三的市场份额，广泛应用于电信、金融、电力、石化、互联网等行业，不仅保障了我国数据通信基础设施的自主可控和安全，同时还规模出口到欧洲、日韩、拉美等国家和地区。

**三、创建华为欧洲业务的产品创新和市场模式，构建了"基于生命周期价值工程评估模型"，改变移动运营商网络建设和采购模式**

2005年，面对欧洲市场极高的技术门槛和市场壁垒、竞争对手百年的本土和市场格局优势，徐文伟作为华为公司欧洲片区总裁，制定了"超越单产品竞争，以系统工程改变格局"的总体思路，提出生命周期价值工程评估模型，以网络建设和运营周期的总成本来衡量产品创新的客户总价值；引导客户不再以单产品价格而是以"生命周期价值"作为选择依据，改变了移动运营商网络建设和采购模式，成功打入了欧洲主流运营商市场。

# Awardee of Industrial Innovation Prize, Xu Wenwei

Xu Wenwei was born in Changzhou City of Jiangsu Province in 1963. In 1980, he was admitted to the Automatic Control Department of Nanjing Institute of Technology (NIT). He received his bachelor's degree from NIT and master's degree from Southeast University (SEU). Mr. Xu joined Huawei's R&D Department in 1991 and currently serves as a board director and Chair of the Scientist Advisory Committee of Huawei.

Committed to the R&D of communication products and the development of the communication industry, Mr. Xu has directed and participated in the R&D of multiple core technologies and products over the past three decades. He led the development of Huawei's first generation of public program-controlled switches, first global system for mobile communications (GSM), and first data center core switch, among other important products. He established Huawei's chip design center (the predecessor to HiSilicon) and served as its president, and created a product R&D model of "system innovation + chip design integration". This laid a solid foundation for Huawei's product competitiveness, and paved the way for HiSilicon to become one of the world's leading chip design companies.

Mr. Xu has served, among others, as Director of Huawei's General Technology Office, General Manager of Wireless Product R&D, Founding President of the Pre-research Department, First President of the European Area, Chief Sales & Service Officer, Founding President of HiSilicon, Founding CEO of the Enterprise BG, Chairman of the Investment Review Board (IRB), and President of the Institute of Strategic Research. Playing an instrumental role in the growth of Huawei from a startup in China to a large international company, Mr. Xu has also made outstanding contributions to the development of China's communication industry into a self-reliant sector and a leading power globally.

# 产业创新奖获得者

# 徐 佐

徐佐，1965年10月出生于湖北省大悟县。1987年获昆明理工大学金属材料专业工学学士学位。1987—2016年先后在渤海铝业有限公司、中信戴卡股份有限公司工作。2016年至今在中国中信集团有限公司工作，历任总经理助理、副总经理，兼总工程师，中信戴卡董事长。其间（2007—2009年），在中国人民大学学习，获EMBA学位。2014—2020年兼任中国铸造协会副会长、中国汽车工业协会第八届理事会副会长。曾获国家科技进步奖二等奖1项、省部级科技进步奖一等奖3项，并获国际镁协"最佳工艺制造"奖和德国iF设计奖等。

徐佐始终专注于汽车零部件用轻合金材料、工艺技术、制造装备及产业化基础与应用研究，为我国铝车轮产业发展并取得全球主导地位作出突出贡献，是我国绿色和智能制造技术的推进者。

## 一、创新研发高强韧轻合金材料、复杂结构件高致密控压铸造成型关键技术及短流程工艺

解决了轻合金应用于汽车结构件的高强韧性和大规模制造质量一致性的行业难题，创建了铝合金车轮材料标准和制造技术新体系。①提出了A356铝合金强韧化技术新方案，合金塑性显著提升；②发明了铝车轮高致密控压铸造成型关键技术，实现了车轮整体的高致密化和组织细化；③发明了"铸造→均温→旋压"复合成型短流程制造技术，工艺流程由7步减至3步，减少300℃升温能耗；④发明了低成本新型高延展性免热处理镁合金，解决了大直径镁铸棒热裂难题和商用大规格镁合金铸棒质量稳定性问题。该技术应用于锻旋镁合金车轮生产，实现国内镁合金车轮首次用于F1赛车以及行业内唯一获得镁合金车轮OEM配套资质。

## 二、突破关键技术，研发了铝合金控压铸造成套装备，实现核心装备自主研制并反向输出

针对传统铸造装备精度低、柔性化差和自动化程度低，不能满足大尺寸复杂结构件低成本大规模稳定生产的迫切需求，自主研发了精密铸造、自动放过滤网、转运、旋压、刻码等成套智能化装备和生产线。①发明了可持续供给铝液的自净化双室保温炉、四导杠高刚度高精密开合模执行机构等关键技术，研发出铝车轮全自动高精密双室型低压铸造成套装备，实现24″大尺寸铝车轮低压铸造，解决了小拔模角车轮铸造面易拉伤难题；②发明了液压机械双同步、三级稳速开合模控制系统以及均匀水冷导向套等关键技术，研发出转向节双缸同步高精密差压铸造成套装备，同时发明了大容量、无空腔密封坩埚炉及其快速更换等技术，减少了铝液氧化夹渣和温降；③提出短流程"U"形工艺新布局，研发了熔炼-铸造-热处理-涂装能源梯度利用新途径，开发了分布式去浇口、变形自适应加工、一体化检测、二维码质量追溯等多项产线关键共性技术，建成全自动数字化高效流转生产线。

## 三、创建了高效、低碳铝车轮全流程智能制造管控技术体系

针对传统铝车轮制造存在的低效、高能耗等难题，开发了AI控制技术与数据管理逻辑，构建了铝车轮生产工序信息闭环和工序间有机融合的全流程智能制造系统。①发明了铸造过程模具温度场实时采集、智能分析和控制技术，建立了铸造过程机理解析与工艺优化模型，实现了数据驱动的铸造质量闭环管理，铸造单机小时平均产能提升35%；②开发了以知识图谱为核心的闭环尺寸自控调整系统，建立了高效多品种车轮柔性加工新模式，单一机加工夹具可适配多种车轮规格；③开发了智能化岛式互通涂装工艺技术，构建了基于涂层厚度及缺陷检测结果的工艺动态调整系统，实现零延时切换涂装品种达100多种；④通过AI和信息技术将各生产工序系统集成，建立了基于大数据分析的精益协同智能制造新模式，实现了全流程柔性智能制造。

## 四、首创车轮及悬架模拟实况安全性测试与评价技术体系

针对双轴疲劳试验国外行业垄断和滥用试验真车路试危险性高、成本高、周期长等难题，研发出被世界同行采用的实况模拟试验技术体系。①研发了外传鼓表征道路的车轮道路模拟疲劳试验技术，发明了外转鼓表征道路的载荷块高效切换实验平台；②开发了道路载荷谱设计新方案，代替整车试车场疲劳试验更加精准，打破了国外技术独家垄断；③研发了模拟车轮滥用试验技术，开发与目标汽车底盘特征等效的试验测试底盘和模拟多种极限坏路的标准障碍物，试验结果与真车实际路况冲击结果一致性好；④研发了乘用车车轮径向冲击安全评价技术和操作方便、测量精密的试验机，该装备技术国内首创、技术领先，打破欧洲的技术垄断并反向输出欧美市场。

# Awardee of Industrial Innovation Prize, Xu Zuo

Xu Zuo was born in Dawu County of Hubei Province in October 1965. He received his bachelor's degree in Metal Materials from Kunming University of Science and Technology in 1987 and received his EMBA degree from the Renmin University of China in 2009. Currently, he serves as the vice president and senior engineer of CITIC Group, and the chairman of CITIC Dicastal Co., Ltd.

Xu Zuo has been dedicated to the research of light alloy materials, process technologies, manufacturing equipment, and intelligent and green manufacturing for automotive parts. He has won many honors and recognition in his field, including 1 Second Prize in the National Science and Technology Progress Award, 3 First Prizes for the Provincial or Ministerial Science and Technology Progress Award, the International Magnesium Association Awards of Excellence for Process, and the German iF Design Award.

He invented an ultra-high strengthening and toughening technology for the A356 alloy by systematically investigating the influence mechanism of the Mg, Si on strength and fluidity of the alloy, and La, Ce on grain refinement and modification.

He invented a two-chamber self-purification holding furnace for a continuous supply of molten aluminum alloy, and high precision and stiffness casting machines. An automatic production line that equipped the automatic equipment, 70% of which was self-developed, was built following the proposed "U"-shaped process layout that investigated for improving energy efficiency.

He has independently developed a complete set of AI control technology, and data management logic, and constructed a thorough-process intelligent manufacturing system for Al wheels production. In the system, the self-established technologies are real-time acquisition, intelligent analysis, control technology of the mold temperature, and autonomous detection of casting defects on basis of machine learning. The efficiency of the intelligent plant increased by 35%.

He established an outer-drum test bench for fatigue tests on different road types and developed a new design scheme for the load spectrum of roads. He established standards for test chassis and obstacles to simulate the performance of wheels and suspension components in actual driving.

# 附 录

APPENDICES

# 何梁何利基金评选章程

（2020年5月27日何梁何利基金信托委员会全体会议通过）

## 一、总　　则

第一条　何梁何利基金（以下称"本基金"）由何善衡慈善基金会有限公司、梁銶琚博士、何添博士、利国伟博士之伟伦基金有限公司于1994年3月30日捐款成立。2005年10月24日经香港高等法院批准。基金捐款人，除了何善衡慈善基金会有限公司及利国伟博士之伟伦基金有限公司外，梁銶琚慈善基金会有限公司和何添基金有限公司各自分别为已故梁銶琚博士及已故何添博士之遗产承办人指定之慈善机构，以便根据本基金信托契约之条款行使有关权力或给予所需批准。

第二条　本基金的宗旨是：

（一）促进中国的科学与技术发展；

（二）奖励取得杰出成就和重大创新的科学技术工作者。

第三条　本基金依法登记设立何梁何利基金（香港）北京代表处，负责何梁何利基金科学技术奖评选工作，执行基金在中国内地的相关业务。

何梁何利基金（香港）北京代表处的业务主管部门为中华人民共和国科学技术部。

## 二、评奖条件

第四条　本基金奖励和资助致力于推进中国科学技术取得成就及进步与创新的个人。

第五条　本基金奖励和资助具备下列条件的中华人民共和国公民：

（一）对推动科学技术事业发展有杰出贡献；

（二）热爱祖国，积极为国家现代化建设服务，有高尚的社会公德和职业道德；

（三）在我国科学技术研究院（所）、大专院校、企业以及信托委员会认为适当的其他机构从事科学研究、教学或技术工作已满5年。

第六条　获奖候选人须由评选委员会选定的提名人以书面形式推荐。

提名人由科学技术领域具有一定资格的专家包括海外学者组成。

## 三、奖　　项

第七条　本基金设"何梁何利基金科学与技术成就奖""何梁何利基金科学与技术进步奖""何梁何利基金科学与技术创新奖"，每年评奖一次。

第八条　何梁何利基金科学与技术成就奖授予下列杰出科学技术工作者：

（一）长期致力于推进国家科学技术进步，贡献卓著，历史上取得国际高水准学术成就者；

（二）在科学技术前沿，取得重大科技突破，攀登当今科技高峰，领先世界先进水平者；

（三）推进技术创新，建立强大自主知识产权和自主品牌，其产业居于当今世界前列者。

何梁何利基金科学与技术成就奖获奖人每人颁发奖励证书和奖金100万港元。

第九条　何梁何利基金科学与技术进步奖授予在特定学科领域取得重大发明、发现和科技成果者，尤其是在近年内有突出贡献者。

何梁何利基金科学与技术进步奖按学科领域分设下列奖项：

（一）数学力学奖

（二）物理学奖

（三）化学奖

（四）天文学奖

（五）气象学奖

（六）地球科学奖

（七）生命科学奖

（八）农学奖

（九）医学药学奖

（十）古生物学、考古学奖

（十一）机械电力技术奖

（十二）电子信息技术奖

（十三）交通运输技术奖

（十四）冶金材料技术奖

（十五）化学工程技术奖

（十六）资源能源技术奖

（十七）生态环保技术奖

（十八）工程建设技术奖

何梁何利基金科学与技术进步奖获奖人每人颁发奖励证书和奖金20万港元。

第十条　何梁何利基金科学与技术创新奖授予具有高水平科技成就而通过技术创新和管理创新，创建自主知识产权产业和著名品牌，创造重大经济效益和社会效益的杰出贡献者。

何梁何利基金科学与技术创新奖分设下列奖项：

（一）青年创新奖

（二）产业创新奖

（三）区域创新奖

何梁何利基金科学与技术创新奖获奖人每人颁发奖励证书和奖金20万港元。

第十一条　本基金每年各奖项名额如下：

何梁何利基金科学与技术成就奖不超过 5 名；何梁何利基金科学与技术进步奖、何梁何利基金科学与技术创新奖总数不超过 65 名（原则上科学与技术进步奖和科学与技术创新奖名额的比例为 3 比 1 至 2 比 1）。而奖金总额不超过该年度信托委员会审议通过的奖金总额。

具体名额根据年度资金运作情况和评选情况确定。

## 四、评选委员会

第十二条　本基金成立由各相关领域具有高尚道德情操、精深学术造诣、热心科技奖励事业的专家组成的评选委员会。

评选委员会委员经过信托委员会批准、颁发聘任书后，独立行使职能，负责评选工作。

第十三条　评选委员会委员最多不超过 24 人，其中主任一人、副主任二人、秘书长一人，由内地学者和海外学者出任。

评选委员会委员内地学者和海外学者的比例，原则上每四名委员中，内地学者为三人，海外学者为一人。

评选委员会主任、副主任由基金信托契约补充条款规定的信托委员兼任。其中主任由补充契约所指明的与科技部有关的信托委员兼任，副主任二人分别由补充契约所指明的与教育部有关的信托委员和补充契约所指明的国际学者信托委员兼任。评选委员会秘书长由信托委员会任命并征得捐款人同意的人选担任。

评选委员会委员实行任期制，一任三年，可以连聘连任。

评选委员会委员原则上每三年更换四分之一（不包括主任、副主任及秘书长）。

此外，评选委员会委员的聘任，贯彻相对稳定和适度更新的原则。其办法由评选委员会制定。

评选委员会办公室设在北京，挂靠科学技术部。

第十四条　评选委员会根据评选工作需要，可组织若干专业评审组、奖项评审组，根据提名人的提名推荐材料对被提名人进行初评，产生获奖候选人，提交评选委员会终评。

专业评审组、奖项评审组的评委由评选委员会任命。

第十五条　本基金各奖项获奖人由评选委员会会议评定。

何梁何利基金科学与技术进步奖、何梁何利基金科学与技术创新奖的获奖人，由评选委员会根据专业评审组、奖项评审组的评选结果，评选审定。

何梁何利基金科学与技术成就奖获奖人，由评选委员会全体会议根据评选委员提名评选产生。评选委员会设立预审小组，必要时对候选人进行考察和听证。

第十六条　评选委员会会议贯彻"公平、公正、公开"原则，实行一人一票制，以无记名形式表决确定获奖人。何梁何利基金科学与技术进步奖、何梁何利基金科学与技术创新奖的候选人，获半数赞成票为获奖人。何梁何利基金科学与技术成就奖的候选人，获三分之二多数赞成票为获奖人。

第十七条　评选委员会在评定获奖人名额时，应适当考虑奖种、学科和区域之间的平衡。

## 五、授　　奖

第十八条　评选委员会评选结果揭晓前须征求获奖人本人意愿，并通知捐款人及信托委员会。遵照捐款人意愿，获奖人应承诺于获奖后，继续在国内从事科学研究和技术工作不少于三年。

第十九条　本基金每年适当时候举行颁奖仪式，由评选委员会安排向何梁何利基金各奖项获得者颁发证书和奖金，并通过新闻媒体公布获奖人员名单及其主要贡献。

## 六、出版物和学术会议

第二十条　本基金每年出版介绍获奖人及其主要科学技术成就的出版物。

出版物的编辑、出版工作由评选委员会负责。

第二十一条　本基金每年举办学术报告会、研讨会，由评选委员会委员、获奖人代表介绍其学术成就及相关学科领域的进展。

根据基金财政状况，本基金各专业领域专题学术讨论会可在海外举办。

本基金学术论坛由评选委员会负责组织。

## 七、附　　则

第二十二条　本基金评选委员会每年例会一次，总结当年工作，部署下一年度工作，研究和决定重大事宜。

第二十三条　本章程由本基金评选委员会解释。

第二十四条　本章程自 2020 年 5 月 27 日施行。

# REGULATIONS OF HO LEUNG HO LEE FOUNDATION ON THE EVALUATION AND EXAMINATION OF ITS PRIZES AND AWARDS

(Adopted at the Plenary Meeting of the Trust Board on May 27, 2020)

## I  General Provisions

Article 1  Ho Leung Ho Lee Foundation (hereinafter referred to as "the Foundation") was established on March 30, 1994 in Hong Kong with funds donated by the S H Ho Foundation Limited, Dr. Leung Kau-Kui, Dr. Ho Tim and Dr. Lee Quo-Wei's Wei Lun Foundation Limited. With the approval of the High Court of Hong Kong, apart from S H Ho Foundation Limited and Wei Lun Foundation Limited (donors of the Foundation), Leung Kau-Kui Foundation Limited and Ho Tim Foundation Limited have respectively been nominated by the estates of the late Dr. Leung Kau-Kui and Dr. Ho Tim to and they can as from October 24, 2005 exercise the powers or give the necessary approvals under the terms of the Foundation's trust deed.

Article 2  Purposes of the Foundation are:
(1) To promote the development of science and technology in China.
(2) To reward the scientific and technical personnel with outstanding achievements and great innovations.

Article 3  The Beijing Representative Office of the Ho Leung Ho Lee Foundation (Hong Kong) is established through registration in accordance with the law. It is responsible for selecting the winners of science and technology prizes and awards granted by the Ho Leung Ho Lee Foundation, and carries out the works related to the Foundation on the mainland of China.

The Ministry of Science and Technology of the People's Republic of China acts as the competent authority responsible for the work of the Beijing Representative Office of the Ho Leung Ho Lee Foundation (Hong Kong).

## II  Criteria for Awards

Article 4  The Foundation shall grant awards and prizes to individuals who are devoted to the achievements, progress and innovations of China's science and technology.

Article 5  The Foundation shall grant awards and prizes to the citizens of the People's Re-

public of China who meet the following criteria:
- (1) Having made outstanding contributions in promoting the development of science and technology.
- (2) Being patriotic, vigorously working for the modernization drive of the country, and preserving lofty social morality and professional ethics.
- (3) Being with at least five years of scientific researches, teaching or technical working experience in China's science and technology research institutes, institutions for higher learning and universities, enterprises and other organizations which the Board of Trustees regards as appropriate.

Article 6  Candidates for the awards and prizes of the Foundation shall be recommended in writing by nominators identified by the Selection Board.

Nominators should be qualified experts (including those overseas) in various fields of sciences and technology.

## III  Awards and Prizes

Article 7  The Foundation sets three annual prizes. They are the Prize for Scientific and Technological Achievements of Ho Leung Ho Lee Foundation, the Prize for Scientific and Technological Progress of Ho Leung Ho Lee Foundation, and the Prize for Scientific and Technological Innovation of Ho Leung Ho Lee Foundation.

Article 8  The Prize for Scientific and Technological Achievements of Ho Leung Ho Lee Foundation shall be awarded to the outstanding science and technology personnel as follows:
- (1) Those who have devoted to scientific and technological progress in China for a long time, having made significant contributions and world-class academic achievements.
- (2) Those who have made great breakthroughs in the frontline of science and technology, attaining high levels in science and technology and leading the trend in specific areas in the world.
- (3) Those who have made great efforts in pushing forward the technology innovation and have built up powerful self intellectual property and brand of its own so that its industry ranks the top of today's world.

Each winner of the Prize for Scientific and Technological Achievements of Ho Leung Ho Lee Foundation will receive a certificate and the amount of the prize of HK $ 1000000.

Article 9  The Prize for Scientific and Technological Progress of Ho Leung Ho Lee Foundation is for those who have made important inventions, discoveries and achievements in specific subject areas, especially having remarkable contributions in recent years.

The following prizes of the Prize for Scientific and Technological Progress of Ho Leung Ho Lee Foundation are set up by subjects:
- (1) Award for Mathematics and Mechanics

(2) Award for Physics

(3) Award for Chemistry

(4) Award for Astronomy

(5) Award for Meteorology

(6) Award for Earth Sciences

(7) Award for Life Sciences

(8) Award for Agronomy

(9) Award for Medical Sciences and Materia Medica

(10) Award for Paleontology and Archaeology

(11) Award for Machinery and Electric Technology

(12) Award for Electronics and Information Technology

(13) Award for Communication and Transportation Technology

(14) Award for Metallurgy and Materials Technology

(15) Award for Chemical Engineering Technology

(16) Award for Resources and Energies Technology

(17) Award for Ecology and Environmental Protection Technology

(18) Award for Engineering and Construction Technology

Each winner of the Prize for Science and Technological Progress of Ho Leung Ho Lee Foundation will be awarded a certificate and the amount of the prize of HK $ 200000.

Article 10  The Prize for Scientific and Technological Innovation of Ho Leung Ho Lee Foundation is for the outstanding contributors who have made high level achievements in science and technology, created industry with self intellectual property and famous brands through technology and management innovation, and thus have created great economic and social benefits for the society.

The following prizes of the Prize for Scientific and Technological Innovation of Ho Leung Ho Lee Foundation are set up:

(1) Award for Youth Innovation

(2) Award for Industrial Innovation

(3) Award for Region Innovation

Each winner of the Prize for Scientific and Technological Innovation of Ho Leung Ho Lee Foundation will be awarded a certificate and the amount of the prize of HK $ 200000.

Article 11  Annual quotas of awardees of each prize of Ho Leung Ho Lee Foundation are as follows:

There should be no more than 5 awardees each year for the Prize for Scientific and Technological Achievements of Ho Leung Ho Lee Foundation; and the total number of the winners of the Prize for Scientific and Technological Progress of Ho Leung Ho Lee Foundation and the Prize for Scientific and Technological Innovation of Ho Leung Ho Lee Foundation should be no more than 65 (The proportion of the awardees of the Prize for Scientific and Technological Progress of Ho Leung Ho Lee Foundation and the Prize for Scientific and Technological Innovation of Ho Leung Ho Lee Foundation is in principle from 3 to 1 to 2 to 1). And the total amount of all the Prizes awarded should not exceed the total amount of prize moneys of the year as approved by the Board of Trustees for that year.

The number of winners of each prize should be decided according to the situation each year of the operation of the Foundation's funds and the results of evaluation and selection for the year.

## Ⅳ Selection Board

Article 12   A Selection Board shall be constituted under the Foundation, consisting of scholars who are highly respected in ethics, with accomplishments in academic researches and devotion to the work of award of science and technology prizes.

Members of the Selection Board shall independently exercise the powers and are responsible for the evaluation work after they have been appointed with the approval of the Board of Trustees and received the letters of appointment.

Article 13   The total number of the members of the Selection Board should be no more than 24. Among them, there will be one Chair, two Vice Chairs and one Secretary-General. Both local and overseas scholars could be members of the Selection Board.

For every four members of the Selection Board, the ratio between local and overseas scholars should in principle be 3 to 1.

The Chair and the two Vice Chairs of the Selection Board should also be members of the Board of Trustees as stated in the Foundation's Supplemental trust deed. Among them, the Chair should be the member of the Board of Trustees who is related, as stated in the Foundation's Supplemental trust deed, to the Ministry of Science and Technology. And the two Vice Chairs should respectively be the member of the Board of Trustees who is related, as stated in the Foundation's Supplemental trust deed, to the Ministry of Education and the international scholar member of the Board of Trustees as mentioned in the Foundation's Supplemental trust deed.

Secretary General of the Selection Board should be appointed by the Board of Trustees with the agreement of the donors as well.

A system of the set term of office is instituted for members of the Selection Board. Each term of office of the members of the Selection Board is 3 years. A member of the Selection Board may serve consecutive terms.

In principle, the members of the Selection Board shall be altered a quarter every 3 years (except Chair, Vice Chair and Secretary General.)

Besides, the appointment of the members of the Selection Board should be in line with the principles of comparative stability and proper renewal. The Selection Board will be responsible for formulation of the ways of selection.

The office of the Selection Board is located in Beijing and affiliated to the Ministry of Science and Technology of China.

Article 14    Several specific professional evaluation panels or prize evaluation panels may be set up under the Selection Board when it is necessary. The first round of evaluation is done according to recommendation materials submitted by the nominators with a candidate list as the results. This list will be submitted to the Selection Board for a final evaluation.

Members of the professional evaluation panels and prize evaluation panels shall be appointed by the Selection Board.

Article 15    Winners of the prizes of the Foundation are evaluated and decided by the Selection Board.

The Selection Board shall evaluate and determine the winners of the Prize for Scientific and Technological Progress of Ho Leung Ho Lee Foundation and the Prize for Scientific and Technological Innovation of Ho Leung Ho Lee Foundation on the basis of results of the work of the professional evaluation panels or the prize evaluation panels.

The Prize for Scientific and Technological Achievements of Ho Leung Ho Lee Foundation should be decided on a plenary meeting of the Selection Board and on the basis of the nomination of the Selection Board. The Selection Board may set up preliminary evaluation panel to exercise the right of examination and hearing of the candidates when necessary.

Article 16    The Selection Board shall work with the principles of "Fairness, Justness and Openness" and "One Member One Vote". Decisions on winners of prizes of the Foundation are made in a way of anonymous ballot by the members of the Selection Board. The endorsement of at least half of the members of the Selection Board is a must for a candidate to win the Prize for Scientific and Technological Progress of Ho Leung Ho Lee Foundation and the Prize for Scientific and Technological Innovation of Ho Leung Ho Lee Foundation; while at least two-third of favorable votes of the total number is a must for candidates to win the Prize for Scientific and Technological Achievements of Ho Leung Ho Lee Foundation.

Article 17    The Selection Board should take the balance between types of prize, between subjects and between regions into consideration in the process of evaluation.

## V    Awarding

Article 18    The Selection Board must ask for the winners' willingness prior to any public announcement of the results of evaluation and selection, and notify both the donors and the Board of Trustees. According to the wishes of the donors, the winners are required to stay in China and continue to carry on scientific researches or technological work for no less than 3 years after receiving the prizes.

Article 19    An award granting ceremony will be held each year at a proper time, in which the winners shall be granted with certificates and prizes as arranged by the Selection Board. The list of awardees and their major contributions will be publicized through media.

## VI  Publications and Academic Seminars

Article 20   The Foundation shall make a publication yearly to introduce the awardees and their major scientific and technological achievements.

The Selection Board is responsible for editing and publication of the publications.

Article 21   The Foundation shall organize academic seminars every year, in which members of the Selection Board and representatives of the awardees introduce their academic achievements and updated progress in the related areas and make relevant reports where appropriate.

Should the financial situation of the Foundation permits, the academic seminars of specific subjects of the Foundation may be held abroad.

The Selection Board is responsible for the organizing academic forums of the Foundation.

## VII  Supplementary Provisions

Article 22   The Selection Board of the Foundation holds a meeting annually to summarize the work of the year, to plan the work of the following year and to study and decide on the relevant important issues.

Article 23   The Selection Board of the Foundation shall have the right of explanation of the Articles of this regulation.

Article 24   This regulation becomes effective on May 27, 2020.

# 关于何梁何利基金获奖科学家异议处理若干规定

（2009年5月20日何梁何利基金信托委员会会议通过）

## 一、总　　则

为了正确处理对何梁何利基金获奖人提出异议的投诉事件，弘扬科学精神，崇尚科学道德，抵御社会不正之风和科研不端行为，提升何梁何利基金科学与技术奖的权威性和公信力，制定本规定。

## 二、基本原则

处理对获奖人投诉事件，贯彻以事实为依据，以法律为准绳的原则，遵循科学共同体认同的道德准则，区别情况，妥善处置。

## 三、受　　理

涉及对获奖科学家主要科技成果评价、知识产权权属以及与奖项有关事项提出异议的署名投诉信件，由评选委员会受理，并调查处理。

匿名投诉信件，原则上不予受理。但涉及获奖人因科研不端行为受到处分、学术资格被取消或与其学术著作、奖项评选相关重要情况的，应由评选委员会跟进调查核实处理。

## 四、调　　查

评选委员会受理投诉后，由评选委员会秘书长指定评选委员会办公室专人按以下工作程序办理：

1. 将投诉信函复印件送交该获奖人的专业评审组负责人，征求意见。
2. 专业评审组负责人有足够理由认为投诉异议不成立，没有必要调查的，评选委员会秘书长可决定终止处理。

专业评审组负责人认为投诉异议有一定依据，有必要进一步调查的，由评选委员会办公室向获奖人所在部门或单位发函听证。

3. 获奖人所在部门或单位经调查，认为投诉异议不成立或基本不能成立的，应请该单位出具书面意见。评选委员会秘书长可据此决定终止处理。

获奖人所在部门或单位根据投诉认为获奖人涉嫌科研不端行为的，评选委员会应建议该部门或单位根据国家有关规定调查处理，并反馈查处信息。

4. 调查结果应向信托委员会报告。

## 五、处理决定

获奖人所在部门或单位经调查认定获奖人确属科研不端行为，并作出相应处理的，评选委员会秘书长应当参照《中华人民共和国科学技术进步法》第七十一条规定，提出撤销其奖励决定（草案），经评选委员会主任批准后，提交信托委员会审议。

## 六、公　　告

因获奖人科研不端行为，撤销其奖励的决定经信托委员会审议通过后，由评选委员会在何梁何利基金年报上公告，并通知本人，返回奖励证书、奖金。

信托委员会对获奖人撤销奖励的决定是终局决定。

## 七、附　　则

本规定自 2009 年 6 月 1 日起试行。

附：《中华人民共和国科学技术进步法》第七十一条：

"违反本法规定，骗取国家科学技术奖励的，由主管部门依法撤销奖励，追回奖金，并依法给予处分。

违反本法规定，推荐的单位或者个人提供虚假数据、材料，协助他人骗取国家科学技术奖励的，由主管部门给予通报批评；情节严重的，暂停或者取消其推荐资格，并依法给予处分。"

# REGULATIONS ON HANDLING THE COMPLAINT LODGED AGAINST THE PRIZE-WINNER WITH HO LEUNG HO LEE FOUNDATION

(Adopted at the Meeting of the Board of Trustees on May 20, 2009)

## I  General Principle

For the purpose of handling properly the objection lodged against the prize-winner with Ho Leung Ho Lee Foundation, promoting scientific spirits and upholding scientific ethics, preventing social malpractice or misconduct in scientific research, and improving the public credibility and authority of Ho Leung Ho Lee Foundation with respect to awards for science and technology, the Selection Board hereby formulates the regulations as stipulated below.

## II  Basic Principle

The Selection Board shall handle the complaint lodged against any prize-winner in accordance with the principle of taking the facts as the basis and taking the law as the criterion, and deal with each case properly by following the moral standard recognized by the scientific community.

## III  Acceptance

For any duly signed letter of objection against a prize-wining scientist with respect to the appraisal of his major scientific and technological achievement, the ownership of intellectual property right and other prize-related matter, the Selection Board shall be responsible for acceptance of the letter of objection and for further investigation and handling thereof.

The Selection Board shall, in principle, not accept a letter of objection written or sent in an anonymous manner. However, if it is mentioned in the letter of objection that, due to misconduct of the prize-winner in the scientific research, the discipline measure is imposed against him, or his academic qualification is cancelled, or there is any other important matter concerning his academic publication and prize selection, such a letter of objection must be accepted by the Selection Board, followed by further investigation, verification and handling.

## IV  Investigation

Upon acceptance of a letter of objection, the Secretary General of the Selection Board shall designate a special person in the Office of Selection Board to handle the letter of objection according to the procedures as follows:

1. A copy of the letter of complaint shall be sent to the person-in-charge of the specialized evaluation team determining to grant the award to the prize-winner for soliciting his comment.

2. When the person-in-charge of the specialized evaluation team concludes with sufficient reason that the objection cannot be established and it is not necessary to make further investigation, the Secretary General of the Selection Board can make a decision as to terminate the handling of the letter of objection.

When the person-in-charge of the specialized evaluation team deems that the objection can be established on basis of facts but should be proved by further investigation, the office of the Selection Board shall issue a notification to the working unit of the prize-winner to request his presence at a hearing to be held.

3. If the working unit of the prize-winner deems that the objection cannot be established or basically cannot be established after investigation, the working unit is obligated to produce a formal document in writing to state its opinion. Then the Secretary General of the Selection Board has the right to make a decision as to the termination of the handling of the letter of objection.

In case the working unit of the prize-winner deems that the prize-winner commits malpractice or misconduct in proof of the letter of objection, the Selection Board is obligated to propose that the working unit carry out investigation in accordance with government regulations before making a response by sending a feedback to the Selection Board.

4. The investigation results should be reported to Ho Leung Ho Lee Foundation's Board of Trustees.

## V  Decision

Once the working unit of the prize-winner proves with further investigation that the prize-winner commits malpractice or misconduct, and takes discipline measure against the prize-winner, the Secretary General of the Selection Board should draft a proposal, in accordance with Article 71 of the *Law of the PRC on, Science and Technology Progress*, on withdrawal of the prize awarded to the prize-winner. The proposal needs to be further approved by the Director of the Selection Board before being submitted to Ho Leung Ho Lee Foundation's Board of Trustees for deliberation.

## VI  Announcement

The Selection Board shall announce its decision with respect to withdrawal of the prize from the prize-winner, due to his malpractice or misconduct, in its annual report with approval of the Ho Leung Ho Lee Foundation's Board of Trustees, and shall notify the prize-winner that the prize and prize-winning certificate are to be cancelled. The decision to withdraw the prize from the prize-winner made by Ho Leung Ho Lee Foundation's Board of Trustees shall be final.

## VII  Appendix

These regulations shall enter into trial implementation on June 1, 2009.

Appendix: Article 71 of the *Law of the People's Republic of China on Science and Technology Progress* stipulates as follows:

The competent authority shall, in accordance with law, withdraw a prize and a bonus and take disciplinary action against anyone who is engaged in fraudulent practice for winning the National Science and Technology Prize.

For anyone or any working unit, which offers false data, false material, or conspire with others in fraudulent practice for winning the National Science and Technology Prize, the competent authority shall circulate a notice of criticism of such malpractice or misconduct; if the circumstances are serious, the competent authority shall suspend or cancel the working unit's eligibility for recommendation of any prize-winning candidate, and shall punish it in accordance with law.

# 关于何梁何利基金评选工作若干问题的说明

何梁何利基金是由香港爱国金融实业家何善衡、梁銶琚先生、何添先生、利国伟先生于1994年3月30日在香港创立的，以奖励中华人民共和国杰出科学技术工作者为宗旨的科技奖励基金。截至2010年，已有901位获奖科学家获得此项殊荣。经过16年的成功实践，何梁何利基金科技奖已经成为我国规模大、层次高、影响广、在国内外享有巨大权威性和公信力的科学技术大奖。为便于科技界、教育界和社会各界进一步了解基金宗旨、基本原则、评选标准和运行机制，在2010年10月颁奖大会期间，何梁何利基金评选委员会秘书长段瑞春就基金评选章程、评选工作以及社会各界所关心的有关问题，做了如下说明。

## 一、什么是何梁何利基金评选章程？

何梁何利基金评选章程是评选工作的基本准则。评选章程以基金《信托契约》为依据，由何梁何利基金信托委员会全体会议审议通过和发布。第一部评选章程诞生于1994年3月30日基金成立之时，保障了评选工作从一开始就步入科学、规范、健康的轨道运行。1998年5月11日适应香港九七回归和国内形势发展，对评选章程做过一次修订。2007年5月15日基金信托委员会会议决定再次修改评选章程，其主要目的，一是根据2005年10月12日香港高等法院批准生效的《补充契约条款》，对评选章程有关条款做相应修改，使之与基金《信托契约》及其《补充契约条款》保持一致。二是将评选委员会适应我国创新国策、改革评选工作的成功经验上升为章程，使之条文化、规范化、制度化，进一步提升各奖项的科学性、权威性。

## 二、根据《补充契约条款》，评选章程做了哪些重要修改？

何梁何利基金是依据香港法律创立的慈善基金。当初，根据香港普通法原则，实行信任委托制度，由捐款人与信托人签订《信托契约》，经香港终审法院批准成立。信托委员会是基金的最高权力机构，决定基金投资、评选和管理等重大事项。自1994年3月基金成立以来，当年四位创立者中，梁銶琚先生、何善衡先生、何添先生都在九旬高寿与世长辞。我们永远缅怀他们的崇高精神。由于他们的离去，《信托契约》有关捐款人的权利与义务主体出现缺位，从法律意义上影响到基金决策程序的进行。2005年10月，经香港高等法院批准《信托契约补充条款》将基金"捐款人"统一修订为原捐款人或者其遗产承办人指定的慈善基金，从而实现了捐款人从老一辈爱国金融家向其下一代的平稳过渡。依据此项修订，现基金捐款人为4个法人，即何善衡慈善基金有限公司、梁銶琚慈善基金有限公司、何添基金有限公司、利国伟先生和其夫人的伟伦基金有限公司。为此，评选章程也做了相应修改。

### 三、何梁何利基金奖励对象应当具备什么条件？

何梁何利基金奖励对象为中华人民共和国公民，获奖人应具备下列三个条件：一是对推动科学技术事业发展有杰出贡献；二是热爱祖国，有高尚的社会公德和职业道德；三是在国内从事科研、教学或技术工作已满5年。

1994年3月30日，何梁何利基金成立时，香港、澳门尚未回归祖国。鉴于当时历史状况，评选章程关于奖励对象为中华人民共和国公民的规定，仅适用祖国内地科技工作者，不包括在香港、澳门地区工作的科技人员。在"一国两制"的原则下，香港和澳门先后于1997年7月1日和1999年12月20日回归祖国。祖国内地与港澳特区科技合作与交流出现崭新局面。而今，香港、澳门特别行政区科技人员，是中华人民共和国公民中的"港人""澳人"，符合章程的要求。为此，自2007年起，何梁何利基金奖励对象扩大到符合上述条件的香港特别行政区、澳门特别行政区科学技术人员。

### 四、现行评选章程对基金奖项结构是如何规定的？

在中央人民政府和香港特区政府的关怀和指导下，16年来，何梁何利基金已经形成了科学合理的奖项结构和严谨、高效、便捷的评选程序。始终保持客观、公正、权威和具有公信力的评选纪录。现行评选章程规定基金设"科学与技术成就奖""科学与技术进步奖""科学与技术创新奖"。

每年，"科学与技术成就奖"不超过5名，授予奖牌、奖金100万港元；"科学与技术进步奖"和"科学与技术创新奖"总数不超过65名，分别授予相应的奖牌、奖金20万港元，其中，"科学与技术进步奖"和"科学与技术创新奖"的数量按3∶1至2∶1的比例，由评选委员会具体掌握。

### 五、"科学与技术成就奖"的评选标准是什么？

根据评选章程，符合下列三类条件的杰出科技工作者，均可获得"科学与技术成就奖"。一是长期致力于推进国家科学技术进步，贡献卓著，历史上取得国际高水平学术成就者；二是在科学技术前沿，取得重大科技突破，攀登当今科技高峰，领先世界先进水平者；三是推进技术创新，建立强大自主知识产权和自主品牌，其产业居于当今世界前列者。符合上述标准的获奖人选，既包括毕生奉献我国科技事业、其卓越成就曾达到世界一流水平的资深科学家，也包括以科学研究或技术创新领域的重大突破或突出业绩，使我国取得世界领先地位的中青年杰出人才。在征求意见过程中，我国科技界对此普遍赞同，认为这样修订丝毫没有降低标准，而是使基金的科技大奖进一步向国际规范靠拢，为在研究开发和创新第一线拔尖人才的脱颖而出注入强大精神动力，也使基金科技奖励更加贴近建设创新型国家的主旋律。

## 六、"科学与技术进步奖"的评选标准是怎样规定的？

评选章程规定，"科学与技术进步奖"授予在特定学科领域取得重大发明、发现和科技成果者，尤其是在近年内有突出贡献者。需要说明的，一是这里所说的"特定学科"包括：数学力学、物理学、化学、天文学、气象学、地球科学、生命科学、农学、医学和药学、古生物学和考古学、机械电力技术、电子信息技术、交通运输技术、冶金材料技术、化学工程技术、资源环保技术、工程建设技术等17个领域，每一领域设一个奖项。原评选章程用"技术科学奖"涵盖了机电、信息、冶金、材料、工程、环保等技术领域，修订后的章程从学科领域之间平衡考虑，将其分别设立奖项。二是"科学与技术进步奖"评选政策，重在考察被提名人"近年内"的突出贡献。所谓"近年内"是指近10年内。三是随着科学技术飞速发展，新兴学科、交叉学科、边缘学科层出不穷。这些学科的被提名人宜按其最主要成就、最接近学科领域归类。关注新兴、交叉、边缘学科优秀人才，是评选委员会的一项政策。有些确实需要跨学科评议的特殊情况，将作为个案协调处理，但不专门设立新兴学科、交叉学科、边缘学科等奖项。

## 七、"科学与技术创新奖"的评选标准是怎样规定的？

设立"科学与技术创新奖"是基金评选工作的重要改革。评选章程规定："科学与技术创新奖"授予具有高水平科技成就而通过技术创新和管理创新，创建自主知识产权产业和著名品牌，创造重大经济效益和社会效益的杰出贡献者。这里需要说明的是，创新，是一个经济学的范畴，指的是有明确经济、社会目标的行为。有人解释为"科学思想在市场的首次出现"。何梁何利基金为适应我国提高自主创新能力，建设创新型国家的重大决策设立这个奖项，评选章程所称的"科学与技术创新"，第一，要以高水平的科学技术成就为起点，实现科技成果转化为现实生产力，完成科技产业化的过程。第二，就创新活动而言，是指在高水平科技成就基础上的技术创新和管理创新，包括原始创新、集成创新和在他人先进技术之上的再创新，但应有自主知识产权产业和著名品牌，创造出重大经济效益和社会效益，对于创新成果在教育、节能环保、生态平衡、国家安全、社会公益事业等领域产生的巨大社会效益，将和可计量的经济效益一样，获得评选委员会的认可。第三，任何一项重大创新都是团队作战的成果，"科学与技术创新奖"的得主，可以是发挥核心作用的领军人物，也可以是实现技术突破的关键人物。当然，这里所说的领军人物本身要有科技成就，而不只是行政管理和组织协调工作。

## 八、怎样理解"科学技术创新奖"所分设的奖项？

根据评选章程，"科学技术创新奖"分设青年创新奖、产业创新奖和区域创新奖等三个奖项。青年创新奖授予在技术创新和管理创新方面业绩突出、年龄不超过45周岁的优秀科技人才；区域创新奖授予通过技术创新、管理创新和区域创新，对区域经济发展和技术进步，尤其是对祖国内地、边远、艰苦地区和少数民族地区发展作出突出贡献的人物；产业创新是指通过创新、创业，大幅度推进技术进步和产业升级，包括对传统产业技术改造和新兴产业的腾飞跨越作出贡献的优秀人才。分设上述三个奖项，是评选政策的安排，其本身并不是相互独立的创新门类。因此，"科学技术创新奖"仍然按照创新奖的基本要求统一评选，适当注意三类奖项的结构平衡，不按区域创新奖、产业创新奖、青年创新奖分组切块进行评审。

## 九、"科学与技术进步奖"和"科学与技术创新奖"评选标准有何差别？

从原则上讲，"科学与技术进步奖"按照学科领域设置，"科学与技术创新奖"基于创新业绩设置，二者有交叉和关联之处，又有重要区别，评选标准的政策取向和侧重有所不同。《评选章程》要求"科学与技术进步奖"获奖人必须是重大发明、发现和科技成果的完成人或主要完成人。而"科学与技术创新奖"的获奖人是在高水平科技成就基础上的创新实践者。前者，重在考察其发明、发现和其他科技成就的水平及其在国内国际的学术地位；而后者，重点考察其产业高端技术创新和管理创新的业绩，包括经济社会效益、自主知识产权和著名品牌建设。当然，"科学与技术创新奖"得主的领军人物本身要有高水平的科技成就，而不只是战略决策、行政管理和组织协调工作。

## 十、"科学与技术进步奖""科学与技术创新奖"获奖人能否获得"科学与技术成就奖"？

何梁何利基金的宗旨是鼓励我国优秀科学技术工作者，无所畏惧地追求科学真理，勇攀当代科学技术高峰。已经获得"科学与技术进步奖""科学与技术创新奖"的科技工作者，在获奖后，再接再厉，开拓进取，在科学技术前沿取得新的重大科技突破，领先世界先进水平者；或者在产业高端作出新的重大技术创新，建立强大自主知识产权和自主品牌，使得我国产业跃居当今世界前列者；如果在前次获奖后取得的新的杰出成就达到"科学与技术成就奖"标准，可以推荐为"科学与技术成就奖"被提名人的人选，按照《评选章程》规定程序参评，也有望摘取"科学与技术成就奖"的桂冠。

## 十一、评选委员会按照怎样的程序进行各奖项评选工作？

每年，基金评选委员会按照下列程序开展评选工作：

（一）提名

每年年初，评选委员会向国内外2000多位提名人发去提名表，由其提名推荐获奖人选，并于3月31日前将提名表返回评选委员会。评选办公室将对提名材料进行形式审查、整理、分组、印刷成册。

（二）初评

每年7月中旬，评选委员会召开当年专业评审会，进行"科学与技术进步奖""科学与技术创新奖"的初评。其中，"科学与技术进步奖"初评，按照学科设立若干专业评审组进行；"科学与技术创新奖"成立一个由不同行业和领域专家组成的评审组进行初评。经过初评，以无记名投票方式，产生一定差额比例的候选人，提交评选委员会会议终评。

（三）预审

根据《评选章程》，"科学与技术成就奖"候选人由评选委员会委员在初评结束后提名。每年8月，评选委员会成立预审小组进行协调、评议，必要时进行考察和听证，产生"科学与技术成就奖"候选人，并形成预审报告，提交评选委员会会议终评。

（四）终评

每年9月中旬评选委员会召开全体会议进行终评。对候选人逐一评议，最后，根据基金信托委员会确定的当年获奖名额，进行无记名投票表决。"科学与技术进步奖""科学与技术创新奖"的候选人，获半数以上赞成票为获奖人。"科学与技术成就奖"的候选人，获三分之二多数赞成票为获奖人。

（五）授奖

每年10月的适当时候，何梁何利基金举行颁奖大会，向获奖人颁发奖牌、奖金。

## 十二、何梁何利基金获奖人有哪些权利和义务？

《世界人权宣言》宣布："人人对他所创造的任何科学、文学或艺术成果所产生的精神的和物质的权利，享有受保护的权利。"知识产权是精神权利和经济权利的总和，其本原和第一要义，是给人的智慧、才能和创造性劳动注入强大精神动力。科技奖励是确认和保护精神权利的重要制度，何梁何利基金"科学与技术成就奖""科学与技术进步奖""科学与技术创新奖"获奖人的权利是，享有何梁何利基金获奖科学家的身份权、荣誉权；享有接受何梁何利基金颁发的奖金的权利，该奖金个人所有；有从第二年起成为基金提名人，向基金提名推荐被提名人的权利。根据基金《信托契约》和评选章程，获奖人有义务在获得基金奖励后继续在中华人民共和国从事科学与技术工作不少于三年，为我国科技进步与创新作出更多贡献。

## 十三、评选委员会委员和专业评委是怎样产生的?

评选委员会是何梁何利基金评选工作的执行机构，通过全体会议审议、决定各奖项获奖人，行使最终评选决定权。根据评选章程，评选委员会由最多不超过20名委员组成。评选委员会主任由科技系统的信托委员担任，副主任委员两人，分别由教育部系统的信托委员和补充契约所指明的国际学者信托委员担任。评选委员会秘书长由信托委员会任命并征得捐款人代表同意的人选担任。

评选委员会委员由信托委员会任命，委员名单通过何梁何利基金出版物、网站公布。

按《评选章程》规定，评选委员会委员的聘任条件是：第一，要具备高尚道德情操，能够公正履行评选委员的职责；第二，要具备精深学术造诣，能够对其所属领域科技成就作出科学性和权威性评价；第三，要热心祖国科技奖励事业，愿意为之作出无私奉献；第四，评选委员会委员的结构配置，原则上每一领域有一名委员，国内评委和海外评委按照三比一的比例安排；第五，评选章程还规定了评选委员会委员的更新和替换制度，以保障评选委员会的生机和活力。

每年7月何梁何利基金召开专业评审会议，进行初评。初评是评选工作的第一道关口。其十多个"科学与技术进步奖"评审组和"科学与技术创新奖"的专业评委，由评选委员会根据工作需要，从250人左右的评审专家库或历年获奖科学家中，按《评选章程》规定的上述条件遴选。

## 十四、怎样理解基金公平、公正、公开的评选原则?

科学精神的精髓是求实、求是、求真。科技奖励评选工作必须坚持以诚信为本，践行实事求是的方针。何梁何利基金从一开始就贯彻"公平、公正、公开"的评选原则，保持良好的评选记录，得到社会各界的高度评价和充分肯定。所谓公平，体现在所有被提名者，不论职务、职位、学衔、资历，也不论年龄、民族、性别，在评选章程确定的评选标准面前一律平等。所谓公正，是指评选工作严格按照章程确定的评选标准和评选程序进行，无论初评的专业评委，还是终评的评选委员会委员，有权作出独立判断，按一人一票的制度行使表决权，最终依据评委共同体的意志决定获奖人，不受任何单位或个人的干扰。所谓公开，是指何梁何利基金评选章程、评选标准及其解释、评选委员会委员、逐年获奖人材料等，通过年报、网站等向社会公开，接受社会公众的监督和指导。自2006年起，评选委员会在部分省市和部门建立联络员，加强同社会各界的联系。何梁何利基金评选实践经验凝练到一点，就是贯彻"公平、公正、公开"的评选原则，是何梁何利基金的指导方针，是评选委员会的工作纪律，是基金的立业之本、权威之根、公信力之源泉，是一个具有国内和国际影响力的科技大奖的生命线。今后，基金将一如既往恪守"三公"原则，本着对科学负责、对基金负责、对科技共同体负责的精神，做好评选工作，使何梁何利基金科学与技术奖经得起历史的检验。

## 十五、何梁何利基金有无异议处理程序？

为了弘扬科学精神，崇尚科学道德，抵御社会不正之风和科研不端行为，提升何梁何利基金科学与技术奖的权威性和公信力，基金于2009年5月20日制定并发布了《关于何梁何利基金获奖科学家异议处理若干规定》，自发布之日起试行。

根据该项决定，凡涉及对获奖科学家主要科技成果评价、知识产权权属以及与奖项有关事项提出异议的署名投诉信件，由评选委员会受理，并调查处理。匿名投诉信件，原则上不予受理。但涉及获奖人因科研不端行为受到处分、学术资格被取消或与奖项评选相关重要情况的，应跟进调查核实，酌情处理。

评选委员会的处理原则是，以事实为依据，以法律为准绳，遵循科学共同体认同的道德准则，区别情况，正确处置。经调查，认定获奖人确属科研不端行为，将参照《中华人民共和国科学技术进步法》第七十一条规定，报基金信托委员会审议并作出相应的处分决定，直至公告撤销其奖励的决定，并通知本人，返回奖励证书、奖金。

## 十六、何梁何利基金未来发展目标是什么？

在中央人民政府和香港特别行政区政府的指导下，在我国科技界、教育界和社会各界的共同努力下，何梁何利基金已经成为我国规模大、权威性高、公信力强的社会力量奖励，成为推进我国科技进步与创新的强大杠杆，在国内外影响和声誉与日俱增。在历年颁奖大会上，党和国家领导人亲临颁奖，发表重要讲话，给予基金同人极大鼓舞和力量。何梁何利基金同人将不负众望，不辱使命，承前启后，继往开来，在新的起点上总结经验，开拓创新，突出特色，丰富内涵，朝着办成国际一流的科技奖励的方向迈进，为祖国的科技进步和创新，为建设富强民主、文明和谐的社会主义现代化国家而不懈努力！

# EXPLANATIONS ON SEVERAL ISSUES ON THE SELECTION WORK OF HO LEUNG HO LEE FOUNDATION

Ho Leung Ho Lee Foundation ("the Foundation") is a scientific and technological award foundation established on March 30, 1994 in Hong Kong by patriotic Hong Kong financial industrialists Ho Sin Hang, Leung Kau-Kui, Ho Tim, Lee Quo-Wei for the purpose of awarding prominent scientific and technological workers of the People's Republic of China. Up to 2010, there were 901 scientists who received this special honor. Within the 16 years of successful practice, HLHL Foundation Scientific and Technological Awards have become major scientific and technological awards of large scale, high standard and extensive influence in China that enjoy enormous prestige and public trust both domestically and abroad. In order for the circle of science and technology, the circle of education, and other various social circles to further understand the Foundation's purpose, basic principles, award selection criteria and operation mechanisms, Mr. Duan Ruichun, secretary general of the Selection Board of HLHL Foundation, made the following explanations during the awards ceremony in October 2010 with respect to the Foundation's selection regulation, selection work and other issues that various social circles are concerned about.

## I. What is the Regulation of Ho Leung Ho Lee Foundation on the Selection of the Award Winners of its Prizes?

The Regulation of Ho Leung Ho Lee Foundation on the Selection of the Award Winners of its Prizes ("Selection Regulation") is the fundamental guideline of the award selection work. The Selection Regulation is based on the Foundation's Trust Agreement and deliberated, adopted and published by the plenary meeting of HLHL Foundation Broad of Trustees. The birth of the first selection regulation on March 30, 1994, the very day when the Foundation was established, guaranteed the operation of the selection work in a scientific, regulated and healthy track from the very beginning. On May 11, 1998, a revision was made to the Selection Regulation to adapt to the return of Hong Kong to China and the development of domestic situation. On May 15, 2007, it was resolved at the meeting of the Foundation's Broad of Trustees that another revision would be made to the Selection Regulation. The main purpose of the revision was that, on the one hand, relevant modifications would be made to certain terms and conditions in the Selection Regulation in accordance with the Supplementary Terms to the Trust Agreement which took effect upon approval by the Hong Kong SAR High Court on October 12, 2005 so that the Foundation's Trust Agreement became consistent with its Supplementary Terms to the Trust Agreement while, on the other hand, the successful experience of the Selection Board in adapting to China's national innovation policy and reforming its selection work was elevated to become part of the selection regulation so that the experience was embodied in agreement terms, standards and systems to further improve the scientific and authoritative features of different award categories.

## II. What are the Important Modifications to the Selection Regulation Made in Accordance with the Supplementary Terms of the Trust Agreement?

HLHL Foundation is a charity foundation established in accordance with the laws of the Hong Kong SAR. In its early days, the trust system was established in accordance with the principles in Hong Kong's common law and the foundation was established upon the approval of the Hong Kong Supreme Court after the donors and the trustees signed the Trust Agreement. The Board of Trustees is the supreme body of power of the Foundation that decides on major matters of the foundation in investment, award selection and management. After the foundation was established in March 1994, Mr. Ho Sin Hang, Mr. Leung Kau-Kui and Mr. Ho Tim of the four founders, whose sublime and noble spirits we will all cherish forever, passed away in their nineties. Due to their decease, the main parties to the rights and obligations of donors in the Trust Agreement became absent, which affected the operation of the Foundation's decision-making procedures in terms of law. In October 2005, it was uniformly revised in the Supplementary Terms of the Trust Agreement, upon the approval of the Hong Kong SAR High Court, that the "donors" of the Foundation became the charity foundations designated by the original donors or their estate administrator. Thus a peaceful and smooth transition was achieved with respect to donors from the old generation patriotic financers to the charity foundations run by their next generation. According to the revision, the current donors of the Foundation are four legal persons, namely the S. H. Ho Foundation Limited, the Leung Kau-Kui Foundation Limited, the Ho Tim Foundation Limited, and the Wei Lun Foundation Limited of Mr. Lee Quo-Wei and his wife. And the relevant modifications were made to the Selection Regulation accordingly.

## III. What Conditions Need the Winners of the Awards of HLHL Foundation Have?

The winners of the awards of HLHL Foundation shall be the citizens of the People's Republic of China. And they also need to meet the following three conditions: First, they shall have made prominent contributions in the development of the undertakings in science and technology. Second, they shall love the motherland and exhibit noble social ethics and good professional ethics. Third, they shall have engaged in scientific and technological research work, teaching work or technical work for no less than five years in China.

When HLHL Foundation was established on March 30, 1994, Hong Kong and Macao were not returned to the motherland yet. In view of the historical situation then, the provision in the Selection Regulation that the winners of the awards shall be citizens of the People's Republic of China only applied to scientific and technological workers in China's mainland and scientific and technological workers in Hong Kong and Macao were excluded. Then Hong Kong and Macao were returned to the motherland under the principle of "one country, two systems" respectively on July 1st, 1997 and December 20, 1999. And a brand new situation emerged in the cooperation and exchange between the mainland of China and the Hong Kong and Macao SARs. Now, the scientific and technological workers in the Hong Kong and Macao SARs are " Hong Kong people" and " Macao people" among the citizens of the People's Republic of China and thus meet the conditions in the Selection Regulation. Therefore, the scope of the scientists eligible to the awards of HLHL Foundation was expanded from 2007 to include scientific and technological personnel in the Hong Kong and Macao SARs who meet the above conditions.

## IV. What are the Provisions on the Structure of the Award Categories in the Prevailing Selection Regulation?

Under the care and guidance of the Central People's Government and the government of the Hong Kong SAR, HLHL Foundation has formed during 16 years a scientific and rational structure of the award categories and a selection regulation of meticulousness, high efficiency, convenience and swiftness. It has always retained its objective, fair, authoritative selection performance and won good public trust. As provided in the prevailing Selection Regulation, the Foundation sets up the Prize for Scientific and Technological Achievements, the Prize for Scientific and Technological Progress, and the Prize for Scientific and Technological Innovation.

Each year there will be no more than five winners of the Prize for Scientific and Technological Achievements. Each of them will be given a medal and a prize of HKMYM one million. The total number of the winners of the Prize for Scientific and Technological Progress and the Prize for Scientific and Technological Innovation will not exceed 65. Each winner will be given a corresponding medal and a prize of HKMYM 200000. Among these, the proportion of the winners of the Prize for Scientific and Technological Progress to those of the Prize for Scientific and Technological Innovation will range from 3 : 1 to 2 : 1. The proportion will be determined by the Selection Board on the basis of specific situation.

## V. What are the Selection Criteria on the Prize for Scientific and Technological Achievements?

According to the Selection Regulation, all outstanding scientific and technological workers who meet the following three conditions are eligible to be honored with the Prize for Scientific and Technological Achievements. The first condition is that the scientist has been committed for a long time to promoting the scientific and technological achievements of the state in China and he or she has made eminent contribution and obtained high-level international academic achievements in his career. The second condition is that the scientist has obtained major scientific and technological breakthroughs in the frontiers of science and technology, mounted the peak of the science and technology of the present age, and obtained achievements of a world-leading standard. Third, the scientist has promoted technological innovation and established powerful independently-owned intellectual property and brand. And the industry in which the scientist works is one of the leading industries in the world. The candidates who meet the above standards include both senior scientists who have devoted their whole life to Chinese scientific and technological undertakings and obtained eminent achievements that were once first-rate in the world and youth and middle-aged outstanding talents who have made major breakthroughs or prominent achievements in the area of scientific and technological research and technical innovation so that China got a world-leading position in the area. During the process of opinion solicitation, the Chinese scientific and technological circle expressed general approval of the revision and indicated that such revision lowered the standard by not a slight bit while pushing the Foundation's awards one step further and closer to international standards. It injected powerful spiritual impetus for top-level talents to excel in the frontline of research and development and innovation. The revision also drew the Foundation's scientific and technological awards more closer to the mainstream ideology of building an innovative country.

## VI. What are the Provisions on the Selection Criteria of the Prize for Scientific and Technological Progress?

It is provided in the Selection Regulation that the Prize for Scientific and Technological Progress will be honored to scientists who have made major inventions, discoveries and scientific and technological results in particular disciplinary areas, particularly those who have made prominent contributions in recent years. First, it needs to be noted that the "particular disciplines" stated here include 17 disciplines, namely mathematics and mechanics, physics, chemistry, astronomy, meteorology, earth sciences, life sciences, agronomy, medical sciences and materia medica, paleontology and archeology, technology of machinery and electronics, information technology, communication and transportation technology, metallurgical materials technology, chemical engineering technology, resources and environment protection technology, and engineering and construction technology. One award category is established for each of these areas. In the original selection regulation, the Award of Technical Sciences is set up to cover various technical areas including machinery, electronics, information, metallurgy, material science, engineering and environment protection. The revised procedure sets up different award categories for these areas out of the consideration on the balance between various disciplinary areas. Second, the selection policy on the Prize for Scientific and Technological Progress focuses on examining and reviewing the prominent contribution of the nominees "within recent years". And "within recent years" refers to within the recent ten years. Third, as emerging disciplines, interdisciplines, and fringe disciplines come up one after another with the rapid development of science and technology, the nominees from these disciplines should desirably be classified according to their most important achievements and the closest disciplines to which these belong. To pay more attention to the excellent talents from emerging disciplines, interdisciplines and fringe disciplines is one policy of the Selection Board. The special cases that truly need cross-disciplinary review and deliberation will be processed through coordination as separate cases. But no prize category will be established particularly for emerging disciplines, interdisciplines and fringe disciplines.

## VII. What are the Provisions on the Selection Criteria of the Prize for Scientific and Technological Innovation?

Setting up the Prize for Scientific and Technological Innovation is an important reform of the Foundation's selection work. It is provided in the Selection Regulation that " the Prize for Scientific and Technological Innovation will be awarded to scientists who have high-level scientific and technological accomplishments and who have established an industry with independently-owned intellectual property and famous brand, created significant economic and social benefits, and made prominent contribution". It needs to be noted here that, as a term in economics, innovation refers to acts with specific economic and social goals. Some people defines it as the "first presence of an idea in science on the market". HLHL Foundation set up the innovation award to adapt to China's important decision to improve the ability to independent innovation and build an innovative country. For the purpose of the Selection Regulation, to make "scientific and technological innovation" first needs to make high-level scientific and technological achievements as its starting point to realize the transformation of scientific and technological achievements into real productive force and complete the process of scientific and technological industrialization. Second, innovation activities refer to technological and managerial innovations on the basis of high-level scientific and technological achievements. These include original innovation, integration innovation and re-innovation on the basis of other people's advanced technology. And such innovations should create independently-owned intellectual properties and famous brands and create significant economic and social benefits. Besides, the Selection Board also accepts and approves, in the same way as measurable economic benefits, the enormous social benefits created by innovation results in the areas of education, energy preservation and environment protection, ecological balance, national security, and social public interest undertakings. Third, as any major innovation is the result of teamwork, the winner of the Prize for Scientific and Technological Innovation may be either a leading person that plays the key role or a key person who has achieved technical breakthroughs. Naturally, the leading person here needs to have his or her own scientific and technological accomplishments in addition to conducting administrative management, organization and coordination work.

## VIII. How should the Award Categories Set Up in the Prize for Scientific and Technological Innovation be Understood?

In accordance with the Selection Regulation, the Prize for Scientific and Technological Innovation includes three award categories of the Award for Youth Innovation, the Award for Region Innovation and the Award for Industrial Innovation. The Award for Youth Innovation will be given to excellent scientific and technological talents not older than 45 years old who have achieved prominent performance in technical and managerial innovation. The Award for Region Innovation will be given to people who have made prominent contributions to regional economic development and technological progress through technical, managerial and regional innovations, particularly those who have made contributions to China's inland, remote regions, regions of harsh conditions, and regions of ethic minorities. The Prize for Industrial Innovation will be given to excellent talents who have made contributions through innovation and entrepreneurship to greatly promote technical progress and industrial upgrading, which include both the technical transformation of traditional industries and the leap-forwards of emerging industries. The above three award categories are set up according to the arrangement in selection policy. These do not define mutually-independent types of innovation. Therefore, the selection of the winners of the Prize for Scientific and Technological Innovation will be conducted as a whole part in accordance with the basic requirements on the Prize while proper attention will be paid to retain the structural balance between these three award categories. Selection and evaluation will not be conducted in a manner that the Award for Region Innovation, the Award for Industrial Innovation and the Award for Youth Innovation are separated and form different groups.

## IX. What are the Differences in the Selection Criteria of the Prize for Scientific and Technological Progress and the Prize for Scientific and Technological Innovation?

In principle, the Prize for Scientific and Technological Progress has award categories set up in accordance with different disciplines while the Prize for Scientific and Technological Innovation has award categories based on innovation results. The two prizes have overlaps and connections while there are important differences between them. And the policy orientations and stresses in their selection criteria are also different. The Selection Regulation requires that the winners of the Prize for Scientific and Technological Achievements must be completers or major completers of major inventions, discoveries and scientific and technological research results while the winners of the Prize for Scientific and Technological Innovation are scientists in innovative practices on the basis of high-level scientific and technological achievements. The former focuses on examining the standard and value of a scientist's invention, discovery or other scientific and technological achievement and its domestic and international academic status. The latter focuses on examining a person's performance in high-end industrial technical and managerial innovations, including economic and social benefits, independently-owned intellectual properties and building of famous brands. Naturally, the winners of the Prize for Scientific and Technological Innovations need to have high-level scientific and technological achievements as leading persons in addition to just conducting strategic decision making, administrative management, organization and coordination work.

## X. Can the Winners of the Prize for Scientific and Technological Progress and the Prize for Scientific and Technological Innovation Be Honored with the Prize for Scientific and Technological Achievements?

The purpose of HLHL Foundation is to encourage excellent Chinese scientific and technological workers to dauntlessly pursue the truth of science and courageously mount the peaks in modern science and technology. The scientific and technological workers who have won the Prize for Scientific and Technological Progress and the Prize for Scientific and Technological Innovation may continue to forge ahead and break new grounds. And they may achieve new important breakthroughs in the frontiers of science and technology and lead in the cutting edge area of the world. Or they may make new important technical innovations in the high-end areas of an industry and create powerful independent intellectual properties and independent brands so that China's relevant industries become industrial leaders in the world. If such scientists' new outstanding achievements obtained after the previous prize winning meet the criteria for the Prize for Scientific and Technological Achievement, these scientists may be recommended as candidates to be nominated to the Prize for Scientific and Technological Achievements. They will participate in the evaluation in accordance with the procedures as provided in the Selection Regulation. And it is hopeful that they may become the laureates of the Prize for Scientific and Technological Achievements.

## XI. In Accordance with What Procedures Will the Selection Board Conduct the Selection Work for Various Award Categories?

Each year, the Foundation's Selection Board will carry out selection work in accordance with the following procedure:

A. Nomination. In the beginning of each year, the Selection Board will send nomination forms to over 2000 domestic and foreign nominators. The nominators will recommend candidates for award winners and return the nomination form to the Selection Board by March 31st. The Selection Office will conduct the formal examination, arranging, assorting, and printing of the nomination materials and bind them into booklets.

B. Preliminary Evaluation. In the middle of July each year, the Selection Board will hold the year's specialized evaluation meeting and conduct the preliminary evaluation for the Prize of Scientific and Technological Progress and the Prize for Scientific and Technological Innovation. In the preliminary evaluation, that of the Prize for Scientific and Technological Progress will be conducted with a number of specialized evaluation groups formed according to different disciplines. The preliminary evaluation of the Prize for Scientific and Technological Innovation will be conducted by an evaluation group consisting of experts from different industries and areas. After the preliminary evaluation, candidates will be determined with a proportion of competitive selection by means of secret ballot and submitted to the meeting of the Selection Board for final evaluation.

C. Preliminary Review. In accordance with the Selection Regulation, the candidates of the Prize for Scientific and Technological Achievements will be nominated by the members of the Selection Board upon the conclusion of the preliminary evaluation. Each August, the Selection Board will form a preliminary evaluation group to conduct coordination and evaluation. Inspection tours and hearings will be made when necessary. Then the candidates for the Prize for Scientific and Technological Achievements will be determined and a preliminary review report will be prepared and submitted to the meeting of the Selection Board for final evaluation.

D. Final Evaluation. In the middle of September each year, the Selection Board will hold a plenary meeting to conduct final evaluation. Candidates will be evaluated one by one. And finally a secret ballot will be made on the selection in accordance with the numbers of prize winners of the year determined by the Trust Board of the Foundation. The candidates for the Prize for Scientific and Technological Progress and the Prize for Scientific and Technological Innovation will become prize winners with over half of the votes in favor. The candidates for the Prize for Scientific and Technological Achievements will become prize winners with over two thirds of the votes in favor.

E. Award Ceremony. At a proper time in October each year, HLHL Foundation will hold an award ceremony to present medals and prizes to the winners.

## XII. What Are the Rights and Obligations of the Winners of the Awards of HLHL Foundation?

The *Universal Declaration of Human Rights* states that "Everyone has the right to the protection of the moral and material interests resulting from any scientific, literary or artistic production of which he is the author. " Intellectual property rights are the sum of both spiritual and economic rights. Its origin and primary significance is to inject powerful spiritual drive to people's wisdom, talent and creative labor. Scientific and technological awards are important systems to recognize and protect spiritual rights. The rights of the winners of the Prize of Scientific and Technological Achievements, the Prize for Scientific and Technological Progress, and the Prize for Scientific and Technological Innovation of HLHL Foundation are the enjoyment of the right of status and the right of honor of the prize-winning scientists of HLHL Foundation, the enjoyment of the right to accept the prize money granted by HLHL Foundation which shall be owned personally by the prize winners, and the right to become a nominator of the Foundation from the year next to the prize winning to recommend nominees to the Foundation. In accordance with the Foundation's Trust Agreement and Selection Regulation, the prize winner is obligated to continue to engage in scientific and technological work in the People's Republic of China for three years after prize winning so as to make more contribution to China's scientific and technological advancement and innovation.

## XIII. How are the Members of the Selection Board and the Specialized Evaluators Selected?

The Selection Board is the implementing body of the selection work of HLHL Foundation. It conducts deliberation through plenary meeting, decides on the winners of the award categories, and exercises the right of decision in final evaluation. In accordance with the Selection Regulation, the Selection Board consists of no more than twenty members at the most. The chairman of the Selection Board shall be a member of the Board of Trustees for the circle of science and technology. The two vice chairmen of the board shall be a member of the Board of Trustees from the bodies under the Ministry of Education and a member of the Board of Trustees who is an international scholar as specified in the Supplementary Terms to the Trust Agreement. The secretary general of the Selection Boards shall be appointed by the Board of Trustees upon the consent of the representatives of the donors.

The members of the Selection Board are appointed by the Board of Trustees. And the list of such members will be published through the publications and website of HLHL Foundation.

As provided in the Selection Regulation, the conditions for the appointment of a member of the Selection Board are: First, the person needs to have noble ethics and the ability to fairly perform the duties of the member of the Selection Board. Second, the person needs to have sophisticated academic accomplishment and the ability to make scientific and authoritative evaluation on the scientific and technological achievements in his or her own specialized field. Third, the person needs to have enthusiasm on the motherland's undertakings in scientific and technological awards and the willingness to make selfless contributions to these undertakings. Fourth, with respect to the structural distribution of the members of the Selection Board, there shall be one member from each area in principle and the proportion between domestic and overseas members shall be 3 : 1. Fifth, the Selection Regulation provides for the renewal and replacement system of the members of the Selection Board so as to ensure the liveliness and vigor of the board.

Each July, HLHL Foundation holds a specialized evaluation meeting to conduct the preliminary evaluation. The preliminary evaluation is the very first step in the selection work. About a dozen of evaluation groups for the Prize for Scientific and Technological Progress and the specialized evaluators of the Prize for Scientific and Technological Innovation will be selected by the Selection Board on the basis of working needs and in accordance with the above conditions as provided in the Selection Regulation from an evaluation expert pool containing about 250 persons or the prize winners in previous years.

## XIV. How should People Understand the Foundation's Selection Principles of Fairness, Justice and Openness?

The essence of the scientific spirit is to be practical, honest and truth-seeking. The selection work for the scientific and technological awards must adhere to the principle of sincerity and follow the guideline of doing things with a realistic and pragmatic approach. HLHL Foundation persistently carries out the selection principle of fairness, justice and openness from the very beginning. It retains good selection records and wins high praises and full recognition from various social circles. The principle of fairness is embodied in the provision that all the nominees, regardless of their jobs, positions, academic titles or work experiences and also their age, ethnic group or gender, are equal with respect to the selection criteria determined in the Selection Regulation. The principle of justice refers to the provision that the selection work is carried out strictly in accordance with the selection criteria and procedures determined in accordance with the Selection Regulation. Any person as either a specialized evaluator in the preliminary evaluation or a member of the Selection Board in final evaluation has the right to make independent judgment and exercise the right to vote under the system of one vote for one person. The prize winners are eventually determined according to the common will of all the evaluators free from the intervention of any entity or individual. The principle of openness refers to the practice that HLHL Foundation's Selection Regulation, Selection Criteria, and their explanations and the information about the members of the Selection Board and the prize winners of different years are published to the society through annual report and website to receive supervision and guidance from the public in the society. From 2006, the Selection Board has appointed liaison persons in some governmental departments, provinces and cities to strengthen its contact with various social circles. One viewpoint that can summarize the practical experience of the award selection of HLHL Foundation is to carry out the selection principle of "fairness, justice and openness." It is the guideline of HLHL Foundation, the working discipline of the Selection Board, and the cornerstone of the Foundation, the root of its authoritativeness and the source of its public trust. It is the lifeline of this major scientific and technological award with both domestic and international influence. From now on, the Foundation will adhere to this three-word principle as always. It will carry out the selection work well with the spirit of being responsible to science, to the Foundation, and to the scientific and technological community so that the scientific and technological awards of HLHL Foundation can stand the test of the history.

## XV. Does HLHL Foundation Have Dispute Handling Procedures?

With a view to carrying forward the spirit of the science, advocating the ethics of the science, guarding against the unhealthy tendencies in the society and the improper conducts in scientific and technological research, and enhancing the authoritativeness and public trust of HLHL Foundation's scientific and technological awards, the Foundation formulated and published on May 20th, 2009 *Several Provisions on Handling the Disputes on the Prize-Winning Scientists of Ho Leung Ho Lee Foundation*. It took effect from the date of publication.

In accordance with the resolution on the document, the Selection Board will accept, investigate and handle all the signed complaint letters on the disputes with respect to the evaluation of the main scientific and technological research results, the ownership of relevant intellectual properties, and the matters about award categories related to a prize-winning scientist. In principle, anonymous complaint letters will not be accepted and handled. However, where such anonymous complaint letters involve the information that a prize winner has been punished due to improper conducts in scientific and technological research, that his academic title or qualification was cancelled, or other information related to the award evaluation, follow-up action shall be taken to investigate and verify. Such disputes shall then be handled according to actual situation.

The complaint handling principle of the Selection Board is to take facts as the basis and the law as the criterion, follow the ethical principles commonly accepted by the science community, distinguish different situations, and handle correctly. Where it is determined upon investigation that a prize winner really involves in improper conducts in scientific and technological research, the case will be referred to the Board of Trustees of the Foundation for deliberation with reference to the provisions in Article 71 of the *Law of the People's Republic of China on, Science and Technology Progress*. The board will make resolutions on corresponding punishment up to that of a public announcement to cancel its reward. The person involved will be notified of the decision and required to return his certificate and prize money.

## XVI. What are the Goals of HLHL Foundation on Its Future Development?

Under the guidance of the Central People's Government and the government of the Hong Kong SAR and with the joint efforts of China's scientific and technological circle, education circle and various social circles, HLHL Foundation has already become an awarding organization founded with social resources that is of large scale, high authoritativeness, and strong public trust in China. It becomes a powerful lever to push forward China's scientific and technological advancement and innovation. Its domestic and foreign influence and reputation also grow constantly. China's state and CPC leaders attended in person the award ceremonies in the previous years. They presented the awards and delivered important speeches to give great encouragement and power to our colleagues working with the Foundation. The people of HLHL Foundation will live up to the expectations of the people and their own commitment. They will build on the past and usher in the future. They will summarize their experiences and move on from a new starting point. They will explore and innovate, highlight the Foundation's features, enrich its connotations, and advance in the direction of making it an internationally first-rate scientific and technological award. They will work hard and relentlessly for the motherland's scientific and technological advancement and innovation and for building China into a wealthy, democratic, civilized and harmonious socialist modern country!

# 关于何梁何利基金（香港）北京代表处公告

（2019年11月20日北京市公安局批准）

何梁何利基金是香港爱国金融家何善衡、梁銶琚、何添、利国伟先生基于崇尚科学、振兴中华的热忱，各捐资1亿港元于1994年3月30日在香港注册成立的社会公益性慈善基金。其宗旨是奖励中华人民共和国杰出科学技术工作者，服务祖国科技进步与创新伟业。

根据《中华人民共和国境外非政府组织管理法》，经申请，并经北京市公安局批准，何梁何利基金（香港）代表处自2019年11月20日在北京宣告成立。

何梁何利基金（香港）代表处负责基金在中国境内开展活动，执行评选委员会指定提名、初评、终评和颁奖大会等日常事务。举办基金学术论坛、图片展。出版《何梁何利奖》等刊物。

特此公告。

何梁何利基金（香港）北京代表处<br>2020年1月1日

# PUBLIC ANNOUNCEMENT OF THE BEIJING REPRESENTATIVE OFFICE OF THE HO LEUNG HO LEE FOUNDATION (HONG KONG)

(Approved by Beijing Municipal Public Security Bureau on November 20, 2019)

With their fervor for advocating science and rejuvenating the Chinese nation, four patriotic financial industrialists in Hong Kong—Mr. Ho Sin-Hang, Mr. Leung Kau-kui, Mr. Ho Tim and Mr. Lee Quo-Wei—each donated 100 million HK dollars to register the establishment of the Ho Leung Ho Lee Foundation in Hong Kong on March 30, 1994. The Ho Leung Ho Lee Foundation is aimed to reward the outstanding science and technology workers of the People's Republic of China and to serve the great undertaking of advancing scientific and technological progress and innovation in the motherland.

The Ho Leung Ho Lee Foundation submitted an application in accordance with *The Law of the People's Republic of China on Administration of Activities of Overseas Nongovernmental Organizations in the Mainland of China*. With the approval of the application by the Beijing Municipal Public Security Bureau, the Beijing Representative Office of the Ho Leung Ho Lee Foundation (Hong Kong) was announced to be established on November 20, 2019 in Beijing.

The Beijing Representative Office of the Ho Leung Ho Lee Foundation (Hong Kong) is responsible for conducting activities of the Ho Leung Ho Lee Foundation in the mainland of China, and handling day-to-day affairs of the Selection Board of Ho Leung Ho Lee Foundation such as designating nominees, holding preliminary and final evaluations, and holding the awarding ceremony of the Ho Leung Ho Lee Foundation. It is also responsible for organizing academic forum and photo exhibition of the Ho Leung Ho Lee Foundation, and publishing periodicals including the *Ho Leung Ho Lee Prize*.

The public announcement is hereby given.

Beijing Representative Office of the
Ho Leung Ho Lee Foundation (Hong Kong)
January 1, 2020

# 何梁何利基金捐款人简历

捐款者何善衡慈善基金会有限公司之创办人

## 何 善 衡

何善衡博士，1900 年出生，广东番禺市人。

何博士于 1933 年创办香港恒生银号，其后又创办恒昌企业及大昌贸易行。1952 年恒生银号改为有限公司，1959 年改称恒生银行，何氏一直担任董事长一职。1983 年，于恒生银行成立 50 周年时，何氏因年事关系，改任恒生银行名誉董事长至病逝。

何博士经营之业务包括银行、贸易、信托、财务、酒店、保险、地产、船务、投资等。

何博士热心慈善公益不遗余力。1970 年设立何善衡慈善基金会，资助国内外慈善事业，包括地方建设、教育、医疗、科学等，帮助社会造就人才，尤其对广州市及其家乡一带贡献很多。1978 年创办恒生商学书院，免费提供教学，并曾任多所学校校董。1971 年获香港中文大学荣誉社会科学博士衔，1983 年获香港大学荣誉法律博士衔，1990 年及 1995 年分别获广州市中山大学荣誉顾问衔及名誉博士学位，1993 年获广州市荣誉市民及番禺市荣誉市民称谓。

何善衡博士于 1997 年 12 月 4 日在香港病逝，享年 97 岁。

## 梁 銶 琚

梁銶琚博士，1903 年出生，广东顺德人。

梁博士为恒昌企业之创办人，曾任恒生银行董事、大昌贸易行副董事长，亦为美丽华酒店企业有限公司、富丽华酒店有限公司、Milford 国际投资有限公司等董事以及恒生商学书院校董等。

梁博士早年在穗、港、澳等地经营银号和贸易，为大昌贸易行创办人之一，为工作经常往返国内各大商埠及海外大城市，或开设分行，或推进业务，并与合伙股东制订运作规章，积极培育人才；梁博士领导华商参与国际贸易，并于20世纪60年代协助香港政府重新厘定米业政策，对香港的安定繁荣有卓越贡献。

梁博士宅心仁厚，精于事业，淡薄声名，热心公益。数十年来对社会福利、教育、医疗事业捐助良多，堪称楷模。较为显著者包括捐款建成纪念其先父之圣高隆庞女修会梁式芝书院，纪念其先母之保良局梁周顺琴学校，香港大学梁銶琚楼，香港中文大学梁銶琚楼，香港浸会学院"梁銶琚汉语中心"，岭南学院梁銶琚楼，广州中山大学捐建两千两百座位的梁銶琚堂与梁李秀娱图书馆，赞助杨振宁博士倡议之中山大学高级学术研究中心基金会及中国教育交流协会留学名额，为清华大学设立"梁銶琚博士图书基金"，中国人民解放军第四军医大学"梁銶琚脑研究中心"，清华大学建筑馆——梁銶琚楼。

在香港的其他教育捐助包括：顺德联谊总会梁銶琚中学，顺德联谊总会梁李秀娱幼稚园（屯门），顺德联谊总会梁李秀娱幼稚园（沙田），香港励志会梁李秀娱小学，恒生商学书院，劳工子弟学校新校，九龙乐善堂陈祖泽学校礼堂，乐善堂梁銶琚学校，乐善堂梁銶琚书院，香港大学黄丽松学术基金，香港女童军总会沙田扬坑营地及梁李秀娱花园；在医疗卫生方面包括：医务卫生署土瓜湾顺德联谊总会梁銶琚诊所，香港防癌会，香港放射诊断科医生协会，玛丽医院"梁銶琚糖尿病中心"，玛丽医院放射学图书博物馆教学资料和医院员工的福利，香港大学医院在山东省为胃癌研究工作经费，支持张力正医生在葛量洪医院的心脏病手术和医疗的发展经费及捐助圣保禄医院设立心脏中心并以"梁銶琚心脏中心"命名；在社会福利捐献包括：九龙乐善堂梁銶琚敬老之家，东区妇女福利会梁李秀娱晚晴中心，香港明爱，西区少年警讯活动及跑马地鹅颈桥区街坊福利会等；向宗教团体的捐助包括：资助基督教"突破机构"开设青年村——信息站，赞助"志莲净苑"重建基金及大屿山"宝莲禅寺"筹募兴建天坛大佛基金等。

多年来，梁博士对家乡顺德的地方建设、科技教育、医疗事业亦大量资助，其中包括捐资成立国家级重点中学梁銶琚中学，中学的科学楼并增置教学仪器，北头学校，梁銶琚图书馆及图书，增设杏坛医院230张病床、独立手术室及分科设备仪器等，杏坛康乐活动中心，北头大会堂及北头老人康乐中心，北头乡每户开建水井一口，修葺北头主路及河道两岸，北头乡蚕房四座，梁銶琚夫人保健中心（即妇产幼儿医院），梁銶琚夫人幼儿园及梁銶琚福利基金会。

1987年梁博士荣获香港中文大学颁授荣誉社会科学博士学位，1990年被广州中山大学聘为名誉顾问，1992年获顺德市（今顺德区）颁授为首位荣誉市民，1994年国务院学位委员会批准清华大学授予梁博士名誉博士学位；同年4月，国务院总理李鹏为梁博士题词"热心公益，发展教育"，以赞扬其贡献。1995年6月21日，香港大学向已故梁銶琚博士追授名誉法学博士文凭。

在海外方面，梁博士亦曾捐助英国牛津大学、苏格兰Aberdeen大学医学院与加拿大多伦多颐康护理中心。

梁銶琚博士于1994年11月10日在香港病逝，享年91岁。

# 何　　添

何添博士于1933年加入香港恒生银行有限公司（前为恒生银号），于1953年任董事兼总经理，1967—1979年任恒生银行副董事长。何添博士于2004年4月退任恒生银行董事，同时获该行委任为名誉资深顾问。何添博士曾任多个上市公司董事职位，包括美丽华酒店企业有限公司（董事长）、新世界发展有限公司、新鸿基地产有限公司、熊谷组（香港）有限公司及景福集团有限公司。

何添博士积极参与公职服务，他为香港中文大学联合书院永久校董、香港中文大学校董会校董、恒生商学书院校董、邓肇坚何添慈善基金创办人之一、香港何氏宗亲总会永久会长、旅港番禺会所永久名誉会长及金银业贸易场永远名誉会长。

何添博士于1982年获香港中文大学颁授荣誉社会科学博士学位；1997年获香港城市大学颁授名誉工商管理学博士学位；1999年获香港大学颁授荣誉法律博士学位；于1988年、1993年、1995年及2004年分别获广州市、番禺市、顺德市及佛山市授予荣誉市民的称号；又于1996年11月出任中华人民共和国香港特别行政区第一届政府推选委员会委员。

何添博士于2004年11月6日在香港病逝，享年95岁。

### 捐款者伟伦基金有限公司之创办人
## 利　国　伟

利国伟博士于1946年加入香港恒生银行有限公司（前为恒生银号），1959年12月任该行董事，1976年1月任副董事长，1983—1996年2月做执行董事长，1996年3月至1997年12月任非执行董事长，1998年1月至2004年4月任名誉董事长，退任后续任名誉资深顾问。

在公职方面，利国伟博士1963—1982年为香港中文大学司库，1982—1997年为该大学校董会主席，并于1994年11月30日起被该校委为终身校董。利博士亦曾先后任香港李宝椿联合世界书院创校主席及名誉主席。此外，亦曾任江门市五邑大学名誉校长。

利国伟博士曾先后任香港行政局议员7年，立法局议员10年，银行业务咨询委员会委员 14 年，教育委员会主席 7 年，教育统筹委员会主席 5 年。

利国伟博士历年获香港及海外多所大学颁授荣誉博士学位，这些学校分别为香港中文大学（1972）、英国赫尔大学（University of Hull）(1985)、英国伯明翰大学（University of Birmingham）(1989)、香港大学及香港城市理工学院（即现时之香港城市大学）(1990)、香港理工学院（即现时之香港理工大学）及香港浸会学院（即现时之香港浸会大学）(1992)、英国伦敦市政厅大学（London Guildhall University）(1993)、清华大学及香港公开进修学院（即现时之香港公开大学）(1995)。利博士于 1971 年及 1995 年分别获选为英国银行学会及美国塔夫斯大学（Tufts University）院士，并于 1991 年、1993 年、1995 年、1996 年及 2003 年分别获选为英国牛津大学圣休学院（St Hugh's College，Oxford University）、爱丁堡皇家医学院（Royal College of Physicians of Edinburgh）、香港心脏专科学院、香港内科医学院以及英国剑桥李约瑟研究所荣誉院士，并于 1993 年获广州市政府、开平市政府及江门市政府颁授荣誉市民名衔。此外，利博士在南华早报及敦豪国际（香港）有限公司主办之 1994 年香港商业奖中获商业成就奖。利博士于 1995—2003 年受聘为中国老教授协会名誉会长，并于 1997 年荣获香港特别行政区政府颁授"大紫荆勋章"，2006 年获香港证券专业学院授予荣誉会员衔。

多年来，利国伟博士对其原籍之开平地方建设、教育及医疗事务多所资助，对江门市亦捐赠不少。此外，对清华大学、上海市和广州市之其他机构亦分别作出捐献。

利国伟博士于 2013 年 8 月 10 日在香港病逝，享年 95 岁。

# BRIEF INTRODUCTION TO THE DONORS TO HO LEUNG HO LEE FOUNDATION

## Brief Biography of Dr. S. H. Ho

Dr. S. H. Ho, the founder of the S. H. Ho Foundation Ltd. which donated to Ho Leung Ho Lee Foundation, born in 1900, was a native of Panyu, Guangdong Province. He cofounded Hang Seng Ngan Ho in Hong Kong in 1933 and later, the Hang Chong Investment Co Ltd. and the Dah Chong Hong Ltd. In 1952, Hang Seng Ngan Ho was incorporated and in 1959, was renamed Hang Seng Bank Ltd. From 1960 until 1983, Dr. Ho served as Chairman of the Bank. In 1983, on the 50th anniversary of the Bank, he became its Honorary Chairman until he passed away.

Dr. Ho was involved in a wide range of businesses, including banking, trade, trusteeship, financing, hotels, insurance, property, shipping and investment.

Dr. Ho was a philanthropist who was committed to promoting charitable causes. In 1970, he founded the S. H. Ho Foundation Ltd to support charitable causes in China and overseas, including regional construction, education, medical services, scientific research and the training of new talent. His contributions to Guangzhou and his homeland were particularly notable. In 1978, he founded the Hang Seng School of Commerce to provide free education to aspiring youths. He also sat as director on many school boards. In 1971, he was conferred the Honorary Degree of Doctor of Social Science by The Chinese University of Hong Kong and in 1983, an Honorary Degree of Doctor of Laws by The University of Hong Kong. In 1990, he became an Honorary Adviser to the Zhongshan University in Guangzhou and was conferred the Honorary Doctorate's degree by that University in 1995. He was made an Honorary Citizen of Guangzhou and of Panyu in 1993.

Dr. S. H. Ho passed away peacefully in Hong Kong on December 4, 1997 at the age of 97.

## Brief Biography of Dr. Leung Kau-Kui

The late Dr. Leung Kau-Kui was born in 1903, a native of the City of Shunde in Guangdong Province. Dr. Leung made his mark in the businesses of foreign exchange and trading in Guangzhou, Hong Kong and Macau early in his career. He was a pioneer in leading Chinese businessmen to participate in international trades.

Throughout his career, Dr. Leung held directorships in various companies. He was a director of the Hang Seng Bank, founder of Hang Chong Investment Co. Ltd., and one of the founders and Vice-Chairman of the Dah Chong Hong Ltd. —a leading Chinese-owned trading firm in Hong Kong during the colonial days. He was also a director of Miramar Hotel and Investment Co. Ltd. Furama Hotel Co. Ltd., Milford (International) Investment Co. Ltd., and a director of the Hang Seng School of Commerce.

Dr. Leung travelled regularly and extensively to cities in China and overseas to set up branches for Dah Chong Hong Ltd. as well as to promote and develop businesses for his partners. During the 60's, he helped to restructure the import procedures of rice to Hong Kong from Thailand contributing significantly to the stability and prosperity of Hong Kong.

Benevolent, enterprising and self-effacing, Dr. Leung was a committed contributor to charitable causes. He gave generously to education, medical social services and religious organisations. Among the charitable causes which he had supported were: the Missionary Sisters St. Columban Leung Shek Chee College in memory of his late father, the Po Leung Kuk Leung Chou Shun Kam Primary School in memory of his late mother, The University of Hong Kong's KK Leung Building, The Chinese University of Hong Kong's Leung Kau-Kui Building, Lingnan College's Leung Kau-Kui Building, the Hong Kong Baptist College's (now the Hong Kong Baptist University) School of Continuing Education Leung Kau-Kui Hanyu Institute, K. K. Leung Architectural Building of Beijing's Tsinghua University, Guangzhou's Zhongshan University's Leung Kau-Kui Hall and Leung Lee Sau Yu Library, and The K. K. Leung Brain Research Centre of the Fourth Military Medical University in Xian, China. He also sponsored the Foundation of Zhongshan University Advanced Research Centre and the China Educational Exchange Association's Scholarships for Overseas Studies, both of which were promoted by Professor Yang Chen Ning. He also set up the Book Foundation of Dr. Leung Kau-Kui for Tsinghua University.

In Hong Kong, his other contributions were supports given to: Shun Tak Fraternal Association Leung Kau-Kui College, Shun Tak Fraternal Association Leung Lee Sau Yu Kindergarten (Tuen Mun), Shun Tak Fraternal Association Leung Lee Sau Yu Kindergarten (Shatin), The Endeavourers Leung Lee Sau Yu Memorial Primary School, Hang Seng School of Commerce, the assembly hall of Lok Sin Tong Chan Cho Chak Primary School, Lok Sin Tong Leung Kau-Kui Primary School, Lok Sin Tong Leung Kau-Kui College, Dr. Raymond Huang Foundation of the University of Hong Kong, S. T. F. A. Leung Kau-Kui Clinic of the Medical and Health Department, The Hong Kong Anti-Cancer Society, Queen Mary Hospital's Leung Kau-Kui Diabetes Centre and donations to upgrade the Radiology Library/Museum as well as teaching materials and staff welfare of the Hospital. He also contributed to the Department of Medicine of the University of Hong Kong to do research work on gastric cancer in Shandong Province, China. Dr. Leung also made generous contributions to the religions bodies, which included assisting the Christian Break-through Organization in establishing and donating to the Youth Village-Information Centre, redevelopment foundation of the Buddhist Chi Lin Nunnery, as well as the construction fund of the Buddha Statue at Po Lin Monastery on Lantau Island.

Dr. Leung was generous and zealous in promoting education in science and technology and medical services in his hometown, Shunde. In particular, he was the first donor working to improve the public amenities of his native Beitou Village. Notable projects which he supported in Shunde included multipurpose halls, hospitals, child care and nursery centres, schools, kindergartens, libraries, sports and recreational centres as well as welfare institutions.

Dr. Leung received an Honorary Degree of Doctor of Social Sciences from The Chinese University of Hong Kong in 1987 and became an Honorary Adviser to Guangzhou's Zhongshan University in 1990. In 1992, the government of Shunde named him an Honorary Citizen. He was conferred an Honorary Doctorate by Tsinghua University in 1994. In April 1994, Premier Li Peng praised him for his enthusiastic support of charitable causes and development of education in China.

Dr. Leung had also donated to overseas institutions such as the Oxford University of United Kingdom, the medical school of Aberdeen University in Scotland, and the Yee Hong Geriatric Centre in Toronto, Canada.

Dr. Leung passed away peacefully in Hong Kong on November 10, 1994 at the age of 91.

## Brief Biography of Dr. Ho Tim

Dr. Ho Tim joined Hang Seng Bank Ltd (formerly Hang Seng Ngan Ho) in Hong Kong in 1933, was appointed its Director and General Manager in 1953 and Vice-Chairman from 1967 to 1979. In April 2004, he retired from the Board of Hang Seng Bank Limited and was named one of the Bank's Honorary Senior Advisers. Dr. Ho held directorships in a number of listed companies. He was the Chairman of Miramar Hotel and Investment Co. Ltd.; a Director of New World Development Co. Ltd., Sun Hung Kai Properties Ltd., Kumagai Gumi (Hong Kong) Ltd. and King Fook Holdings Ltd.

Dr. Ho was active in public service. He was a Permanent Member of the Board of Trustees of the United College of The Chinese University of Hong Kong, a Council Member of The Chinese University of Hong Kong, a Board Member of the Hang Seng School of Commerce, one of the founders of the Tang Shiu Kin and Ho Tim Charitable Fund, Permanent President of the Ho's Clansmen Association Ltd., Honorary President of the Panyu District Association of Hong Kong and Honorary Permanent President of the Chinese Gold & Silver Exchange Society.

In 1982, The Chinese University of Hong Kong conferred on Dr. Ho the Honorary Degree of Doctor of Social Science; in 1997, an Honorary Doctorate Degree of Business Administration by The City University of Hong Kong; and in 1999, an Honorary Degree of Doctor of Laws by The University of Hong Kong. He was made an Honorary Citizen of Guangzhou, Panyu, Shunde and Foshan in 1988, 1993, 1995 and 2004 respectively by the respective municipal governments. He was appointed a member of the Selection Committee of the First Government of the Hong Kong

Special Administrative Region of the People's Republic of China in November 1996.

Dr. Ho Tim passed away peacefully in Hong Kong on November 6, 2004 at the age of 95.

## Brief Biography of Dr. Lee Quo-Wei

Dr. Lee Quo-Wei, the founder of Wei Lun Foundation Limited which donated to Ho Leung Ho Lee Foundation, joined Hang Seng Bank (formerly Hang Seng Ngan Ho) in Hong Kong in 1946. He was appointed a Director of the Bank in December 1959 and elected Vice-Chairman in January 1976. He became Executive Chairman of the Bank from 1983 until February 1996; non-executive Chairman from March 1996 to December 1997. He was appointed Honorary Senior Advisor of the Bank after his appointment as Honorary Chairman from January 1998 to April 2004.

Dr. Lee was well-known for his active involvement in public services. He had been Treasurer of the Chinese University of Hong Kong from 1963 to 1982, the Chairman of the Council of the University from 1982 to 1997 and a Life Member of the Council of the University since 30 November 1994. He was the Founding Chairman and later the Honorary Chairman of the Li Po Chun United World College of Hong Kong as well as the Honorary President of Jiangmen's Wuyi University.

He was a member of the Executive Council in Hong Kong for 7 years and a member of the Legislative Council for 10 years. He was also a member of the Banking Advisory Committee for 14 years, Chairman of the Board of Education for 7 years and Chairman of the Education Commission for 5 years.

Several universities in Hong Kong and overseas had conferred Honorary Doctorate Degrees on Dr Lee, including The Chinese University of Hong Kong in 1972, University of Hull (United Kingdom) in 1985, University of Birmingham (United Kingdom) in 1989, University of Hong Kong in 1990, City Polytechnic of Hong Kong (presently known as the City University of Hong Kong) in 1990, Hong Kong Polytechnic (now the Hong Kong Polytechnic University) and Hong Kong Baptist College (now the Hong Kong Baptist University) in 1972, London Guildhall University (United Kingdom) in 1993, Tsinghua University (Beijing of China) and the Open Learning Institute (now the Open University of Hong Kong) in 1995. Dr Lee was also elected to a fellowship of the Chartered Institute of Bankers, London in 1971 and Tufts University (USA) in 1995 as well as honorary fellowships of St Hugh's College, Oxford University; Royal College of Physicians of Edinburgh; Hong Kong College of Cardiology; and Hong Kong College of Physicians; and Needham Research Institute, Cambridge in 1991, 1993, 1995, 1996 and 2003 respectively. In 1993, he was made an Honorary Citizen of Guangzhou, Kaiping and Jiangmen by the three municipal governments. In the 1994 South China Morning Post/DHL Hong Kong Business Awards, he was awarded Businessman of the year. Dr Lee had been engaged Honorary President of

China Senior Professors Association from 1995 to 2003. In July 1997, he was awarded the Grand Bauhinia Medal by the Hong Kong Special Administrative Region Government. In 2006, he was elected Honorary Fellow for the year by the Hong Kong Securities Institute.

Over the years, Dr Lee had donated generously to his homeland Kaiping, helping to improve infrastructure, education and medical services. He had also made significant contributions to Jiangmen. In addition, he had made donations to Tsinghua University in Beijing and other institutions in the cities of Shanghai and Guangzhou.

Dr Lee Quo-Wei passed away peacefully in Hong Kong on August 10, 2013 at the age of 95.

# 何梁何利基金信托人简历

## 朱 丽 兰

朱丽兰，女，1935年8月出生于上海。教授，原科学技术部部长，现任全国人大常委会委员、全国人大教科文卫委员会主任委员。曾就读于上海中西小学，毕业于第三女中。1956年在苏联敖德萨大学高分子物理化学专业学习，1961年获优秀毕业生文凭。回国后在中国科学院化学研究所工作到1986年。长期从事高分子反应动力学、高分子材料剖析及结构表征研究。所承担的高分子材料剖析、性能结构形态关系的研究项目曾分别获国家级重大科研成果奖及应用成果奖，多次在国内外发表学术论文。曾任中国科学院化学研究所研究室主任和所长职务。

1979—1980年，在德国费拉堡大学高分子化学研究所做访问学者。在科研工作中，发展了一种新的染色技术用于制备样品，被称为一种突破，在国内外同行中享有较高声誉。

1986—2001年，曾任国家科委副主任、常务副主任、科学技术部部长。任国家科委、科技部领导期间，组织制定并实施了国家高技术研究发展计划（"863"计划）、国家发展基础研究的攀登计划以及高技术产业化的火炬计划等。倡导和推行新的专家管理机制，提出了一系列适应当代高技术发展规律并结合中国国情的管理理论与政策、方法，出版了专著《当代高技术与发展战略》《发展与挑战》等，并获中国材料研究学会成就奖。由于在推动国际科技合作以及促进中国国家高技术研究发展与产业化方面成绩卓著，1993年获美洲中国工程师协会颁发的杰出服务奖；1998年获德国联邦总统星级大十字勋章。

朱丽兰曾任中国工程院主席团顾问，中国科学院学部主席团顾问，国家科技领导小组成员，中央农村工作领导小组成员，国家信息化领导小组成员，国家奖励委员会主任委员等职。现任中国化学会常务理事会理事，中国对外友好协会常务理事，中国自然辩证法研究会理事，中国材料研究学会理事，并被聘为北京理工大学、国家行政学院、清华大学、中国科学院化学研究所兼职教授。

朱丽兰是国际欧亚科学院院士、亚太材料科学院院士。

# 孙　　煜

孙煜自 2020 年 12 月起任中银香港（控股）有限公司及中国银行（香港）有限公司副董事长兼总裁。彼时为战略及预算委员会和可持续发展委员会委员。调任前，于 2020 年 3 月—2020 年 12 月出任集团非执行董事和风险委员会委员。

孙煜于 1998 年加入中国银行，2012 年 7 月—2014 年 12 月任中银香港全球市场总经理，2015 年 3 月—2018 年 11 月任中国银行伦敦分行行长、中国银行（英国）有限公司行长，2015 年 12 月—2018 年 11 月兼任中国银行伦敦交易中心总经理。此前，先后担任中国银行全球金融市场部总监、金融市场总部总监（代客）、金融市场总部总监（证券投资）和上海市分行副行长。2018 年 9 月—2019 年 2 月任中国银行海外业务总监，2019 年 2 月—2020 年 12 月任中国银行副行长，并于 2019 年 2 月—2020 年 12 月兼任中银航空租赁有限公司（于香港上市）董事长，于 2019 年 11 月—2020 年 12 月兼任中国银行上海人民币交易业务总部总裁，于 2019 年 12 月—2020 年 12 月兼任中国银行北京市分行行长。

孙煜目前亦兼任多项职务，包括中国银行（英国）有限公司董事长、中银保险（国际）控股有限公司董事长、中银集团人寿保险有限公司董事长以及中银香港慈善基金董事局主席。孙煜现任多项公职，包括香港中资银行业协会会长、外汇基金咨询委员会委员、银行业务咨询委员会委员、财资市场公会议会委员、香港总商会理事会理事、香港贸易发展局"一带一路"及大湾区委员会委员、香港交易所风险管理委员会成员、香港印钞有限公司董事、香港银行学会副会长等。

孙煜于 1998 年毕业于南开大学，获经济学硕士学位。

# 钟　登　华

钟登华，1963 年 11 月出生。天津大学工学博士。现任教育部党组成员、副部长。曾任天津大学党委副书记、校长。2009 年当选中国工程院院士。

长期从事水利工程领域的人才培养和科学研究工作。提出了水利工程智能仿真与实时控制理论方法与技术、水利工程地质精细建模与分析理论方法与技术、水利工程建设智能控制数字大坝理论方法与技术。

先后承担并完成 10 余项国家重大工程的科技攻关或技术开发任务，研究成果在我国 80 多项水利水电工程中得到推广应用，在提高工程设计水平与效率、保证工程质量和节省工程投资方面发挥了重要作用。作为第一完成人获国家科技进步奖二等奖 2 项。

# 郑 慧 敏

郑慧敏女士为恒生银行副董事长兼行政总裁、恒生银行（中国）及恒生集团内若干附属公司之董事长、恒生指数顾问委员会主席、澳洲 Treasury Wine Estates Limited（富邑葡萄酒集团）独立非执行董事以及何梁何利基金信托委员会委员。郑慧敏亦为汇丰控股集团总经理。

郑慧敏于 1999 年加入汇丰集团，曾出任个人理财服务及市场推广业务多个要职。2007 年获委任为香港个人理财服务主管；2009 年为亚太区个人理财服务董事；2010 年为亚太区零售银行及财富管理业务主管。2014 年被委任为汇丰集团环球零售银行业务主管，至 2017 年出任恒生银行副董事长兼行政总裁。2017—2020 年出任香港上海汇丰银行董事。

郑慧敏目前亦出任下列机构职务：
- 香港恒生大学校董会主席
- 香港大学校董
- 江苏省港商投资企业服务协会荣誉会长
- 中国银联国际顾问
- 第十二届江苏省政协委员
- 中国（广东）自由贸易试验区深圳前海蛇口片区暨深圳市前海深港现代服务业合作区咨询委员会委员
- 香港银行学会副会长

其过往职务包括：
- 美国花旗银行市场总监
- 香港按揭证券有限公司董事
- 汇丰集团多间公司董事
- 香港公益金董事及执行委员会委员

郑慧敏毕业于香港大学并取得社会科学学士学位，为 Beta Gamma Sigma 香港大学分会终身荣誉会员。

## 霍　泰　辉

霍泰辉毕业于香港大学医学院，后于香港中文大学取得医学博士学位，专研新生儿科。曾在香港大学及玛丽医院担任儿科学系讲师，后于英国牛津大学约翰拉德克利夫医院及加拿大麦克马斯特大学医疗中心的初生儿科部门工作多年。于1984年加入香港中文大学，曾任多项重要职务，包括1995—2004年出任儿科学系主任，2004—2012年出任医学院院长，2013—2021年出任大学副校长，负责对外事务及大学拓展筹募。现为香港中文大学儿科学系荣休教授。

致力推动医学教育，培养新一代的医疗专业人才。其研究范畴是新生儿科，包括小儿呼吸系统疾病、传染性疾病、生长发育及医学教育。曾于国际医学期刊发表多篇研究论文，并为国内外多份学术期刊的编委会成员。英国皇家内科医学院（伦敦及爱丁堡）及英国皇家儿科医学院荣授院士，香港医学专科学院院士（儿科）及香港儿科医学院院士，香港儿科医学会终身荣誉会员。

积极参与社会服务，曾出任政府及专业团体多个委员会顾问，建树良多。曾任香港儿科医学院主席（2003—2006年）、香港医院管理局医疗服务发展委员会主席（2005—2012年）、香港医学专科学院副主席（一般事务）（2012—2016年）。现为香港医务委员会初步侦讯委员会主席、香港中文大学医院董事局成员及香港儿童医院管治委员会成员。

曾获多项奖誉，包括亚洲杰出儿科医生奖、中大校长模范教学奖、中大医学院杰出教学奖以及五次荣获医学院最杰出教师奖。此外，亦获香港特别行政区政府委任为太平绅士及颁授银紫荆星章，表扬其对公共医疗服务的杰出贡献。

# BRIEF INTRODUCTION TO THE TRUSTEES OF HO LEUNG HO LEE FOUNDATION

### Brief Biography of Professor Zhu Lilan

Professor Zhu Lilan, female, born in Shanghai in August 1935, is the member of the Standing Committee of the National People's Congress, the director of the Science, Education, Culture and Health Commission of the National People's Congress, former minister of the Ministry of Science and Technology of China. From 1956 to 1961, Professor Zhu studied in the Aodesa University of former Soviet Union majoring in macromolecule physical chemistry. After graduated from the university as an excellent student, Professor Zhu worked in the Institute of Chemistry, Chinese Academy of Sciences till 1986. For a long time, Professor Zhu had been conducted the research of macromolecule reactivity dynamics, macromolecule material analysis and structure token. The research project had got the national award of Grand Research Achievements and Award of Application Achievements. During this period, Professor Zhu served as the director of the research department and the director of the Institute of Chemistry, Chinese Academy of Sciences.

From 1979 to 1980, Professor Zhu was a visiting scholar in macromolecule institute in Fleberg University in Germany. In her research, she developed a kind of new dyeing technique for the sample producing, which was considered a break through at that time and won high reputation in the research circle.

From 1986 to 2001, Professor Zhu was appointed vice-minister of the State Science and Technology Commission and minister of the Ministry of Science and Technology of China. During this period, Professor Zhu organized the formulating and implementation of the National High-Tech Development Plan (863 Plan), National Climbing Plan for the Basic Research, and Torch Program for the High-Tech Industrialization. Professor Zhu advocated and implemented the new expertise management mechanism, put forward a series of management theories and policies which suit to the development of high-tech and the situation of China, published her monograph *High-tech, Development Strategy in the Contemporary Era, Development and Challenge*. Owing to her outstanding contribution to promoting international science and technology cooperation and the development of China's high-tech research and industrialization, Professor Zhu was awarded the Outstanding Service Prize in 1993 by the American Association of Chinese Engineers, and the Germany Federal President Star Great Cross Medal in 1998.

Professor Zhu has been the counselor of Chinese Academy of Engineering Presidium, the counselor of Chinese Academy of Science Presidium, the member of State Science and Education Steering Group, member of Central Rural Work Steering Group, member of State Informationalization Steering Group, director-commissioner of State Award Commission. Professor Zhu is now the member of China Chemistry Society Administrative Council, the administrative member of the board of the Association of China Foreign Friendship Relations, the member of board of China Natural Dialectic Seminar, the director of China Material Seminar. Professor Zhu is also the concurrent Professors of Beijing University of Science and Technology, National Administration College, Tsinghua University, Chemistry Institute of Chinese Academy of Sciences. Professor Zhu is the academician of International Europe and Asia Academy of Science, and the academician of Asian and Pacific Material Academy of Science.

## Brief Biography of Mr. Sun Yu

Mr. Sun has been appointed as Vice Chairman and Chief Executive of BOC Hong Kong (Holdings) Limited and Bank of China (Hong Kong) Limited since December 2020. He is a member of each of the Strategy and Budget Committee and the Sustainability Committee. Prior to the re-designation, Mr.Sun was a Non-executive Director and a member of the Risk Committee of the Group from March 2020 to December 2020.

Mr. Sun joined BOC in 1998. He served as the Executive Vice President of BOC from February 2019 to December 2020, and as Chief Overseas Business Officer of BOC from September 2018 to February 2019. From March 2015 to November 2018, Mr.Sun served as General Manager of London Branch of BOC, CEO of Bank of China (UK) Limited, and also served as General Manager of London Trading Center of BOC from December 2015 to November 2018. Mr.Sun previously served as Director of Global Financial Markets Department, Director of Financial Markets Unit (Client Business), Director of Financial Markets Unit (Securities Investments) and Deputy General Manager of the Shanghai Branch of BOC. He served as General Manager of Global Markets of BOCHK from July 2012 to December 2014. He was also Chairman of the Board of Directors of BOC Aviation Limited (listed in Hong Kong) from February 2019 to December 2020, President of Shanghai RMB Trading Unit of BOC from November 2019 to December 2020 and General Manager of Beijing Branch of BOC from December 2019 to December 2020.

Mr. Sun holds other roles with the group, including Chairman of the Board of Directors of Bank of China (UK) Limited, Chairman of BOC Insurance (International) Holdings Company Limited, Chairman of BOC Group Life Assurance Company Limited and Chairman of BOCHK Charitable Foundation. Mr.Sun also holds a number of public offices in Hong Kong. He serves as Chairman of the Chinese Banking Association of Hong Kong, and sits on the Exchange Fund Advisory Committee, the Banking Advisory Committee, the Council of Treasury Markets Association, the General Committee of the Hong Kong General Chamber of Commerce, the Belt and Road and Greater Bay Area Committee of the Hong Kong Trade Development Council, and the Risk Management Committee of the Hong Kong Exchanges and Clearing Limited. He is also Director of Hong Kong Note Printing Limited, as well as Vice President of the Hong Kong Institute of Bankers, etc.

Mr. Sun graduated from Nankai University with a Master's Degree in Economics in 1998.

## Brief Biography of Mr. Zhong Denghua

Zhong Denghua was born in November 1963. He earned a doctorate in engineering from Tianjin University. He is currently Vice Minister and member of CPC Leading Group of Ministry of Education. He served as the deputy secretary of the CPC committee and president of Tianjin University. He was elected a member of the Chinese Academy of Engineering in 2009.

Zhong Denghua has long been engaged in the training of talents and scientific research in the field of hydraulic engineering. He put forward theories, methodologies and developed technologies in the following areas: intelligent simulation and real-time control of hydraulic projects, precision modeling and analysis of the geological conditions of hydraulic projects, and intelligent control in the construction of hydraulic projects and digital dam.

Zhong Denghua has undertaken and completed the tasks of tackling hard-nut problems or technological development in more than 10 national major projects. The research achievements he has scored have been applied in more than 80 hydraulic and hydroelectric power projects in China, and have played important roles in improving the level and efficiency of project design, guaranteeing project quality and saving project investment. He was presented with 2 second-prizes of the State Science and Technology Advancement Award as the first complete person.

## Brief Biography of Ms Louisa Cheang

Ms Louisa Cheang is Vice-Chairman and Chief Executive of Hang Seng Bank, and Chairman of Hang Seng Bank (China) and various subsidiaries in Hang Seng Group. She is Chairman of Hang Seng Index Advisory Committee of Hang Seng Indexes, an Independent Non-executive Director of Treasury Wine Estates Limited, Australia and a Member of the Board of Trustees of the Ho Leung Ho Lee Foundation. She is also a Group General Manager of HSBC.

Ms Cheang joined HSBC in 1999, and has worked across a wide range of Personal Financial Services and Marketing positions. She was appointed Head of Personal Financial Services, Hong

Kong in 2007; Regional Director of Personal Financial Services, Asia Pacific in 2009; and Regional Head of Retail Banking and Wealth Management, Asia Pacific in 2010. Ms Cheang became Group Head of Retail Banking, HSBC in 2014 prior to her appointment as Vice-Chairman and Chief Executive of Hang Seng Bank in 2017. She was also a Director of The Hongkong and Shanghai Banking Corporation from 2017 to 2020.

Ms Cheang currently also holds the following appointments:
- Chairman of the Board of Governors of The Hang Seng University of Hong Kong
- Member of the Court of The University of Hong Kong
- Honorary President of Jiangsu Service Association for Hong Kong Enterprise Investment
- International Advisor of China Union Pay
- Member of The Twelfth Jiangsu Provincial Committee of the Chinese People's Political Consultative Conference
- Member of the Consulting Committee of Qianhai & Shekou Area of Shenzhen, China (Guangdong) Pilot Free Trade Zone, and Qianhai Shenzhen-Hong Kong Modern Service Industry Cooperation Zone of Shenzhen
- Vice President of The Hong Kong Institute of Bankers

Her previous appointments include:
- Marketing Director of Citibank N.A.
- Director of The Hong Kong Mortgage Corporation Limited
- Director of various subsidiaries in HSBC
- Board Member and Member of Executive Committee of The Community Chest of Hong Kong

Ms Cheang graduated from The University of Hong Kong receiving a Bachelor of Social Sciences degree. She was made a Chapter Honoree of Beta Gamma Sigma of The University of Hong Kong Chapter.

## Brief Biography of Mr. Fok Tai-Fai

Fok Tai-Fai graduated in Medicine from The University of Hong Kong (HKU) and received his Doctor of Medicine (MD) from The Chinese University of Hong Kong (CUHK). A paediatrician by training, he served in HKU and Queen Mary Hospital as a Lecturer in Paediatrics, and spent a number of years working in the Neonatal Units at the John Radcliffe Hospital in the University of Oxford, UK and the McMaster University Medical Centre, Canada. Professor Fok joined CUHK in 1984 and had served in various key positions including Chairman of the Department of Paediatrics (1995—2004), Dean of the Faculty of Medicine (2004—2012), and Pro-Vice-Chancellor/Vice-President (External Affairs and Institutional Advancement) from 2013 to 2021. Professor Fok is the Emeritus Professor in the Department of Paediatrics of CUHK.

Professor Fok is dedicated to nurturing the next generation of medical professionals. His research interest is in newborn care, especially the prevention and management of respiratory conditions, newborn infection, newborn growth, and medical education. Professor Fok has published extensively in international journals, and served on the editorial boards of international and national medical journals. He is a Fellow of the Royal College of Physicians of Edinburgh, Royal College of Physicians of London, Royal College of Paediatrics and Child Health, Hong Kong Academy of Medicine (Paediatrics) and Hong Kong College of Paediatricians. He has also been elected as Honorary Life Member of the Hong Kong Paediatric Society.

Professor Fok has served on many government committees and advisory bodies and has contributed significantly to the community. He was the President of the Hong Kong College of Paediatricians (2003—2006), Chairman of the Medical Services Development Committee of Hong Kong Hospital Authority (2005—2012), and Vice-President (General Affairs) of the Hong Kong Academy of Medicine (2012—2016). He is the Chairman of the deemed Preliminary Investigation Committee of the Medical Council of Hong Kong, and a member of the Board of Directors of CUHK Medical Centre and the Hospital Governing Committee of the Hong Kong Children's Hospital.

Professor Fok has received many honours and awards throughout his career, including the Outstanding Asian Paediatrician Award, the Vice-Chancellor's Exemplary Teaching Award of CUHK, and Master Teaching Award of the Faculty of Medicine. He received the Outstanding Teacher Award of the Faculty of Medicine five times. He was also awarded the honours of Justice of Peace and Silver Bauhinia Star by the HKSAR Government for his distinguished contribution to the public healthcare sector.

# 何梁何利基金评选委员会成员简历

### 评选委员会主任
### 朱 丽 兰

朱丽兰，女，1935年8月出生，浙江湖州人，教授。现任中国发明协会理事长，澳门特别行政区科技奖励委员会主任。曾任国家科委副主任（1986年）、国家科学技术部部长（1998年），全国人大常委会教科文卫委员会主任委员（2001年），中国工程院主席团顾问，中国科学院学部主席团顾问，国家科教领导小组成员，国家科技奖励委员会主任委员，澳门特别行政区科学技术委员会顾问等职。

在中国科学院化学所从事高分子材料剖析及结构形态表征、反应动力学研究期间，承担了多项国家、国防重点科研攻关项目，曾获国家级、省部级重大科研成果奖及应用成果奖。担任全国人大常委会教科文卫委员会主任委员期间，负责组织完成《科技进步法》《义务教育法》的修订和实施；组织实施一批关系到社会、民生、科技、文化、卫生等重要法律的立法调研与修法任务，为法制建设奠定重要基础。

发表了多篇有关高技术发展现状及对策和管理方面的文章，出版了《当代高技术与发展战略》《发展与挑战》等专著。曾获中国材料研究学会成就奖。由于在推动中国高技术发展及国际科技合作方面成绩显著，获美洲中国工程师协会颁发的杰出服务奖、德国总统颁发的德意志联邦共和国大十字勋章、乌克兰总统二级勋章。

### 评选委员会副主任
### 钟 登 华

钟登华，1963年11月出生。天津大学工学博士。现任教育部党组成员、副部长。曾任天津大学党委副书记、校长。2009 年当选中国工程院院士。

长期从事水利工程领域的人才培养和科学研究工作。提出了水利工程智能仿真与实时控制理论方法与技术、水利工程地质精细建模与分析理论方法与技术、水利工程建设智能控制数字大坝理论方法与技术。

先后承担并完成 10 余项国家重大工程的科技攻关或技术开发任务，研究成果在我国 80 多项水利水电工程中得到推广应用，在提高工程设计水平与效率、保证工程质量和节省工程投资方面发挥了重要作用。作为第一完成人获国家科技进步奖二等奖 2 项。

## 评选委员会副主任
## 霍 泰 辉

霍泰辉毕业于香港大学医学院，后于香港中文大学取得医学博士学位，专研新生儿科。曾在香港大学及玛丽医院担任儿科学系讲师，后于英国牛津大学约翰拉德克利夫医院及加拿大麦克马斯特大学医疗中心的初生儿科部门工作多年。于 1984 年加入香港中文大学，曾任多项重要职务，包括 1995—2004 年出任儿科学系系主任，2004—2012 年出任医学院院长，2013—2021 年出任大学副校长，负责对外事务及大学拓展筹募。现为香港中文大学儿科学系荣休教授。

致力推动医学教育，培养新一代的医疗专业人才。其研究范畴是新生儿科，包括小儿呼吸系统疾病、传染性疾病、生长发育及医学教育。曾于国际医学期刊发表多篇研究论文，并为国内外多份学术期刊的编委会成员。英国皇家内科医学院（伦敦及爱丁堡）及英国皇家儿科医学院荣授院士，香港医学专科学院院士（儿科）及香港儿科医学院院士，香港儿科医学会终身荣誉会员。

积极参与社会服务，曾出任政府及专业团体多个委员会顾问，建树良多。曾任香港儿科医学院主席（2003—2006 年）、香港医院管理局医疗服务发展委员会主席（2005—2012 年）、香港医学专科学院副主席（一般事务）（2012—2016 年）。现为香港医务委员会初步侦讯委员会主席、香港中文大学医院董事局成员及香港儿童医院管治委员会成员。

曾获多项奖誉，包括亚洲杰出儿科医生奖、中大校长模范教学奖、中大医学院杰出教学奖以及五次荣获医学院最杰出教师奖。此外，亦获香港特别行政区政府委任为太平绅士及颁授银紫荆星章，表扬其对公共医疗服务的杰出贡献。

## 评选委员会秘书长
## 段 瑞 春

段瑞春，1943年2月出生。上海交通大学工学学士，中国科学院研究生院理学硕士，北京大学法学硕士。20世纪90年代，任国家科委政策法规与体制改革司司长、国务院知识产权办公会议办公室主任，2000—2007年任国务院国有重点大型企业监事会主席。现任中国科学技术法学会名誉会长，曾任中国民营科技促进会会长、中国产学研合作促进会常务副会长。

我国知识产权、科技政策和企业创新领域著名专家，具有自然科学、经济管理和法律科学复合型知识结构。曾主持起草我国《技术合同法》《科学技术进步法》《促进科技成果转化法》《国家科技奖励条例》等法律法规；参加多项知识产权法律的制定和修改工作；担任中美、中欧、中俄科技合作知识产权谈判首席代表、中国"入世"知识产权谈判主要代表；《国家知识产权战略》总报告评审组组长；何梁何利基金《信托契约》《评选章程》主要制定者之一。

其研究成果于1992年获得国家科委科技进步奖一等奖、1993年获得国家科技进步奖二等奖，均为第一完成人。2004年获我国技术市场建设功勋奖，2008年获中国科技法学会杰出贡献奖，2017年获中国科技法学会终身成就奖。撰写出版《国际合作与知识产权》《技术合同原理与实践》《技术创新读本》《科技政策多维思考》等多部著作。主编《光荣、责任与梦想》《情系科学春天》等何梁何利基金文献。

## 评选委员会委员
## 马 永 生

马永生，1961年10月出生于内蒙古自治区呼和浩特市。石油地质学家、沉积学家。1980年至1990年先后就读于中国地质大学（原武汉地质学院）和中国地质科学院，获博士学位。现任中国石化集团公司副总经理、总地质师。2009年当选中国工程院院士。

长期从事中国油气资源勘探理论研究和生产实践，

在中国海相碳酸盐岩油气勘探理论和技术方面取得了多项创新性成果，成功指导发现了普光、元坝等多个大型、特大型天然气田，为国家重大工程"川气东送"提供了扎实的资源基础。他在非常规天然气领域的前瞻性研究，为中国第一个页岩气田——涪陵页岩气田的发现作出了重要贡献。他的科研成果对缓解我国天然气供需矛盾、发展地区经济与环境保护起到了重要的促进作用。

获国家科技进步奖一等奖 2 项；2007 年获何梁何利科学与技术成就奖，同年获第十次李四光地质科学奖；2013 年被评为国家首批"万人计划"杰出人才。由于他在石油工业界的杰出成果，2017 年国际小行星中心将国际编号为 210292 号小行星命名为"马永生星"。

## 评选委员会委员
## 王 小 凡

王小凡，著名癌症生物学家。1955 年出生于乌鲁木齐市，1982 年毕业于武汉大学生物化学专业，同年考入中国科学院遗传研究所，并在当年举办的首届"中美生物化学联合招生项目"（CUSBEA）中取得第一名的成绩赴美留学。1986 年获加州大学洛杉矶分校博士学位，之后在麻省理工学院师从癌症生物学家 Robert A. Weinberg 从事博士后研究。1992 年被聘为杜克大学药理学和肿瘤生物学系助理教授，成为最早在杜克大学执教的华人教授之一。1998 年成为终身教授，2003 年晋升为正教授。现任杜克大学医学中心药理学和肿瘤生物学 Donald and Elizabeth Cooke 终身讲席教授。

王小凡在细胞信号转导、DNA 损伤与修复、癌症转移分子机制、肿瘤微环境等多个领域均有重要学术贡献，尤其在 TGF-β 相关研究领域取得了令人瞩目的成绩。先后发表了 100 多篇学术论文，其中在 *Cell*、*Nature*、*Science*、*Cancer Cell*、*Nature Cell Biology* 等高水平杂志上发表论文 20 余篇。王小凡长期坚持通过多种渠道为中国的教育科技事业建言献策，推动、促成了一系列改善中国教育科研环境的政策制度，目前担任中国国务院侨办海外专家咨询委员会委员。

## 评选委员会委员
## 杨 祖 佑

  杨祖佑，1940年出生。获美国康奈尔大学博士学位。先后任普度大学航空宇宙工程系主任、工学院院长；曾兼任美国国家科学基金会智能制造工程中心共同主任，同时任阿姆斯特朗（首位登陆月球者）杰出宇航讲座教授。现任美国圣塔芭芭拉加州大学校长（1994年始任），美国国家工程院院士，美国航天、机械学会Fellow，中国工程院海外院士。兼任美、中、印、日、加"三十米望远镜"计划（简称TMT计划）主席，太平洋滨42所大学联盟主席（包括北大、清华、复旦、科大、浙大、南京），美国总统科学奖章评委，科维理科学基金会理事，曾任美国大学联盟（AAU，包括62所顶尖研究型大学）主席，芬兰千禧科技奖评委。共获7所大学荣誉博士。

  长期致力于教学及科研。从事宇航结构、颤振、控制转型至地震、制造、材料（LED）及生物工程等方面的研究，亲任博士论文主席指导60篇，发表期刊论文200余篇，学术会议论文200余篇，有限元教科书1本（被40余所美国大学采用，有中文、日文版）。

  曾获2008年美国航天学会结构、振动、材料奖（SDM Award），美国工程教育学会最高李梅金质奖章以及十余次最佳教学奖。

## 评选委员会委员
## 杨 纲 凯

  杨纲凯，1948年7月出生于上海市。自1973年起任职香港中文大学，曾任物理系主任、理学院院长、研究院院长、副校长。现任香港中文大学敬文书院院长、物理系教授，香港特别行政区教育统筹委员会委员、课程发展议会主席。曾任香港特别行政区大学教育资助委员会委员及香港研究资助局主席，亚太物理联会秘书长、副会长。1965—1972年就读于美国加州理工学院，

主修物理，1969 年获学士学位，1972 年获博士学位。1972—1973 年在美国普林斯顿大学从事教学及研究。

长期从事理论物理学研究，包括基本粒子、场论、高能唯象、耗散系统及其本征态展开，对光学、引力波等开放系统的应用作出贡献，其主要研究成果载于有关国际杂志，包括 Microscopic derivation of the Helmholtz force density, Phys Rev Lett 47, 77; Late time tail of wave propagation on curved spacetime, Phys Rev Lett 74, 2414; Quasinormal mode expansion for linearized waves in gravitational systems, Phys Rev Lett 74, 4588; Quasinormal modes of dirty black holes, Phys Rev Lett 78, 289 等。1999 年被选为美国物理学会院士，2004 年被选为国际欧亚科学院院士。

## 评选委员会委员
## 吴 伟 仁

吴伟仁，1953 年出生，中国探月工程总设计师，航天测控通信和深空探测工程总体技术专家。中国工程院院士，国际宇航科学院院士，全国政协常委。我国深空探测领域主要开拓者之一和航天战略科学家。

先后获国家科技进步奖特等奖 3 项，一等奖 2 项；获首届全国创新争先奖章，何梁何利科学与技术成就奖，钱学森最高成就奖等。2020 年获国际宇航联合会最高奖——世界航天奖。鉴于他在航天领域的杰出贡献，国际天文学联合会将国际永久编号 281880 小行星命名为"吴伟仁星"。

## 评选委员会委员
## 张 立 同

张立同，女，1938 年 4 月出生于重庆，著名航空航天材料专家。1961 年毕业于西北工业大学。1989—1991 年在美国 NASA 空间结构材料商业发展中心做高级访问学者。现任西北工业大学教授、博士生导师、超高温结构复合材料技术国家重点实验室学术委员会副主

任。1995年当选中国工程院院士。

致力于航空航天材料及其制造技术研究,在薄壁复杂高温合金和铝合金铸件的无余量熔模精密铸造技术及其理论基础研究中取得丰硕成果。揭示了叶片变形规律、粗糙度形成规律和陶瓷型壳中温和高温软化变形机理。创新发展了高温合金无余量熔模铸造技术、铝合金石膏型熔模铸造技术、高温合金熔模铸造用中温和高温抗蠕变陶瓷型壳材料、高温合金泡沫陶瓷过滤净化材料技术等。相关成果成功用于航空发动机和飞机构件生产中。

突破大型空间站用陶瓷基复合材料技术,建立了具有自主知识产权的制造工艺、制造设备与材料环境性能考核三个技术平台,打破了国际技术封锁。

获国家技术发明奖一等奖1项,国家科技进步奖一、二、三等奖4项,国家级教学成果奖二等奖1项,获授权国家发明专利64项。

## 评选委员会委员
## 张 恭 庆

张恭庆,1936年5月29日出生于上海。1959年毕业于北京大学数学系,毕业后留校工作至今。1978年作为我国改革开放后第一批赴美访问学者赴美进修。现为北京大学教授、中国科学院院士、发展中国家(第三世界)科学院院士、高校数学研究与人才培养中心主任,还担任多个国际核心刊物的编委。

著名数学家。发展无穷维 Morse 理论为临界点理论的统一框架,并首次将其应用于偏微分方程的多解问题,其著作成为该领域的基本文献。发展了集值映射的拓扑度理论以及不可微泛函的临界点理论,使之成为研究数学物理方程以及非光滑力学中的一类自由边界问题的有效方法。

曾荣获全国科技大会奖(1978)、国家自然科学奖三等奖(1982)、国家自然科学奖二等奖(1987)、陈省身数学奖(1986)、有突出贡献的中青年科学家(1984)、第三世界科学院数学奖(1993)、华罗庚数学奖(2009)、北京大学国华奖、方正教学特等奖(2011)等。

## 评选委员会委员
## 陈 佳 洱

陈佳洱，1934年10月1日出生于上海。中国科学院院士、第三世界科学院院士。现任北京大学物理学教授，国家重点基础研究计划（"973"计划）专家顾问组副组长，国际科联中国协调委员会副主席等职。

曾任北京大学校长和研究生院院长、国家自然科学基金委员会主任、中国科学院数理学部主任和中科院主席团成员以及中科院研究生院物理科学学院院长等职。

长期致力于低能粒子加速器及其应用的教学与科研工作，善于把握学科前沿发展与国家需求的结合，前瞻性地部署物理研究与人才培养，开拓发展我国的射频超导加速器、超灵敏加速器质谱计、射频四极场加速器、高压静电加速器等，是我国低能粒子加速器的奠基者和领头人之一。

陈佳洱长期在北京大学和国家自然科学基金委等单位担任领导工作，并曾担任国家中长期科技规划领导小组成员等职，为我国科学技术中长期规划的制订与相关的科教事业的发展作出了重要贡献。

## 评选委员会委员
## 郝 吉 明

郝吉明，1946年8月出生于山东省，著名环境工程专家。1970年毕业于清华大学，1981年获清华大学硕士学位，1984年获美国辛辛那提大学博士学位。现任清华大学教授、博士生导师、教学委员会副主任、环境科学与工程研究院院长，兼任国家环境咨询委员会委员、中国环境与发展国际合作委员会委员。2005年当选中国工程院院士，2018年当选美国国家工程院外籍院士。

致力于中国空气污染控制研究40余年，主要研究领域为能源与环境、大气污染控制工程。主持全国酸沉降控制规划与对策研究，划定酸雨和二氧化硫控制区，被国务院采

纳实施，为确定我国酸雨防治对策起到主导作用。建立了城市机动车污染控制规划方法，推动了我国机动车污染控制进程。深入开展大气复合污染特征、成因及控制策略研究，发展了特大城市空气质量改善的理论与技术方法，推动我国区域性大气复合污染的联防联控。长期开展大气污染控制关键技术研究，在燃煤烟气除尘脱硫脱硝、机动车污染控制等领域作出贡献。

获国家科技进步奖一等奖1项、二等奖2项，国家自然科学奖二等奖和国家技术发明奖二等奖各1项，国家教学成果奖一等奖2项。2006年获国家教学名师称号，获2015年度哈根-斯密特清洁空气奖及2016年IBM全球杰出学者奖。

## 评选委员会委员
### 赵宇亮

1985年获四川大学放射化学学士学位，从事核燃料研究。1989年赴日本原子力研究所进修，在东京都立大学获硕士、博士学位，从事原子核裂变碎片质量测量的研究，与日本同事一起发现了113号新元素（Nh），是元素周期表中亚洲国家发现的唯一元素。

2001年回国，率先提出纳米生物安全性问题并创建第一个实验室。率先揭示了无机和碳纳米材料的生物安全性规律与肿瘤纳米药物的化学生物学机制。部分研究成果被ISO颁布为国际标准。曾获国家自然科学奖二等奖（2012年，2018年）、中国科学院杰出科技成就奖（2019年）、何梁何利基金科学与技术进步奖（2020年）、中国侨界贡献奖（2020年）、TWAS化学奖、中国毒理学杰出贡献奖、全国优秀科技工作者等。2015年创建中国药学会纳米药物专业委员会，2011年创建中国毒理学会纳米毒理学专业委员会，大力推动了纳米生物学这个学科交叉前沿在我国的起步和发展。

中国科学院院士，发展中国家科学院院士，中国医学科学院学部委员，国家纳米科学中心主任。目前担任中国生物材料学会候任理事长，中国化学会副理事长，中国药学会副理事长，爱思唯尔学术期刊 *Nano Today* 主编等。

## 评选委员会委员
## 钱 绍 钧

钱绍钧，1934年出生于浙江平湖。1951年考入清华大学物理系，后在北京俄语专科学校和北京大学物理系、物理研究室（现技术物理系）学习。现任原总装备部科技委顾问，研究员，中国工程院院士。曾任核试验基地副司令员、司令员，国防科工委科技委常任委员。

长期从事核试验放射化学诊断工作，参与了由原子弹到氢弹、由大气层到地下的一系列核试验，建立完善多项诊断方法和技术，显著提升测量精度。多次参加国防科技和武器装备发展战略研究，参与组织国家中长期科学技术发展规划专题研究。指导开展国防应用基础研究，努力促进与国家基础研究的协调链接。指导军用核技术发展，长期跟踪研究国际态势及主要国家政策演变，参与军备控制研究和"全面禁止核试验条约"谈判。

出版译著1部，主编专著2部，撰写科技论文和重要科技档案多篇，获国家科技进步奖特等奖、二等奖各1项，国家发明奖二等奖、三等奖各1项，军队科技进步奖多项。

## 评选委员会委员
## 倪 军

倪军，1961年11月出生于青海，著名制造科学专家。1982年获上海交通大学学士学位。1984年和1987年分别获得美国威斯康星大学硕士和博士学位。1987年起在美国密歇根大学任教至今。现为美国密歇根大学吴贤铭制造科学冠名教授及机械工程系终身教授；上海交通大学校长特聘顾问、交大密西根学院荣誉院长，并同时担任美国密西根大学吴贤铭制造研究中心主任及美国国家科学基金会产学研"智能维护系统中心"共同主任。倪军教授目前担任世界经济论坛（达沃斯论坛）未来制造委员会主席。

曾担任美国国家科学基金会"可重组制造系统中心"执行主任及美国国家科学基金会产学研"制造质量测量与控制中心"主任。倪军教授主要从事先进制造科学领域中智能制造技术的研究，包括基于工业大数据分析和人工智能技术在精密质量控制、制造过程效率优化、重大装备的可靠性和健康预测管理、智能维护系统等研究。他的研究成果在众多工业领域得到成功应用。

倪军教授获得40多项学术成就奖。2013年获中华人民共和国国际科技合作奖；1994年获克林顿颁发的美国总统教授奖；2013年获国际制造工程师协会金奖，是该奖1955年设立之后首位获此殊荣的华人学者；2009年获美国机械工程学会William T. Ennor最高制造技术奖；2002年当选为美国制造工程师学会FELLOW；2004年当选为美国机械工程学会FELLOW；1991年获国际制造工程师学会杰出制造工程师奖。

# 评选委员会委员
## 桑 国 卫

桑国卫，1941年11月出生，浙江湖州人。临床药理学家，中国工程院院士。中国药学会理事长，"十一五""十二五""十三五"国家"重大新药创制"重大专项技术总师，工信部"医药工业'十三五'发展规划"专家咨询委员会主任，中国药品生物制品检定所资深研究员，上海中医药大学名誉校长。曾任十一届全国人大常委会副委员长、农工民主党中央主席。

对长效注射与口服甾体避孕药及抗孕激素的药代动力学、种族差异及临床药理学做了系统研究，取得多项重大成果。近年来，在新药的安全性评价、质量控制和临床试验等方面进行了卓有成效的工作，为加强我国GLP、GCP平台建设作出了重要贡献。

获全国科技大会奖2项，国家科学技术进步奖二等奖3项，部委级科技进步奖一等奖1项、二等奖4项。1997年获何梁何利科学与技术进步奖（医学药学奖）。2008年获吴阶平—保罗·杨森奖特殊贡献奖。2014年获国际药学联合会药学科学终身成就奖。

## 评选委员会委员
## 曹 雪 涛

曹雪涛，1964年7月出生，山东济南人。1990年毕业于第二军医大学。现为中国医学科学院院长、中国工程院院士、医学免疫学国家重点实验室主任，兼任中国免疫学会理事长、全球慢性疾病防控联盟主席、亚洲大洋洲免疫学会联盟主席等。担任 Cell 等杂志编委。

主要从事天然免疫识别及其免疫调节的基础研究、肿瘤免疫治疗应用性研究。发现了具有重要免疫调控功能的树突状细胞新型亚群；独立发现了 22 种免疫相关分子；系统研究了天然免疫识别与干扰素产生调控的新机制；探讨了表观分子在炎症与肿瘤发生发展中的作用；建立了肿瘤免疫治疗新途径并开展了临床试验。

以第一完成人获国家自然科学奖二等奖 1 项，中华医学科技奖一等奖 1 项，军队科技进步奖一等奖 1 项，上海市自然科学奖一等奖 3 项，已获得国家发明专利 16 项，获得 2 个国家 II 类新药证书。研究成果入选 2011 年中国十大科技进展。获得光华工程奖、长江学者成就奖、中国青年科学家奖、中国十大杰出青年等。以通讯作者发表 SCI 收录论文 220 余篇，包括 Cell、Science、Nature Immunology、Cancer Cell、Immunity 等。论文被 SCI 他引 5600 多次；编写和共同主编专著 8 部。

## 评选委员会委员
## 程　　序

程序，1944 年出生，江苏无锡人。1965 年毕业于北京农业大学（现中国农业大学）农学系，后入中国农业科学院作物育种栽培研究所从事研究工作。现为中国农业大学教授，博导。曾就职于北京市农科院、农业部等单位。主要研究方向为可持续农业与农村发展、农业生态与生态农业以及生物能源等。

曾主持农业现代化规律和实验基地建设（实验基地：北京市房山区窦店村）以及生态农业两个研究项目。1985 年率先引进农业可持续发展的理论，此后开始研究中国条件下农业可持续发展的途径。重点放在农牧交错生态脆弱带的生态恢复途径，以及探索可持续的集约化农业模式的研究两个方面。

作为第一完成人，先后被授予北京市科技进步奖一等奖及国家星火科技奖（等同科技进步奖）一等奖。累计获省部级科技进步奖二、三等奖7项，1988年被批准为国家级有突出贡献的中青年专家。

著有《可持续农业导论》和《中国可持续发展总纲第13卷：中国农业与可持续发展》两部专著。

# 评选委员会委员
## 曾 庆 存

曾庆存，1935年5月出生于广东省阳江市（原阳江县）。1956年毕业于北京大学物理系。1961年在苏联科学院应用地球物理研究所获副博士（现称博士即Ph.D）学位。回国后先后在中国科学院地球物理研究所和大气物理研究所工作。1980年当选中国科学院院士。现为中国科学院大气物理研究所研究员。

主要研究领域为大气科学和地球流体力学。致力于大气环流和地球流体动力学基础理论和数值模式及模拟、地球系统动力学模式、数值天气预报和气候预测理论、气候动力学和季风理论、大气边界层动力学、卫星遥感理论方法、应用数学和计算数学以及自然控制论等的研究工作。在国际上最早提出半隐式差分法和平方守恒格式，最早成功将原始方程应用于实际数值天气预告（1961）和研制成大气海洋耦合模式并用作跨季度气候预测（1990，1994），提出系统的卫星大气遥感理论（1974）以及自然控制论理论方法（1995）。

曾获国家自然科学奖二等奖2项和三等奖1项，中国科学院自然科学奖一等奖6项和杰出贡献奖1项。出版专著包括《大气红外遥测原理》《数值天气预报的数学物理基础》《短期数值气候预测原理》《千里黄云——东亚沙尘暴研究》等。发表学术文章约百篇。

## 评选委员会委员
## 蒲 慕 明

蒲慕明，1948年10月出生。1970年毕业于台湾清华大学物理系；1974年在美国Johns Hopkins大学生物物理系获博士学位；1974—1976年先后在美国Woods Hole海洋生物研究所、美国Purdue大学生命科学系做博士后研究；1976年9月—1985年3月在美国加州大学Irvine分校生物物理系任助理教授、副教授、教授；1985年4月—1988年8月在美国耶鲁大学医学院分子神经生物学系任教授；1988年7月—1995年12月在美国哥伦比亚大学生物学系任教授；1996年1月—2000年10月在美国加州大学圣地亚哥分校生物学系任Stephen W. Kuffler讲座教授。1998年7月筹建神经科学研究所；2000年9月起任美国加州大学Berkeley分校分子与细胞生物学系1933级讲座教授，2002年起任神经生物学部主任。中国科学院外籍院士（2011年），美国科学院院士（2009年），台湾"中央研究院"院士。现任中国科学院上海生命科学研究院神经科学研究所所长，中国科学院脑科学卓越创新中心主任。

蒲慕明教授主要从事轴突导向和突触可塑性的分子与细胞机制研究，以其卓越成就于2005年荣获中华人民共和国国际科学技术合作奖，2016年荣获Gruber神经科学奖。

蒲慕明是一位世界级科学家，曾参与清华大学生物系组建并担任首任系主任，长期担纲中国神经科学研究领军者。

蒲慕明于2017年放弃美国国籍，恢复中国国籍。

# BRIEF INTRODUCTION TO THE MEMBERS OF THE SELECTION BOARD OF HO LEUNG HO LEE FOUNDATION

## Zhu Lilan, Director of the Selection Board

Zhu Lilan, female, was born in August 1935 and is of the origin of Huzhou, Zhejiang Province. At present, she is the Chairman of the China Association of Inventions and the Chairman of the Committee of Science and Technology Awards of Macau Special Administrative Region. She was the vice-minister of the State Science and Technology Commission (1986), the Minister of the Ministry of Science and Technology (1998), the Director of the Education, Science, Culture and Public Health Committee of the National People's Congress (2001), the counselor of Chinese Academy of Engineering Presidium, the Advisor of the Presidential Committee of CAS Academic Board, the Member of the State Leading Group of Science, Technology and Education, the Director of the State Committee of Science and Technology Awards and the Advisor of the Macao Science and Technology Council.

When analyzing polymer materials and researching morphological structure and reaction dynamics in the Institute of Chemistry of the Chinese Academy of Sciences, Zhu Lilan undertook several national and national defense key science and technological projects and was granted the statelevel and provincelevel significant scientific and technological result awards and application result awards. When being the Director of the Education, Science, Culture and Public Health Committee of the National People's Congress, she organized the amendments to and implementation of the Science and Technology Progress Law and the Compulsory Education Law; and organized a series of investigations for making the laws and amending the important laws concerning such matters as society, people's life, science and technology, culture and health, which has provided an important basis for legal construction.

Zhu Lilan has published several articles and books on the status quo of hi-tech development and the corresponding strategies and management measures, including *Modern Hi-tech. Development Strategy in the Contemporary Era* and *Development and Challenge*. She was granted the Achievement Award by the Chinese Materials Research Society. Thanks to her significant contribution to the development of China's hi-tech development and international scientific and technological cooperation, Zhu Lilan obtained the Distinguished Service Award granted by the Chinese Institute of Engineers, USA, the Grand Cross Medal of the Federal Republic of Germany granted by German President and the Medal No. 2 of Ukraine President.

## Zhong Denghua, Deputy Director of the Selection Board

Zhong Denghua was born in November 1963. He earned a doctorate in engineering from Tianjin University. He is currently Vice Minister and member of CPC Leading Group of Ministry of Education. He served as the deputy secretary of the CPC committee and president of Tianjin University. He was elected a member of the Chinese Academy of Engineering in 2009.

Zhong Denghua has long been engaged in the training of talents and scientific research in the field of hydraulic engineering. He put forward theories, methodologies and developed technologies in the following areas: intelligent simulation and real-time control of hydraulic projects, precision modeling and analysis of the geological conditions of hydraulic projects, and intelligent control in the construction of hydraulic projects and digital dam.

Zhong Denghua has undertaken and completed the tasks of tackling hard-nut problems or technological development in more than 10 national major projects. The research achievements he has scored have been applied in more than 80 hydraulic and hydroelectric power projects in China, and have played important roles in improving the level and efficiency of project design, guaranteeing project quality and saving project investment. He was presented with 2 second-prizes of the State Science and Technology Advancement Award as the first complete person.

## Fok Tai-Fai, Deputy Director of the Selection Board

Fok Tai-Fai graduated in Medicine from The University of Hong Kong (HKU) and received his Doctor of Medicine (MD) from The Chinese University of Hong Kong (CUHK). A paediatrician by training, he served in HKU and Queen Mary Hospital as a Lecturer in Paediatrics, and spent a number of years working in the Neonatal Units at the John Radcliffe Hospital in the University of Oxford, UK and the McMaster University Medical Centre, Canada. Professor Fok joined CUHK in 1984 and had served in various key positions including Chairman of the Department of Paediatrics (1995—2004), Dean of the Faculty of Medicine (2004—2012), and Pro-Vice-Chancellor/Vice-President (External Affairs and Institutional Advancement) from 2013 to 2021. Professor Fok is the Emeritus Professor in the Department of Paediatrics of CUHK.

Professor Fok is dedicated to nurturing the next generation of medical professionals. His research interest is in newborn care, especially the prevention and management of respiratory conditions, newborn infection, newborn growth, and medical education. Professor Fok has published extensively in international journals, and served on the editorial boards of international and national medical journals. He is a Fellow of the Royal College of Physicians of Edinburgh, Royal College of Physicians of London, Royal College of Paediatrics and Child Health, Hong Kong

Academy of Medicine (Paediatrics) and Hong Kong College of Paediatricians. He has also been elected as Honorary Life Member of the Hong Kong Paediatric Society.

Professor Fok has served on many government committees and advisory bodies and has contributed significantly to the community. He was the President of the Hong Kong College of Paediatricians (2003—2006), Chairman of the Medical Services Development Committee of Hong Kong Hospital Authority (2005—2012), and Vice-President (General Affairs) of the Hong Kong Academy of Medicine (2012—2016). He is the Chairman of the deemed Preliminary Investigation Committee of the Medical Council of Hong Kong, and a member of the Board of Directors of CUHK Medical Centre and the Hospital Governing Committee of the Hong Kong Children's Hospital.

Professor Fok has received many honours and awards throughout his career, including the Outstanding Asian Paediatrician Award, the Vice-Chancellor's Exemplary Teaching Award of CUHK, and Master Teaching Award of the Faculty of Medicine. He received the Outstanding Teacher Award of the Faculty of Medicine five times. He was also awarded the honours of Justice of Peace and Silver Bauhinia Star by the HKSAR Government for his distinguished contribution to the public healthcare sector.

## Duan Ruichun, Secretary-General of the Selection Board

Duan Ruichun, born in February 1943, is a bachelor of engineer from Shanghai Jiaotong University, a master of science from Graduate University of Chinese Academy of Science and a master of law from Peking University. In the 1990s, he was the Director of the Policy, Law and System Reform Department of the State Science and Technology Commission and the Director of the Intellectual Property Working Meeting Office of the State Council. From 2000 to 2007, he was the Chairman of the Board of Supervisors for Key Large State-Owned Enterprises of the State Council. At present, Duan Ruichun is the Chairman of the China Association for Science and Technology and the permanent vice chairman of the China Association for Promotion of Cooperation among Industries, Universities & Research Institutes.

As a famous expert in China's intellectual property rights, scientific and technological policies and enterprise innovation, Duan Ruichun possesses interdisciplinary knowledge in natural science, economic management and legal science. He has led the drafting of many Chinese laws and regulations such as the Technology Contract Law, the Scientific and Technological Progress Law and the Regulation on National Awards for Science and Technology; he has participated in drafting of and amendments to many laws on intellectual property rights; he was the chief representative of the Intellectual Property Negotiations for Scientific and Technological Cooperation between China and the United States and the main representative of intellectual property negotiations in the process of China's entry into WTO; he was the Leader of the Review Team of the general report of the National IP Strategy; and he was one of the main person formulating the Trust Deed and the Selection Articles of the Ho Leung Ho Lee Foundation.

Due to his research results, Duan Ruichun was granted the first prize of the Science and Technology Progress Award by the State Science and Technology Commission in 1992 and granted the second prize of the Science and Technology Progress Award in 1993. He was granted the recognition award of China's technology market in 2004 and the significant contribution award of the China Law Association on Science and Technology in 2008. He has written and published several books such as *International Cooperation and Intellectual Property Rights*, *Principles and Practice of Technology Contracts*, *Guidelines on Technology Innovation* and *Multi-Dimensional Thinking of Scientific and Technological Policies*.

## Ma Yongsheng, Member of the Selection Board

Ma Yongsheng, a petroleum geologist and sedimentologist, was born in Hohhot City of Inner Mongolia in October 1961. He obtained his bachelor's and master's degrees from China University of Geosciences (previously known as Wuhan College of Geology) and received his Ph.D from Chinese Academy of Geological Sciences in 1990. He is now the Vice President and Chief Geologist of China Petroleum & Chemical Corporation (Sinopec Group). He has been elected as academician of Chinese Academy of Engineering in 2009.

Over the past few decades, he devoted his career to the research and application of the petroleum and natural gas exploration theory. He has made great contributions to the marine carbonates hydrocarbon exploration theory with a number of leading technological and theoretical achievements. For instance, he led the successful discovery of several giant natural gas reservoirs in China, such as the Puguang and Yuanba gas fields, establishing solid foundations for the Sichuan-to-East China Gas Transmission Project. His pioneering research in unconventional natural gas contributed significantly to the discovery of Fuling shale gas field in Chongqing, China's first large-scale shale gas field. His research accomplishments have also remarkably facilitated the mitigation of natural gas supply-demand imbalance, as well as the promotion of regional economy and environmental protection in China.

Ma has won the 1st Prize of the National Science & Technology Progress Award twice. In 2007, he won the Scientific & Technological Achievements Award granted by the Ho Leung Ho Lee Foundation. In the same year, he won Li Siguang Geoscience Prize for the 10th time. In 2013, he was selected as one of China's first six outstanding scientists supported by the National Ten-Thousand Talents Program. For his distinguished achievement in the petroleum industry, the Minor Planet Center named No. 210292 asteroid officially after him as "Ma Yongsheng Planet" in 2017.

## Wang Xiaofan, Member of the Selection Board

Wang Xiaofan is a renowned cancer biologist. He was born in Urumqi in 1955.

In 1982, he graduated from Wuhan University after completing an undergraduate program in biological chemistry, and was admitted into the Institute of Genetics, the Chinese Academy of Sciences.

In the same year, he ranked the highest in the first China-United States Biochemistry Examination and Application (CUSBEA) and went to the U.S. to pursue further studies.

In 1986, he obtained the doctoral degree from the University of California, Los Angeles (UCLA). Later he engaged in post-doctoral study by following Robert A. Weinberg, an eminent cancer biologist, at Massachusetts Institute of Technology (MIT).

In 1992, he was engaged as an assistant professor by the Department of Pharmacology and Tumor Biology at Duke University, becoming one of the earliest Chinese professors who taught at Duke University.

He became a tenure-track professor in 1998 and was promoted to be a full professor in 2003.

He is the Donald and Elizabeth Cooke Professor of Cancer Research at the Department of Pharmacology and Cancer Biology, School of Medicine, Duke University.

Professor Wang Xiaofan has made important academic contributions in many fields including cell signal transduction, repair of DNA damage, molecular mechanism of cancer metastasis and tumor microenvironment. In particular, he has made eye-catching achievements in the field related to TGF-$\beta$. He has published more than 100 academic papers, of which more than 20 were published in high-level academic periodicals such as *Cell*, *Nature*, *Science*, *Cancer Cell* and *Nature Cell Biology*.

Over a long period of time, professor Wang Xiaofan has insisted on offering advice and putting forward suggestions on education and science and technology undertakings in China through various channels. He has promoted or brought about a series of policies and systems for improving the environment of education and scientific research in China. He currently serves as a member of the Overseas Expert Consultant Committee of Overseas Chinese Affairs Office of the State Council.

## Henry T. Yang, Member of the Selection Board

Henry T. Yang was born in 1940. He obtained a Ph.D from Cornell University. He has served as Dean of the Aerospace Engineering Department and Head of the Engineering College of Purdue University. He used to be a co-director of the Smart Manufacturing Engineering center of the National Science Foundation (U. S.) and an outstanding professor of Armstrong (the first Moon lander) Astronautics Lectures. Currently, he is President of University of California Santa Barbara (since 1994), an academician of American Academy of Engineering, a fellow of both American Institute of Aeronautics and Astronautics and American Society of Mechanical Engineers, an overseas academician of Chinese Academy of Engineering and an academician of the Taiwan Academia Sinica. He is the chairman of the Thirty-metre Telescope Program (TMT Program) jointly sponsored by the United States, China, India, Japan and Canada. He is the chairman of the Association of Pacific Rim 42 Universities (including Peking University, Tsinghua University, Fudan University, University of Science and Technology of China, Zhejiang University and Nanjing University), a member of the Selection Board of the United States Presidential Medal of Science and a member of council of the Kavli Foundation. He used to be the Chairman of Association of American Universities (AAU) that consists of 62 top universities and a member of the Selection Board of Finnish Millennium Technology Grand Prize. He has been conferred seven honorary doctoral degrees.

He has been involved in teaching and research in aerospace structure, oscillation, control transition to earthquake, manufacturing, material (LED) and biological engineering. He has served as doctoral supervisor for sixty dissertations. He has published over 200 papers in journals, over 200 papers for academic conferences and one textbook on finite element (used by over forty American universities and translated into Chinese and Japanese).

He won the SDM Award granted by the American Institute of Aeronautics and Astronautics in 2008. He won Benjamin Garver Lamme Gold Metal, the highest one granted by the American Society for Engineering Education, and over ten excellent awards for education.

## Kenneth Young, Member of the Selection Board

Born in July 1948 in Shanghai, Kenneth Young has been working at The Chinese University of Hong Kong (CUHK) since 1973, and has held the position of Chairman of the Department of Physics, Dean of the Faculty of Science, Dean of the Graduate School and Pro-Vice-Chancellor/Vice-President. At present, Kenneth Young is Master of the CW Chu College and professor of physics at CUHK. He is also a member of the Education Commission (EC) and the Chairman of the Curriculum Development Council of the Hong Kong SAR. He was a member of the Hong Kong University Grants Committee and Chairman its Research Grants Council. He was the Secretary and later Vice-President of the Association of Asia Pacific Physical Societies. Kenneth Young studied at the California Institute of Technology from 1965 to 1972 and obtained the BS in physics in 1969 and the Ph.D in physics and mathematics in 1972. He was engaged in teaching and research at Princeton University from 1972 to 1973.

Kenneth Young has been engaged in physics research for a long time, on topics including elementary particles, field theory, high energy phenomenology, dissipation system and their eigenfunctions expansion, with applications to such open systems as optics and gravitational waves. Some of his publications include "Microscopic derivation of the Helmholtz force density", Phys Rev Lett 47, 77; "Late time tail of wave propagation on curved spacetime", Phys Rev Lett 74, 2414; "Quasinormal mode expansion for linearized waves in gravitational systems", Phys Rev Lett 74, 4588; "Quasinormal modes of dirty black holes", Phys Rev Lett 78, 289. Kenneth Young was elected as a Fellow of the American Physical Society in 1999 and an academician of International Eurasian Academy of Science in 2004.


### Wu Weiren, Member of the Selection Board

Wu Weiren was born in 1953. He is the designer-in-chief of China's Lunar Exploration Program, expert in aerospace TT&C and communication area and overall design technology in deep space exploration program; Prof. Wu is the academician of Chinese Academy of Engineering (CAE) and the member of International Academy of Astronautics (IAA), member of the standing committee of the National Committee of the Chinese People's Political Consultative Conference (CPPCC). He is also one of the main pioneers in the Chinese deep space exploration area and aerospace strategy scientist in China.

Prof. Wu has won 3 special awards and 2 first awards of national science and technology progress award, the first national innovation award, Ho Leung Ho Lee foundation for scientific and technological achievement award and Qian Xuesen's highest achievement award, etc. Also, Prof. Wu has been given the World Space Award, the highest award of the International Astronautical Federation (IAF) in 2020. For his outstanding contributions to the field of aerospace, the International Astronomical Union (IAU) approved the official name of the asteroid numbered 281880 as "Wu Weiren star".


### Zhang Litong, Member of the Selection Board

Zhang Litong, female, born in Chongqing in April of 1938, is a famous expert in aerospace materials. She graduated from Northwestern Polytechnical University in 1961. She was a senior visiting scholar in the Business Development Center of Spatial Structure Materials of NASA of the US from April 1989 to January 1991. Now, she acts as a professor and doctoral supervisor of Northwestern Polytechnical University and the deputy director of the Academic Committee of National Key Laboratory on Ultra-temperature Structure Composite Material Technology. She was elected as an academician of the Chinese Academy of Engineering in 1995.

She has been devoting himself to the research of aerospace materials and the technologies of manufacturing aerospace materials for many years and has achieved abundant research results in marginless melted module precise casting technologies and their fundamental theory research of thin-wall complex high-temperature alloy and aluminum alloy castings. She reveals the blade deformation rules, roughness generation rules and middle/high-temperature softening deformation mechanism of ceramic shells. Through independent innovation, she develops marginless melted module casting technology of high-temperature alloy, plaster-mold melted module casting technology of aluminum alloy, technology of middle/high-temperature creep-resisting ceramic shell materials for melted module casting of high-temperature alloy, and technology of foamed ceramic filtering and purifying materials for high-temperature alloy. Relevant achievements have been applied to production of aero-engines and aircraft components successfully.

After returning to China, she establishes three technology platforms with independent intellectual property rights (manufacturing process, manufacturing equipment and material and environment performance assessment), breaking international blockade on technologies.

She was awarded with one first-class prize of National Award for Technological Invention, four first-class, second-class and third-class prizes of National Award for Scientific and Technological Progress, one second-class prize of State-level Teaching Award. She is authorized with 64 national invention patents.

## Zhang Gongqing, Member of the Selection Board

Zhang Gongqing was born on May 29, 1936 in Shanghai. After he graduated from the Department of Mathematics of Peking University in 1959 he worked in his university. In the year of 1978, as one of the first visiting scholars since the reform and opening-up, he made further study in the United States. Now he is a professor of Peking University, an academician of Chinese Academy of Sciences, an academician of the Academy of Sciences for the Developing World, the Director of the Research and Talent Training Center for Teaching and Learning Mathematics in Universities and Colleges, and he also serves as a member in the editorial board of many international core academic journals.

As a famous mathematician, he develops infinite dimensional Morse theory into a unified framework of the critical point theory, and is the first one to employ Morse theory as a tool to study multiple solutions to partial differential equations. His monograph is the fundamental literature of the related field. He also develops the topological degree theory of set-valued mappings and the critical point theory of non-differential functional, making them a kind of free boundary problem in the study on equations of mathematical physics and on non-smooth mechanics.

He won the Award of National Science & Technology Conference (1978), the third prize of the State Natural Sciences Award (1982), the second prize of the State Natural Sciences Award (1987), Chen Xingshen Mathematics Prize (1986), the title of the Young Scientist with Outstanding Contributions (1984), the Third World Academy of Sciences Award in Mathematics (1993), Hua Luogeng Mathematics Prize (2009), Guohua Award of Peking University, and Special Award for Teaching presented by Founder Group (2011), etc.

## Chen Jiaer, Member of the Selection Board

Chen Jiaer, born on October 1, 1934 in Shanghai, is an academician of Chinese Academy of Sciences, an academician of the Academy of Sciences for the Developing World. He is currently a professor of physics at Peking University, the vice director of the Advisory Group of the National Basic Research Program of China (or 973 Program), and the vice chairman of the China Coordination Committee of the International Council of Scientific Unions.

He was the president of the Peking University and the dean of the Graduate School of Peking University, the director of the Committee of the National Natural Sciences Foundation, the director of the Division of Mathematics and Physics of the Chinese Academy of Sciences (CAS), a member of the CAS presidium, and the dean of the School of Physics of the Graduate University of CAS.

For a long time he has been devoting himself to the teaching and scientific research of the low-energy particle accelerator and its application. He is good at combining the cutting-edge development of an academic subject with national demands and planning the research in physics and talent training in a forward-looking way. He pioneered the development of RF superconducting accelerator, ultra-sensitive accelerator mass spectrometry, RF quadrupole field accelerator and electrostatic accelerator in China. He is a founder and one of the leaders in researching and developing low-energy particle accelerator in China.

Chen Jiaer was a long-time leader in Peking University and the Committee of the National Natural Science Foundation, and was also a member of the Leadership Group of Medium and Long Term Planning for Development of Science and Technology. He made important contribution to the formulation of the National Medium and Long Term Planning of Development of Science and Technology and the development of relevant science and education causes in China.

## Hao Jiming, Member of the Selection Board

Hao Jiming, a well-known expert in environmental engineering, was born in Shandong

Province in August 1946. He graduated from Tsinghua University in 1970. He earned a master degree from Tsinghua University in 1981, and obtained a Ph.D from University of Cincinnati in 1984. At Tsinghua University, he is a professor, tutor for doctoral candidates, deputy director of the teaching committee, and director of the Research Institute of Environmental Science and Engineering. He is also a member on the National Environmental Consultation Committee and China Council for International Cooperation on Environment and Development. He was elected as academician of the Chinese Academy of Engineering in 2005, and was elected as foreign academician of the National Academy of Engineering in the U.S. in 2018.

Hao Jiming has dedicated himself to the research in controlling air pollution in China for more than 40 years. His main fields of research include energy and environment, and air pollution control engineering. He is in charge of national acid deposition control planning and the research in countermeasures against acid deposition. His research result on dividing the areas for controlling acid rain and carbon dioxide has been adopted by the State Council, playing a guiding role in formulating China's policies on preventing and treating acid rain pollution. He has developed the planning and methods for controlling pollution caused by motor-driven vehicles in urban areas, promoting the control of the pollution caused by motor-driven vehicles in China. He has conducted in-depth research in the characteristics, causes and control policy on air compound pollution, further developed the theoretical and technological methods on improving the air quality in mega cities, and promoted the joint efforts to prevent and control the regional air compound pollution in China. He has conducted the research in the key technologies for controlling air pollution for a long period of time, and has made contributions in the fields such as dust control, desulfurization and denitration in coal-fired flue gas, and control of the pollution caused by motor-driven vehicles.

Hao Jiming won one first-prize and two second prizes of National Award for Scientific and Technological Progress, one second prize of National Award for Natural Science and two second prizes of National Award for Technical Invention, and two first prizes of National Award in Teaching Achievement. He was granted the title of national famous teacher in 2006. He won the Haagen-Smit Clean Air Award in 2015, and the IBM Global Faculty Award in 2016.

## Zhao Yuliang, Member of the Selection Board

Zhao Yuliang is a pioneer in the study of nano safety, having proposed the toxicology study of engineered nanomaterials and establishment of the first research laboratory in 2001. His work focuses on understanding the biological effects of nanomaterials, with a particular emphasis on establishing reliable and valid analytical methods for discovering their effects *in vivo*. Dr. Zhao also aims to understand the chemical mechanisms of nanosafety and ensure the safe application of nanomaterials. As a result of his research, a list of ISO standard analytical methods has been adapted by ISO/IEC 168 member countries. He has also established a nanosafety assessment framework for occupational exposure to nanomaterials, and has made significant contributions to the development of a new-concept nanomedicine for cancer therapeutics.

Dr. Zhao has received many honours and awards throughout his career, including TWAS Prize in Chemistry, CAS Outstanding Science and Technology Achievement Prize, National Prize for Natural Sciences (twice), Ho Leung Ho Lee Foundation Science and Technology Progress Prize, China Award for Outstanding Contribution on Toxicology, Beijing Award for Leading Talent in Science & Technology, etc.

Prof. Yuliang Zhao is the Director-General of National Center for Nanosciences and Technology, China. He is also Academician of Chinese Academy of Sciences, Academician of the World Academy of Sciences (TWAS), Academician of Chinese Academy of Medical Sciences, Elected President of Chinese Association for Biomaterials, Vice President of Chinese Chemical Society, Vice President of Chinese Pharmaceutical Association, Editor-in-Chief of *Nano Today*, Elsevier, Netherlands.

## Qian Shaojun, Member of the Selection Board

Qian Shaojun was born in 1934 in Pinghu, Zhejiang Province. In 1951, he was admitted to the Department of Physics of Tsinghua University, and later studied Beijing Russian Language College, Department of Physics and the Research Section of Physics (now the Department of Technical Physics) of Peking University. He currently works as a consultant and research fellow of the Committee of Science and Technology of General Armament Department of the PLA, a research fellow and an academician of the Chinese Academy of Engineering. He used to be the deputy commander and the commander of the Nuclear Test Base, and was a standing member of the Committee of Science and Technology in the State Commission of Science and Technology for National Defense Industry.

He has been long engaged in the radiochemical diagnostic work of nuclear test and participated in a series of atomic bomb and hydrogen bomb nuclear tests conducted in the atmosphere or underground, in which he remarkably enhanced the measurement accuracy by establishing and improving many diagnostic approach and technology. For many times he took part in the study on the development strategy of science and technology and weaponry and equipment for national defence and participated in organizing the special research in national medium and long term scientific and technical development planning. He guided the basic study on applying research results in national defense, and worked hard to make such basic study consistent with the national basic research programs. He was put in charge of developing nuclear technology for military use, kept track of long-term changes with international situations and the policy evolvement of some leading nations, and instructed and took part in the study of arms control. He participated in the negotiation of the Comprehensive Nuclear Test Ban Treaty and guided the preparatory work for the performance of the treaty after it was signed.

His published works include a translated work, two monographs, wrote many scientific and technical papers and important scientific and technical articles for archival purpose. He won the Top Prize of the State Scientific and Technological Progress Award and the second prize of the State Scientific and Technological Progress Award once, the second prize of the State Award for Inventions and the third prize of the State Award for Inventions once, and the Military Progress Prize in Science and Technology many times.

## Ni Jun, Member of the Selection Board

Ni Jun was born in Qinghai Province in November 1961. He is the Shien-Ming (Sam) Wu Collegiate Professor of Manufacturing Science and Professor of Mechanical Engineering at the University of Michigan, USA. He is the director of the Wu Manufacturing Research Center and the co-director of a National Science Foundation sponsored Industry/University Cooperative Research Center for Intelligent Maintenance Systems at the University of Michigan. Professor Ni served as the founding Dean of the University of Michigan – Shanghai Jiao Tong University Joint Institute located in Shanghai, China and is currently the Honorary Dean and Special Advisor to the President of Shanghai Jiao Tong University. Professor Ni is currently the Chairman of Global Future Council on Production at the World Economic Forum. Professor Ni served as the Deputy Director of the National Science Foundation Engineering Research Center for Reconfigurable Manufacturing Systems, and the Director of a National Science Foundation sponsored Industry/University Cooperative Research Center for Dimensional Measurement and Control in Manufacturing.

Professor Ni's research covers many topics in advanced manufacturing, including smart manufacturing technologies, and applications of industrial big data analytics and artificial intelligence in quality assurance, precision manufacturing, and intelligent maintenance systems. His research has been successfully applied by various industrial companies.

Selected honors and awards that Professor Ni received are 2013 International Science and Technology Cooperation Award from the President of People's Republic of China, 2013 Gold Medal from Society of Manufacturing Engineers, 2009 Ennor Manufacturing Technology Award from American Society of Mechanical Engineers, and 1994 Presidential Faculty Fellows Award from President Clinton. He is an elected Fellow of International Society of Engineering Asset Management, International Society for Nano-manufacturing, American Society of Mechanical Engineers, and Society of Manufacturing Engineers.

## Sang Guowei, Member of the Selection Board

Sang Guowei was born in Huzhou, Zhejiang in November 1941. He is a clinical pharmacologist, an academician of the Chinese Academy of Engineering, Chairman of Chinese Pharmaceutical Association, Chief Engineer for the important specific techniques for the national "development of important new medicines" in the "11th Five-Year Plan", "12th Five-Year Plan" and "13th Five-Year Plan". He is also the director of the Expert Consultation Committee of the "Development Program of the Pharmaceuticals Industry in the 13th Five-Year Plan" of the Ministry of Industry and Information Technology, senior research fellow of National Institute for the Control of Pharmaceutical and Biological Products (NICPBP), honorary president of Shanghai University of Traditional Chinese Medicine (SHUTCM), and was the vice chairman of the 11th National People's Congress Standing Committee, and chairman of Chinese Peasants' and Workers' Democratic Party.

He has systematically studied the pharmacokinetics, race differences and clinical pharmacology of steroidal contraceptives and antiprogestogens for long-acting injection and for oral taking, and made a number of important achievements. He has done fruitful work in terms of safety evaluation, quality control and clinical trial etc. for new drugs in recent years, and has made great contributions in strengthening China's construction of the GLP and GCP platforms.

He has won two National Scientific Conference Awards (in 1978), three Second Prizes of National Science and Technology Progress Award (in 1987, 1997 and 2008), one First Prize and four Second Prizes of Science and Technology Progress Award at the ministerial and commission levels, the Science and Technology Awards of the Ho Leung Ho Lee Foundation in 1997 (Medical-Pharmaceutical Award), the Special Contribution Award of the Wu Jieping-Paul Janssen Medical-Pharmaceutical Award in 2008, and the Lifetime Achievement Award in Pharmacy Science of the Federation International Pharmaceutical (FIP) in 2014.

## Cao Xuetao, Member of the Selection Board

Cao Xuetao, was born in July 1964 in Jinan City, Shandong Province. In 1990, he graduated from the Second Military Medical University. He is the President of Chinese Academy of Medical Sciences (CAMS), member of the Chinese Academy of Engineering, and the Director of National Key Laboratory of Medical Immunology. Concurrently he is the President of the Chinese Society for Immunology, Chairperson of Global Alliance of Chronic Diseases (GACD), and President of the Federation of Immunological Societies of Asia-Oceania (FIMSA). He also serves as a member of the editorial board of magazines including Cell.

He is mainly engaged in fundamental research on innate immune recognition and relevant immune regulation, and applicability research on tumor immunotherapy. He has found a new dendritic cell (DC) subset with an important immune regulation function, independently identified 22 immune-related molecules, systematically studied innate immune recognition and the new mechanism for interferon production regulation, explored apparent molecular action on inflammation and cancer development and progression, established new approaches for tumor immunotherapy, and carried out relevant clinical trials.

He won the second-class prize of National Science and Technology Awards as the primary participant of a research project, a first-class prize of Chinese Medical Science and Technology Awards, a first-class prize of Military Science and Technology Progress Awards, three first-class prizes of Shanghai Science and Technology Progress Awards. He has obtained 16 national invention patents and two national category-II new medicine certificates. His research result was selected as one of the top ten results representing the scientific and technological progress in China in 2011. He was presented with Guanghua Engineering Science and Technology Award, Cheng Kong Scholar Achievement Award, China Young Scientist Award, and others. As corresponding author, he published over 220 papers in SCI-cited journals including Cell, Science, Nature Immunology, Cancer Cell, Immunity and others. His papers have been non-self-cited for over 5600 times in SCI-cited journals; he has written and served as a co-chief-editor for eight monographs. Of all the doctoral candidates under his tutorship, 11 have been presented with the awards of "national 100 excellent dissertations for doctoral degrees."

## Cheng Xu, Member of the Selection Board

Cheng Xu, born in 1944, is of the origin of Wuxi, Jiangsu Province. He graduated from the Department of Agronomy of Beijing Agricultural University (Now China Agricultural University), later he worked in the Institute of Crop Breeding and Cultivation of the Chinese Academy of Agricultural Science. He is currently a professor of the China Agricultural University, and a tutor for doctoral candidates. He worked in the Beijing Academy of Agricultural Science and the Ministry of Agriculture. His major fields of research include sustainable agriculture and rural development, agricultural ecology and ecological agriculture.

He was put in charge of two research projects: one is the construction of the Agricultural Modernization and Experimental Base (location: Doudian village, Fangshan County, Beijing) and the other is Ecological Agriculture Program. In 1985, he took the lead in introducing the theory of sustainable agricultural development. From then on he started to study the way to realize sustainable agricultural development in China. He focused his research on the ecological restoration in the fragile farming-pastoral transitional zones and the exploration of the sustainable intensive agriculture.

As the main participant in completing the research project, he won the first prize of the Beijing

Science and Technology Progress Awards and the first prize of the National Sparkle Technology Award (equivalent to Science and Technology Progress Award). He was totally presented with seven second or third prizes of science and technology progress awards at provincial and ministerial level. In 1988, he was approved as a National Young & Middle-Aged Expert with Outstanding Contribution.

His works include *An Introduction to Sustainable Agriculture* and *General Program on Sustainable Development in China Volume* 13: *Agriculture in China and the Sustainable Development*.

## Zeng Qingcun, Member of the Selection Board

Zeng Qingcun, born in May 1935 in Yangjiang County of Guangdong Province, graduated from the Department of Physics of Peking University in 1956. In 1961, he completed his Licentiate (namely Ph.D now) in the Institute of Applied Geophysics of the Soviet Academy of Science. After he returned to China he worked in the Institute of Geophysics and then the Institute of Atmospheric Physics of the Chinese Academy of Sciences (CAS). He was elected as an academician of the Chinese Academy of Sciences in 1980. Currently he is a research fellow of the Institute of Atmospheric physics of the CAS.

His major research field includes atmospheric sciences and geophysical fluid dynamics. He has been devoting himself to the study of the basic theory and numerical model and simulation of general atmospheric circulation and fluid dynamics, earth system dynamics model, numerical weather prediction and climatic prediction theory, climate dynamics and monsoon theory, dynamics of atmospheric boundary layer, theoretical method of satellite remote sensing, applied mathematics and numerical mathematics, and natural cybernetics. He is the first one in the world to put forward half-implicit difference scheme and square conservative scheme, applied the original equation into the actual numerical climate prediction (1961), developed the marine-atmosphere coupled mode for the extra-seasonal climate predictions (1990, 1994), and put forward the systematic theory of satellite remote sensing (1974) and the Theoretical method of natural control (1995).

He won the second prize of the State Natural Sciences Award twice and the third prize of the State Natural Sciences Awards once, the first prize of the Natural Science Award of the CAS six times and Outstanding Contribution Award once. His monographs include *Principles of the Atmospheric Remote Sensing in Infrared*, *Mathematical Physics Foundations of the Numerical Weather Prediction*, *Principles of the Short-term Numerical Climatic Prediction*, *Yellow Clouds Stretching Thousands of Miles—The research on Dust-storm in East Asia*. He has also published hundreds of academic articles.

## Pu Muming, Member of the Selection Board

Pu Muming, born in October 1948, graduated from the Department of Physics, Tsing Hua University, Taiwan in 1970; He received his Ph. D. degree in biophysics from Johns Hopkins University in 1974. From 1974 to 1976, he did postdoctoral research in Woods Hole Institute of Marine Biology and Department of Life Sciences, Purdue University. From September 1976 to March 1985, he served as assistant professor, associate professor and professor in the Department of Biophysics, University of California, Irvine, USA; professor, Department of Molecular Neurobiology, Yale University School of Medicine, USA, from April 1985 to August 1988; professor, Department of Biology, Columbia University, USA, from July 1988 to December 1995; he was Stephen W.Kuffler's Chair Professor in the Department of Biology, University of California, San Diego, USA, from January 1996 to October 2000. In July 1998, he founded the Institute of Neuroscience. Since September 2000, he has been the Chair professor of the Department of Molecular and Cell Biology, University of California, Berkeley, Class 1933, and the director of the Department of Neurobiology since 2002. He is a foreign member of the Chinese Academy of Sciences (2011), a member of the American Academy of Sciences (2009), and a member of the Academia Sinica, Taiwan. He is currently the director of the Institute of Neuroscience, Shanghai Institutes for Biological Sciences, Chinese Academy of Sciences, and Director of the Center for Excellence in Brain Science Innovation, Chinese Academy of Sciences.

Professor Pu Muming, who is mainly engaged in molecular and cellular mechanisms of axon orientation and synaptic plasticity, was awarded the People's Republic of China International Science and Technology Cooperation Award in 2005 and the Gruber Neuroscience Award in 2016 for his outstanding achievements.

Professor Pu is a world-class scientist who was born in Nanjing and grew up in Taiwan. He has been engaged in scientific research in the United States for a long time. He participated in the establishment of the Department of Biology of Tsinghua University and served as the first chair of the department.

Pu renounced his US citizenship and restored his Chinese citizenship in 2017.